MATH TRAILBLAZERS

Grade

1

Teacher Implementation Guide

Second Edition

A Mathematical Journey Using Science and Language Arts

KENDALL/HUNT PUBLISHING COMPANY
4050 Westmark Drive   Dubuque, Iowa   52002

A TIMS® Curriculum
University of Illinois at Chicago

Teacher Implementation Guide

Math Trailblazers™

A Mathematical Journey Using Science and Language Arts

A TIMS® Curriculum from the University of Illinois at Chicago

Dedication

This book is dedicated to the children and teachers who let us see the magic in their classrooms and to our families who wholeheartedly supported us while we searched for ways to make it happen.

—The TIMS Project—

UIC The University of Illinois at Chicago

The original edition was based on work supported by the National Science Foundation under grant No. MDR 9050226 and the University of Illinois at Chicago. Any opinions, findings, and conclusions or recommendations expressed in this publication are those of the authors and do not necessarily reflect the views of the granting agencies.

Cover photo by Design Photography

Printed in the United States of America

2 3 4 5 6 7 8 9 10   07 06 05 04

Acknowledgments

TIMS Elementary Mathematics Curriculum Project

Teaching Integrated Mathematics and Science (TIMS) Project Directors

Philip Wagreich, Principal Investigator
Joan L. Bieler
Marty Gartzman
Howard Goldberg (emeritus)
Catherine Randall Kelso

Director, Second Edition

Catherine Randall Kelso

Curriculum Developers, Second Edition

Lindy M. Chambers-Boucher
Elizabeth Colligan
Marty Gartzman
Carol Inzerillo
Catherine Randall Kelso
Georganne E. Marsh
Leona Peters
Philip Wagreich

Editorial and Production Staff, Second Edition

Kathleen R. Anderson
Ai-Ai C. Cojuangco
Andrada Costoiu
Erika Larson
Georganne E. Marsh
Cosmina Menghes
Anne Roby
Kathy Vondracek

TIMS Professional Developers

Barbara Crum
Craig Cleve
Elizabeth Colligan
Pamela Guyton
Carol Inzerillo
Linda Miceli
Leona Peters
Jane Schlichting

TIMS Director of Media Services

Henrique Cirne-Lima

TIMS Research Staff

Catherine Randall Kelso
Barry Booton
Dibyen Majumdar

TIMS Administrative Staff

Ora Benton
David Cirillo
Enrique Puente

Principal Investigators, First Edition

Philip Wagreich, Project Director
Howard Goldberg

Senior Curriculum Developers, First Edition

Joan L. Bieler
Janet Simpson Beissinger
Astrida Cirulis
Marty Gartzman
Howard Goldberg

Carol Inzerillo
Andy Isaacs
Catherine Randall Kelso
Leona Peters
Philip Wagreich

Curriculum Developers, First Edition

Janice C. Banasiak
Lynne Beauprez
Andy Carter
Lindy M. Chambers-Boucher
Kathryn Chval
Diane Czerwinski

Jenny Knight
Sandy Niemiera
Janice Ozima
Polly Tangora
Paul Trafton

Illustrator, First Edition

Kris Dresen

Research Consultant, First Edition

Andy Isaacs

Mathematics Education Consultant, First Edition

Paul Trafton

National Advisory Committee, First Edition

Carl Berger
Tom Berger
Hugh Burkhardt
Donald Chambers
Naomi Fisher
Glenda Lappan

Mary Lindquist
Eugene Maier
Lourdes Monteagudo
Elizabeth Phillips
Thomas Post

Preface

This second edition of *Math Trailblazers* is the product of more than twelve years of concerted effort by the TIMS (Teaching Integrated Mathematics and Science) Project. The TIMS Project has its roots in the pioneering work of Howard Goldberg, Professor of Physics at the University of Illinois at Chicago and a Carnegie Foundation Professor of the Year in 1995. Over the past two decades, the TIMS Project has worked with children, teachers, and administrators to improve the quality of mathematics and science curriculum and instruction in the Chicago area and nationwide. In 1990, the TIMS Project was awarded a grant by the National Science Foundation to develop a new elementary mathematics curriculum to meet the needs of children who will be entering the world of work in the 21st century. After years of research and development, including pilot- and field-testing in hundreds of classrooms, the first edition of the curriculum was published as *Math Trailblazers* in 1997 and 1998.

The primary goal of *Math Trailblazers* has been to create an educational experience that results in children who are flexible mathematical thinkers, who see the connections between the mathematics they learn in school and the thinking they do in everyday life, and who enjoy mathematics. We believe that children can succeed in mathematics and that if more is expected of them, more will be achieved. This curriculum incorporates the best of traditional mathematics, while widening the horizons of students' mathematical thinking.

Since the initial publication of *Math Trailblazers,* the TIMS Project has continued its research and development work, studying how to implement the curriculum in the most effective ways. We have learned considerably more about the importance of teacher professional development and whole-school change. The dedication and insight of our teacher collaborators constantly encouraged us. Feedback from hundreds of teachers who tested early versions of *Math Trailblazers* and thousands of others who used the program over the past five years significantly reshaped our view of the curriculum and inspires our continuing efforts to improve it.

The first edition of *Math Trailblazers* was grounded in mathematics education research literature as well as our own research and experience as curriculum and staff developers. It was also inspired by the 1989 publication of the National Council of Teachers of Mathematics *Curriculum and Evaluation Standards for School Mathematics.* In this edition we drew from advances in research over the decade as well as NCTM's updated vision for school mathematics, as embodied in the NCTM's *Principles and Standards for School Mathematics.*

The second edition of *Math Trailblazers* makes the curriculum easier for teachers to use. It also realigns the math facts program and strengthens and highlights the assessment and review components that were hard for some teachers to identify in the first edition. The result is a stronger curriculum for teachers and students. We hope that teaching *Math Trailblazers* will be an enjoyable experience for you and a productive experience for your students.

Philip Wagreich

Philip Wagreich
Professor, Department of Mathematics, Statistics, and Computer Science
Director, Institute for Mathematics and Science Education
University of Illinois at Chicago

Teacher Implementation Guide
Table of Contents

Grade 1 *Math Trailblazers* Table of Contents

This Table of Contents includes page numbers for the teacher material in the *Unit Resource Guide* plus corresponding page numbers in the student books (*Student Guide* and *Adventure Book*).

Introduction

The Introduction outlines the various sections of this document and explains how to get the most out of them.

A teacher and a student explore equivalent fractions.

Introduction

PART I | ## What Is the *Teacher Implementation Guide?*

The *Teacher Implementation Guide* (TIG) is the reference manual for *Math Trailblazers*. The *Teacher Implementation Guide*, combined with the *Unit Resource Guide* (URG), provides teachers and schools with a comprehensive set of resources to assist in the implementation of the curriculum. The *Unit Resource Guide* is the teacher's working guide, providing information and instructions related to the planning and teaching of units and individual lessons—it is intended to be used on a day-to-day basis. The *Teacher Implementation Guide* supplements the *Unit Resource Guide* by addressing larger issues related to the curriculum. Information in the *Teacher Implementation Guide* can be roughly categorized into three groups: general background about *Math Trailblazers*; specific information about the program; and deep background about important math and science concepts. The *Teacher Implementation Guide* is a valuable resource for use in long-range planning regarding math instruction, curriculum, related implementation issues, and staff development.

Below are brief descriptions of sections found in the *Teacher Implementation Guide*:

- **Foundations of *Math Trailblazers***
  The underlying philosophy of the program is described.

- **Components and Features Guide**
  Math Trailblazers is a multicomponent program. Grade 1 includes two books for students (the *Student Guide* and the *Adventure Book*) and two volumes for teachers (the *Teacher Implementation Guide* and the *Unit Resource Guide*). A *Teacher Resource CD* is also available for teachers. The Components and Features Guide is a road map to help you understand the purposes of the various components and where to find key information. Examples of important features taken from actual student and teacher pages are illustrated.

- **Grade 1 Overview**
  The Overview is an extended table of contents for the Grade 1 curriculum. Pacing Suggestions in unit outlines help in planning your instruction schedule. Unit summaries include a narrative description of the content for each unit and a list of important math concepts covered in the individual units. This provides a snapshot view of the curriculum for your grade.

- **Connections with the NCTM *Principles and Standards***
  Math Trailblazers was developed to reflect the goals and approaches outlined in the *Principles and Standards for School Mathematics* of the National Council of Teachers of Mathematics (NCTM). The *Teacher*

Implementation Guide includes detailed information, using text and tables, about how the program aligns with the *Principles and Standards.*

- **Scope and Sequence**

  The curriculum's scope and sequence is presented in the *Teacher Implementation Guide.* The Scope and Sequence is organized to correspond with the NCTM *Principles and Standards,* providing additional detailed information about *Math Trailblazers'* alignment with the *Standards.* The scope and sequence chart is divided into two sections—one section for the unit lessons and one section for the Daily Practice and Problems.

- **Summary of Approaches to Math Facts and Whole-Number Operations**

  The *Math Trailblazers* program for presenting the math facts and whole-number operations is summarized in the *Teacher Implementation Guide.* Background information about our approach and expectations for the grades are outlined.

- **Daily Practice and Problems**

  An essential component of *Math Trailblazers* is a carefully designed sequence of short problems in Grades 1–5, called the Daily Practice and Problems (DPP). Beginning in third grade, a component called Home Practice is introduced. This component provides additional practice with skills and concepts.

- **Assessment**

  Math Trailblazers includes a comprehensive program of student assessment. The philosophy and components of the assessment program are described in the *Teacher Implementation Guide.* Assessment materials from the curriculum are used to illustrate key ideas. Specific suggestions for implementing the assessment program are included.

- **TIMS Tutors: Background Information for Teachers**

  The *Teacher Implementation Guide* includes a series of documents called TIMS Tutors. The tutors provide extensive information on topics in pedagogy, mathematics, and science. The tutors serve as a source of deep background information for teachers and others. Some tutors, such as the tutor on math facts, supply specific information needed by teachers to plan particular portions of the *Math Trailblazers* program. Other tutors, such as the tutor on mass, focus on math and science content. Still others, such as the tutor on portfolios, address teaching strategies.

- **Manipulatives List**

  A listing of the manipulatives required for program implementation is included in the *Teacher Implementation Guide.*

- **Literature List**

  Math Trailblazers incorporates the use of commercially available trade books in many lessons. A listing of these trade books is included in the *Teacher Implementation Guide.*

- **Games List**

  Games are often used in *Math Trailblazers* to engage students in practicing basic arithmetic skills and other math concepts. Once introduced, these games can be used throughout the year for ongoing practice. A complete listing of the games for your grade and a description of the games are provided.

- **Software List**

  Math Trailblazers does not require the use of computers. We do, instead, suggest the use of some software programs that can supplement the curriculum. A listing of these programs and some suggested uses for them are provided.

- **Suggestions for Working with Parents**

  When adopting a math program that is new and different, such as *Math Trailblazers*, it is important to keep parents informed and educated about the program. Some hints for working with parents regarding *Math Trailblazers* are outlined in the *Teacher Implementation Guide*. A brochure about the curriculum and a parent letter that describes the math facts program are also provided. The documents are written in both English and Spanish.

- **Glossary**

  Most *Math Trailblazers* lessons include mathematical terms relevant to the lesson. Many of these terms are defined in the glossary. The glossary can also be used to locate key vocabulary in the lessons. Most definitions cite the locations of the term in the curriculum.

- **Index**

  The index is a list of major mathematical topics and their locations in the curriculum. The *Student Guide* and *Teacher Implementation Guide* are all referenced in this index.

PART II | How to Use the *Teacher Implementation Guide*

Use of the *Teacher Implementation Guide* will differ depending upon your purpose. Suggestions for using the *Teacher Implementation Guide* for different purposes are described below.

If you are a teacher considering whether to use *Math Trailblazers*:

The *Teacher Implementation Guide* provides useful information for adoption committees or individual teachers who are considering *Math Trailblazers*. General information about the program that will be most helpful for this group includes the Foundations, alignment with the NCTM *Principles and Standards,* Scope and Sequence, and the Overview. The Components and Features Guide will help reviewers understand the purposes of the different student and teacher books. Other specific information, such as the Math Facts and Whole-Number Operations section and the Assessment section, may also be useful for potential users of the curriculum.

If you are a teacher who is about to use *Math Trailblazers* for the first time:

There is too much information in the *Teacher Implementation Guide* and the *Unit Resource Guide* for any teacher to digest all at once. To make effective use of the *Teacher Implementation Guide*, it is best to select portions of the manual to examine at different points in the curriculum implementation. Prior to using *Math Trailblazers*, it would be useful to glance at the Foundations section to get a sense of our overall philosophy. However, you will probably want to spend more time reviewing the sections that provide specific information about using the curriculum. This information will help you get started and plan for the year.

Carefully review the Components and Features Guide so that you see the big picture of the program's components and features. This information will eventually become second nature to you as you gain experience with the curriculum, but it will be helpful at first to at least see what is included in the program. We suggest that you review the Overview so that you get a feel for what is covered over the course of the year and can plan ahead. It will

be easier to make instructional decisions at any given moment if you know what is planned for later lessons. The Assessment section and the Daily Practice and Problems Guide are essential and should be read prior to beginning the curriculum. Among the TIMS Tutors, we suggest that you first review *Math Facts*. It outlines our philosophy and plan for introducing the math facts. The manipulatives and literature lists are useful tools if you are ordering manipulatives. The section on working with parents will also be useful to read prior to using the curriculum. Use the rest of the *Teacher Implementation Guide* as the need arises.

If you are a teacher who is already using *Math Trailblazers*:

During your first several years of using *Math Trailblazers*, you will likely refer to the *Teacher Implementation Guide* on a regular and ongoing basis. You will find the TIMS Tutors particularly valuable in helping you better understand the content and approaches of key parts of the curriculum. There are numerous pointers in the *Unit Resource Guide* that refer you to individual tutors. The Scope and Sequence supplements the Overview in providing detailed information about when specific concepts are covered. The Games List and

Software List can be reviewed periodically to help you in lesson planning. If there is background information that you do not find in the *Unit Resource Guide,* there is a good chance you will find it in the *Teacher Implementation Guide.*

If you are a school administrator in a school that is using *Math Trailblazers:*

Principals and other school administrators are likely, at some point, to be queried by parents or even the media about the school's math program. It is therefore useful to have some familiarity with the program's philosophy and a general view of the program's content. The Foundations of *Math Trailblazers* section of the *Teacher Implementation Guide* is a good start for this. The sections that outline the curriculum's alignment with the NCTM *Principles and Standards* provide useful information about the national recommendations that underlie *Math Trailblazers.* We strongly recommend that administrators read the section on working with parents. This section provides suggestions and resources for communicating the goals of the curriculum to parents. Administrators may also want to review the section that outlines our approaches to teaching math facts and whole-number operations; most potential parental concerns are likely to address that topic.

If you are planning staff development sessions about *Math Trailblazers:*

Implementation of *Math Trailblazers* will be much more effective if it is accompanied by a good staff development program. An orientation to *Math Trailblazers* is made available to schools through Kendall/Hunt Publishing Company. We recommend that schools supplement this with additional staff development, preferably to support teachers at least through the initial years of implementation. Several sections of the *Teacher Implementation Guide*—especially the TIMS Tutors, Assessment, Foundations of *Math Trailblazers,* and the portions that outline the curriculum's alignment with the NCTM *Principles and Standards*—are ready-made for use in a staff development program. For specific suggestions about planning local staff development related to *Math Trailblazers,* contact the Teaching Integrated Mathematics and Science (TIMS) Project at 800-454-TIMS or Kendall/Hunt Publishing Company at 800-542-6657. Information is also available on the *Math Trailblazers* Implementation Center website at *www.math.uic.edu/IMSE* and at *www.mathtrailblazers.com.*

2

Foundations of Math Trailblazers™

The Foundations of *Math Trailblazers* describes the principles behind *Math Trailblazers* and discusses the curriculum's key features.

Students work together to solve problems.

Foundations of *Math Trailblazers*

Math Trailblazers is an elementary mathematics curriculum for schools that want their math programs to reflect the goals and ideas of the National Council of Teachers of Mathematics (NCTM) *Principles and Standards for School Mathematics.* With funding from the National Science Foundation (NSF) the TIMS (Teaching Integrated Mathematics and Science) Project at the University of Illinois at Chicago created a comprehensive program that embodies the *Principles and Standards.*

Math Trailblazers is based on the ideas that mathematics is best learned in real-world contexts that make sense to children; that all students deserve a richer and more challenging curriculum; and that a balanced and practical approach to mathematics learning is what students need and what teachers want.

Features of *Math Trailblazers*
Alignment with Reform Recommendations

NCTM's *Principles and Standards* provides the most current and comprehensive set of recommendations for improving the teaching and learning of mathematics. The *Principles and Standards* is an update of three, groundbreaking volumes published a decade earlier that collectively became known as the "NCTM *Standards.*" The *Principles and Standards,* which was released in 2000, largely reflects the same consensus about how to reform mathematics education as found in the earlier NCTM recommendations.

The NCTM documents outline a vision for school mathematics that includes: a curriculum that is mathematically challenging, coherent, and covers a broad range of mathematical content; a strong focus on engaging students in mathematical problem solving; instruction that is conceptually oriented and stresses thinking, reasoning, and applying; appropriate uses of calculators and computers; and a strong commitment to promoting success in mathematics among all students—not merely those who traditionally have done well. This vision for mathematics teaching and learning was incorporated into the mathematics standards of most states.

The first edition of *Math Trailblazers* was the result of more than six years of work, that included extensive pilot and field testing of the materials. After publication of the first edition, continued NSF support enabled the TIMS Project to develop implementation models and professional development materials that assisted teachers and schools as they adopted the program. TIMS researchers also studied how the program impacted student achievement. The second edition of *Math Trailblazers* therefore represents over twelve years of NSF-supported work related to the curriculum.

In developing the second edition of *Math Trailblazers,* we looked carefully at the NCTM *Principles and Standards.* The reorganization of the *Math Trailblazers* math facts program in the second edition reflects new recommendations in the *Principles and Standards* and keeps *Math Trailblazers* closely aligned with NCTM recommendations for mathematics curricula.

The importance of a coherent, well-developed curriculum is clearly articulated in the *Principles and Standards* which states:

> ***A curriculum is more than a collection of activities: it must be coherent, focused on important mathematics, and well articulated across the grades.*** *A school mathematics curriculum is a strong determinant of what students have an opportunity to learn and what they do learn. In a coherent curriculum, mathematical ideas are linked to and build on one another so that students' understanding and knowledge deepens and their ability to apply mathematics expands. An effective mathematics curriculum focuses on important mathematics—mathematics that will prepare students for continued study and for solving problems in a variety of school, home, and work settings. A well-articulated curriculum challenges students to learn increasingly more sophisticated mathematical ideas as they continue their studies.* (NCTM, 2000, p. 14)

Math Trailblazers was developed with that goal in mind. It is a *Standards*-based curriculum in the truest sense—developed explicitly to reflect national standards for K–5 mathematics, and now revised to maintain close alignment with those standards as they have evolved.

More specific connections between *Math Trailblazers* and the NCTM *Principles and Standards* are discussed in Scope and Sequence & the NCTM *Principles and Standards* (Section 5).

High Expectations and Equity

The first principle in the *Principles and Standards* is the Equity Principle. It challenges a myth prevalent in the United States that only a few students are capable of rigorous mathematics. The Equity Principles states:

> *Excellence in mathematics education requires equity—high expectations and strong support for all students.* (NCTM, 2000, p. 12)

Accordingly, we introduce challenging content in every grade: computation, measurement, data collection, statistics, geometry, ratio, probability, graphing, algebraic concepts, estimation, mental arithmetic, and patterns and relationships.

Contexts for this demanding content begin with students' lives. Lessons are grounded in everyday situations, so abstractions build on experience. By presenting mathematics in rich contexts, the curriculum helps students make connections among real situations, words, pictures, data, graphs, and symbols. The curriculum also validates students' current understandings while new understandings develop. Students can solve problems in ways they understand while being encouraged to connect those ways to more abstract and powerful methods. Within the same lesson, some students may work directly with the manipulatives to solve the problems while other students may solve the same problems using graphs or symbols. The use of varied contexts and diverse representations of concepts allows children of varying abilities to access the mathematics.

Problem Solving

A fundamental principle of *Math Trailblazers* is that mathematics is best learned through active involvement in solving real problems. Questions a student can answer immediately may be worthwhile exercises, but *problems,* by definition, are difficult, but not impossible.

The importance of problem solving is echoed in the NCTM *Principles and Standards,* which states:

> *Problem solving is the cornerstone of school mathematics. . . . The goal of school mathematics should be for all students to become increasingly able and willing to engage with and solve problems.*

> *Problem solving is also important because it can serve as a vehicle for learning new mathematical ideas and skills (Schroeder and Lester). A problem-centered approach to teaching mathematics uses interesting and well-selected problems to launch mathematical lessons and engage students. In this way, new ideas, techniques, and mathematical relationships emerge and become the focus of discussion.* (NCTM, 2000, p. 182)

As recommended by NCTM, problem solving in *Math Trailblazers* is not a distinct topic but permeates the entire program, providing a context for learning concepts and skills. Throughout the curriculum, students apply the mathematics they know and construct new mathematics as needed. Students' skills, procedures, and concepts emerge and develop as they solve complex problems.

Connections to Science and Language Arts

Real-world problems are naturally interdisciplinary, so that any problem-solving curriculum should integrate topics that are traditionally separated. Accordingly, we have integrated mathematics with many disciplines, especially science and language arts.

Connections to Science

Math Trailblazers is a full mathematics program that incorporates many important scientific ideas. Traditionally, school science has focused on 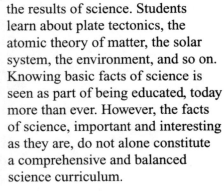 the results of science. Students learn about plate tectonics, the atomic theory of matter, the solar system, the environment, and so on. Knowing basic facts of science is seen as part of being educated, today more than ever. However, the facts of science, important and interesting as they are, do not alone constitute a comprehensive and balanced science curriculum.

Science has two aspects: results and method. The results of scientific inquiry have enriched human life the world over. More marvelous than the results of science, however, is the

method that has established those results. Without the method, the results would never have been achieved. *Math Trailblazers* aims to teach students the method of science through scientific investigation of everyday phenomena. During these investigations, students learn both mathematics and science.

The method scientists use is powerful, flexible, and quantitative. The TIMS Project has organized this method in a way that is simple enough for elementary school children to use. Students use the TIMS Laboratory Method in a rich variety of mathematical investigations. In these investigations, students develop and apply important mathematical skills and concepts in meaningful situations. Their understanding of fundamental scientific concepts is also enhanced through the use of quantitative tools.

Investigations begin with discussions of experimental situations, variables, and procedures. Then, students draw pictures in which they indicate the experimental procedures and identify key variables. Next, students gather data and organize it in data tables. Then, they graph their data. By analyzing their data or studying their graphs, students are able to see patterns in the data. These patterns show any relationships between the variables. The relationships can be used to make predictions about future data. The last phase of the experiment is an in-depth analysis of the experimental results, structured as a series of exploratory questions. Some questions ask students to make predictions and then to verify them. Other questions probe students' understanding of underlying concepts and explore the role of controlled variables. As students advance through the curriculum, the questions progress from simple to complex, building eventually to problems that require proportional reasoning, multiple-step logic, and algebra.

The TIMS Laboratory Method initiates children into the authentic practice of science. Identifying variables, drawing pictures, measuring, organizing data in tables, graphing data, and looking for and using patterns are a major part of many scientists' work. This is a major goal of science: to discover and use relationships between variables—usually expressed in some mathematical form—in order to understand and make predictions about the world.

The science content in *Math Trailblazers* focuses on a small set of simple variables that are fundamental to both math and science: length, area, volume, mass, and time. Understanding these basic variables is an essential step to achieving scientific understanding of more complex concepts. Measurement is presented in meaningful, experimental situations.

Emphasizing the scientific method and fundamental science concepts helps students develop an understanding of how scientists and mathematicians think. These habits of mind will be important in all aspects of life in the 21st century. See the TIMS Tutor: *The TIMS Laboratory Method* for more discussion of these ideas.

Connections to Language Arts

Reading, writing, and talking belong in mathematics class, not only because real mathematicians and scientists read, write, and talk mathematics and science constantly, but also because these activities help students learn. The NCTM *Principles and Standards* emphasizes the importance of communication and discourse for students to achieve at higher levels.

In school mathematics, results should be accepted not merely because someone in authority says so, but rather because persuasive arguments can be made for them. A result and a reason are often easier to remember than the result alone. By discussing the mathematics they are doing, students increase their understanding of that mathematics. They also extend their abilities to discuss mathematics and so to participate in a community of mathematicians. Talking and writing about mathematics, accordingly, are part of every lesson. Journal and discussion prompts are standard features in the teacher's guide for each lesson.

Reading is also built into this curriculum. Many lessons, especially in the primary grades, use trade books to launch or extend mathematical investigations. The curriculum also includes many original stories, called *Adventure Books,* that show applications of concepts being studied or sketch episodes from the history of mathematics and science. Literature is used to portray mathematics as a human endeavor, so that students come to think of mathematicians and scientists as people like themselves. Mathematics embedded in a narrative structure is also easier to understand, remember, and discuss. And, of course, everyone loves a good story. In addition, students regularly write about their mathematical investigations, even in the early grades.

Collaborative Work

Scientists, mathematicians, and most others who solve complex problems in business and industry have always worked in groups. The reasons for this are not hard to understand: Most interesting problems are too difficult for one person working alone. Explaining one's work to another person can help clarify one's own thinking. Another person's perspective can suggest a new approach to an unsolved problem. Ideas that have been tested through public scrutiny are more trustworthy than private notions.

All these are reasons for collaborating in schools as well. But there are other reasons, too. Students can learn both by receiving and by giving explanations. The communication that goes with group work provides practice in verbal and symbolic communication skills. In group discussion, a basic assumption is that mathematics and science ought to make sense—something, unfortunately, that many students cease to believe after only a few years of schooling. Social skills, especially cooperation and tolerance, increase, and the classroom community becomes more oriented towards learning and academic achievement.

Assessment

There are three major purposes for assessment. First, assessment helps teachers learn about students' thinking and knowledge; this information can then be used to guide instruction. Secondly, it communicates the goals of instruction to students and parents. Finally, it informs students and parents about progress toward these goals and suggests directions for further efforts.

Assessment in *Math Trailblazers* reflects the breadth and balance of the curriculum. Numerous opportunities for both formal and informal assessment of student learning are integrated into the program. Many of the assessment activities are incorporated into the daily lessons; others are included in formal assessment units. Assessment activities include a mix of short, medium-length, and extended activities. Some are hands-on investigations, others are paper-and-pencil tasks. In all cases, assessment activities further students' learning.

For a detailed discussion of assessment in *Math Trailblazers,* refer to Assessment (Section 8) and the TIMS Tutor: *Portfolios.*

More Time Studying Mathematics

One cannot reasonably expect to cover all the concepts in a traditional program, add many new topics, and utilize an approach that emphasizes problem solving, communication, reasoning, and connections in the same amount of time that is used to teach a traditional math curriculum. In developing *Math Trailblazers,* we have attempted to achieve some efficiencies, such as building review into new concepts and making use of effective strategies to ease the learning of math facts and procedures. However, we make no appeal to magic with *Math Trailblazers.* Implementing a comprehensive, reform mathematics curriculum will require a significant amount of time. **We assume that in Grades 1–5 one hour every day will be devoted to teaching mathematics.** In Kindergarten, the make-up of the class and the activity will determine the length of the class.

In some schools, finding an hour per day for math instruction may require a restructuring of the daily school schedule. Please note, however, that because *Math Trailblazers* includes extensive connections with science and language arts, *some* time spent with *Math Trailblazers* can be incorporated within science or language arts time. Thus, it may be possible to allot the one hour per day of mathematics instruction by simply scheduling math and science instruction back to back or including literature connections and journal writing in language arts.

Hard work on the part of students and more time spent engaged in mathematical problem solving are important ingredients to success in mathematics—no matter what program you are using. Because students using *Math Trailblazers* will be actively involved in applying mathematics in meaningful contexts, our experience is that students will be highly motivated to spend this extra time studying mathematics.

Staff Development and Broad School Support: Essential Ingredients

Our experience developing the curriculum and working with schools over the last decade has taught us that implementing a *Standards*-based mathematics program will go much more smoothly if it is accompanied by a solid support system for teachers. Ideally, this includes a professional development program that includes workshops on content and pedagogy, leadership development, in-school support, and the means to address a variety of concerns as they arise.

Overall implementation of *Math Trailblazers* will be much easier in a school that organizes support for the new program. Necessary tools such as manipulatives, overhead projectors, and transparency masters need to be provided in adequate quantities. Institutional considerations, such as classroom schedules that allot necessary time for instruction and provide time for teachers to meet and plan together, need to be implemented. In-classroom support from resource teachers is extremely helpful. Storage and check-out systems for shared manipulatives need to be in place. Ways to engender parental support for the program, including possible ways to involve some parents in providing classroom assistance to interested teachers during math time, should be developed.

Administrators need to maintain a long-term perspective on program implementation, recognizing that it will take some time before teachers and students are in "full gear" with the program—and they need to communicate this clearly to teachers. In short, schools need to examine their current situations and make necessary modifications to develop a school environment that supports the kind of teaching and learning that characterizes *Math Trailblazers*.

A Balanced Approach

A reform mathematics program should take a balanced and moderate approach. *Math Trailblazers* is balanced in many different ways. Whole-class instruction, small-group activities, and individual work each have a place. New mathematical content is included, but traditional topics are not neglected. Children construct their own knowledge in rich problem-solving situations, but they are not expected to reinvent 5000 years of mathematics on their own. Concepts, procedures, and facts are important, but these are introduced thoughtfully to engender the positive attitudes, beliefs, and self-image that are also important in the long run. Hands-on activities of varied length and depth, as well as paper-and-pencil tasks, all have their place. The program's rich variety of assessment activities has been designed to reflect this broad balance.

Either-or rhetoric has too often short-circuited real progress in education: problem solving vs. back-to-basics, conceptual understanding vs. procedural skill, paper-and-pencil computation vs. calculators. *Math Trailblazers* is based on the view that these are false dichotomies. Students must solve problems, but of course they need basic skills to do so. Both concepts and procedures are important, and neglecting one will undermine the other. There is a place in the curriculum both for paper-and-pencil algorithms and for calculators, and for mental arithmetic and estimation. The careful balance in *Math Trailblazers* allows teachers and schools to move forward with a reform mathematics curriculum while maintaining the strengths of their current teaching practices.

Research Foundations of *Math Trailblazers*

The first edition of *Math Trailblazers* was completed in 1997. The roots of the curriculum, however, date back to the late 1970s and the work of Howard Goldberg, a particle physicist at the University of Illinois at Chicago (UIC). Building on the work of Robert Karplus and others, Goldberg developed a framework for adapting the scientific method for elementary school children and applied that framework within a series of elementary laboratory investigations (Goldberg & Boulanger, 1981). Goldberg was joined in 1985 by UIC mathematician Philip Wagreich and, together with others, formed the Teaching Integrated Mathematics and Science Project (TIMS).

Thus, the motivation behind TIMS came from two sources, one with roots in science and one with roots in mathematics. The scientific impetus stemmed from the desire to teach science to children in a manner that reflects the practice of scientists. Modern science is fundamentally quantitative; therefore, quantitative investigations should have an important role in children's science education. The mathematical impetus was to find a way to make mathematics meaningful to children. Engaging children in quantitative investigations of common phenomena harnesses their curiosity in a way that builds upon their understanding of the natural world, which, in turn, helps promote study of rigorous mathematics (Isaacs, Wagreich, & Gartzman, 1997).

Initially, TIMS focused primarily on the development and implementation of a series of quantitative, hands-on activities, the *TIMS Laboratory Investigations* (Goldberg, 1997). The laboratory investigations continue the tradition of Dewey (1910) and others in focusing on the method of science and on exploring a relatively small set of fundamental scientific concepts in depth. Several studies provided clear evidence that the *TIMS Laboratory Investigations* are effective in promoting students' development of mathematics and science concepts (Goldberg & Wagreich, 1990; Goldberg, 1993).

Based largely upon the success with the supplemental *TIMS Laboratory Investigations,* the National Science Foundation (NSF) supported the TIMS Project to develop a comprehensive, elementary mathematics curriculum that would align with the National Council of Teachers of Mathematics (NCTM)

Curriculum and Evaluation Standards for School Mathematics (NCTM, 1989). The first edition of *Math Trailblazers* is the result of this work. As part of the revision process for the second edition, the authors made changes so that the new edition aligns with the current NCTM recommendations as outlined in the *Principles and Standards for School Mathematics* (NCTM, 2000).

In developing *Math Trailblazers,* the authors drew upon research findings from a wide variety of sources, as well as from the broad experiences of the authoring group. In this section we highlight a portion of the research that helped guide the curriculum's development and other current research that validates the approaches used.

A Problem-Solving Curriculum

A distinguishing element of any *Standards*-based mathematics curriculum is that problem solving is used as a context for students to learn new concepts and skills. Throughout *Math Trailblazers,* students apply the mathematics they know and construct new mathematics as needed. Students' skills, procedures, and concepts emerge and develop as they solve problems. Students also practice skills and procedures as they apply them in diverse and increasingly challenging contexts. Problem-solving contexts can emerge from real-life investigations or from more mathematical situations. The problems serve as the motivation for purposeful use of mathematics.

Using problem solving as a cornerstone of the mathematics curriculum has been promoted by educators dating back to Dewey and has received considerable support from current mathematics education researchers. (See Hiebert et al., 1996; Schoenfeld, 1985 and 1994; National Research Council, 2001; and NCTM 1989 and 2000 for a discussion of problem solving in the curriculum.)

A curriculum that emphasizes solving problems can use many different contexts for problem situations. In developing *Math Trailblazers,* the authors first identified the key mathematical concepts and skills to be developed and then selected problem-solving contexts that would support student learning in these areas. Our earlier work and that of others (e.g., Cognition and Technology Group at Vanderbilt, 1997) had confirmed the value of using quantitative laboratory investigations for this purpose. Drawing from this work, eight to ten laboratory investigations were adapted and integrated into *Math Trailblazers* in each grade, beginning with first grade. These investigations are supplemented by many other contexts for problem solving.

Challenging Mathematics in All Grades for All Students

An assumption in the development of *Math Trailblazers* was that students can learn more challenging mathematics than is covered in traditional mathematics curricula. This has been underscored in international comparison studies (Heibert, 1999; McKnight et al., 1987; Stigler & Perry, 1988; Schmidt, McKnight, & Raizen, 1996; Stigler & Hiebert, 1997; Stevenson & Stigler, 1992) and in analyses of U.S. mathematics instruction (Flanders, 1987; Lindquist, 1989). Maintaining high expectations and providing access to rigorous mathematics for all students has proven effective regardless of the socioeconomic status and ethnicity of the students (National Research Council, 2001; Newmann, Bryk, & Nagaoka, 2001; Smith, Lee,

& Newmann, 2001). Therefore, mathematical expectations in *Math Trailblazers* are high and grow steadily over time. Review of concepts and skills is carefully built into new and increasingly challenging problems as the program builds upon itself both within and across grades.

Balancing Concept and Skill Development

The importance of developing a strong conceptual foundation is emphasized in research that guided the development of all content strands in *Math Trailblazers*. Many educators have long recognized the importance of balancing conceptual and skill development. New conceptual understandings are built upon existing skills and concepts; these new understandings in turn support the further development of skills and concepts.

A wide body of research affirms that instructional programs that emphasize conceptual development can facilitate significant mathematics learning without sacrificing skill proficiency (see Hiebert, 1999). Research affirms that well-designed and implemented instructional programs can facilitate both conceptual understanding and procedural skill.

This research had a profound effect on development of *Math Trailblazers*. For example, such research helped define the curriculum's program for developing number sense and estimation skills (Sowder, 1992) and for learning math facts and whole-number operations (Carpenter, Carey, & Kouba, 1990; Carpenter, et al., 1999; Fuson, 1987, 1992; Fuson & Briars, 1990; Fuson et al., 1997; Isaacs & Carroll, 1999; Lampert, 1986a, 1986b; Thornton, 1978, 1990a, 1990b). Work with fractions and decimals was informed by research that stressed the need to develop conceptual understandings of fractions and decimals prior to introducing procedures with the four arithmetic operations (see Behr & Post, 1992; Ball, 1993; Cramer, Post, & del Mas, 2002; Lesh, Post, & Behr, 1987; Mack, 1990; Hoffer & Hoffer, 1992). Similar research findings on student understanding of geometric concepts shaped the development of lessons in geometry (see Burger & Shaughnessy, 1986; Crowley, 1987; Fuys, Geddes, & Tishler, 1988).

In direct response to research such as that cited here, every content strand within *Math Trailblazers* interweaves the promotion of conceptual understanding with distributed practice of skills and procedures.

Field Testing and Research on the Curriculum in Classrooms

NSF funding allowed sequential development of the program to be coupled with extensive field testing in schools. As a result, curriculum development became an iterative process involving considerable interaction between the developers and field-test teachers. Comments and suggestions from teachers were incorporated into revisions that were often retested in classrooms one or more times before final revisions were made. Field-test teachers met regularly with the program's authors, and classrooms were often visited as part of the development process. Content, language, format, practical considerations, and other issues related to each lesson were addressed by teachers who were using the early versions in their classrooms.

In addition to assessing feedback from field-test teachers, independent researchers and TIMS Project staff conducted preliminary studies that helped affirm the efficacy of the content placement and approaches in the early versions of the materials (Burghardt, 1994; Perry, Whiteaker, & Waddoups, 1996; Whiteaker, Waddoups, & Perry, 1994). These preliminary studies provided an additional means for the authors to monitor the effectiveness of the developing program.

Early studies of student achievement in *Math Trailblazers* classrooms in both urban and suburban schools have shown that students using the curriculum performed as well, and often better, on mandated standardized tests than students in those schools prior to implementation of *Math Trailblazers*. (Carter, et al., 2003; Putnam, 2003) "[The results] indicate that the balanced problem-solving approach found in *Math Trailblazers* has been successful in improving student learning and achievement in mathematics." (Carter, et al., 2003)

In developing the second edition, we benefited from the suggestions and comments of teachers throughout the country who were using the published *Math Trailblazers* materials. Input from teachers, for example, resulted in the major changes to the second edition's teacher guides. Teachers' feedback also directed us to modify or eliminate some lessons.

Extensive field testing during the program's development, current research and evaluation in schools, and our ongoing conversations with *Math Trailblazers* teachers have helped us develop a challenging, yet grade-level-appropriate program that reflects the needs and realities of teachers and students.

References

The following references are cited in the above document. Additional references to research literature are included in many *Unit Resource Guides* following the Background and in many sections of the *Teacher Implementation Guide* including the Assessment section and the TIMS Tutors.

Ball, D. "Halves, Pieces, and Twoths: Constructing and Using Representational Contexts in Teaching Fractions." In T. P. Carpenter, E. Fennema, and T.A. Romberg (Eds.), *Rational Numbers: An Integration of Research,* pp. 157–195. Lawrence Erlbaum Associates, Hillsdale, NJ, 1993.

Behr, M.J., and T.R. Post. "Teaching Rational Number and Decimal Concepts." In *Teaching Mathematics in Grades K–8: Research Based Methods.* Allyn and Bacon, Boston, 1992.

Burger, W., and J.M. Shaughnessy. "Characterizing the Van Hiele Levels of Development in Geometry." *Journal for Research in Mathematics Education,* 17, pp. 31–48, National Council of Teachers of Mathematics, Reston, VA, 1986.

Burghardt, B. Results of Some Summative Evaluation Studies: 1993–1994 Evaluation Report. (An unpublished report to the National Science Foundation.) 1994.

Carpenter, T.P., D. Carey, and V. Kouba. "A Problem-Solving Approach to the Operations." J.N. Payne, ed., *Mathematics for the Young Child.* National Council of Teachers of Mathematics, Reston, VA, 1990.

Carpenter, T.P., E. Fennema, M.L. Franke, L. Levi, and S.E. Empson. *Children's Mathematics: Cognitively Guided Instruction.* Heinemann, Westport, CT, 1999.

Carter, M.A., J.S. Beissinger, A. Cirulis, M. Gartzman, C.R. Kelso, and P. Wagreich. "Student Learning and Achievement with *Math Trailblazers.*" S.L. Senk and D.R. Thompson, eds., *Standards-Based School Mathematics Curricula: What Does the Research Say about Student Outcomes?* Lawrence Erlbaum Associates, Inc., Hillsdale, NJ, 2003.

Cognition and Technology Group at Vanderbilt. *The Jasper Project: Lessons in Curriculum, Instruction, Assessment, and Professional Development.* Erlbaum, Mahwah, NJ, 1997.

Cramer, K., T. Post, and R. del Mas. "Initial Fraction Learning by Fourth- and Fifth-Grade Students: A Comparison of the Effects of Using Commercial Curricula with the Effects of Using the Rational Number Project Curriculum." *Journal for Research in Mathematics Education,* 33(2), pp. 111–144.

Crowley, M.L. "The Van Hiele Model of Development of Geometric Thought." *Learning and Teaching Geometry, K–12, 1987 Yearbook.* Edited by Mary Montgomery Lindquist. National Council of Teachers of Mathematics, Reston, VA, 1987.

Curriculum and Evaluation Standards for School Mathematics. National Council of Teachers of Mathematics, Reston, VA, 1989.

Dewey, J. "Science as Subject-Matter and as Method." *Science,* 31(787), pp. 121–127, 1910.

Flanders, J. "How Much of the Content in Mathematics Textbooks Is New?" *The Arithmetic Teacher,* 35(1), pp. 18–23, 1987.

Fuson, K.C. "Teaching Addition, Subtraction, and Place-Value Concepts." L. Wirszup and R. Streit (eds.), *Proceedings of the UCSMP International Conference on Mathematics Education: Developments in School Mathematics Education Around the World: Applications-Oriented Curricula and Technology-Supported Learning for All Students.* National Council of Teachers of Mathematics, Reston, VA, 1987.

Fuson, K.C. "Research on Whole Number Addition and Subtraction." *Handbook of Research on Mathematics Teaching and Learning,* pp. 243–275, D.A. Grouws, ed. Macmillan Publishing Company, New York, 1992.

Fuson, K.C., and D.J. Briars. "Using a Base-Ten Blocks Learning/Teaching Approach for First- and Second-Grade Place-Value and Multidigit Addition and Subtraction." *Journal for Research in Mathematics Education,* 21, pp. 180–206, 1990.

Fuson, K.C., D. Wearne, J. Hiebert, H. Murray, P. Human, A. Olivier, T. Carpenter, and E. Fennema. "Children's Conceptual Structures for Multidigit Numbers and Methods of Multidigit Addition and Subtraction." *Journal for Research in Mathematics Education,* 28, pp. 130–162, 1997.

Fuys, D., D. Geddes, and R. Tishler. "The Van Hiele Model of Thinking in Geometry among Adolescents." *Journal for Research in Mathematics Education, Monograph Number 3.* National Council of Teachers of Mathematics, Reston, VA, 1988.

Goldberg, H. *A Four Year Achievement Study: The TIMS Program.* University of Illinois at Chicago Institute for Mathematics and Science Education, Chicago, IL, 1993.

Goldberg, H. *The TIMS Laboratory Investigations.* Kendall/Hunt, Dubuque, IA, 1997.

Goldberg, H.S., and F.D. Boulanger. "Science for Elementary School Teachers: A Quantitative Approach." *American Journal of Physics,* 19(2), pp. 120–124, 1981.

Goldberg, H., and P. Wagreich. "A Model Integrated Mathematics Science Program for the Elementary School." *International Journal of Educational Research,* 14(2), pp. 193–214, 1990.

Goldberg, H., and P. Wagreich. "Teaching Integrated Math and Science: A Curriculum and Staff Development Project for the Elementary School." *Issues in Mathematics Education: Mathematicians and Education Reform.* N. Fisher, H. Keynes, and P. Wagreich, eds., American Mathematical Society, Providence, RI, 1990.

Hiebert, J. "Relationships between Research and the NCTM Standards." *Journal for Research in Mathematics Education,* 30(1), pp. 3–19, 1999.

Hiebert, J., T.P. Carpenter, E. Fennema, K.C. Fuson, P. Human, H. Murray, A. Olivier, D. Wearne. "Problem Solving as a Basis for Reform in Curriculum and Instruction: The Case of Mathematics." *Educational Researcher,* 25(4), pp. 12–21, 1996.

Hoffer, A.R., and S.A.K. Hoffer. "Ratios and Proportional Thinking." In *Teaching Mathematics in Grades K–8: Research Based Methods.* Allyn and Bacon, Boston, 1992.

Isaacs, A.C., and W.M. Carroll. "Strategies for Basic-Facts Instruction." *Teaching Children Mathematics,* 5(9), pp. 508–515, 1999.

Isaacs, A.C., P. Wagreich, and M. Gartzman. The Quest for Integration: School Mathematics and Science. *American Journal of Education,* 106(1), pp. 179–206, 1997.

Lampert, M. "Knowing, Doing, and Teaching Multiplication." *Cognition and Instruction,* 3 (4), pp. 305–342, 1986a.

Lampert, M. "Teaching Multiplication." *Journal of Mathematical Behavior,* 5, pp. 241–280, 1986b.

Lesh, R., T. Post, and M. Behr. "Representations and Translations Among Representations in Mathematics Learning and Problem Solving." C. Janvier, ed., *Problems of Representation in the Teaching and Learning of Mathematics.* Lawrence Erlbaum Associates, Hillsdale, NJ, 1987.

Lindquist, M.M., ed. *Results from the Fourth Mathematics Assessment of the National Assessment of Educational Progress.* National Council of Teachers of Mathematics. Reston, VA, 1989.

Mack, N.K. "Learning Fractions with Understanding: Building on Informal Knowledge." *Journal for Research in Mathematics Education,* 21(1), National Council of Teachers of Mathematics, Reston, VA, January 1990.

McKnight, C.C., F.J. Crosswhite, J.A. Dossey, E. Kifer, J.O. Swafford, K.T. Travers, and T.J. Cooney, *The Underachieving Curriculum: Assessing U.S. School Mathematics from an International Perspective.* Stipes Publishing Company, Champaign, IL, 1987.

National Research Council. *Adding It Up: Helping Children Learn Mathematics.* J. Kilpatrick, J. Swafford, and B. Findell, eds. National Academy Press, Washington, DC, 2001.

Newmann, F.M., A.S. Bryk, and J.K. Nagaoka. *Authentic Intellectual Work and Standardized Tests: Conflict or Coexistence?* Consortium on Chicago School Research, Chicago, 2001.

Perry, M., M. Whiteaker, and G.L. Waddoups. "Students' Participation in a Reform Mathematics Classroom: Learning to Become Mathematicians." In K. Fuson (Chair), *Effects of Reform Mathematics Curricula on Children's Mathematical Understanding.* Symposia conducted at the annual meeting of the American Educational Research Association, New York, 1996.

Principles and Standards for School Mathematics. National Council of Teachers of Mathematics, Reston, VA, 2000.

Putnam, R.T. "Commentary on Four Elementary Mathematics Curricula." S.L. Senk and D.R. Thompson, eds., *Standards-Based School Mathematics Curricula: What Does the Research Say about Student Outcomes?* Lawrence Erlbaum Associates, Inc., Hillsdale, NJ, 2003.

Schmidt, W.H., C.C. McKnight, and S.A. Raizen. *A Splintered Vision: An Investigation of U.S. Science and Mathematics Education.* Kluwer, Norwell, MA, 1996.

Schoenfeld, A.H. *Mathematical Problem Solving.* Academic Press, Orlando, FL, 1985.

Schoenfeld, A.H. "What Do We Know about Mathematics Curricula?" *Journal of Mathematical Behavior,* 13(1), pp. 55–80, 1994.

Schroeder, T.L., and F.K. Lester, Jr. "Developing Understanding in Mathematics via Problem Solving." In *New Directions for Elementary School Mathematics,* 1989 Yearbook. National Council of Teachers of Mathematics, Reston, VA, 1989.

Smith, J.B., V.E. Lee, and F.M. Newmann. *Instruction and Achievement in Chicago Elementary Schools.* Consortium on Chicago School Research, Chicago, 2001.

Sowder, J. "Estimation and Number Sense." *Handbook of Research on Mathematics Teaching and Learning,* pp. 243–275, D.A. Grouws, ed., Macmillan Publishing Company, New York, 1992.

Stevenson, H.W., and J.W. Stigler. *The Learning Gap.* Simon & Schuster, New York, NY, 1992.

Stigler, J.W., and J. Hiebert. "Understanding and Improving Classroom Mathematics Instruction: An Overview of the TIMSS Study." *Phi Delta Kappan,* 79(1), pp. 14–21.

Stigler, J.W., and M. Perry. "Mathematics Learning in Japanese, Chinese, and American Classrooms." G.B. Saxe and M. Gearhart, eds., *New Directions for Child Development, No. 41: Children's Mathematics.* Jossey Bass, San Francisco, CA, 1988.

Thornton, C.A. "Emphasizing Thinking Strategies in Basic Fact Instruction." *Journal for Research in Mathematics Education,* 9 (3), pp. 214–227, 1978.

Thornton, C.A. "Solution Strategies: Subtraction Number Facts." *Educational Studies in Mathematics,* 21 (1), pp. 241–263, 1990a.

Thornton, C.A. "Strategies for the Basic Facts." *Mathematics for the Young Child,* pp. 133–151, J.N. Payne, ed. National Council of Teachers of Mathematics, Reston, VA, 1990b.

3

Components and Features Guide

The Components and Features Guide presents reduced-size curriculum pages and descriptive boxes which cover each element of *Math Trailblazers*.

Students use Activity, Lab, and Game Pages, which are provided in the student books.

Components of *Math Trailblazers*

The following pages offer a walk-through of the *Teacher Implementation Guide, Teacher Resource CD, Unit Resource Guide, Student Guide,* and *Adventure Book.*

Teacher Materials

TEACHER IMPLEMENTATION GUIDE (TIG)

- reference guide for teachers, containing program philosophy, overview, and in-depth reference documents, including a section on assessment
- black and white, nonconsumable
- glossary, including locations of key vocabulary terms in the curriculum
- curriculum index with page references to key vocabulary terms

TEACHER RESOURCE CD

Teacher resource containing:

- Daily Practice and Problems items
- Observational Assessment Record
- Individual Assessment Record Sheet
- Letters Home (English and Spanish)
- Assessment, Transparency, and Blackline Masters
- Generic Pages
- Student and Teacher Rubrics

UNIT RESOURCE GUIDE (URG)

- comprehensive guide providing essential background information and materials for day-to-day planning, instruction, and assessment
- black and white, nonconsumable
- contains:
  Letters Home
  Unit Outlines
  Daily Practice and Problems
  Observational Assessment
    Record
  Lesson Guides
  Materials Lists
  Assessment Pages
  Transparency and
    Blackline Masters
  Answer Keys
  Generic Pages

Student Materials

STUDENT GUIDE (SG)

- core material for students
- four-color
- soft cover, consumable in 2 volumes: Grades 1, 2
- hard cover, nonconsumable: Grades 3, 4, 5
- glossary and index: Grades 1, 2
- glossary-embedded index: Grades 3, 4, 5

ADVENTURE BOOK (AB)

- collections of illustrated stories focused on math and science concepts
- available in four-color Big Adventure Book and consumable black-and-white books in Grades 1, 2
- available in soft cover, four-color, nonconsumable format in Grades 3, 4, 5

Unit Resource Guide
Letter Home (Parent Letter)

The Letter Home is designed to go out under the teacher's signature. It explains what students will study and how their families can help. Spanish versions of letters are also provided and can be found in a separate booklet in the *Unit Resource Guide* File.

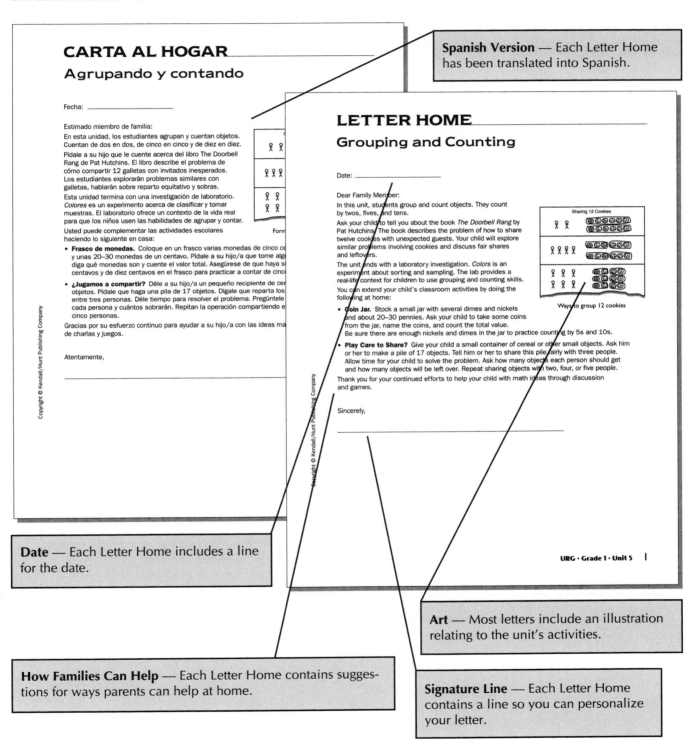

Spanish Version — Each Letter Home has been translated into Spanish.

CARTA AL HOGAR
Agrupando y contando

Fecha: _____

Estimado miembro de familia:

En esta unidad, los estudiantes agrupan y cuentan objetos. Cuentan de dos en dos, de cinco en cinco y de diez en diez. Pídale a su hijo que le cuente acerca de su libro The Doorbell Rang de Pat Hutchins. El libro describe el problema de cómo compartir 12 galletas con invitados inesperados. Los estudiantes explorarán problemas similares con galletas, hablarán sobre reparto equitativo y sobras.

Esta unidad termina con una investigación de laboratorio. *Colores* es un experimento acerca de clasificar y tomar muestras. El laboratorio ofrece un contexto de la vida real para que los niños usen las habilidades de agrupar y contar.

Usted puede complementar las actividades escolares haciendo lo siguiente en casa:

- **Frasco de monedas.** Coloque en un frasco varias monedas de cinco ce... y unas 20–30 monedas de un centavo. Pídale a su hijo/a que tome alg... diga qué monedas son y cuente el valor total. Asegúrese de que haya s... centavos y de diez centavos en el frasco para practicar a contar de cinc...

- **¿Jugamos a compartir?** Déle a su hijo/a un pequeño recipiente de cer... objetos. Pídale que haga una pila de 17 objetos. Dígale que reparta los... entre tres personas. Déle tiempo para resolver el problema. Pregúntele... cada persona y cuántos sobrarán. Repitan la operación compartiendo e... cinco personas.

Gracias por su esfuerzo continuo para ayudar a su hijo/a con las ideas ma... de charlas y juegos.

Atentamente,

_____

Copyright © Kendall/Hunt Publishing Company

LETTER HOME
Grouping and Counting

Date: _____

Dear Family Member:

In this unit, students group and count objects. They count by twos, fives, and tens. Ask your child to tell you about the book *The Doorbell Rang* by Pat Hutchins. The book describes the problem of how to share twelve cookies with unexpected guests. Your child will explore similar problems involving cookies and discuss fair shares and leftovers.

The unit ends with a laboratory investigation. *Colors* is an experiment about sorting and sampling. The lab provides a real-life context for children to use grouping and counting skills.

You can extend your child's classroom activities by doing the following at home:

- **Coin Jar.** Stock a small jar with several dimes and nickels and about 20–30 pennies. Ask your child to take some coins from the jar, name the coins, and count the total value. Be sure there are enough nickels and dimes in the jar to practice counting by 5s and 10s.

- **Play Care to Share?** Give your child a small container of cereal or other small objects. Ask him or her to make a pile of 17 objects. Tell him or her to share this pile fairly with three people. Allow time for your child to solve the problem. Ask how many objects each person should get and how many objects will be left over. Repeat sharing objects with two, four, or five people.

Thank you for your continued efforts to help your child with math ideas through discussion and games.

Sincerely,

_____

Copyright © Kendall/Hunt Publishing Company

Sharing 12 Cookies

Ways to group 12 cookies

Date — Each Letter Home includes a line for the date.

Art — Most letters include an illustration relating to the unit's activities.

How Families Can Help — Each Letter Home contains suggestions for ways parents can help at home.

Signature Line — Each Letter Home contains a line so you can personalize your letter.

Unit Resource Guide
Unit Outline

The Unit Outline indicates the number of lessons, what they are about, what you will need to do them, how much time they will take, and other materials you may want to introduce.

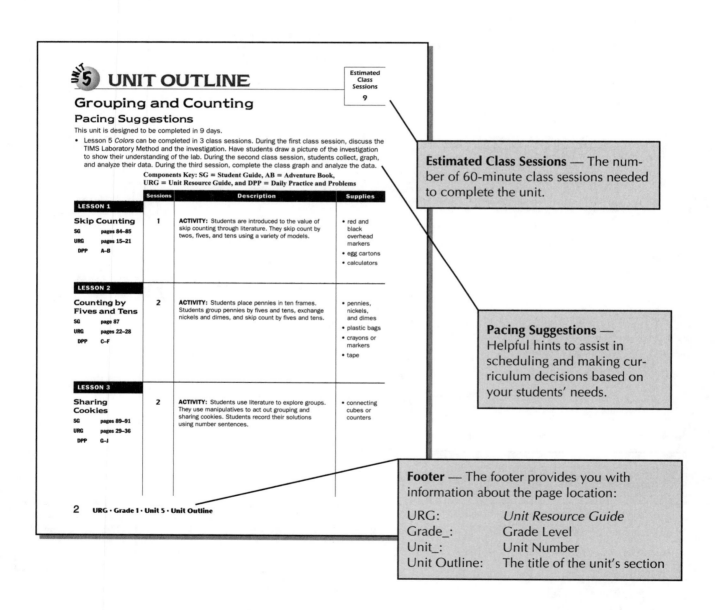

Estimated Class Sessions — The number of 60-minute class sessions needed to complete the unit.

Pacing Suggestions — Helpful hints to assist in scheduling and making curriculum decisions based on your students' needs.

Footer — The footer provides you with information about the page location:

URG:	*Unit Resource Guide*
Grade_:	Grade Level
Unit_:	Unit Number
Unit Outline:	The title of the unit's section

Sessions — The number of 60-minute class sessions needed to complete the lesson.

Assessment Pages — Listed here to help you prepare and plan.

Supplies — Describes the type of manipulatives, lab equipment, and other materials essential for each lesson.

Daily Practice and Problems Letters — These letters indicate the suggested DPP items for each lesson.

Sessions	Description	Supplies
LESSON 4		
I've Got a Little List AB pages 9–18 URG pages 37–40 DPP K–L	1	**ADVENTURE BOOK:** Students read a story while learning the importance of labeling data tables.	
LESSON 5		
Colors SG pages 93–97 URG pages 41–50 DPP M–R	3	**LAB:** Students sample cereal to determine the colors in a population. The TIMS Laboratory Method is introduced.	• Froot Loops® (or substitute) • $\frac{1}{4}$ measuring cup • large bowl • calculators • crayons or markers • scissors • tape

CONNECTIONS

A current list of connections is available at www.mathtrailblazers.com.

Literature   **Essential Titles**
- Dee, Ruby. *Two Ways to Count to Ten.* Econo-Clad Books, Topeka, KS, 1999.
- Hutchins, Pat. *The Doorbell Rang.* Mulberry Books, New York, 1994.

Software
- *Grouping and Place Value* practices grouping objects by twos, fives, and tens.
- *Kid Pix* helps students draw, write, and illustrate math concepts.
- *Math Concepts One . . . Two . . . Three!* provides practice with number sense, addition and subtraction with manipulatives and money, sorting objects, and making simple bar graphs.
- *Mighty Math Carnival Countdown* provides practice with place value, counting, and basic operations.
- *Mighty Math Zoo Zillions* provides practice with basic operations (adding and subtracting) with money, rounding, skip counting, and identifying even/odd numbers.
- *Money Challenge* provides practice with money.

PREPARING FOR UPCOMING LESSONS

Ask students to bring in toy cars or other things with wheels for use in the *Rolling Along with Links* lab in Unit 6.

URG · Grade 1 · Unit 5 · Unit Outline   **3**

Component — Tells you where to find student and teacher print materials for each lesson.

Connections — The material in *Math Trailblazers* lessons often can be related to books, magazine articles and computer programs. When a Connection is recommended for use with a specific lesson, it is included in the Lesson Guide.

Optional Lessons — Shaded banner highlights optional lessons and review materials.

Lesson Description — Indicates the type of lesson (Activity, Adventure Book, Assessment, Game, or Lab) and outlines its contents.

Preparing for Upcoming Lessons — Suggestions to help you plan ahead.

Unit Resource Guide
Background

The Background explains what students will learn in the unit and places the material in the larger context of the *Math Trailblazers* curriculum.

 BACKGROUND

Grouping and Counting

Grouping and Counting, Sorting, and Sampling

In this unit, students group and count objects. They skip count by twos, fives, and tens. This experience strengthens students' number sense so that they can use a range of numbers in future units to explore measurement, concepts of addition and subtraction, and computation.

Students count by twos through counting hands, arms, and other objects that are naturally grouped by twos. Counting by fives occurs in the context of counting fingers on one hand, grouping pennies by fives, and substituting a nickel for every group of five pennies. Counting by tens is motivated by counting fingers on both hands, grouping pennies by tens, and substituting a dime for every group of ten pennies.

Children will also describe and name numbers in terms of groups. It is important for children to think about groups of numbers. Work with 12, for example, includes far more than the fact that it is twelve ones or the number that comes after eleven. Twelve is also two 6s, three 4s, and two 5s with 2 left over. This helps students establish a foundation for working with place value ideas.

Children will apply their grouping and skip counting experiences in the *Colors* laboratory investigation. In *Colors,* students explore sorting and sampling. Through this activity and others like it, students begin to understand what can be said about a collection by looking at a sample. The investigation provides an example of sampling techniques that are used by scientists, journalists, health professionals, business people, and others who regularly analyze data. Two familiar examples of this type of work include election polls and health surveys.

TIMS Laboratory Method

Students are in the process of developing facility with different problem-solving tools, such as graphs, tables, manipulatives, diagrams, and calculators. With *Colors,* some of these tools are put together into a process that is similar to one used regularly by scientists—the scientific method.

Students portray a problem situation using a picture. They collect data, organize it in a data table, and graph it. Then, they use tools to look for patterns and analyze the data carefully. This simplified version of the scientific method is characteristic of TIMS laboratory investigations. It is a powerful way to examine many different problems. For additional information, see the TIMS Tutor: *The TIMS Laboratory Method* in the *Teacher Implementation Guide.*

Math Journals and Portfolios

Before students begin the *Colors* lab, they read an adventure book story about a boy who didn't label his data table during the experiment. When he cannot answer the questions, his mother helps him find a solution and discusses the importance of making lists to help one remember. In the adventure book guide, the first journal prompt for first grade is listed. This is a good opportunity for students to begin math journals. Math journals are a rich assessment source. Many of the journal prompts listed in future Lesson Guides elicit information about students' understanding of specific concepts, their ability to communicate this understanding in writing, and their attitudes about mathematics. Students' first journal entries may be sketchy, but experience suggests that their efforts will improve. See the TIMS Tutor: *Journals* for more information. Math portfolios also provide a rich assessment source. Students may begin collecting materials that can be added to their portfolios throughout the year as a record of progress. See the TIMS Tutor: *Portfolios* for additional information.

Assessment Indicators

- Can students group and count objects by twos, fives, and tens?
- Can students divide a collection of objects into groups of a given size and count the leftovers?
- Can students collect and organize data in a table?
- Can students identify the relationships among pennies, nickels, and dimes?

Assessment Indicators — A list that orients teachers to some of the key skills and concepts covered in the unit.

Resources — Pointers to additional information on the ideas covered in the unit are included.

Unit Resource Guide
Observational Assessment Record

The *Observational Assessment Record* is a form used to record observations of students' progress.

Assessment Indicators — These are the Assessment Indicators listed in the Background. They highlight the skills and concepts you should look for as you observe students working on activities in the unit.

Additional lines are provided to help document students' progress with other content.

OBSERVATIONAL ASSESSMENT RECORD

(A1) Can students group and count objects by twos, fives, and tens?

(A2) Can students divide a collection of objects into groups of a given size and count the leftovers?

(A3) Can students collect and organize data in a table?

(A4) Can students identify the relationships among pennies, nickels, and dimes?

(A5) _____

Assessment Icons — Each of the Assessment Indicators is numbered and labeled with an icon (e.g., (A1)–(A5)).

Name	A1	A2	A3	A4	A5	Comments
1.						
2.						
3.						
4.						
5.						
6.						
7.						
8.						
9.						
10.						
11.						
12.						
13.						

URG · Grade 1 · Unit 5 · Observational Assessment Record   **5**

Unit Resource Guide
Daily Practice and Problems

The Daily Practice and Problems (DPP) is a series of short exercises that provide continuing review of math concepts, skills, and facts. Each set of DPP includes a Teacher's Guide, which provides specific information on the study and assessment of the math facts in the current unit.

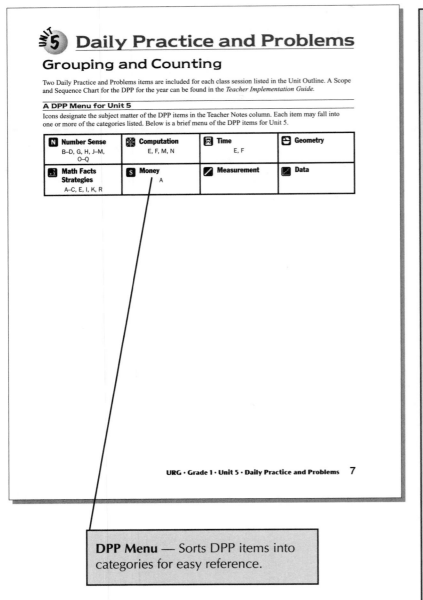

Daily Practice and Problems
UNIT 5

Grouping and Counting

Two Daily Practice and Problems items are included for each class session listed in the Unit Outline. A Scope and Sequence Chart for the DPP for the year can be found in the *Teacher Implementation Guide*.

A DPP Menu for Unit 5

Icons designate the subject matter of the DPP items in the Teacher Notes column. Each item may fall into one or more of the categories listed. Below is a brief menu of the DPP items for Unit 5.

N Number Sense B–D, G, H, J–M, O–Q	**※** Computation E, F, M, N	**⌛** Time E, F	**⬢** Geometry
7+3 Math Facts Strategies A–C, E, I, K, R	**$** Money A	**▧** Measurement	**▨** Data

URG · Grade 1 · Unit 5 · Daily Practice and Problems   7

DPP Menu — Sorts DPP items into categories for easy reference.

The Daily Practice and Problems may be used in class for practice and review, as assessment, or for homework. Notes for teachers provide the answers as well as suggestions for using the items.

Eight icons indicate the subject matter of each item:

N **Number Sense** (estimating, partitioning numbers, skip counting, etc.);

※ **Computation** (problems which may be solved using paper-and-pencil methods, estimation, mental math, or calculators);

⌛ **Time** (exploring time concepts including time of day, days, weeks, months, and using the calendar);

⬢ **Geometry** (work with shapes, measurement, coordinates, or other geometric topics);

7+3 **Math Facts Strategies** (practice with addition, subtraction, multiplication, or division facts strategies);

$ **Money** (counting change, combining various coins, or estimating total cost);

▧ **Measurement** (measuring length, area, or volume); and

▨ **Data** (collecting, organizing, graphing, or analyzing data).

For each nonoptional class session noted in a Unit Outline, there are two Daily Practice and Problems items.

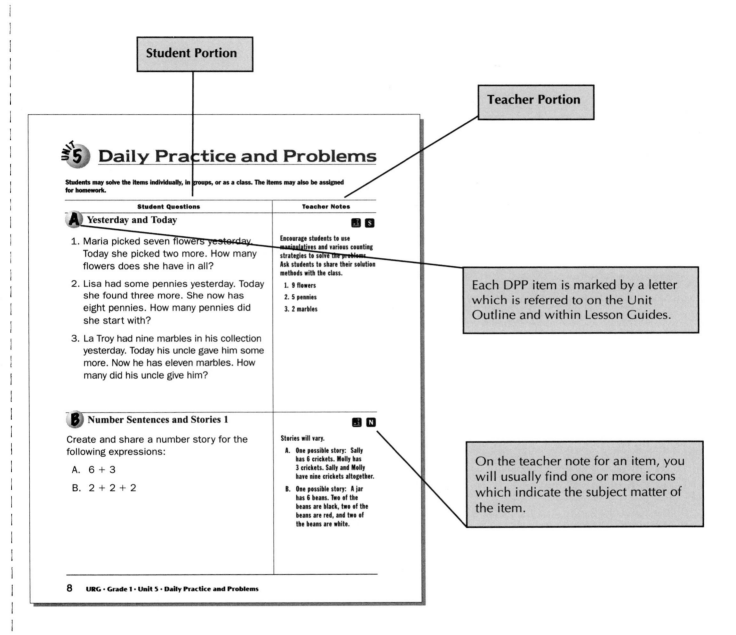

Student Portion

Teacher Portion

^{UNIT}5 Daily Practice and Problems

Students may solve the items individually, in groups, or as a class. The items may also be assigned for homework.

Student Questions	Teacher Notes
A Yesterday and Today	
1. Maria picked seven flowers yesterday. Today she picked two more. How many flowers does she have in all?	Encourage students to use manipulatives and various counting strategies to solve the problems. Ask students to share their solution methods with the class.
2. Lisa had some pennies yesterday. Today she found three more. She now has eight pennies. How many pennies did she start with?	1. 9 flowers 2. 5 pennies 3. 2 marbles
3. La Troy had nine marbles in his collection yesterday. Today his uncle gave him some more. Now he has eleven marbles. How many did his uncle give him?	
B Number Sentences and Stories 1	
Create and share a number story for the following expressions:	Stories will vary.
A. 6 + 3	A. One possible story: Sally has 6 crickets. Molly has 3 crickets. Sally and Molly have nine crickets altogether.
B. 2 + 2 + 2	B. One possible story: A jar has 6 beans. Two of the beans are black, two of the beans are red, and two of the beans are white.

8   URG · Grade 1 · Unit 5 · Daily Practice and Problems

Each DPP item is marked by a letter which is referred to on the Unit Outline and within Lesson Guides.

On the teacher note for an item, you will usually find one or more icons which indicate the subject matter of the item.

Unit Resource Guide
Lesson Guide

The Lesson Guide is a how-to manual explaining what you need and what is involved in each lesson.

Estimated Class Sessions — Indicates the number of 60-minute class sessions needed to complete the lesson.

Lesson Description — A summary of the lesson orients you quickly.

Key Content — Lists important mathematical ideas students will encounter.

Key Vocabulary — Words to watch for.

DPP Items — DPP items to be completed as a warm-up or review.

DPP Information — Page numbers for further information on how and when to use the DPP.

Curriculum Sequence

Before This Unit — Describes material students have covered on this topic in previous grades or previous units.

After This Unit — Describes material students will cover on this topic in succeeding units.

LESSON GUIDE 5
Colors

Estimated
Class
Sessions:
3

Colors is a laboratory investigation about sorting and sampling. The TIMS Laboratory Method, a four-step adaptation of the scientific method, is introduced. Using a colored breakfast cereal, students investigate the color distribution in a box of cereal by studying smaller samples. They also explore how the size of the sample can have an effect on experimental results. In addition, the experiment provides a context for applying grouping and skip counting.

Key Content

- Connecting mathematics and real-world events: investigating colors in cereals.
- Sampling a population.
- Collecting, organizing, graphing, and analyzing data.
- Using number patterns to count objects.
- Translating among different representations of numbers.

Key Vocabulary

prediction
sample

Curriculum Sequence

After This Unit

TIMS Laboratory Method. This lesson introduces the TIMS Laboratory Method. In Grade 1, students will use this four-step scientific method in labs in Units 6, 9, 11, 14, 16, and 19. Students will continue to use the TIMS Laboratory Method in Grades 2–5.

Portfolios. Keep students' work for this lab in a portfolio so that their baseline work on this lab can be compared to their work on other labs, including *Rolling Along with Links* in Unit 6, *Full of Beans* in Unit 9, *Pets* in Unit 14, and *Healthy Kids* in Unit 16.

Daily Practice and Problems

M. Sharing Stickers (URG p. 12) **N** **※**

Draw eight stickers. Show how you would share these stickers with . . .

A. four friends: 4 groups of __ and __ left over

B. three friends: 3 groups of __ and __ left over

C. five friends: 5 groups of __ and __ left over

N. Who Is at the Door? (URG p. 12) **※**

The Samsons are having a party. There were sixteen people in their house. Then, the doorbell rang and three more people entered the house.

1. How many people are there now?
2. Write a number sentence to go with your answer.
3. Create another story to go along with this number sentence.

O. Grandma's Cookies 1 (URG p. 13) **N**

Grandma made 27 cookies. Only ten fit in one box. Help Grandma pack her cookies. Draw a rectangle for each box Grandma can fill with ten cookies. Draw one circle for each leftover cookie.

P. Grandma's Cookies 2 (URG p. 13) **N**

Grandma made 42 cookies. Only ten fit in one box. Help Grandma pack her cookies. Draw a rectangle for each box Grandma can fill with ten cookies. Draw one circle for each leftover cookie.

Q. My Pencils/Your Pencils (URG p. 13) **N**

1. How many pencils are in your desk?
2. Is the number of pencils even or odd? How did you decide?
3. Put your pencils in a pile with your partner's pencils.
4. Is the number of pencils even or odd? How did you decide?

R. Spoonful of Cereal (URG p. 14)

1. Alex took a sample of cereal with a teaspoon. He grabbed five red pieces and two green pieces. How many pieces of cereal did Alex grab with his spoon?
2. Tanya's sample of cereal had three red pieces, three green pieces, and two yellow pieces. How many pieces of cereal did Tanya grab?

Suggestions for using the DPPs are on page 47.

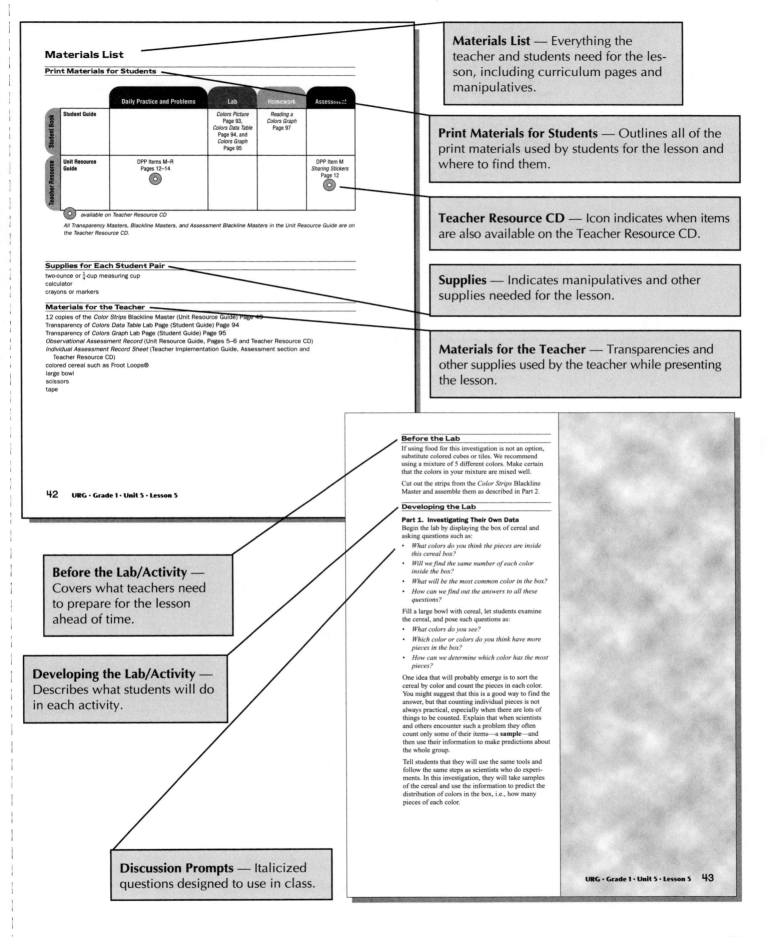

Materials List

Print Materials for Students

		Daily Practice and Problems	Lab	Homework	Assessment
Student Book	Student Guide		Colors Picture Page 93, Colors Data Table Page 94, and Colors Graph Page 95	Reading a Colors Graph Page 97	
Teacher Resource	Unit Resource Guide	DPP Items M–R Pages 12–14			DPP Item M Sharing Stickers Page 12

available on Teacher Resource CD

All Transparency Masters, Blackline Masters, and Assessment Blackline Masters in the Unit Resource Guide are on the Teacher Resource CD.

Supplies for Each Student Pair

two-ounce or $\frac{1}{4}$-cup measuring cup
calculator
crayons or markers

Materials for the Teacher

12 copies of the *Color Strips* Blackline Master (Unit Resource Guide) Page 49
Transparency of *Colors Data Table* Lab Page (Student Guide) Page 94
Transparency of *Colors Graph* Lab Page (Student Guide) Page 95
Observational Assessment Record (Unit Resource Guide, Pages 5–6 and Teacher Resource CD)
Individual Assessment Record Sheet (Teacher Implementation Guide, Assessment section and Teacher Resource CD)
colored cereal such as Froot Loops®
large bowl
scissors
tape

42   URG · Grade 1 · Unit 5 · Lesson 5

Materials List — Everything the teacher and students need for the lesson, including curriculum pages and manipulatives.

Print Materials for Students — Outlines all of the print materials used by students for the lesson and where to find them.

Teacher Resource CD — Icon indicates when items are also available on the Teacher Resource CD.

Supplies — Indicates manipulatives and other supplies needed for the lesson.

Materials for the Teacher — Transparencies and other supplies used by the teacher while presenting the lesson.

Before the Lab

If using food for this investigation is not an option, substitute colored cubes or tiles. We recommend using a mixture of 5 different colors. Make certain that the colors in your mixture are mixed well.

Cut out the strips from the *Color Strips* Blackline Master and assemble them as described in Part 2.

Developing the Lab

Part 1. Investigating Their Own Data
Begin the lab by displaying the box of cereal and asking questions such as:

* *What colors do you think the pieces are inside this cereal box?*
* *Will we find the same number of each color inside the box?*
* *What will be the most common color in the box?*
* *How can we find out the answers to all these questions?*

Fill a large bowl with cereal, let students examine the cereal, and pose such questions as:

* *What colors do you see?*
* *Which color or colors do you think have more pieces in the box?*
* *How can we determine which color has the most pieces?*

One idea that will probably emerge is to sort the cereal by color and count the pieces in each color. You might suggest that this is a good way to find the answer, but that counting individual pieces is not always practical, especially when there are lots of things to be counted. Explain that when scientists and others encounter such a problem they often count only some of their items—a **sample**—and then use their information to make predictions about the whole group.

Tell students that they will use the same tools and follow the same steps as scientists who do experiments. In this investigation, they will take samples of the cereal and use the information to predict the distribution of colors in the box, i.e., how many pieces of each color.

Before the Lab/Activity — Covers what teachers need to prepare for the lesson ahead of time.

Developing the Lab/Activity — Describes what students will do in each activity.

Discussion Prompts — Italicized questions designed to use in class.

URG · Grade 1 · Unit 5 · Lesson 5   43

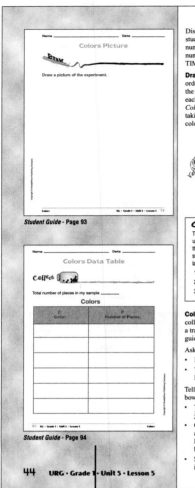

Student Guide - Page 93

Student Guide - Page 94

Discuss the procedure for the investigation with students: take a sample of the cereal, count the total number in the sample, sort it by color, and count the number of pieces of each color. They will use the TIMS Laboratory Method as described below.

Draw. The first step in a lab is drawing a picture. In order to facilitate the drawing of the picture, model the procedure, clearly demonstrating and discussing each step. Ask each child to draw a picture on the *Colors Picture* Lab Page that shows themselves taking a scoop of cereal, sorting it according to color, and counting the pieces of each color.

Figure 6: *A picture communicating the variables in the lab*

Content Note

The picture allows students to plan and organize the procedure used in the lab and provides a way for them to communicate this procedure. It can also provide you with some insight into students' understanding. To assess their understanding of the lab, look for each of these important elements:

1. each cereal color
2. sampling the cereal
3. sorting and counting the cereal

Collect. The second step in the lab procedure is collecting data and organizing it in a data table. Use a transparency of the *Colors Data Table* Lab Page to guide students as needed.

Ask the class to:

- Identify all the colors in the cereal.
- Write each color on the *Colors Data Table* Lab Page.

Tell the class you are going to walk around with a bowl of cereal and a scoop. Each pair should:

- Take one scoop of cereal. (A two-ounce cup or $\frac{1}{4}$-cup measuring cup works well.)
- Count the total number of pieces in their sample and write this total on the *Colors Data Table* Lab Page. Encourage students to group their pieces by twos, fives, or tens.
- Sort their sample by color and count the pieces in each pile.

- Record this data in the data table.

After pairs have finished their data tables, pose questions such as:

In your sample,

- *Are there more yellow or red pieces? How can you tell?*
- *What color has the most pieces? How can you tell?*
- *Was this the most common color in all the samples?*
- *When you add all the numbers with a calculator, predict what the total number of pieces will be. Try it.*

Graph. The third step is to use the data table to create a graph. Guide students by using a transparency of the *Colors Graph.* Say:

- *A data table is one way to organize the data. Sometimes it is easier to see patterns if the data is organized on a graph.*
- *Look at the Colors Graph. Notice the graph has a title at the top of the graph.*
- *Notice the label "Color" at the bottom. This is the same label that is in one column of the data table. You will fill in a color name in each box or use a crayon to mark the color as needed.*
- *Notice the label "Number of Pieces" on the left side. This is the same label that is in the other column on the data table. The numbers along the left side help us read a graph.*
- *Color in each bar between the dotted lines. If your sample had 13 yellow pieces, I should be able to look at your graph and see that the yellow bar goes up to the 13.*

C Color	P Number of Pieces
yellow	13
red	7
orange	10
green	7
purple	8

Figure 7: *A student data table*

TIMS Tip

When filling in the data table and graph, children can use a crayon or marker of the appropriate color in place of writing the color name.

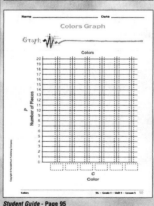

Student Guide - Page 95

Content Note

The data table is a numerical representation of the data; the graph is a pictorial representation of the same data. Often, patterns in the data emerge more clearly when shown on a graph. Point out how the axis labels on the graph correspond to the columns of the data table.

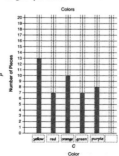

Figure 8: *A graph for the data in Figure 7*

URG · Grade 1 · Unit 5 · Lesson 5 **45**

Math Facts Strategies — DPP items that are designed to review, practice, or assess math facts strategies are highlighted.

Homework and Practice — Suggested homework assignments, review, and practice.

Assessment — How to evaluate your students' skills and their understanding of concepts.

At A Glance — Summarizes suggested steps for teaching the lesson and highlights math facts, practice, other DPP items, homework, and assessment.

Pose questions concerning the class graph:
- *What color has the most pieces, according to the class graph?*
- *Do you think the same color is most common in all boxes of this kind of cereal?*
- *Why is it better to base our prediction on the class graph instead of the pairs' graphs?*

These questions focus on these important ideas:
- Samples can be used to make predictions;
- The size of the sample affects the accuracy of the prediction.

The larger the sample, the more likely it is that the prediction will be accurate. In this light, students may see that it is better to make a prediction from the class data than from their own data. A larger sample size will provide more accurate information about what might be in the cereal box.

Suggestions for Teaching the Lesson

Math Facts Strategies

DPP item R includes two word problems with addition situations.

Homework and Practice

- Students complete the *Reading a Colors Graph* Activity Page.
- DPP item N practices addition. Items O and P review dividing cookies into groups of ten and counting leftovers. Item Q practices identifying even and odd numbers.

Assessment

- Save pictures for students' portfolios so that you will see their growth over time.
- Save journal entries for portfolios. Students record their thinking about the big ideas in the lab. It is important that they can express their thinking in writing as well as orally. Their first attempts may be sketchy, but experience suggests that their efforts will improve.
- Use DPP item M as an assessment of students' abilities to divide objects among three, four, and five friends and count leftovers.
- Use the *Observational Assessment Record* to document students' abilities to group and count objects and to collect and organize data in a table.
- Transfer appropriate assessment documentation from the Unit 5 *Observational Assessment Record* to students' *Individual Assessment Record Sheets*.

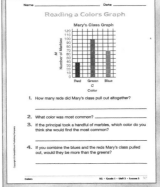

Student Guide - Page 97

📓 **Journal Prompt**
What did I learn in the *Colors* Lab?

AT A GLANCE

Math Facts Strategies and Daily Practice and Problems

DPP items N and R are addition story problems. Items O and P review packaging Grandma's cookies into boxes of 10 cookies. Item Q explores even and odd numbers in the context of pencils.

Part 1. Investigating Their Own Data (A1) (A3)

1. Students predict what colors will be in a box of cereal.
2. Students predict which colors will be the most common and least common.
3. Students examine a large bowl of cereal and discuss how to find the most popular color.
4. Discuss taking a sample to make predictions about the box.
5. Discuss and model the procedure for the lab.
6. Students draw a picture of the lab setup on the *Colors Picture* Lab Page.
7. Student pairs take their sample and complete the *Colors Data Table*.
8. Discuss the data in the table using the prompts in the Lesson Guide.
9. Students complete the *Colors Graph* Lab Page.
10. Students discuss and analyze their graphs.

Part 2. Investigating Class Data (A1)

1. Each pair of students adds their data for each color to the appropriate color strip.
2. Post the color strips on a bulletin board.
3. Children skip count to find the total for each strip.
4. Students answer questions about the class graph.

Homework

Students analyze a different graph using the *Reading a Colors Graph* Homework Page.

Assessment

1. Save children's pictures and journal entries in a portfolio to document their growth over time.
2. Use DPP item M as an assessment. Record your observations on the *Observational Assessment Record*.
3. Use the Assessment Indicators (A1, A3) and the *Observational Assessment Record* to document students' abilities to group and count objects and to collect and organize data in a table.
4. Transfer appropriate documentation from the Unit 5 *Observational Assessment Record* to students' *Individual Assessment Record Sheets* in the *Teacher Implementation Guide*.

Notes:

Journal Prompts — Suggested prompts for writing that can be assigned to students in class or for homework.

Extensions — Activities or suggestions for further exploration on the same topic.

Connections — How to connect the lesson to children's literature, computer programs, and other content areas such as science and social studies.

Unit Resource Guide
Lesson Guide for the Adventure Book

The Lesson Guide is a how-to manual explaining what you need and what is involved in each lesson.

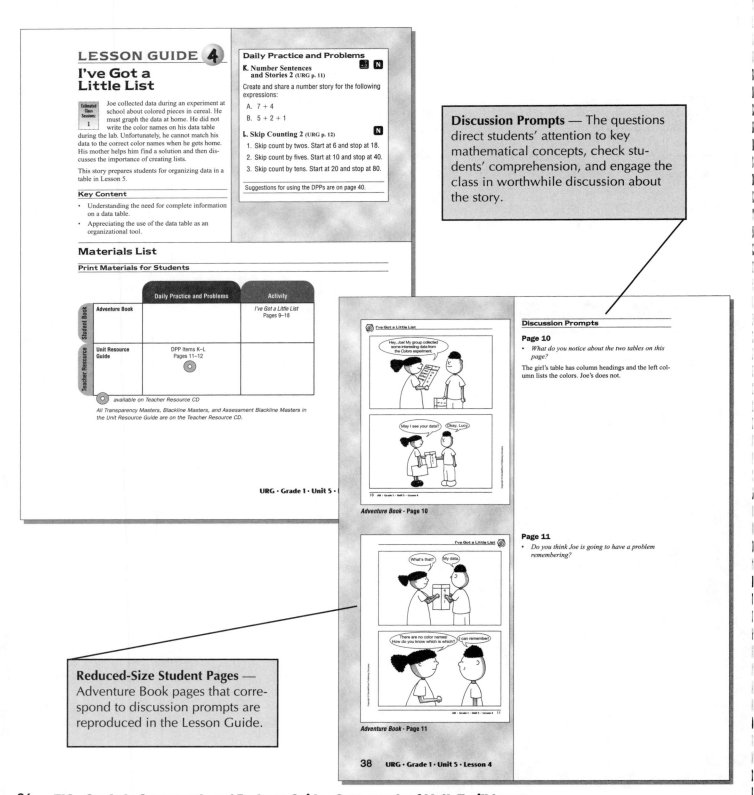

LESSON GUIDE 4

I've Got a Little List

Estimated Class Sessions: 1

Joe collected data during an experiment at school about colored pieces in cereal. He must graph the data at home. He did not write the color names on his data table during the lab. Unfortunately, he cannot match his data to the correct color names when he gets home. His mother helps him find a solution and then discusses the importance of creating lists.

This story prepares students for organizing data in a table in Lesson 5.

Key Content

* Understanding the need for complete information on a data table.
* Appreciating the use of the data table as an organizational tool.

Materials List

Print Materials for Students

	Daily Practice and Problems	Activity
Adventure Book (Student Book)		*I've Got a Little List* Pages 9–18
Unit Resource Guide (Teacher Resource)	DPP Items K–L Pages 11–12	

available on Teacher Resource CD

All Transparency Masters, Blackline Masters, and Assessment Blackline Masters in the Unit Resource Guide are on the Teacher Resource CD.

Daily Practice and Problems

K. Number Sentences and Stories 2 (URG p. 11)

Create and share a number story for the following expressions:

A. 7 + 4

B. 5 + 2 + 1

L. Skip Counting 2 (URG p. 12)

1. Skip count by twos. Start at 6 and stop at 18.

2. Skip count by fives. Start at 10 and stop at 40.

3. Skip count by tens. Start at 20 and stop at 80.

Suggestions for using the DPPs are on page 40.

URG · Grade 1 · Unit 5 ·

Discussion Prompts — The questions direct students' attention to key mathematical concepts, check students' comprehension, and engage the class in worthwhile discussion about the story.

I've Got a Little List

Hey, Joe! My group collected some interesting data from the Colors experiment.

May I see your data? Okay, Lucy.

10 AB · Grade 1 · Unit 5 · Lesson 4

Adventure Book - Page 10

Discussion Prompts

Page 10

* *What do you notice about the two tables on this page?*

The girl's table has column headings and the left column lists the colors. Joe's does not.

I've Got a Little List

What's that? My data.

There are no color names! How do you know which is which? I can remember.

AB · Grade 1 · Unit 5 · Lesson 4 11

Adventure Book - Page 11

Page 11

* *Do you think Joe is going to have a problem remembering?*

38 URG · Grade 1 · Unit 5 · Lesson 4

Reduced-Size Student Pages — Adventure Book pages that correspond to discussion prompts are reproduced in the Lesson Guide.

Unit Resource Guide
Student Pages

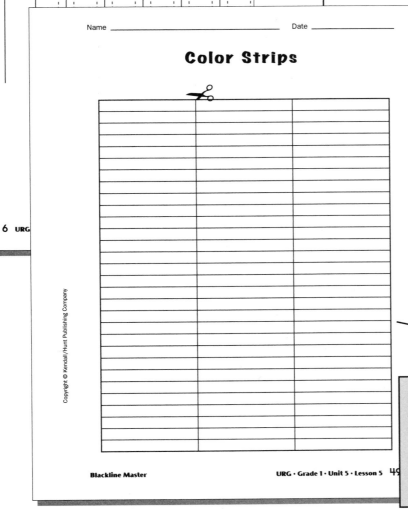

Name _____ Date _____

Name _____ Date _____

Color Strips

Copyright © Kendall/Hunt Publishing Company

Blackline Master

6 URG

URG · Grade 1 · Generic Section   3

URG · Grade 1 · Unit 5 · Lesson 5   49

Generic Pages — Laminated pages to be photocopied for use with various activities and labs. These pages are located in a separate section in the *Unit Resource Guide Filebox.* They can also be printed from the *Teacher Resource CD.*

Blackline Masters, Transparency Masters, and Assessment Blackline Masters — Pages to be photocopied as review, assessment, or transparency masters; located at the end of the Lesson Guide. They can also be printed from the *Teacher Resource CD.*

Unit Resource Guide
Answer Key

An Answer Key at the end of each lesson provides answers to questions in the *Student Guide* and *Unit Resource Guide* pages.

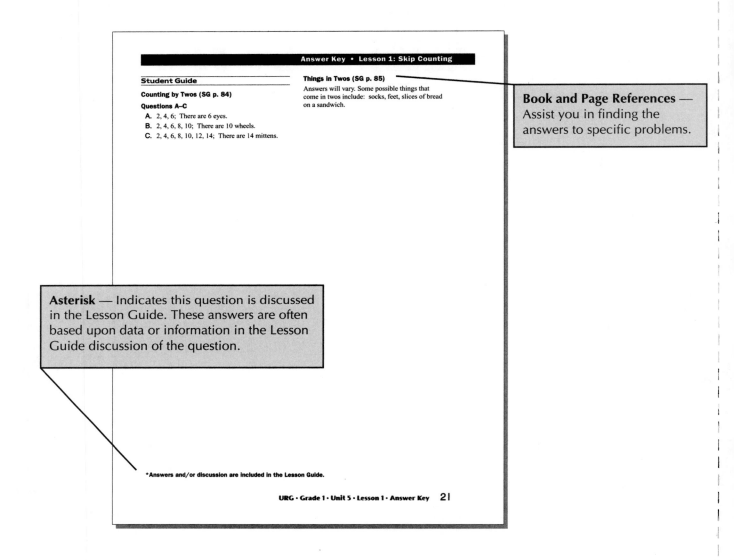

Answer Key • Lesson 1: Skip Counting

Student Guide

Counting by Twos (SG p. 84)

Questions A–C

A. 2, 4, 6; There are 6 eyes.

B. 2, 4, 6, 8, 10; There are 10 wheels.

C. 2, 4, 6, 8, 10, 12, 14; There are 14 mittens.

Things in Twos (SG p. 85)

Answers will vary. Some possible things that come in twos include: socks, feet, slices of bread on a sandwich.

Book and Page References — Assist you in finding the answers to specific problems.

Asterisk — Indicates this question is discussed in the Lesson Guide. These answers are often based upon data or information in the Lesson Guide discussion of the question.

*Answers and/or discussion are included in the Lesson Guide.

URG • Grade 1 • Unit 5 • Lesson 1 • Answer Key   21

Student Guide

The *Student Guide* contains most nonconsumable student materials, including activities, labs, and games. Book 1 includes Units 1–10 and Book 2 includes Units 11–20.

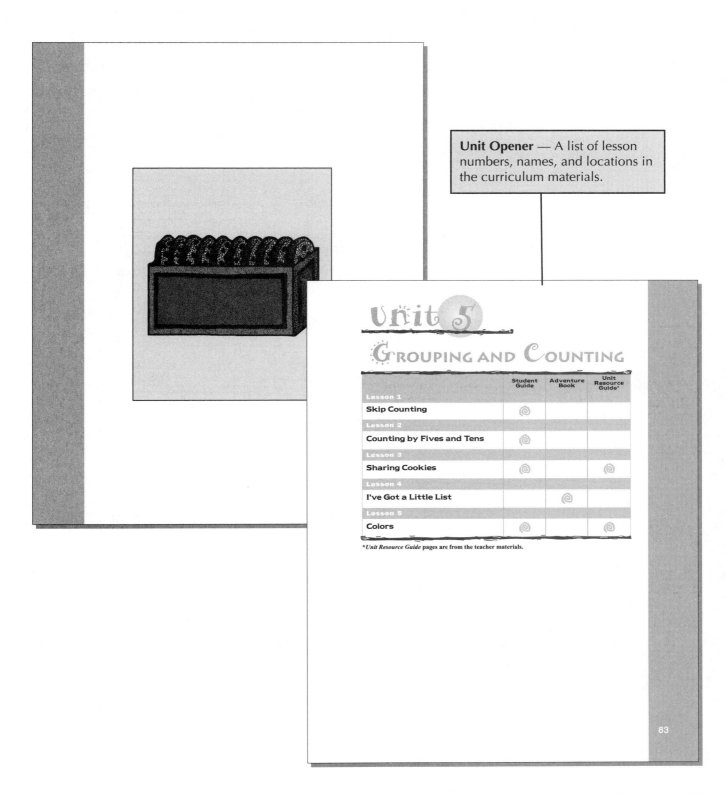

Unit Opener — A list of lesson numbers, names, and locations in the curriculum materials.

Unit 5
GROUPING AND COUNTING

	Student Guide	Adventure Book	Unit Resource Guide*
Lesson 1			
Skip Counting	◎		
Lesson 2			
Counting by Fives and Tens	◎		
Lesson 3			
Sharing Cookies	◎		◎
Lesson 4			
I've Got a Little List		◎	
Lesson 5			
Colors	◎		◎

*Unit Resource Guide pages are from the teacher materials.

83

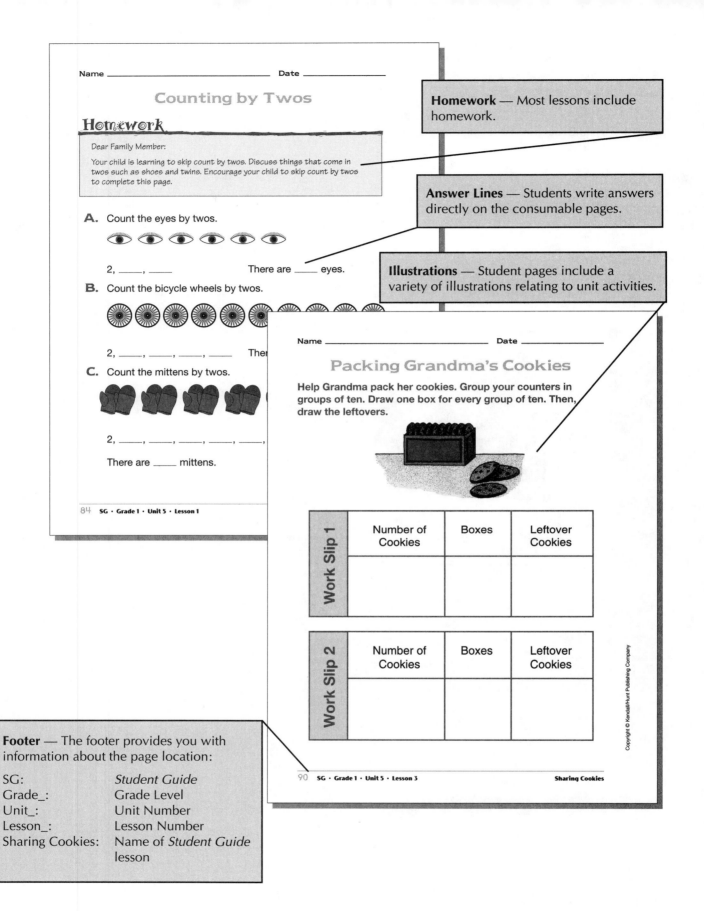

Homework — Most lessons include homework.

Answer Lines — Students write answers directly on the consumable pages.

Illustrations — Student pages include a variety of illustrations relating to unit activities.

Name _____ Date _____

Counting by Twos

Homework

Dear Family Member:

Your child is learning to skip count by twos. Discuss things that come in twos such as shoes and twins. Encourage your child to skip count by twos to complete this page.

A. Count the eyes by twos.

2, _____, _____   There are _____ eyes.

B. Count the bicycle wheels by twos.

2, _____, _____, _____, _____   Ther

C. Count the mittens by twos.

2, _____, _____, _____, _____, _____,

There are _____ mittens.

Name _____ Date _____

Packing Grandma's Cookies

Help Grandma pack her cookies. Group your counters in groups of ten. Draw one box for every group of ten. Then, draw the leftovers.

Work Slip 1	Number of Cookies	Boxes	Leftover Cookies

Work Slip 2	Number of Cookies	Boxes	Leftover Cookies

Copyright © Kendall/Hunt Publishing Company

Footer — The footer provides you with information about the page location:

SG: *Student Guide*
Grade_: Grade Level
Unit_: Unit Number
Lesson_: Lesson Number
Sharing Cookies: Name of *Student Guide* lesson

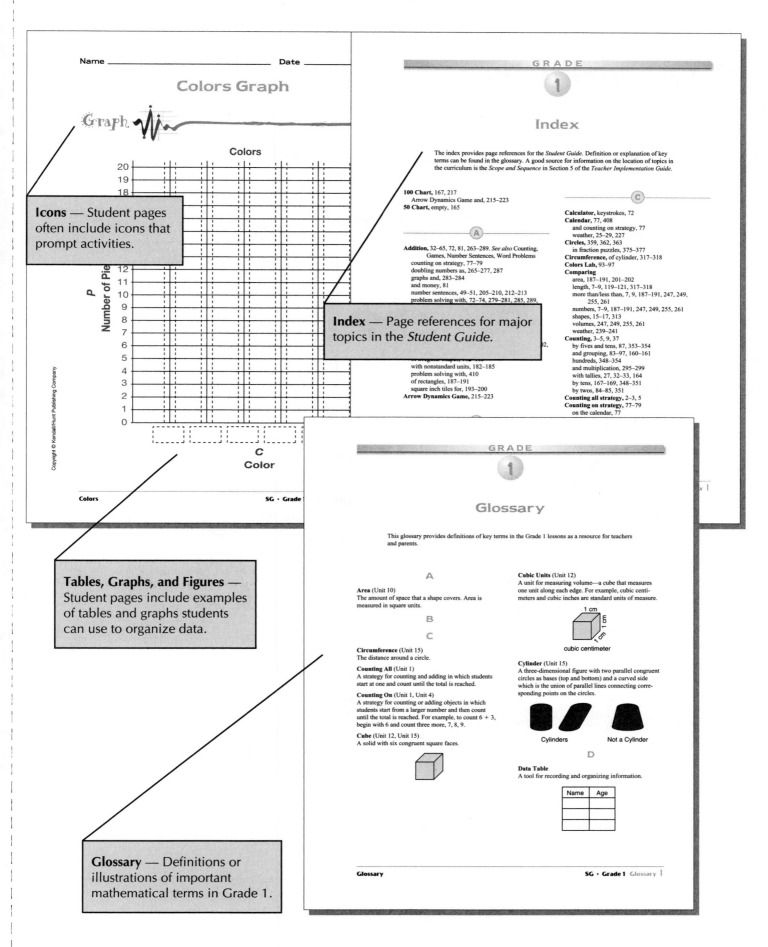

Icons — Student pages often include icons that prompt activities.

Index — Page references for major topics in the *Student Guide*.

Tables, Graphs, and Figures — Student pages include examples of tables and graphs students can use to organize data.

Glossary — Definitions or illustrations of important mathematical terms in Grade 1.

Colors Graph

Colors

Graph

Number of Pieces

Color

Colors

SG · Grade 1

Copyright © Kendall/Hunt Publishing Company

GRADE 1

Index

The index provides page references for the *Student Guide*. Definition or explanation of key terms can be found in the glossary. A good source for information on the location of topics in the curriculum is the *Scope and Sequence* in Section 5 of the *Teacher Implementation Guide*.

100 Chart, 167, 217
　Arrow Dynamics Game and, 215–223
50 Chart, empty, 165

A

Addition, 32–65, 72, 81, 263–289. *See also* Counting,
　　Games, Number Sentences, Word Problems
　counting on strategy, 77–79
　doubling numbers as, 265–277, 287
　graphs and, 283–284
　and money, 81
　number sentences, 49–51, 205–210, 212–213
　problem solving with, 72–74, 279–281, 285, 289,

of irregular shapes, 410
　with nonstandard units, 182–185
　problem solving with, 410
　of rectangles, 187–191
　square inch tiles for, 193–200
Arrow Dynamics Game, 215–223

C

Calculator, keystrokes, 72
Calendar, 77, 408
　and counting on strategy, 77
　weather, 25–29, 227
Circles, 359, 362, 363
　in fraction puzzles, 375–377
Circumference, of cylinder, 317–318
Colors Lab, 93–97
Comparing
　area, 187–191, 201–202
　length, 7–9, 119–121, 317–318
　more than/less than, 7, 9, 187–191, 247, 249,
　　255, 261
　numbers, 7–9, 187–191, 247, 249, 255, 261
　shapes, 15–17, 313
　volumes, 247, 249, 255, 261
　weather, 239–241
Counting, 3–5, 9, 37
　by fives and tens, 87, 353–354
　and grouping, 83–97, 160–161
　hundreds, 348–354
　with tallies, 27, 32–33, 164
　by tens, 167–169, 348–351
　by twos, 84–85, 351
Counting all strategy, 2–3, 5
Counting on strategy, 77–79
　on the calendar, 77

GRADE 1

Glossary

This glossary provides definitions of key terms in the Grade 1 lessons as a resource for teachers and parents.

A

Area (Unit 10)
The amount of space that a shape covers. Area is measured in square units.

B

C

Circumference (Unit 15)
The distance around a circle.

Counting All (Unit 1)
A strategy for counting and adding in which students start at one and count until the total is reached.

Counting On (Unit 1, Unit 4)
A strategy for counting or adding objects in which students start from a larger number and then count until the total is reached. For example, to count 6 + 3, begin with 6 and count three more, 7, 8, 9.

Cube (Unit 12, Unit 15)
A solid with six congruent square faces.

Cubic Units (Unit 12)
A unit for measuring volume—a cube that measures one unit along each edge. For example, cubic centimeters and cubic inches are standard units of measure.

cubic centimeter

Cylinder (Unit 15)
A three-dimensional figure with two parallel congruent circles as bases (top and bottom) and a curved side which is the union of parallel lines connecting corresponding points on the circles.

Cylinders　　　Not a Cylinder

D

Data Table
A tool for recording and organizing information.

Name	Age

Glossary

SG · Grade 1 Glossary

Adventure Book

Illustrated stories that present mathematics and science concepts.

Footer — The footer provides you with information about the page location:

AB: *Adventure Book*
Grade_: Grade Level
Unit_: Unit Number
Lesson_: Lesson Number

Quick Reference Guide

What I Want to Know	Where to Find It
What does this lesson cover?	*Unit Resource Guide*–Unit Outline *Unit Resource Guide*–Lesson Guide *Teacher Implementation Guide*–Overview
What are the "big ideas" in this lesson or the entire unit?	*Unit Resource Guide*–Unit Outline *Unit Resource Guide*–Unit Background *Unit Resource Guide*–Lesson Guide–Key Content *Teacher Implementation Guide*–Overview
What do I need to prepare for this lesson?	*Unit Resource Guide*–Unit Outline–Preparing for Upcoming Lessons *Unit Resource Guide*–Lesson Guide–Before the Activity *Unit Resource Guide*–Lesson Guide–Materials List
What manipulatives do I need for this lesson?	*Unit Resource Guide*–Unit Outline *Unit Resource Guide*–Lesson Guide–Materials List
What have students covered on this topic in previous grades or previous units?	*Unit Resource Guide*–Lesson Guide–Curriculum Sequence– Before This Unit *Teacher Implementation Guide*–Scope and Sequence *Teacher Implementation Guide*–Overview
What will students cover on this topic in later units?	*Unit Resource Guide*–Lesson Guide–Curriculum Sequence– After This Unit *Teacher Implementation Guide*–Scope and Sequence *Teacher Implementation Guide*–Overview
How do I teach this lesson?	*Unit Resource Guide*–Lesson Guide
Where is a quick summary of each lesson to help teach the lesson?	*Unit Resource Guide*–Lesson Guide–At a Glance
How long will it take to do this lesson (or the entire unit)?	*Unit Resource Guide*–Unit Outline–Estimated Class Sessions *Unit Resource Guide*–Lesson Guide *Teacher Implementation Guide*–Overview
How do I deal with potential trouble spots?	*Unit Resource Guide*–Lesson Guide–TIMS Tip *Unit Resource Guide*–Lesson Guide–Content Notes *Teacher Implementation Guide*–TIMS Tutors
How do I organize my class to do this lesson?	*Unit Resource Guide*–Lesson Guide
Where are the Blackline and Transparency Masters?	*Unit Resource Guide*–Letter Home *Unit Resource Guide*–Lesson Guide *Unit Resource Guide File*–Generic Section *Teacher Resource CD*
Where are Journal Prompts?	*Unit Resource Guide*–Lesson Guide
Where is the skill practice and review?	*Unit Resource Guide*–Daily Practice and Problems *Student Guide*–Homework sections
Where are the enrichment activities?	*Unit Resource Guide*–Lesson Guide–Extensions

What I Want to Know	Where to Find It
What information is available for parents?	*Unit Resource Guide*–Letter Home
	Unit Resource Guide File–Letter Home (Spanish)
	Unit Resource Guide–Unit 11–Information for Parents: Math Facts Philosophy
	Teacher Implementation Guide–Parents and *Math Trailblazers*– Parent Brochure; Information for Parents: Math Facts Philosophy (English and Spanish)
What should I assign as homework?	*Unit Resource Guide*–Lesson Guide–Suggestions for Teaching the Lesson–Homework and Practice–At a Glance
How do I assess students' progress?	*Unit Resource Guide*–Unit Background–Assessment Indicators
	Unit Resource Guide–Daily Practice and Problems–Facts Quizzes
	Unit Resource Guide–*Observational Assessment Record*
	Unit Resource Guide–Assessment Units
	Unit Resource Guide–Assessment Lessons
	Unit Resource Guide–Lesson Guide–Assessment Pages
	Unit Resource Guide–Lesson Guide–Suggestions for Teaching the Lesson–Assessment
	Unit Resource Guide–Lesson Guide–Journal Prompts
	Teacher Implementation Guide–Assessment section
	Teacher Implementation Guide–Assessment section– *Individual Assessment Record Sheet*
Where do I find connections to literature, computer software, and other content areas such as social studies and science?	*Unit Resource Guide*–Unit Outline
	Unit Resource Guide–Lesson Guide–Connections
	Teacher Implementation Guide–Literature List
	Teacher Implementation Guide–Software List
How do I find background information about concepts underlying each activity?	*Unit Resource Guide*–Unit Background
	Unit Resource Guide–Lesson Guide–Content Notes
	Teacher Implementation Guide–TIMS Tutors
How does this activity or unit fit into the "big picture" for my grade?	*Unit Resource Guide*–Unit Background
	Unit Resource Guide–Lesson Guide–Curriculum Sequence
	Teacher Implementation Guide–Overview
	Teacher Implementation Guide–Scope and Sequence
What will my students do this year?	*Teacher Implementation Guide*–Overview
	Teacher Implementation Guide–Scope and Sequence
What manipulatives do I need for the entire year?	*Teacher Implementation Guide*–Manipulatives List
Where is the scope and sequence?	*Teacher Implementation Guide*–Scope and Sequence
Does this curriculum match my district's objectives?	*Teacher Implementation Guide*–Scope and Sequence & the NCTM *Principles and Standards*
	Teacher Implementation Guide–Overview
	Unit Resource Guide–Unit Background–Assessment Indicators
	Teacher Implementation Guide–Assessment section– *Individual Assessment Record Sheet*
Where is the *Student Guide* Index?	*Student Guide*—Index
Where is the index for the curriculum?	*Teacher Implementation Guide*—Index

Overview

The Overview presents brief descriptions and lists of featured concepts for each unit. It provides a quick reference to locate concepts and activities.

Students solve a problem using money.

Overview

The overview reflects the scope, sequence, and tone of the first-grade curriculum. The fundamental assumption of all the units is that math concepts and skills are best acquired through active involvement in problem solving. In every unit, students practice computation and estimation while solving problems. The TIMS Laboratory Method, used in laboratory experiments throughout the curriculum, incorporates experiences with important tools for investigation and experimentation: drawing a picture, measuring, collecting and organizing data, constructing a graph, and posing and answering questions about the data.

Units also include:

- Suggestions for journal writing;
- Recommended homework assignments for most lessons;
- Parent letters that discuss the important ideas within the unit and provide suggestions for home activities that support lessons in school;
- Special notes to parents on individual homework activities;
- Assessment, both through formal instruments and through the informal observations that a discourse-rich curriculum makes possible.

Many units include Adventure Book stories and recommendations for using related trade books and children's literature. A recommended software list accompanies most units. Some of the units in the first semester include activities that review materials from kindergarten so students new to the curriculum will have the necessary skills and concepts for first grade.

Daily Practice and Problems. The Daily Practice and Problems (DPP) is a vital component of the curriculum and can be found at the beginning of each unit in the *Unit Resource Guide* and on the *Teacher Resource CD*. These short exercises provide ongoing practice, review, and study of a variety of topics. These include basic facts, computation, time, money, number sense, data, measurement, and geometry. Many are word problems. Two DPP items are provided for each class session. The problems require anywhere from

2 to 15 minutes to solve. They can be completed in class, as homework, or for assessment. The content includes:

- addition facts strategies
- addition facts practice
- subtraction facts strategies
- subtraction facts practice
- problem solving

- counting and numeration
- computation
- number sense
- measurement
- estimation

- time
- money
- geometry
- data
- graphs

Summaries, pacing suggestions, and outlines of the first-grade units in the *Math Trailblazers* curriculum follow. Additionally, hints for preparing for upcoming lessons are included in some units.

Unit 1: Welcome to First Grade:
A Baseline Assessment Unit . . . . 8 Sessions

Unit Summary
Children are introduced to mathematics through two clusters of activities, one in which they count objects and one in which they compare lengths using connecting cubes and links. They use counting as they read an interactive poem, *Look Around You*, attach cubes to make ten, and use a chain of six links to compare and classify the lengths of various objects. These activities will help teachers assess children's understanding of number concepts in a cross section of mathematical domains.

Major Concept Focus
- mathematical communication skills
- ordering numbers
- classification
- Adventure Book: counting
- counting
- counting-on strategy
- computation strategies
- measuring by comparison
- more or less

Pacing Suggestions
- Unit 1 contains representative activities from the *Math Trailblazers* kindergarten curriculum as well as a preview of experiences included in first grade. While the activities provide opportunities for students to learn or review important content, this first unit is a baseline assessment unit. The various activities will provide insight into students' abilities at the beginning of the school year. What is the largest number of objects students can comfortably count? Do they understand the process of measurement? Can they represent a quantity symbolically? What strategies do they employ in problem solving? This information will help inform instruction for the remainder of the year.

- Each of the skills and concepts will appear (and reappear) in later units, so when the class has completed an assessment activity, move on to the next lesson. Use the recommended session numbers for each lesson and use the Assessment Indicators as a guide for the appropriate time to assess specific skills. The *Individual Assessment Record Sheet*, which is in the Assessment section (Section 8) of this book, lists the Assessment Indicators for all the Grade 1 units.

- The pacing schedule for the year assumes that mathematics instruction begins on the first day of school and that students receive 60 minutes of mathematics instruction each day through the last day of school. The first lesson is particularly appropriate for the first day of school since it is an *Adventure Book* story that engages students in the exploration of their new surroundings.

Preparing for Upcoming Lessons
Allow students to explore connecting cubes and links before Lessons 3 and 4.

On October 1, your class will begin collecting weather data. See Unit 2 Lesson 6.

In Unit 3 Lesson 6, each student will need ten pennies. Ask students to each bring ten pennies. They can be stored in a class bank.

Unit 1 Outline

	Books & Pages	Sessions	DPP	Description	Supplies
LESSON 1 **Look Around You**	URG pages 15–19 AB pages 1–8	1	DPP A–B	**ADVENTURE BOOK:** Students count objects in this Adventure Book while exploring their own classroom and school.	• pencils • cup • meter-stick or pointer
LESSON 2 **We're Counting on You!**	URG pages 20–25 SG pages 2–5	3	DPP C–H	**ASSESSMENT ACTIVITY:** Students count objects around their classroom and homes. They are introduced to the counting-on strategy. **ASSESSMENT PAGES:** *Counting at the Toy Store* and *How Many Are There?*, Student Guide, pages 2–3.	• beans, pennies, or other manipu-latives
LESSON 3 **The Train Game**	URG pages 26–28	1	DPP I–J	**ASSESSMENT GAME:** Student pairs build a train of connecting cubes by adding one, two, or three cubes at a time. The winner adds the tenth cube.	• connecting cubes
LESSON 4 **More or Less**	URG pages 29–34 SG pages 7–9	3	DPP K–P	**ASSESSMENT ACTIVITY:** Students compare lengths of objects to a chain of six connecting links. Children classify these lengths as *more than*, *less than*, or *about the same* as the chain.	• connecting cubes • connecting links

Unit 2: Exploring Shapes .... 8 Sessions

Unit Summary
Identifying, comparing, and describing shapes in nature help students explore and focus on the attributes of two-dimensional geometric shapes. The *Weather 1: Eye on the Sky* lab is introduced so that children can build a calendar and collect weather data in the month of October.

Major Concept Focus
- problem-solving strategies
- properties of shapes
- identifying shapes
- partitioning shapes
- TIMS Laboratory Method
- data collection using tallies
- using a calendar

Pacing Suggestions
- Unit 2 contains multiple opportunities for children to locate, analyze, and describe shapes in their environment. At this time of the year, when students talk and write about how shapes are alike or different, their verbal descriptions will likely be much richer than their written descriptions. Collect and save early samples of written work so that student growth over time can be observed and documented. Use the Assessment Indicators highlighted in the At a Glance section of each lesson guide for the appropriate time to assess specific skills.
- Begin Unit 2 Lesson 6 *Weather 1: Eye on the Sky* on the first day of October so that students can collect weather data for every day in October. On October 1, the lesson will take a full period. Subsequent days will take only a few minutes per day. On the last day of October, students will spend time graphing and analyzing the data. Save students' data to compare to weather data collected in the month of February.

Preparing for Upcoming Lessons
Set up a learning center with pattern blocks so that students have an opportunity to explore them before they are introduced in Lesson 2.

Provide opportunities for free exploration with the calculator prior to Unit 4.

In Unit 5, student pairs will need fifty pennies, eight nickels, and five dimes. Ask students to bring in these coins and add them to the class bank.

On October 1, start collecting weather data. See Lesson 6.

Unit 2 Outline

Components Key: SG = Student Guide, AB = Adventure Book, URG = Unit Resource Guide, and DPP = Daily Practice and Problems

	Books & Pages	Sessions	DPP	Description	Supplies
LESSON 1 **Shapes Around Us**	URG pages 15–18	1	DPP A–B	**ACTIVITY:** Children identify and record shapes in the environment.	
LESSON 2 **Describing Shapes**	URG pages 19–25 SG pages 12–17	3	DPP C–H	**ACTIVITY:** Children describe shapes without using their names. They also compare and contrast shapes, focusing on the shapes' attributes. **ASSESSMENT PAGE:** *Alike and Different 2*, Student Guide, page 17.	• overhead pattern blocks • pattern blocks • paper bags
LESSON 3 **Seven Ways to Make a Hexagon**	URG pages 26–29 SG page 19	1	DPP I–J	**ACTIVITY:** Children find seven ways to create a hexagon using the rhombus, trapezoid, and triangle pattern blocks.	• pattern blocks • overhead pattern blocks • crayons or markers
LESSON 4 **How Many Does It Take?**	URG pages 30–33 SG pages 20–23	1	DPP K–L	**ACTIVITY:** Children use their pattern blocks to fill in the outlines of figures. Then, they record how many of each pattern block they used. **ASSESSMENT PAGE:** *The Rocket*, Student Guide, page 23.	• pattern blocks • overhead pattern blocks
LESSON 5 **Mystery Figure**	URG pages 34–36	1	DPP M–N	**ACTIVITY:** Children examine the shadow outline of a figure (projected by the overhead) that is formed by combining three or four pattern blocks. Students determine what pattern blocks can comprise the figures.	• pattern blocks
LESSON 6 **Weather 1: Eye on the Sky**	URG pages 37–45 SG pages 25–29	1	DPP O–P	**LAB:** This is an ongoing lab. On the first of the month (October 1 is recommended), students begin recording the type of sky for each day on a calendar. Students also keep track of the data in a table.	

Unit 3: Pennies, Pockets, and Parts . . . . 15 Sessions

Unit Summary
Work with numbers is extended to partitioning. The part-whole relationship is the basis for developing a strong understanding of addition and subtraction and is useful in learning basic facts. Ten frames provide a visual framework for number relationships, emphasizing the use of 5 and 10 as anchors. One primary context of the work is data collection and interpretation. There is also a strong problem-solving orientation to all aspects of the work.

Major Concept Focus
- tally marks
- gathering and recording data in tables and graphs
- ten frames
- exploring relationships among numbers
- using 5 and 10 as benchmarks
- number sentences
- partitioning a number in two or three parts
- word problems
- mathematical communication skills

Pacing Suggestions
Unit 3 introduces mathematical concepts that will be revisited many times over the course of the year. Use the recommended number of class sessions for each lesson as a guide for moving through the unit.

- Lesson 1 *Favorite Colors* and Lesson 4 *Pockets Graph* use data tables and bar graphs, two of the four components of the TIMS Laboratory Method. The complete method is used in Unit 5, so it is not necessary to focus on the other components here.
- Lesson 5 *Pocket Parts* introduces a variety of problem types. Students will solve problems in different ways that are meaningful to them. This is particularly important in Part 3 of the lesson, which challenges students to think about missing addend problems. Some students may be ready to think about this type of problem while others may not. Since this is only an introduction, move on after the allotted number of days has passed.
- It is an appropriate time to begin collecting samples of student work for portfolios. See the Background of this unit and the TIMS Tutor: *Portfolios* in the *Teacher Implementation Guide* for more information.

Preparing for Upcoming Lessons
Remind students to wear clothes with pockets for Lessons 4 and 5. Send home the parent note in Lesson 3 reminding parents to send their children to school with pockets.

In Lesson 7, each child will need pennies. Begin a class bank so that students can help you collect pennies.

Unit 3 Outline

Components Key: SG = Student Guide, AB = Adventure Book, URG = Unit Resource Guide, and DPP = Daily Practice and Problems

	Books & Pages	Sessions	DPP	Description	Supplies
LESSON 1 Favorite Colors	URG pages 18–23 SG pages 32–33	1	DPP A–B	**ACTIVITY:** Students generate and record data in a group data table. They keep track of totals with tally marks.	• self-adhesive notes • easel paper
LESSON 2 Ten Frames	URG pages 24–30 SG pages 35–39	3	DPP C–H	**ACTIVITY:** Students visualize numbers using five and ten as benchmarks. **ASSESSMENT PAGE:** *What's My Sentence?*, Student Guide, page 39.	• counters such as beans or pennies
LESSON 3 Think and Spin	URG pages 31–33 SG pages 41–45	1	DPP I–J	**ACTIVITY:** Students write number sentences that fit ten frames.	• clear spinners • crayons, markers, or colored pencils
LESSON 4 Pockets Graph	URG pages 34–37	2	DPP K–N	**ACTIVITY:** Students collect data and create a group bar graph.	• connecting cubes • self-adhesive notes
LESSON 5 Pocket Parts	URG pages 38–48 SG pages 47–53	4	DPP O–V	**ACTIVITY:** Students solve problems and write number sentences based on the number of pockets in each problem. **ASSESSMENT PAGE:** *Pockets*, Student Guide, page 53.	• connecting cubes
LESSON 6 What's in That Pocket?	URG pages 49–56 SG pages 55–63	3	DPP W–BB	**ACTIVITY:** Students partition numbers into two and three parts using pennies. They record their data in a table. **ASSESSMENT PAGE:** *Nine Pennies Data Table*, Student Guide, page 63.	• pennies • blank transparency
LESSON 7 Purchasing with Pennies	URG pages 57–60 SG pages 35 & 65	1	DPP CC–DD	**ACTIVITY:** Students solve story problems as they use pennies and price tags to "purchase" items in a classroom store. They explore multiple strategies for finding solutions.	• pennies or other counters

Unit 4: Adding to Solve Problems . . . . 5 Sessions

Unit Summary

The concept of addition and the writing of number sentences are major themes of this unit. Addition is not limited to counting-on situations, but is explored in a variety of contexts. A secondary focus is using a variety of numbers (and facts) to extend the work to two-digit numbers in order to familiarize children with the addition of larger numbers. Students also explore even and odd numbers.

Major Concept Focus

- grouping objects in pairs
- even and odd numbers
- creating and sharing addition problems
- number sentences
- counting on
- modeling addition problems with manipulatives

Pacing Suggestions

This unit is designed to be completed in 5 days. Use the recommended session numbers for each lesson as a guide. The skills and concepts in this unit will be revisited in new contexts in later units.

- Lesson 1 introduces the concept of even and odd numbers. Students will revisit this concept in the Daily Practice and Problems throughout the year and again in Unit 13.
- Students use the counting-on strategy in this unit. It requires children to be able to conceptualize a number and then count on from that number. Some children will need more time to leave behind the idea of counting all. The counting-on strategy is a valuable tool for gaining fluency with the addition math facts and will be revisited many times in future units.

Preparing for Upcoming Lessons

Continue collecting coins for the class bank activities in Unit 5.

Ask students to bring in toy cars or other things with wheels for use in the *Rolling Along with Links* Lab in Unit 6.

Unit 4 Outline

	Books & Pages	Sessions	DPP	Description	Supplies
LESSON 1 **Exploring Even and Odd Numbers**	URG pages 14–20 SG pages 68–69	1	DPP A–B	**ACTIVITY:** Students use manipulatives to explore even and odd numbers.	• connecting cubes
LESSON 2 **The Pet Shop**	URG pages 21–27 SG pages 71–74	1	DPP C–D	**ACTIVITY:** A pet shop provides a setting for students to discuss and solve addition problems. The part-whole concept and related language are also introduced. Students use calculators to explore addition problems.	• calculators
LESSON 3 **Parts and Wholes**	URG pages 28–33 SG page 75	1	DPP E–F	**ACTIVITY:** Students write addition number sentences for the numbers 11 and 12. Number partitions that involve more than two addends are emphasized. **ASSESSMENT PAGE:** *More Parts and Wholes,* Unit Resource Guide, page 32.	• connecting cubes • counters • scissors
LESSON 4 **Counting On to Add**	URG pages 34–41 SG pages 77–81	2	DPP G–J	**ACTIVITY:** This activity highlights the counting-on strategy for solving addition problems.	• connecting cubes or counters • self-adhesive dots • large paper cup • classroom calendar • self-adhesive notes

Unit 5: Grouping and Counting .... 9 Sessions

Unit Summary
This unit introduces numbers up to 100 through counting and grouping. Counting by twos, fives, and tens is introduced in purposeful contexts, e.g., counting hands and fingers. There is also a focus on naming numbers in terms of groupings, e.g., 12 is 2 sixes or 2 fives and 2. This leads naturally to naming 23 as 2 tens and 3 ones and using pennies, nickels, and dimes (13¢ is 2 nickels and 3 pennies). The unit continues to build fundamental number relationships, extends ideas of partitioning numbers, and provides informal multiplication and division experiences. The lab *Colors* introduces the sampling of a population. The Adventure Book *I've Got a Little List* stresses the importance of labeling data.

Major Concept Focus
- counting by twos, fives, and tens
- pennies, nickels, dimes
- grouping and naming numbers
- partitioning and describing numbers
- TIMS Laboratory Method
- Adventure Book: labeling data tables
- concepts of multiplication and division

Pacing Suggestions
This unit is designed to be completed in 9 days.

Lesson 5 *Colors* can be completed in 3 class sessions. During the first class session, discuss the TIMS Laboratory Method and the investigation. Have students draw a picture of the investigation to show their understanding of the lab. During the second class session, students collect, graph, and analyze their data. During the third session, they complete the class graph and analyze the data.

Preparing for Upcoming Lessons
Ask students to bring in toy cars or other things with wheels for use in the *Rolling Along with Links* lab in Unit 6.

Unit 5 Outline

	Books & Pages	Sessions	DPP	Description	Supplies
LESSON 1 **Skip Counting**	URG pages 15–21 SG pages 84–85	1	DPP A–B	**ACTIVITY:** Students are introduced to the value of skip counting through literature. They skip count by twos, fives, and tens using a variety of models.	• red and black over-head markers • egg cartons • calculators
LESSON 2 **Counting by Fives and Tens**	URG pages 22–28 SG page 87	2	DPP C–F	**ACTIVITY:** Students place pennies in ten frames. Students group pennies by fives and tens, exchange nickels and dimes, and skip count by fives and tens.	• pennies, nickels, and dimes • plastic bags • crayons or markers • tape
LESSON 3 **Sharing Cookies**	URG pages 29–36 SG pages 89–91	2	DPP G–J	**ACTIVITY:** Students use literature to explore groups. They use manipulatives to act out grouping and sharing cookies. Students record their solutions using number sentences.	• connecting cubes or counters
LESSON 4 **I've Got a Little List**	URG pages 37–40 AB pages 9–18	1	DPP K–L	**ADVENTURE BOOK:** Students read a story while learning the importance of labeling data tables.	
LESSON 5 **Colors**	URG pages 41–50 SG pages 93–97	3	DPP M–R	**LAB:** Students sample cereal to determine the colors in a population. The TIMS Laboratory Method is introduced.	• Froot Loops ® (or substitute) • $\frac{1}{4}$ measuring cup • large bowl • calculators • crayons or markers • scissors • tape

Unit 6: Measurement: Length ....10 Sessions

Unit Summary

This unit focuses on various concepts involving measurement, using both standard and nonstandard units. Comparing and ordering lengths, developing an appreciation of the approximate nature of measurement, and introducing the idea that different sizes of units yield different results are the goals of this section. The problems presented in the lab *Rolling Along with Links* include applications for skip counting and counting on. The Adventure Book *Betty Builds a Better Racer* shows students another application of the techniques they used in the lab.

Major Concept Focus

- measuring with nonstandard units
- measuring, comparing, and ordering lengths
- grouping and counting objects
- TIMS Laboratory Method
- number placement within an interval
- comparing lengths with different units
- measuring with inches
- Adventure Book: techniques used in an experiment

Pacing Suggestions

This unit is designed to be completed in 10 class sessions.

Lesson 2, *Rolling Along with Links* lab, is designed to be completed in 3 class sessions. During the first class session, discuss and model the investigation. Have students draw a picture of the investigation to show their understanding. During the second class session, have students collect their data. In the third session, complete the graph and analyze the results.

Preparing for Upcoming Lessons

Continue collecting small toy cars and roller skates for Lesson 2.

Unit 6 Outline

	Books & Pages	Sessions	DPP	Description	Supplies
LESSON 1 Linking Up	URG pages 15–19 SG pages 100–101	1	DPP A–B	**ACTIVITY:** Students measure a variety of objects using connecting links. Chains of links are arranged in groups of five with alternating colors to encourage students to skip count.	• connecting links
LESSON 2 Rolling Along with Links	URG pages 20–27 SG pages 103–109	3	DPP C–H	**LAB:** Students roll toy cars down ramps and measure how far the cars roll. **ASSESSMENT PAGE:** *Brian's Class*, Student Guide, page 109.	• masking tape • ramp • toy cars • index cards or self-adhesive notes • blocks or books • connecting links
LESSON 3 Betty Builds a Better Racer	URG pages 28–33 AB pages 19–28	1	DPP I–J	**ADVENTURE BOOK:** Betty builds a car to enter in a soap box derby. She uses the same techniques students explored in the lab to determine how far her car rolls.	
LESSON 4 Using Unusual Units	URG pages 34–44 SG pages 111–117	3	DPP K–P	**ACTIVITY:** Students measure objects with different units of measure.	• an assortment of objects (e.g., markers, paper clips, erasers)
LESSON 5 Delightful Dachshunds	URG pages 45–50 SG pages 119–121	1	DPP Q–R	**ACTIVITY:** Students examine pairs of dachshunds, predict the longer dog based on measurements given in links and cubes, and check their predictions. **ASSESSMENT PAGE:** *Comparing Links and Cubes*, Student Guide, page 121.	• connecting links • connecting cubes
LESSON 6 Give 'em an Inch	URG pages 51–56 SG page 123	1	DPP S–T	**ACTIVITY:** Students make the transition from unusual units to standard inches. Students use inch rulers to measure objects in the classroom. **ASSESSMENT PAGE:** *Could Be or Crazy?*, Student Guide, page 123.	• rulers • tape • scissors

Unit 7: Patterns and Designs .... 5-7 Sessions

Unit Summary

Patterns are explored as students use their first names to make patterns on a 10×10 grid. A group graph evolves from organizing the patterns. Students identify, describe, and extend patterns. Characteristics of shapes are emphasized as students use pattern blocks to explore symmetry.

Major Concept Focus

- creating patterns
- describing and generalizing patterns
- naming, recording, and extending patterns
- line symmetry
- spatial problem-solving skills
- Game: symmetry

Pacing Suggestions

This unit reintroduces and extends the experiences with patterns in the kindergarten curriculum. Pattern concepts are typically engaging and accessible to young children so you may find that you can move through the unit at a brisk pace.

Unit 7 Outline

	Books & Pages	Sessions	DPP	Description	Supplies
LESSON 1 Line Up!	URG pages 13–18 SG page 126	1–2	DPP A–D	**ACTIVITY:** Students describe, extend, translate, and record "kid patterns" and patterns they create with links.	• crayons • links • opaque paper sacks
LESSON 2 Pick Apart a Pattern	URG pages 19–24 SG pages 127–131	1–2	DPP E–H	**ACTIVITY:** Students describe, extend, identify, and translate patterns to AB symbols. **ASSESSMENT PAGE:** *Twins,* Student Guide, page 131.	• links • opaque paper sacks
LESSON 3 Name Patterns	URG pages 25–28 SG pages 133–137	1	DPP I–J	**ACTIVITY:** Students repeatedly print their names on a grid to create and examine the resulting two-dimensional patterns. **ASSESSMENT PAGE:** *Names and Grids,* Student Guide, page 137.	
LESSON 4 Pattern Block Symmetry	URG pages 29–33 SG pages 139–143	1	DPP K–L	**ACTIVITY:** Students use pattern blocks to make designs with line symmetry. **ASSESSMENT PAGE:** *Tree,* Student Guide, page 143.	• pattern blocks • overhead pattern blocks
LESSON 5 Balancing Act	URG pages 34–36 SG page 145	1	DPP M–N	**GAME:** Students play a game with pattern blocks and make symmetric designs.	• pattern blocks • overhead pattern blocks

Unit 8: Subtracting to Solve Problems .... 5-6 Sessions

Unit Summary
The concept of subtraction is developed and symbolized in a problem-solving context. The use of counting back to subtract is introduced and applied to two-digit numbers and multiples of ten, as well as basic facts. The part-part-whole model for thinking about problems and number facts is introduced. Several of the lessons parallel the addition activities in Unit 4.

Major Concept Focus
- subtraction stories
- subtraction number sentences
- symbols for subtraction situations
- ten frames
- partitioning numbers from 10 to 20
- connecting addition and subtraction
- counting up or back to find the missing part

Pacing Suggestions
In Lesson 1, you will share a story about the circus with students. If you choose to read *Circus!* by Peter Spier, plan to spend an extra class session on this lesson.

Preparing for Upcoming Lessons
Ask students to bring in newspaper headlines with two-digit numbers in them for use in Unit 9 Lesson 7.

Unit 8 Outline

	Books & Pages	Sessions	DPP	Description	Supplies
LESSON 1 **At the Circus**	URG pages 14–17	1–2	DPP A–B	**ACTIVITY:** A circus context is used to introduce subtraction situations. Students create and solve their own circus-related subtraction stories.	• connecting cubes • children's book about the circus
LESSON 2 **Our Own Stories**	URG pages 18–22 SG pages 148–151	1	DPP C–D	**ACTIVITY:** Students create their own subtraction situations and take-away problems. A whole-part-part mat facilitates modeling of the stories.	• counters
LESSON 3 **Clowning Around**	URG pages 23–28 SG page 153	1	DPP E–F	**ACTIVITY:** Students create a subtraction circus story for a given number sentence. They use a three-frame cartoon format.	
LESSON 4 **How Many in the Bag?**	URG pages 29–34 SG pages 155–158	1	DPP G–H	**ACTIVITY:** Students revisit the ten frame and partitions of ten. Then, take-away subtraction situations are linked to partitioning numbers from 10 to 20.	• paper bags (or opaque substitutes) • counters
LESSON 5 **Making Flip Books**	URG pages 35–40 SG page 155	1	DPP I–J	**ACTIVITY:** Students construct flip books incorporating number sentences generated in the previous activity and use them to model subtraction problems.	• scissors • crayons • counters • opaque bag

Unit 9: Grouping by Tens .... 11-12 Sessions

Unit Summary

This unit explores number relationships and number patterns on the *100 Chart*. It extends the partitioning work begun in Unit 2 to multiples of ten. Students group and count objects by tens and ones. They compare and order two-digit numbers. The lab *Full of Beans* allows students to apply their grouping and counting skills in an investigation of volume and units.

Major Concept Focus

- grouping and counting by tens and ones
- ten frames
- identifying intervals
- representing numbers with tens and ones
- number patterns on the *100 Chart*
- comparing and ordering numbers
- multiple solution strategies
- investigating volume
- TIMS Laboratory Method
- Game: grouping and adding

Pacing Suggestions

This unit is designed to be completed in 11–12 days.

- If your students used *Math Trailblazers* in kindergarten, plan for the minimum number of recommended sessions for each lesson.
- Lesson 8 *Full of Beans* is a laboratory investigation. Make use of *Math Trailblazers* connections to other subjects by having students collect data during science time.

Preparing for Upcoming Lessons

Place square-inch tiles in a learning center for students to explore prior to beginning Unit 10.

Unit 9 Outline

Components Key: SG = Student Guide, AB = Adventure Book, URG = Unit Resource Guide, and DPP = Daily Practice and Problems

	Books & Pages	Sessions	DPP	Description	Supplies
LESSON 1 **Spill the Beans**	URG pages 19–23 SG page 160	1–2	DPP A–B	**ACTIVITY:** Pairs of students count 50–70 beans and then discuss grouping and counting strategies.	• lima beans • small scoop
LESSON 2 **More or Less than 100?**	URG pages 24–28 SG page 161	1	DPP C–D	**ACTIVITY:** Students make stacks of cubes to represent the number of letters in their first names; they group and count to find the class total.	• connecting cubes • calculators
LESSON 3 **Spin for Beans**	URG pages 29–35 SG pages 163–164	1	DPP E–F	**GAME:** Students use ten frames to organize beans in a grouping and recording game.	• clear plastic spinners • baby lima beans

Unit 10 Outline

Components Key: SG = Student Guide, AB = Adventure Book, URG = Unit Resource Guide, and DPP = Daily Practice and Problems

	Books & Pages	Sessions	DPP	Description	Supplies
LESSON 1 **Finding Area with Pennies**	URG pages 12–17 SG pages 182–185	1	DPP A–B	**ACTIVITY:** Students develop a conceptual understanding of area, using the penny as a nonstandard, but uniform, unit.	• pennies • sheets of paper
LESSON 2 **Goldilocks and the Three Rectangles**	URG pages 18–24 SG pages 187–191	1	DPP C–D	**ACTIVITY:** Rectangles are used to illustrate that length or width alone do not impart the size of a two-dimensional figure. The square inch is introduced.	• square-inch tiles • scissors • rulers
LESSON 3 **How Much Area?**	URG pages 25–29 SG pages 193–197	1	DPP E–F	**ACTIVITY:** Students determine the area of various shapes by covering them with inch squares and halves of inch squares. **ASSESSMENT PAGE:** *Tiles 3*, Student Guide, page 197.	• envelopes • scissors
LESSON 4 **The Midnight Visit**	URG pages 30–35 AB pages 29–40	1	DPP G–H	**ADVENTURE BOOK:** Students work with two mice to find the area of a figure in an Adventure Book story.	
LESSON 5 **Unit Designs**	URG pages 36–40 SG pages 199–202	1	DPP I–J	**ACTIVITY:** Students use 1-inch squares and halves to make a design on a piece of paper. **ASSESSMENT PAGES:** *Which Two?*, Student Guide, pages 201–202.	• 1-inch paper squares and half-square-inch pieces • construction paper • scissors • glue or paste

Unit 11: Looking at 100 .... 11 Sessions

Unit Summary
This unit builds number sense by focusing on the quantity of 100. It extends the partitioning work in Unit 9.
A variety of contexts, including time and money, provide problem-solving settings that build ideas about number
relationships to 100. This unit includes the second part of the weather lab, *Weather 2: Winter Skies,* which allows
students to analyze and compare data collected in Unit 3. An Adventure Book *It's Sunny in Arizona* explores the
variability of weather across the United States. The DPP includes items that practice and assess math facts
strategies, especially the counting-on strategy.

Major Concept Focus
- money
- partitioning 100 into two and three parts
- counting on by fives and tens
- number relationships
- *100 Chart*

- exploring the importance of units
- TIMS Laboratory Method
- using a calendar
- Adventure Book: weather changes
- adding and subtracting with multiples of ten

Pacing Suggestions
This unit is designed to be completed in 11 class sessions.

Take advantage of *Math Trailblazers* connections to other subject areas:

- Lesson 6 *Weather 2: Winter Skies* is a laboratory investigation. Students collect weather data in a winter month
  to compare to the data they collected in the fall in Unit 2 Lesson 6 *Weather 1: Eye on the Sky.* We recommend
  that this lab be scheduled for February. Use one math class session on the first day of the month to introduce
  this lesson. Then, continue to collect data during science time.
- Lesson 7 *It's Sunny in Arizona* is an Adventure Book story that reinforces concepts in the Lesson 6 lab. Read
  and discuss the story during language arts or social studies.

Preparing for Upcoming Lessons
Encourage your students to bring quarters to add to the class bank. The class bank will be used throughout the
activities in this unit.

Unit 11 Outline

Components Key: SG = Student Guide, AB = Adventure Book, URG = Unit Resource Guide,
and DPP = Daily Practice and Problems

Books & Pages	Sessions	DPP	Description	Supplies
LESSON 1				
100 Links URG pages 20–25 SG page 204	1	DPP A–B	**ACTIVITY:** Students partition a 100-link chain into two and three parts. They write addition sentences and describe their partitions.	• links
LESSON 2				
Pennies and Dimes URG pages 26–35 SG pages 205–210	2	DPP C–F	**ACTIVITY:** Students explore the relationship between pennies and dimes. They generalize addition and subtraction facts to multiples of ten.	• pennies • dimes • overhead pennies and dimes

	Books & Pages	Sessions	DPP	Description	Supplies
LESSON 3 Dimes, Nickels, and Quarters	URG pages 36–45 SG pages 211–213	2	DPP G–J	**ACTIVITY:** Students compare the values of different coins and determine different combinations of coins that add up to $1.00.	• scissors • pennies • nickels • dimes • quarters • overhead pennies, nickels, dimes, and quarters
LESSON 4 Arrow Dynamics	URG pages 46–50 SG pages 215–223	1	DPP K–L	**GAME:** Students develop their knowledge of number relationships by playing the game *Arrow Dynamics* on the *100 Chart* and writing number sentences. **ASSESSMENT PAGE:** *Follow the Arrows*, Student Guide, page 223.	• spinners or paper clips and pencils • counters or game tokens
LESSON 5 How Long Is 100?	URG pages 51–55 SG page 225	1	DPP M–N	**ACTIVITY:** Students discuss seconds and minutes as they develop number sense for 100. They collect and organize data about time.	• calculators
LESSON 6 Weather 2: Winter Skies	– INTRODUCTORY SESSION –					
Weather 2: Winter Skies	URG pages 56–67 SG pages 227–239	1	DPP O–P	**LAB:** Students use the TIMS Laboratory Method to collect, record, and analyze data about weather. They compare data collected in this lesson to data from Unit 2 Lesson 6. **ASSESSMENT PAGE:** *Winter Weather*, Student Guide, page 239.	
LESSON 7 It's Sunny in Arizona	URG pages 68–76 SG page 241 AB pages 41–56	1	DPP Q–R	**ADVENTURE BOOK:** A family takes a vacation and notes how the weather changes as they travel from state to state.	• crayons
LESSON 8 Maria's Marble Mart	URG pages 77–83 SG pages 242–243	2	DPP S–V	**ASSESSMENT ACTIVITY:** Students' knowledge of addition and subtraction is assessed as they create and solve problems by grouping and counting with tens.	• index cards • connecting cubes

Unit 12: Cubes and Volume . . . . 6-7 Sessions

Unit Summary

Students investigate the variety of buildings that can be constructed from a fixed volume of eight cubes. They make a data table showing the number of floors in their buildings to help plan a model city. They further explore the concept of volume by building models of classroom objects. The Adventure Book *A World of Cubic Animals* is included in this unit. The DPP includes items that practice and assess math facts strategies, especially counting on.

Major Concept Focus

- spatial visualization
- building models
- using models to approximate volume
- communicating solution strategies
- volume in cubic units
- Adventure Book: volume in cubic units
- investigating the relationship between volume and shape
- sorting and classifying cube models

Pacing Suggestions

This unit is designed to be completed in 6–7 class sessions.

Take advantage of *Math Trailblazers* connections to other subject areas:

- Lesson 4 *A World of Cubic Animals* is an *Adventure Book* story that reinforces concepts in the unit. Read and discuss the story during language arts.

Preparing for Upcoming Lessons

Weather 2: Winter Skies: Continue gathering data about the weather.

Unit 12 Outline

Components Key: SG = Student Guide, AB = Adventure Book, URG = Unit Resource Guide, and DPP = Daily Practice and Problems

	Books & Pages	Sessions	DPP	Description	Supplies
LESSON 1 **Skylines**	URG pages 13–21 SG page 246	2	DPP A–D	**ACTIVITY:** Students construct and describe an eight-cube building using different variables: area, volume, and height. They then guide the teacher in making a group data table to display information about a skyline.	• connecting cubes • large sheets of paper • small cardboard box
LESSON 2 **Cubic Classroom**	URG pages 22–26 SG pages 247–249	1–2	DPP E–F	**ACTIVITY:** Students create cube models of classroom objects to estimate their volumes.	• connecting cubes • classroom objects
LESSON 3 **TIMS Towers**	URG pages 27–32 SG pages 251–257	2	DPP G–J	**ACTIVITY:** Students explore strategies for finding the volume of buildings depicted in three-dimensional drawings. **ASSESSMENT PAGE:** *TIMS Radio Tower,* Student Guide, page 257.	• connecting cubes • calculators
LESSON 4 **A World of Cubic Animals**	URG pages 33–38 SG pages 259–261 AB pages 57–68	1	DPP K–L	**ADVENTURE BOOK:** Students use an interactive book about a young boy's dream to find the volume of imaginary animals made of cubes. **ASSESSMENT PAGE:** *Comparing Ruffy and the Snake,* Student Guide, page 261.	• connecting cubes

Unit 13: Thinking About Addition and Subtraction ....8 Sessions

Unit Summary

Doubling numbers is explored, beginning with children creating various representations of doubles. They investigate other doubles of their choosing and, from this, develop the inverse notion of "halving a number." Informal connections to multiplication and division concepts are made.

The DPP for this unit includes items that practice and assess math facts strategies. In particular, they can reason from known facts by using doubles.

Major Concept Focus

- sums to ten
- number sentences for doubles
- relationships between doubles and halves
- even and odd
- visual imagery of doubles and halves
- communicating solution strategies
- addition and subtraction problems
- Game: sums of ten, doubles

Preparing for Upcoming Lessons

Begin collecting empty toilet paper cylinders, tissue boxes, and other examples of cylinders, prisms, and spheres for use in Unit 15.

Weather 2: Winter Skies: Continue gathering weather data. (Unit 11 Lesson 6)

Unit 13 Outline

Components Key: SG = Student Guide, AB = Adventure Book, URG = Unit Resource Guide, and DPP = Daily Practice and Problems

	Books & Pages	Sessions	DPP	Description	Supplies
LESSON 1 **Make Ten**	URG pages 16–23 SG page 264	1	DPP A–B	**GAME:** Students play an adding game using digit cards to form combinations of numbers whose sum equals 10.	• beans (or other counters) • scissors
LESSON 2 **Seeing Doubles**	URG pages 24–30 SG pages 265–268	2	DPP C–F	**ACTIVITY:** Students create their own examples of doubling numbers and find real-world examples of doubles in their own surroundings. **ASSESSMENT PAGES:** *Doubles Problems*, Student Guide, pages 267–268.	• paint-brushes and jars of paint, hole punches, or scissors • paper • oversize chart paper or newsprint
LESSON 3 **Doubles and Halves**	URG pages 31–38 SG pages 269–277	2	DPP G–J	**ACTIVITY:** Students explore the relationship between doubling and halving. Students also practice doubling and halving numbers in a game called *Doubles Railroad.*	• connecting cubes • clear plastic spinners (or pencils with paper clips) • beans (or other game tokens)
LESSON 4 **Odd and Even Revisited**	URG pages 39–46 SG pages 279–281	1	DPP K–L	**ACTIVITY:** Students classify answers to doubles problems as even or odd and evaluate the results of adding 1 or subtracting 1.	• connecting cubes • tape
LESSON 5 **Problem Solving**	URG pages 47–55 SG pages 283–289	2	DPP M–P	**ACTIVITY:** Students use a variety of strategies to solve problems and interpret data recorded on graphs. **ASSESSMENT PAGES:** *Recipe for Peanut Butter, Jelly, and Banana Sandwiches* and *How Many?*, Student Guide, pages 287 & 289.	• scissors • connecting cubes

Unit 14: Exploring Multiplication and Division ......5-8 Sessions

Unit Summary
Students investigate problem solving using multiplication and division. The lab *Pets* is used to generate numbers with which to create a series of problems. While student-discovered strategies continue to be of paramount importance, doubling and skip counting are emphasized. The DPP includes items that practice and assess math facts strategies. In particular, students can reason from known facts by using a ten or making a ten.

Major Concept Focus
- multiples of 2, 3, and 5
- solving problems based on real data
- TIMS Laboratory Method
- multiplication and division problems

Pacing Suggestions
This unit is designed to be completed in 5–8 class sessions.

Take advantage of *Math Trailblazers* connections to other subject areas:

- Lesson 2 *Pets* is a laboratory investigation that uses science process skills. Students can collect and organize the data during science time.

Preparing for Upcoming Lessons
Begin collecting empty toilet paper cylinders, tissue boxes, and other examples of cylinders, prisms, and spheres for use in Unit 15.

Ask students to bring in clippings of food ads for use in Unit 15 Lesson 4.

Unit 14 Outline

Components Key: SG = Student Guide, AB = Adventure Book, URG = Unit Resource Guide, and DPP = Daily Practice and Problems

	Books & Pages	Sessions	DPP	Description	Supplies
LESSON 1 **Math Mice**	URG pages 14–19 SG pages 293–294	2–3	DPP A–D	**ACTIVITY:** Students build triangular mice from toothpicks and solve problems involving multiplication and division concepts.	• envelopes or bags • glue • crayons • toothpicks • white yarn or string • dark yarn • construction paper
LESSON 2 **Pets**	URG pages 20–27 SG pages 295–299	2–3	DPP E–H	**LAB:** Students collect, classify, organize, and analyze data as they explore types of pets owned by classmates. Students use data to generate numbers for a series of word problems. **ASSESSMENT PAGES:** *Room 222's Pets Graph* and *More Pet Problems,* Student Guide, pages 279 & 299.	• 3-inch square self-adhesive note or 3" by 3" construction paper square and tape
LESSON 3 **Problems That Will Knock Your Socks Off!**	URG pages 28–33 SG pages 301–305	1–2	DPP I–J	**ACTIVITY:** Students choose one of two word problem sets to solve. **ASSESSMENT PAGE:** *Basil the Basset Hound,* Student Guide, page 305.	

Unit 15: Exploring 3-D Shapes ....5 Sessions

Unit Summary

Students explore cylinders, spheres, and prisms in their surroundings and develop necessary vocabulary to work with three-dimensional shapes. They match shape outlines to actual shapes and generate a chart comparing rectangular prisms and cubes by measuring the dimensions of boxes. Students classify objects into shape categories. Then, they create a book of shapes. The DPP includes items that practice and assess math facts strategies, in particular, using doubles.

Major Concept Focus

- naming 3-D shapes
- describing 3-D shapes
- identifying shapes by properties
- length in centimeters

Unit 15 Outline

	Books & Pages	Sessions	DPP	Description	Supplies
LESSON 1 **Tubes, Boxes, Spheres, and Cubes**	URG pages 14–19 SG pages 313–316	1	DPP A–B	**ACTIVITY:** Students explore the attributes of cylinders, prisms, spheres, and cubes. Then, they describe each of these three-dimensional shapes.	• toilet paper cores (cylinders) • boxes (prisms) • balls (spheres) • one-inch cubes • bag • markers • book or short ramp
LESSON 2 **Sizing Cylinders**	URG pages 20–27 SG pages 317–319	1	DPP C–D	**ACTIVITY:** Students compare the height and circumference of cylinders and classify the cylinders into three categories.	• cylindrically shaped objects • string • square paper • tape • blank paper • scissors
LESSON 3 **Looking at Prisms**	URG pages 28–36 SG pages 321–326	2	DPP E–H	**ACTIVITY:** Students match boxes to outlines of six box faces. **ASSESSMENT PAGES:** *Find the Shapes* and *3-D Shapes,* Student Guide, pages 321 and 323–324.	• boxes (rectangular prisms) • cubes • newsprint paper • crayons or markers • chart paper
LESSON 4 **In the Shapes Kitchen**	URG pages 37–41	1	DPP I–J	**ACTIVITY:** Students cut out pictures of foods and food containers from newspaper ads. They then use the pictures to create a shapes book.	• paper • scissors • paste or glue • food ads • crayons or markers • stapler

Unit 16: Collecting and Organizing Data . . . . 5 Sessions

Unit Summary

Offered as an opportunity for teacher-guided assessment, this unit encourages students to work more independently on data collection and analysis. Students review and discuss the TIMS Laboratory Method with *The Martians* Adventure Book before beginning the *Healthy Kids* Lab. Students collect and organize data about their daily eating habits to see if it falls in a range. The DPP includes items that practice and assess students' use of math facts strategies, including using a ten.

Major Concept Focus

- using a survey to study variables
- classification
- comparing two sets of data
- TIMS Laboratory Method
- Adventure Book: TIMS Laboratory Method

Pacing Suggestions

This unit is designed to be completed in 5 class sessions.

Utilize *Math Trailblazers* connections to other subjects:

- Read and discuss the Adventure Book in Lesson 1 *The Martians* during language arts.
- Lesson 3 *Healthy Kids* is a laboratory investigation. Compare and discuss students' data during science time.
- This unit can complement a unit on nutrition in science.

Preparing for Upcoming Lessons

In Unit 17 students will need egg cartons to group objects. Encourage students to bring in egg cartons from home.

Unit 16 Outline

	Books & Pages	Sessions	DPP	Description	Supplies
LESSON 1 **The Martians**	URG pages 12–16 SG page 331 AB pages 69–76	1	DPP A–B	**ADVENTURE BOOK:** A group of Martians decides to travel to Earth and study Earthlings. They land near a school. Curious about the source of the children's energy, the Martians decide to study what the children eat. This Adventure Book provides the setting for the lab *Healthy Kids* in Lesson 3.	
LESSON 2 **Food Sort**	URG pages 17–21 SG pages 333–335	1	DPP C–D	**ACTIVITY:** This activity prepares students for the data collection in the lab *Healthy Kids* in the following lesson. Children become familiar with food groups by sorting ten of their favorite foods into the six food groups. Then, children classify fruits and vegetables.	
LESSON 3 **Healthy Kids**	URG pages 22–31 SG pages 337–345	3	DPP E–J	**LAB:** In this teacher-guided lab, students collect data on what they eat for one day and compare their diets to suggested ranges for each food group. Students then analyze their personal data to see if they need to make changes to achieve a healthy diet. **ASSESSMENT PAGES:** *David's and Cindy's Food,* Student Guide, pages 343–345.	

Unit 17: Moving Beyond 100 .... 5-6 Sessions

Unit Summary

The Adventure Book *Tensland* provides the setting for an investigation of place value. Students explore ones, tens, and hundreds by grouping and counting objects. DPP items assess students' use of math facts strategies, especially using a ten.

Major Concept Focus

- grouping to count objects
- counting objects by ones, tens, and hundreds
- mental math
- representing quantities pictorially and symbolically
- addition and subtraction with multiples of 10 and 100
- Adventure Book: counting and grouping by tens

Pacing Suggestions

This unit is designed to be completed in 5–6 class sessions.

Utilize *Math Trailblazers* connections to other subjects by reading and discussing the Adventure Book in Lesson 1 *Tensland* during language arts.

Unit 17 Outline

Books & Pages	Sessions	DPP	Description	Supplies
LESSON 1 **Tensland**				
URG pages 12–15 AB pages 77–92	1	DPP A–B	**ADVENTURE BOOK:** Students follow the adventures of Hildie and Rosie, two sisters who group and count their way through a magical land.	
LESSON 2 **Our Class in Tensland**				
URG pages 16–22 SG pages 348–351	2	DPP C–F	**ACTIVITY:** Students pretend they are in Tensland by following in the footsteps of Hildie and Rosie. Students group and count an assortment of classroom obects. **ASSESSMENT PAGE:** *Terry in Tensland,* Student Guide, page 351.	• beans, connecting cubes, chain links, or colored tiles • bags or boxes • small cups, egg cartons, or small containers • transparencies and markers or sheets of construction paper
LESSON 3 **Counting One Hundred Seventy-two**				
URG pages 23–26 SG pages 353–354	1–2	DPP G–H	**ACTIVITY:** Students interpret the meaning of the number 172 and illustrate ways of grouping 172 beans. They also use manipulatives to represent the quantity 172. **ASSESSMENT PAGE:** *Pumpkin Patch,* Student Guide, pages 353–354.	• connecting cubes, connecting links, or colored tiles • transparencies and markers or sheets of construction paper • clear container • beans
LESSON 4 **Adding Hundreds**				
URG pages 27–32 SG pages 355–356	1	DPP I–J	**ACTIVITY:** Students use familiar addition strategies to add multiples of 100.	

Unit 18: Pieces, Parts, and Symmetry ....6-7 Sessions

Unit Summary

Students explore halves and fourths by folding paper shapes. They learn to discriminate between fractional parts of areas that are equal and unequal by telling if shapes are halves and fourths or not halves and fourths. Students also explore fractional parts of collections by counting the numbers in the part and the whole. Students use illustrations to demonstrate their understanding of fractions.

Major Concept Focus

- fraction names for $\frac{1}{2}$ and $\frac{1}{4}$
- line symmetry
- part-whole relationship of fractions
- fractional parts of areas
- fractional parts of sets

Pacing Suggestions

This unit is designed to be completed in 6–7 class sessions.

Omit Lesson 2 *Equal and Unequal* if your students show that they understand that fractional parts of a whole (halves and fourths) must have the same area.

Unit 18 Outline

	Books & Pages	Sessions	DPP	Description	Supplies
LESSON 1 **Fold and Color**	URG pages 14–21 SG pages 359–369	1–2	DPP A–B	**ACTIVITY:** Students fold various figures in halves and fourths and describe the parts in terms of their size and shape. They also look for lines of symmetry. **ASSESSMENT PAGE:** *Halves and Fourths*, Student Guide, page 369.	• glue • scissors • crayons • paper
LESSON 2 **Equal and Unequal**	URG pages 22–27 SG pages 371–373	1	DPP C–D	**ACTIVITY:** Students explore the difference between equal and unequal parts. They illustrate halves and not-halves, and fourths and not-fourths. **ASSESSMENT PAGE:** *Halves and Fourths*, Unit Resource Guide, page 27.	• scissors • crayons • tape or thumbtacks
LESSON 3 **Fraction Puzzles**	URG pages 28–33 SG pages 375–385	1	DPP E–F	**ACTIVITY:** Students explore the relationship between parts and the whole by making and solving puzzles. **ASSESSMENT PAGE:** *Which Shape Is It?*, Student Guide, page 385.	• letter-sized envelopes • scissors
LESSON 4 **A Class Full of Fractions**	URG pages 34–38 SG pages 387–388	1	DPP G–H	**ACTIVITY:** Students explore fractional parts of sets, as portrayed by their classmates. **ASSESSMENT PAGES:** *Drawing Fractions*, Student Guide, pages 387–388.	• blank transparency
LESSON 5 **Fraction Finale**	URG pages 39–43 SG page 389	2	DPP I–L	**ACTIVITY:** Teams of students find or make different representations of the fraction one-half. They explore other fractions using a variety of manipulatives. **ASSESSMENT PAGE:** *Pieces of Eighths*, Student Guide, page 389.	• assortment of objects (that can be arranged or partitioned to show halves or fourths, etc.) • tape or glue • newsprint

Unit 19: Measurement and Mapping . . . . 4-5 Sessions

Unit Summary

The plastic figure Mr. Origin provides the vehicle for work with directionality and length measurement in the lab *Mr. Origin Left/Right.* Students, working along one axis, use counting, addition, and subtraction to solve a series of problems. The Adventure Book *Buried Treasure* emphasizes the importance of map reading skills.

Major Concept Focus

- measuring length
- locating objects relative to Mr. Origin
- right and left
- direction and distances on a one-dimensional map (number line)
- TIMS Laboratory Method
- numbering a line right and left of Mr. Origin
- Adventure Book: map reading

Pacing Suggestions

This unit is designed to be completed in 4–5 class sessions.

Utilize *Math Trailblazers* connections to other subjects by reading and discussing the Lesson 3 Adventure Book *Buried Treasure* during language arts.

Unit 19 Outline

	Books & Pages	Sessions	DPP	Description	Supplies
LESSON 1 Meet Mr. Origin and Mr. Origin's Map	URG pages 14–23 SG pages 392–393	1	DPP A–B	**ACTIVITY:** Students are introduced to the manipulative Mr. Origin. They find out how right and left directions and distance are plotted on Mr. Origin's map.	• pattern blocks • penny • Mr. Origins • connecting links • cup and saucer • key
LESSON 2 Mr. Origin Left/Right	URG pages 24–42 SG pages 395–401	2–3	DPP C–F	**LAB:** Students locate various objects relative to Mr. Origin, a reference point. They use connecting links to measure the distances of the objects from Mr. Origin. They record the data they have gathered, plot the location of the objects on a left/right map, and analyze the findings of their investigation. **ASSESSMENT PAGE:** *Vanessa Finds Her Money,* Student Guide, page 401.	• Mr. Origins • pattern blocks • connecting links • tape • scissors
LESSON 3 Buried Treasure	URG pages 43–51 AB pages 93–108	1	DPP G–H	**ADVENTURE BOOK:** In this interactive story, Helen and Johnny use Mr. Origin and their map-reading skills to help them discover buried Native American artifacts.	

Unit 20: Looking Back at First Grade .... 4-7 Sessions

Unit Summary

In this unit, teachers can assess problem-solving progress as students review the concepts and skills learned in first grade with a series of problems. A paper-and-pencil assessment is included.

Major Concept Focus

- Assessment: problem-solving strategies
- Assessment: Grade 1 concepts and skills

Pacing Suggestions

This unit is designed to be completed in 4–7 class sessions.

- Lesson 1 *Problem Solving* is a set of 21 problems for students to solve during four to five class sessions. Allow time for students to share their solutions.
- Lesson 2 *End-of-Year Test* is an optional paper-and-pencil assessment.

Unit 20 Outline

Components Key: SG = Student Guide, AB = Adventure Book, URG = Unit Resource Guide, and DPP = Daily Practice and Problems

	Books & Pages	Sessions	DPP	Description	Supplies
LESSON 1 Problem Solving	**URG** pages 13–20 **SG** pages 404–415	4–5	**DPP** A–H	**ACTIVITY:** Students solve problems involving length, area, volume, and time as they revisit concepts of measurement, geometry, fractions, and arithmetic that they have encountered during the year.	• a variety of manipulatives (e.g., pattern blocks, chain links, connecting cubes, toothpicks, and so on) • calculators
LESSON 2 End-of-Year Test	**URG** pages 21–32	– OPTIONAL LESSON – 1–2	**DPP** I–J	**OPTIONAL ASSESSMENT ACTIVITY:** Students complete a pencil-and-paper assessment that reviews concepts learned throughout the year. **ASSESSMENT PAGES:** *End-of-Year Test*, Unit Resource Guide, pages 25–32.	• variety of manipulatives (e.g., pattern blocks, links, connecting cubes, toothpicks, and play money)

5

Scope and Sequence
& the NCTM *Principles and Standards*

The Scope and Sequence & the NCTM *Principles and Standards* section provides descriptions and tables that show how *Math Trailblazers* relates to the National Council of Teachers of Mathematics *Principles and Standards for School Mathematics*. A comprehensive scope and sequence for Grade 1 units and Daily Practice and Problems is included.

Math Trailblazers and the Principles and Standards

The National Council of Teachers of Mathematics (NCTM) *Principles and Standards for School Mathematics* and *Math Trailblazers* complement each other: The *Principles and Standards* provides a vision of what school mathematics should be. *Math Trailblazers* provides the curricular structure so that teachers can turn that vision into reality. This section starts with an outline of how *Math Trailblazers* complements the five content standards and five process standards in the *Principles and Standards*. It concludes with a scope and sequence that gives specific information on how the Grade 1 curriculum develops through the year. For information on the scope and sequence across the grades, see the *Math Trailblazers Scope and Sequence Chart* available from Kendall/Hunt Publishing Company.

Content Standards

Principles and Standards for School Mathematics outlines an articulated vision of how learning and teaching in each of five content areas should develop across the grades. These content areas are number and operations, algebra, geometry, measurement, and data analysis and probability. In *Math Trailblazers* the standards for all five content areas are addressed appropriately at every grade level, from Kindergarten through Grade 5. Five process standards prescribe a curriculum where problem solving, communication, reasoning, connections, and what the relationship between drop height and bounce height is, and how that relationship is evident in the table and graph. Then, students make predictions and verify those predictions. Finally, students generalize: "What would the graph look like for a Super ball?" "What would happen if the experiment were repeated on a carpeted floor?"

This single experiment involves measurement, data analysis, number sense, estimation, graphing, multiplication, patterns and functions (algebra), and mathematical reasoning. All these topics, moreover, relate to a single context that unites them. By weaving so many themes into one complex whole, that whole becomes more meaningful and the mathematics more powerful.

Lessons such as *Bouncing Ball* are embedded in a careful sequence of lessons and units that address all the standards. Other lessons develop single skills or concepts that students can then practice in the Daily Practice and Problems. These skills and concepts are extended and applied in more complex lessons and investigations. *Math Trailblazers* is therefore a comprehensive and balanced curriculum that includes geometry, statistics and probability, measurement, algebra, estimation, fractions, numeration, and computation—just what the *Principles and Standards* requires.

For more information on the *Math Trailblazers* approach to selected content areas, see the TIMS Tutors in Section 9 of this *Teacher Implementation Guide.*

Process Standards

The process standards highlight ways of acquiring and using content knowledge. Each of the process standards is connected to the others. Moreover, the learning of mathematical processes is deeply embedded in the learning of content.

Problem Solving. A strong emphasis on problem solving is evident in the NCTM recommendations. Throughout *Math Trailblazers,* students are immersed in complex problem situations in which they both apply the mathematics they know and learn new mathematics. Students develop skills, procedures, and concepts as they work on the problems. For example, in the third-grade laboratory experiment, *The Better "Picker Upper,"* students explore the absorbency of various brands of paper towels by dropping water on each type of towel and comparing the areas of the spots. As the students work through this complex problem, they learn about area (by tracing the spots on grid paper and counting square centimeters to find the areas), fractions (as they piece parts of square centimeters together to make whole square centimeters), averaging (as they aggregate the results of several trials), graphing (as they display and interpret their data in graphs), and computation (as they calculate the number of drops of water a whole paper towel absorbs). All this mathematics grows out of one problem: "Which is the more absorbent towel?"

Putting problems first is a different and difficult way to organize a mathematics curriculum. If the focus is on problems, then careful design, meticulous planning, and continual assessment are required to ensure the timely development of skills and concepts. Despite the difficulties, the benefits are clear: students not only master skills and concepts, they can apply them flexibly to solve problems.

Reasoning and Proof. This standard requires that reasoning permeate the curriculum. Students constantly explain their thinking and justify their solutions, first in small groups and then to the class as a whole. Sometimes they explain their thoughts orally and other times in writing or by using pictures and other tools. Students are always encouraged to find solutions in more than one way and to compare and contrast various solution methods. Thus, meaning and understanding are emphasized, and students find that mathematics makes sense. "Mathematical reasoning develops in classrooms where students are encouraged to put forth their own ideas for examination. Teachers and students should be open to questions, reactions, and elaborations from others in the classroom. Students need to explain and justify their thinking and learn how to detect fallacies and critique others' thinking. They need to have ample opportunity to apply their reasoning skills and justify their thinking in mathematical discussion." (NCTM 2000, p. 188)

One example of an important area of mathematical reasoning that receives particular attention in *Math Trailblazers,* especially in Grades 3 through 5, is pre-proportional and proportional reasoning. This kind of reasoning is carefully developed over time through a sequence of real-life problems that can be solved with manipulatives, patterns, graphs, or symbols. Students choose the strategies and tools that make sense to them. Using these tools helps students create visual images of this important mathematical concept, which historically has largely been taught symbolically or procedurally and has been difficult for many students to grasp.

Communication. Students need frequent opportunities to communicate their mathematics. "Communication is an essential part of mathematics and mathematics education… Students gain insight into their thinking when they present their methods for solving problems, when they justify their reasoning to a classmate or teacher, or when they formulate a question about something that is puzzling to them." (NCTM 2000, p. 60) Communication is integral to *Math Trailblazers.* In many activities, students handle manipulatives, draw pictures, make graphs, and grapple with mathematical ideas. Many of the activities are collaborative exercises involving groups of students who work together to obtain, analyze, and generalize their results.

Just as people explain how they solve problems on the job, students who use the labs and activities talk about their mathematics. Students discuss, compare, contrast, and write about their problem-solving methods in both small-group and whole-class settings. This "publication" of students' mathematical thinking gives students access to a broader range of solution strategies and helps them become more reflective about mathematics.

Connections. This standard calls for connections within mathematics, between mathematics and other parts of the school curriculum, and between mathematics and their own interests. Integration of subject matter is a major focus of *Math Trailblazers.* Mathematics arises naturally in science, language, history, and daily life. *Math Trailblazers* does not artificially merge disparate ideas from distinct disciplines, but rather builds up the underlying unity between disciplines that we see in the real world. For example, the basic measurement variables that are covered extensively in the curriculum—length, area, volume, mass, and time—are fundamental not only to mathematics but also to science and in daily life. The TIMS Laboratory Method effectively incorporates the method of science into the mathematics curriculum as a problem-solving tool.

The *Adventure Books* and Literature Connections integrate language arts and social studies with the mathematics curriculum. Some *Adventure Books* recount the history of science and mathematics; others show how the concepts and procedures students are learning apply to the work of real scientists or to everyday life. Students are continually required to communicate their mathematical thinking orally and in writing. *Math Trailblazers* is committed to the ideal of "writing across the curriculum."

Connections within mathematics are equally important. Like most real-world problems, activities in *Math Trailblazers* generally involve a combination of mathematical topics. A single laboratory experiment, for example, might involve arithmetic, data collection, estimation, geometry, probability, and algebraic concepts—each covered at an appropriate level for students.

Representation. "Representing ideas and connecting their representations to mathematics lies at the heart of understanding mathematics." (NCTM 2000, p. 136) *Math Trailblazers* is rich in the many opportunities it gives students to represent mathematical ideas. For example, whole numbers are represented as collections of objects (using manipulatives or drawings), as measurements, as points on a number line, or as items on a *100 Chart*. When children collect data they may organize it in a data table or represent it graphically. If there are patterns in the data, they can be described numerically or graphically. Ultimately, some relations are described symbolically.

Throughout *Math Trailblazers* students are encouraged to draw pictures and diagrams to illustrate their ideas and support their thinking. This communicates their reasoning, and as students create these representations, they clarify and build their thinking.

Developing a *Standards*-Based Classroom

The *Professional Standards for Teaching Mathematics* (NCTM, 1991) and the Teaching Principle in the *Principles and Standards* specify what classroom teachers, supervisors, teacher educators, and policy makers should do to improve mathematics instruction. Much of this discussion concerns four key areas: tasks, discourse, environment, and analysis. Teachers decide what tasks to set for students, foster discourse about mathematics, establish a classroom environment conducive to high achievement and positive attitudes, and engage in analysis of students' thinking and their own teaching. While accomplishing these things depends more on teachers' expertise than on curricula, materials that embody the *Principles and Standards* can make the work easier.

Tasks. *Math Trailblazers* provides a logical sequence of well-conceived tasks. Professional mathematicians and scientists helped develop the curriculum so that lessons focus on significant concepts and skills. Teachers and mathematics educators also helped write the curriculum, so that tasks are engaging, practical, and developmentally appropriate. Lessons develop both skills and concepts, so that they make connections within mathematics and between mathematics and other subjects, portray mathematics as a human endeavor, and promote communication and problem solving.

Discourse. Many features of *Math Trailblazers* support discourse. Tasks in the curriculum have enough depth for significant discussion to be possible. An emphasis on multiple solutions to problems encourages students to talk about their own thinking. The *Student Guide* often displays and discusses multiple solutions to problems. Journal and discussion prompts in the teacher materials stimulate and focus classroom discussions. *Adventure Books* and children's literature help students understand that people really do talk about mathematics and science. The wide range of tools and technology in *Math Trailblazers*—manipulatives, calculators, pictures, tables, graphs, and symbols—enhance discourse by broadening the means of communication beyond what is traditional.

Environment. Creating a classroom environment conducive to the development of each student's mathematical power is necessary for the *Principles and Standards* to come alive. This involves arranging space, time, and materials in ways that maximize student learning. *Math Trailblazers'* diverse range of lessons—activities of varied length, activities for groups and individuals, hands-on and paper-and-pencil investigations, and activities that encourage multiple solution paths—all help teachers develop a classroom that builds mathematical understandings and skills for a wide range of students.

Analysis. The curriculum's activities and assessment program provide teachers with many opportunities to analyze students' learning. Teachers using the curriculum will know more about their students' mathematical abilities than they ever have before. The extensive background information provided in the unit guides and in the *Teacher Implementation Guide* provides accessible ways for teachers to gain additional insight into how students learn mathematics. This enhanced knowledge motivates the teaching of subsequent lessons. *Math Trailblazers* will help you become more attuned both to your students and to your own teaching.

Math Trailblazers: A Standards-Based Curriculum

In summary, NCTM calls for curricula to be coherent within and across the grades, to be conceptually oriented, to involve students actively, to emphasize development of students' mathematical thinking and reasoning abilities, to emphasize applications, to include a broad range of content, and to make appropriate use of calculators and computers.

These are admirable goals and high expectations. No curriculum can finally and fully attain such goals and fulfill such expectations—not only will there always be improvements to be made, but in the end much depends upon individual teachers and students. Yet a curriculum that has been developed specifically to be aligned with the *Principles and Standards* will provide the foundation. The goals and characteristics described above are all hallmarks of *Math Trailblazers*.

The best test of alignment with the *Principles and Standards,* however, is to observe students using the curriculum. Are they actively involved? Do they grapple with significant concepts while learning and applying basic skills? Are they thinking and reasoning? Do they use a broad range of tools to solve realistic problems? We think you will find that *Math Trailblazers* more than meets this test.

References

An Agenda for Action: Recommendations for School Mathematics of the 1980s. National Council of Teachers of Mathematics, Reston, VA, 1980.

Assessment Standards for School Mathematics. National Council of Teachers of Mathematics, Reston, VA, 1995.

Curriculum and Evaluation Standards for School Mathematics. National Council of Teachers of Mathematics, Reston, VA, 1989.

Essential Mathematics for the 21st Century: The Position of the National Council of Supervisors of Mathematics. National Council of Supervisors of Mathematics, Minneapolis, MN, 1988.

National Research Council. "Conclusions and Recommendations." In *Adding It Up: Helping Children Learn Mathematics.* J. Kilpatrick, J. Swafford, and B. Findell (Eds.). National Academy Press, Washington, DC, 2001.

Principles and Standards for School Mathematics. National Council of Teachers of Mathematics, Reston, VA, 2000.

Professional Standards for Teaching Mathematics. National Council of Teachers of Mathematics, Reston, VA, 1991.

Scope and Sequence

Scope and Sequence for Units

Math Trailblazers has been developed to meet the NCTM *Principles and Standards for School Mathematics*. The scope and sequence in white on the top of the following pages indicates how each unit aligns with the *Principles and Standards*. By reading the chart horizontally, you will be able to see the integration of the various standards within a given unit. By reading the chart vertically, you will be able to track the development of a specific standard throughout the first-grade curriculum.

Scope and Sequence for the Daily Practice and Problems

Every unit includes a series of Daily Practice and Problems (DPP). The scope and sequence chart in gray on the following pages indicates how the DPP aligns with the *Principles and Standards*. By reading the chart vertically, you will be able to track the development of a specific standard throughout the first-grade DPP. Each DPP item, which is denoted by a letter, has been correlated with one or more of the standards. The appropriate letters are indicated in parentheses following each entry. Thus, the scope and sequence can also serve as a content map for the DPP.

For more information about the Daily Practice and Problems, see the Daily Practice and Problems Guide (Section 7).

	Number and Operations	Algebra	Geometry	Measurement	Data Analysis and Probability
Unit 1: Welcome to First Grade: A Baseline Assessment Unit **Lessons**	• Translating between different representations of small numbers (concrete, pictorial, and symbolic). • Developing number sense for small numbers. • Counting using one-to-one correspondence. • Using the strategies of counting all and counting on to add. • Comparing numbers using *more, less,* or *about the same.* • Identifying the number of objects in a small group without counting.	• Using patterns to solve problems.		• Measuring length using nonstandard units (links).	• Collecting and organizing data.
Daily Practice and Problems	• Developing number sense for small numbers. (A, B, E, F, K, N) • Counting using one-to-one correspondence. (A, B, L, M, P) • Estimating quantities. (B, K, N) • Counting forward or backward by ones. (C, D, G, I, L, O, P) • Comparing quantities. (L, N) • Counting on from a given number. (C, E, F, G, H, I, J, M, O, P)				

Problem Solving	Reasoning and Proof	Communication	Connections	Representation
• Using patterns to solve problems.		• Communicating mathematics verbally and in writing.	• Connecting mathematics to real-world situations: counting and measuring objects at school and at home.	• Translating between different representations of small numbers (concrete, pictorial, and symbolic).
• Solving problems involving money. (H, J, O)				• Using counters to represent numbers. (A, B, H, J, K, L, M, N, O, P)

	Number and Operations	Algebra	Geometry	Measurement	Data Analysis and Probability
Unit 2: Exploring Shapes **Lessons**	• Using tallies and symbols to represent numbers.	• Using patterns in data to make predictions and solve problems.	• Investigating properties of 2-dimensional shapes. • Translating between representations of shapes (concrete and pictorial). • Identifying and describing 2-dimensional shapes using their properties (number of sides, length of sides, number of corners). • Making and testing conjectures about geometric properties. • Using geometric concepts and skills to solve problems. • Partitioning shapes in different ways. • Investigating, describing, and reasoning about the results of combining shapes. • Drawing 2-dimensional shapes.	• Exploring time concepts (time of day, days, weeks, months). • Using a calendar to measure the passage of time.	• Collecting, organizing, graphing, and analyzing data. • Using patterns in data to make predictions and solve problems.
Daily Practice and Problems	• Developing number sense for small numbers. (E, L, M, N) • Counting on or counting back from a given number. (E, F, G, H, I, J, K) • Comparing quantities. (F, G, H, I, J, K, L, M, N)		• Comparing and describing 2-dimensional shapes using their properties (number of sides, length of sides, number of corners). (O, P)	• Exploring time concepts (days, weeks, months). (A, B, C, D)	

Problem Solving	Reasoning and Proof	Communication	Connections	Representation
• Using geometric concepts and skills to solve problems. • Communicating solutions verbally and pictorially.	• Making and testing conjectures about geometric properties. • Investigating, describing, and reasoning about the results of combining shapes.	• Identifying and describing 2-dimensional shapes. • Investigating, describing, and reasoning about the results of combining shapes. • Communicating solutions verbally and pictorially.	• Connecting mathematics and science to real-world situations: recording weather data. • Connecting mathematics to real-world situations: identifying shapes. • Using a calendar to measure the passage of time.	• Translating between different representations of large numbers (tallies and symbols). • Translating between representations of shapes (concrete and pictorial). • Investigating, describing, and reasoning about the results of combining shapes. • Drawing 2-dimensional shapes.
	• Comparing and describing 2-dimensional shapes. (O, P)	• Comparing and describing 2-dimensional shapes. (O, P) • Comparing quantities using more or less. (I, J, K, L, M, N)		• Using counters to represent numbers. (F, G, H, I, J, K, N)

	Number and Operations	Algebra	Geometry	Measurement	Data Analysis and Probability
Unit 3: Pennies, Pockets, and Parts **Lessons**	• Using tallies, ten frames, words, and symbols to represent numbers. • Developing number sense using part-whole relationships. • Developing number sense using five and ten as benchmarks. • Identifying numbers represented on ten frames. • Partitioning numbers (ten or less) into two and three parts. • Adding using ten frames and counters. • Writing addition number sentences. • Translating between representations of numbers (ten frames, tallies, manipulatives, words, and symbols). • Using counting on to add. • Solving problems involving addition.	• Translating between graphs and real-world events. • Writing number sentences for addition situations.			• Collecting, organizing, graphing, and analyzing data. • Using a bar graph to solve problems. • Translating between graphs and real-world events.
Daily Practice and Problems	• Developing number sense for small numbers. (A, B, C, V, W) • Using the strategies of counting all and counting on to add. (I, J, P, X, Y, Z, CC, DD) • Comparing quantities. (A, F, G) • Writing addition number sentences. (Y, AA, BB) • Partitioning numbers (ten or less) into two and three parts. (AA, BB) • Counting on or counting back from a given number. (B, C, V, W) • Solving addition or subtraction problems with missing parts. (X, Y, CC, DD)	• Solving addition or subtraction problems with missing parts. (X, Y, CC, DD)	• Partitioning shapes. (D, E, K, L, M) • Investigating, describing, and reasoning about the results of combining shapes. (D, E, K, L, M) • Describing 2-dimensional shapes using their properties (number of sides, length of sides, number of corners). (N, O, T, U)	• Measuring length using nonstandard units (links). (F, G) • Exploring time concepts (days, weeks, months). (H, I, J, P, Q, R, S)	• Organizing data in a table. (Z, AA, BB)

Problem Solving	Reasoning and Proof	Communication	Connections	Representation
• Solving word problems involving money. • Exploring, comparing, and contrasting solution methods. • Solving addition problems.	• Communicating solutions verbally and in writing, or with manipulatives. • Exploring, comparing, and contrasting solution methods.	• Communicating solutions verbally and in writing. • Writing addition number sentences.	• Connecting mathematics to real-world situations: pockets in clothing. • Translating between graphs and real-world events.	• Translating between representations of numbers (tallies, ten frames, manipulatives, words, and symbols). • Translating between graphs and real-world events. • Writing number sentences for addition situations.
• Solving word problems involving money. (X, Y, CC, DD) • Solving addition or subtraction problems with missing parts. (X, Y, CC, DD) • Using data to solve problems. (Z)	• Investigating, describing, and reasoning about the results of combining shapes. (D, E, K, L, M)	• Describing 2-dimensional shapes using their properties. (N, O, T, U)		• Investigating, describing, and reasoning about the results of combining shapes. (D, E, K, L, M) • Translating between different representations of numbers (tallies and symbols). (Z) • Writing addition number sentences. (Y, AA, BB) • Using counters to represent numbers. (A, X, Y, AA, BB)

	Number and Operations	Algebra	Geometry	Measurement	Data Analysis and Probability
Unit 4: Adding to Solve Problems **Lessons**	• Writing number sentences for addition situations. • Using manipulatives, pictures, and symbols to represent numbers. • Identifying odd and even numbers. • Developing number sense using part-whole relationships. • Partitioning numbers into two and three parts. • Using the strategies of counting all and counting on to add. • Adding using manipulatives. • Solving problems involving addition. • Choosing appropriate methods and tools to calculate (calculator and pencil and paper). • Translating between different representations of numbers (manipulatives, pictures, words, and symbols).	• Exploring patterns in even and odd numbers. • Writing number sentences for addition situations.		• Using a calendar to measure the passage of time.	
Daily Practice and Problems	• Counting on and counting back from a given number. (A, C) • Using the strategies of counting all and counting on to add. (A, D, F, H, I) • Developing number sense for small numbers. (C) • Comparing quantities. (F) • Identifying odd and even numbers. (E, G) • Writing addition number sentences. (H, I, J) • Partitioning numbers into two and three parts. (J) • Solving addition or subtraction problems with missing parts. (D)	• Solving addition or subtraction problems with missing parts. (D)	• Identifying and describing 2-dimensional shapes using their properties. (B)	• Measuring length using nonstandard units (links). (C)	

Problem Solving	Reasoning and Proof	Communication	Connections	Representation
• Solving addition word problems and explaining the reasoning. • Choosing appropriate methods and tools to calculate (calculator and pencil and paper). • Creating stories for addition number sentences. • Exploring different types of addition problems.	• Solving addition word problems and explaining the reasoning.	• Solving addition word problems and explaining the reasoning. • Creating stories for addition number sentences. • Writing number sentences for addition situations. • Communicating solutions verbally and in writing.	• Connecting mathematics to real-world situations: pet shop. • Using a calendar to measure the passage of time.	• Translating between different representations of numbers (manipulatives, pictures, words, and symbols). • Using the equals sign in number sentences. • Writing number sentences for addition situations.
• Solving problems involving money. (A, D, J) • Solving word problems using math facts strategies. (D, I) • Solving addition or subtraction problems with missing parts. (D)	• Explaining mathematical reasoning using manipulatives. (E)	• Identifying and describing 2-dimensional shapes using their properties. (B) • Explaining mathematical reasoning using manipulatives. (E) • Comparing quantities using more or less. (F)		• Writing addition number sentences. (H, I, J) • Using counters to represent numbers. (E, F, H, J)

	Number and Operations	Algebra	Geometry	Measurement	Data Analysis and Probability
Unit 5: Grouping and Counting **Lessons**	• Grouping and counting objects by twos, fives, and tens. • Dividing a collection of objects into groups of a given size and counting the leftovers. • Using patterns to count objects. • Using pictures, counters, a *100 Chart,* and ten frames to represent numbers. • Translating between different representations of numbers (manipulatives, diagrams, and symbols). • Exploring division using fair shares. • Partitioning numbers into two and three parts. • Identifying relationships among pennies, nickels, and dimes.	• Using patterns to count objects. • Making and interpreting bar graphs. • Translating between graphs and real-world events.			• Sampling a population. • Collecting, organizing, and graphing data. • Making and interpreting bar graphs.
Daily Practice and Problems	• Using the strategies of counting all and counting on to add. (A, E, F, I, R) • Developing number sense for small numbers. (K) • Partitioning numbers into two and three parts. (C, H) • Writing addition number sentences. (C, E, F, H, I, N) • Skip counting by twos, fives, or tens. (D, L) • Identifying odd and even numbers. (G, J, Q) • Dividing a collection of objects into groups of a given size and counting the leftovers. (M, O, P) • Creating stories for addition number sentences. (B, F, K, N) • Grouping and counting objects by tens and ones. (O, P)	• Solving problems with missing parts. (A)		• Using a calendar to measure the passage of time. (E, F)	

Problem Solving	Reasoning and Proof	Communication	Connections	Representation
			• Connecting mathematics and science to real-world situations: investigating colors in cereals. • Translating between graphs and real-world events. • Connecting mathematics to real-world situations: investigating the relationships between pennies, nickles, and dimes.	• Using pictures, counters, *100 Chart,* and ten frames to represent numbers. • Translating between different representations of numbers (manipulatives, diagrams, and symbols). • Collecting, organizing, graphing, and analyzing data. • Representing data using bar graphs. • Translating between graphs and real-world events.
• Solving word problems involving money. (A) • Using math facts strategies to solve word problems. (A, E, F, N, R) • Solving problems with missing parts. (A)	• Explaining mathematical reasoning using manipulatives. (G, J, Q)	• Creating stories for addition number sentences. (B, F, K, N) • Explaining mathematical reasoning using manipulatives. (G, J, Q)		• Writing addition number sentences. (C, E, F, H, I, N) • Using pictures or counters to represent numbers. (A, C, G, H, I, M, O, P)

	Number and Operations	Algebra	Geometry	Measurement	Data Analysis and Probability
Unit 6: Measurement: Length **Lessons**	• Placing numbers into intervals. • Exploring the median as an average measure. • Grouping and counting objects by fives and ones.	• Using patterns to group and count objects. • Using patterns in data to make predictions and solve problems. • Translating between graphs and real-world events. • Making and interpreting bar graphs.		• Using a number and a unit to report a length. • Measuring length in nonstandard units (links, connecting cubes, footprints). • Estimating length in nonstandard units. • Measuring length in inches. • Comparing and ordering lengths. • Exploring the inverse relationship between the size of a unit and the number of units needed to measure an object. • Solving problems involving length.	• Using patterns in data to make predictions and solve problems involving length. • Making and interpreting bar graphs. • Collecting, organizing, graphing, and analyzing data. • Conducting a simple, controlled experiment involving multiple trials. • Translating between graphs and real-world events. • Exploring the median as an average measure.
Daily Practice and Problems	• Skip counting by twos, fives, or tens. (A, C, H, M) • Dividing a collection of objects into groups of a given size and counting the leftovers. (B, G, K, P) • Solving problems involving addition or subtraction. (C, J, N, O) • Using the strategies of counting all and counting on to add. (C, D, J, O, R) • Identifying odd and even numbers. (F) • Writing addition number sentences. (O) • Partitioning numbers into two and three parts. (P) • Grouping and counting objects by tens and ones. (K) • Finding the value of a collection of pennies, nickels, or dimes. (M)			• Measuring length in nonstandard units. (C, E, I, L, N, R, S, T) • Exploring the inverse relationship between the size of a unit and the number of units needed to measure an object. (S, T)	• Exploring the median as an average measure. (Q)

Problem Solving	Reasoning and Proof	Communication	Connections	Representation
• Using patterns in data to make predictions and solve problems involving length.	• Exploring the inverse relationship between the size of a unit and the number of units needed to measure an object.	• Using a number and a unit to report a length.	• Connecting mathematics and science: measuring the distance cars roll, starting on a ramp. • Using patterns in data to make predictions and solve problems involving length. • Translating between graphs and real-world events.	• Translating between graphs and real-world events. • Making and interpreting bar graphs. • Collecting, organizing, graphing, and analyzing data.
• Solving word problems involving money. (M) • Solving problems involving addition or subtraction. (C, J, N, R)				• Using counters or pictures to represent numbers. (B, F, K, P) • Writing addition number sentences. (O)

	Number and Operations	Algebra	Geometry	Measurement	Data Analysis and Probability
Unit 7: Patterns and Designs **Lessons**		• Identifying and describing patterns. • Extending patterns. • Representing patterns using manipulatives pictures, words, and symbols. • Translating between different representations of patterns (concrete, pictorial, symbolic). • Communicating patterns verbally and in writing.	• Constructing designs that have line symmetry. • Using symmetry to solve problems.		
Daily Practice and Problems	• Solving problems involving addition. (H, K) • Partitioning numbers into two and three parts. (E) • Writing addition number sentences. (E) • Dividing a collection of objects into groups of a given size and counting the leftovers. (E) • Using the strategies of counting all and counting on to add. (L) • Counting on or counting back from a given number. (A, C, H, K, L) • Grouping and counting objects by twos, fives, or tens. (I, J) • Skip counting by twos. (I, J)	• Identifying patterns. (G) • Extending a core pattern. (G) • Representing patterns using manipulatives, pictures, words, or symbols. (N) • Solving addition and subtraction problems with missing parts. (K)	• Using geometric concepts and skills to solve problems. (M) • Investigating, describing, and reasoning about the results of combining shapes. (M)	• Predicting and measuring length in nonstandard units (links, pennies, or feet). (B, C, D, F, H) • Exploring the inverse relationship between the size of a unit and the number of units needed to measure an object. (B, D, F) • Using a number and a unit to report a length. (D, F) • Using a calendar to measure the passage of time. (A)	

Problem Solving	Reasoning and Proof	Communication	Connections	Representation
• Extending patterns. • Using symmetry to solve problems.	• Extending repeating patterns. • Constructing designs that have line symmetry.	• Communicating patterns verbally and in writing.	• Connecting mathematics to real-world situations: identifying patterns in the classroom. • Connecting mathematics to real-world situations: identifying name patterns.	• Representing patterns using manipulatives, pictures, words, and symbols. • Translating between different representations of patterns (concrete, pictorial, symbolic).
• Solving word problems involving money. (E, J, K) • Solving word problems involving length. (C, D, F, H) • Solving addition and subtraction problems with missing parts. (K) • Extending a core pattern. (G, N)	• Making predictions based on known information. (B, D, F, M)			• Partitioning numbers into parts and representing them with number sentences. (E) • Representing patterns using pictures, words, or symbols. (N)

	Number and Operations	Algebra	Geometry	Measurement	Data Analysis and Probability
Unit 8: Subtracting to Solve Problems **Lessons**	• Representing subtraction situations using whole-part-part language. • Representing subtraction situations using manipulatives, words, pictures, and symbols. • Using the strategies of counting up and counting back to solve subtraction problems. • Writing number sentences for subtraction situations. • Creating stories for subtraction number sentences. • Solving problems involving subtraction. • Identifying numbers represented on ten frames. • Partitioning numbers (from 10 to 20) into two parts.	• Writing number sentences for subtraction situations.			
Daily Practice and Problems	• Partitioning numbers into two and three parts. (D) • Dividing a collection of objects into groups of a given size and counting the leftovers. (D) • Developing number sense for small numbers. (F) • Using the strategies of counting up and counting back to add and subtract. (F, G, H, I, J) • Writing addition and subtraction number sentences. (I, J)	• Identifying patterns. (A) • Extending repeating patterns. (A, E) • Representing patterns using manipulatives, pictures, words, or symbols. (A, E) • Solving addition and subtraction problems with missing parts. (G, I)		• Exploring time concepts (time of day, days, weeks, months). (B, C)	

Problem Solving	Reasoning and Proof	Communication	Connections	Representation
• Solving problems involving subtraction. • Creating stories for subtraction number sentences. • Exploring different types of subtraction problems.	• Solving subtraction problems and explaining the reasoning.	• Solving problems involving subtraction and communicating solution strategies. • Representing subtraction situations using whole-part-part language. • Creating stories for subtraction number sentences. • Writing number sentences for subtraction situations.	• Connecting mathematics to real-world situations: creating subtraction situations about the circus.	• Representing subtraction situations using part-part-whole language. • Representing subtraction situations using manipulatives, words, pictures, and symbols. • Writing number sentences for subtraction situations. • Creating stories for subtraction number sentences. • Identifying numbers represented on ten frames.
• Solving problems using math facts strategies. (G, I, J) • Extending repeating patterns. (A, E) • Solving addition and subtraction problems with missing parts. (G, I)			• Writing addition and subtraction number sentences. (I, J)	• Representing patterns using manipulatives, pictures, words, or symbols. (A, E) • Writing addition and subtraction number sentences. (I, J)

	Number and Operations	Algebra	Geometry	Measurement	Data Analysis and Probability
Unit 9: Grouping by Tens **Lessons**	• Grouping and counting objects by ones, twos, fives, and tens. • Describing a number in relation to other numbers. • Using a *100 Chart,* ten frames, manipulatives, words, and symbols to represent two-digit numbers. • Representing 100 as 10 tens. • Developing number sense for two-digit numbers. • Placing numbers into intervals. • Comparing and ordering two-digit numbers using more than, less than, about the same as, between, and close.	• Making and interpreting bar graphs. • Using number patterns to solve problems on the *100 Chart.*		• Measuring length using nonstandard units (links). • Using data to solve problems involving volume. • Exploring volume measurement (capacity). • Solving problems involving volume. • Exploring the inverse relationship between the size of the unit and the number of units needed to measure the volume of a container. • Checking the reasonableness of measurements by comparing data.	• Making and interpreting bar graphs. • Using data to solve problems involving volume.
Daily Practice and Problems	• Using the strategies of counting up and counting back to add and subtract. (A, G, H, I, L, N, P) • Solving problems involving addition and subtraction. (D, I, K) • Writing addition and subtraction number sentences. (D) • Dividing a collection of objects into groups of a given size and counting the leftovers. (E, F) • Estimating sums. (K) • Using a *100 Chart* to solve problems. (M, N, O, P, R, S, U) • Developing number sense for two-digit numbers. (N, O, Q, S, T, U) • Comparing and ordering two-digit numbers. (Q, S, T, U) • Skip counting by twos, fives, or tens. (R) • Placing numbers into intervals. (S) • Developing number relationships and place value. (U) • Finding the value of a collection of pennies, nickels, and dimes. (B) • Grouping and counting by tens and ones. (E, F, T) • Using a calculator to add and subtract. (K)	• Identifying patterns. (J, O, R) • Representing a pattern using letters. (J)	• Solving problems involving volume. (V) • Exploring the inverse relationship between the size of the unit and the number of units needed to measure the volume of a container. (V)	• Exploring time concepts (time of day, days, weeks, months). (C) • Measuring length using nonstandard units (links). (E, T) • Solving problems involving volume. (V) • Exploring the inverse relationship between the size of the unit and the number of units needed to measure the volume of a container. (V)	• Interpreting a data table. (I)

Problem Solving	Reasoning and Proof	Communication	Connections	Representation
• Solving problems involving volume. • Using number patterns to solve problems on the *100 Chart*. • Using data to solve problems involving volume.	• Exploring the relationship between the size of a unit and the number of units needed to measure an object.	• Communicating mathematics verbally and in writing. • Comparing and ordering two-digit numbers using more than, less than, about the same as, between, and close.	• Connecting mathematics and science to real-world situations: predicting the total number of letters in first names in the class. • Connecting mathematics to real-world situations: numbers in newspapers. • Using data to solve problems involving volume.	• Using a *100 Chart*, ten frames, manipulatives, words, and symbols to represent two-digit numbers. • Representing 100 as 10 tens. • Making and interpreting bar graphs.
• Solving word problems involving money. (B, F) • Solving word problems using math facts strategies. (C, D, H, I)	• Explaining mathematical reasoning. (K)	• Explaining math facts strategies. (A, G, L) • Explaining mathematical reasoning. (K) • Describing patterns. (O)		• Writing addition and subtraction number sentences. (D, H) • Representing a pattern using letters. (J)

	Number and Operations	Algebra	Geometry	Measurement	Data Analysis and Probability
Unit 10: Measurement: Area **Lessons**	• Introducing the symbol for one-half ($\frac{1}{2}$).		• Comparing the length and width of shapes. • Comparing the areas of shapes. • Estimating area by covering shapes with nonstandard units. • Measuring area by covering shapes with square inches and half-square inches. • Recognizing that different shapes can have the same area.	• Measuring length in inches. • Comparing the length and width of shapes. • Comparing the areas of shapes. • Estimating area by covering shapes with nonstandard units. • Measuring area by covering shapes with square inches and half-square inches. • Recognizing that different shapes can have the same area. • Reporting areas using numbers and units.	• Collecting and organizing data in a table.
Daily Practice and Problems	• Using pictures, counters, a *100 Chart,* or ten frames to represent numbers. (A, B, D, F) • Writing addition and subtraction number sentences. (A, G) • Using a *100 Chart* to solve problems. (B, F) • Grouping and counting objects by tens and ones. (B, F) • Developing number sense for two-digit numbers. (D, E) • Solving problems involving addition and subtraction. (G) • Using the strategies of counting all and counting on to add and subtract. (E, G) • Skip counting by tens. (I)	• Solving addition and subtraction problems with missing parts. (B, F)	• Comparing areas. (H) • Measuring area by covering shapes with square inches and half-square inches. (J)	• Measuring length in inches. (C) • Comparing the length and width of shapes. (H) • Comparing areas. (H) • Measuring area by covering shapes with square inches and half-square inches. (J)	

Problem Solving	Reasoning and Proof	Communication	Connections	Representation
	• Recognizing that different shapes can have the same area.	• Introducing the symbol for one-half ($\frac{1}{2}$). • Reporting areas using numbers and units.	• Connecting geometry and measurement.	• Introducing the symbol for one-half ($\frac{1}{2}$). • Collecting and organizing data in a table.
• Solving word problems using math facts strategies. (B, F, G, H) • Solving addition and subtraction problems with missing parts. (B, F)				• Translating between representations on ten frames and in fact situations and number sentences. (A, G)

	Number and Operations	Algebra	Geometry	Measurement	Data Analysis and Probability
Unit 11: Looking at 100 **Lessons**	• Using math facts strategies to add (direct modeling, counting strategies, or reasoning from known facts). • Using counting on to add. • Grouping and counting objects by fives and tens. • Using multiples of five and ten to solve addition and subtraction problems. • Developing number sense for 100. • Partitioning 100 into groups of ten. • Partitioning $1.00 into two and three parts. • Finding the value of a collection of nickels, dimes, and quarters. • Using a *100 Chart,* ten frames, manipulatives, words, and symbols to represent two-digit numbers. • Using a *100 Chart* to solve problems. • Writing addition and subtraction sentences using two-digit numbers.	• Making and interpreting bar graphs. • Using patterns in data to make predictions and solve problems. • Translating between graphs and real-world events. • Comparing sets of data in which one variable has changed. • Writing number sentences for addition and subtraction situations using two-digit numbers.		• Using seconds and minutes. • Using a calendar to measure the passage of time.	• Collecting, organizing, graphing, and analyzing data. • Making and interpreting bar graphs. • Using patterns in data to make predictions and solve problems. • Comparing sets of data in which one variable has changed.
Daily Practice and Problems	• Using math facts strategies to add (direct modeling, counting strategies, or reasoning from known facts). (E, G, H, J, K, L, M, N, O) • Practicing and assessing the addition facts in Group A.* (E, H, J, K, L, M, N) • Skip counting by fives or tens. (A) • Developing number sense for two-digit numbers. (B, D, F, U, V) • Solving problems involving addition and subtraction. (G, O, T) • Writing addition and subtraction number sentences. (F, G, M, U) • Using related addition facts to subtract. (H) • Dividing a collection of objects into groups of a given size and counting the leftovers. (P) • Using the strategies of counting all and counting on to add. (T) • Using a *100 Chart* to solve problems. (U) • Identifying odd or even numbers. (V) • Finding the value of a collection of pennies, nickels, and dimes. (C, K, M, Q, R) • Grouping and counting objects by tens and ones. (B, F, K)	• Identifying and describing number patterns. (E)	• Estimating area by covering shapes with nonstandard units. (I) • Measuring area by covering shapes with square inches and half-square inches. (I) • Using geometric concepts and skills to solve problems. (S)	• Estimating area by covering shapes with nonstandard units. (I) • Measuring area by covering shapes with square inches and half-square inches. (I) • Comparing areas. (S)	

*See the chart on page 11 in the Grade 1 Unit 11 *Unit Resource Guide* for a list of the facts in each group.

Problem Solving	Reasoning and Proof	Communication	Connections	Representation
• Using math facts strategies to add (direct modeling, counting strategies, or reasoning from known facts). • Using counting on to add. • Using multiples of five and ten to solve addition and subtraction problems. • Using a *100 Chart* to solve problems. • Using patterns in data to make predictions and solve problems.		• Communicating mathematics verbally and in writing. • Writing number sentences for addition and subtraction situations using two-digit numbers.	• Connecting mathematics and science to real-world situations: recording weather data. • Using a calendar to measure the passage of time.	• Using a *100 Chart*, ten frames, manipulatives, words, and symbols to represent two-digit numbers. • Translating between different representations of numbers (ten frames, *100 Charts*, manipulatives, and number sentences). • Translating between different representations of numbers (tallies and symbols). • Making and interpreting bar graphs. • Translating between graphs and real-world events. • Writing number sentences for addition and subtraction situations using two-digit numbers.
• Solving problems involving money. (C, K, M, Q, R) • Solving problems involving addition and subtraction. (G, O, T) • Using geometric concepts and skills to solve problems. (S)		• Explaining math facts strategies. (E, H, J, L, N) • Identifying and describing number patterns. (E)		• Using ten frames to represent numbers. (B) • Using a *100 Chart* to represent numbers. (U) • Using manipulatives to represent numbers. (F, G, K, M, O, P, Q, R) • Writing addition and subtraction number sentences. (F, G, M, U)

	Number and Operations	Algebra	Geometry	Measurement	Data Analysis and Probability
Unit 12: Cubes and Volume **Lessons**	• Grouping and counting objects.		• Measuring volume by counting cubic units. • Recognizing that different shapes can have the same volume. • Sorting and classifying shapes by volume, area of the base, and height. • Estimating volume by building cube models for objects. • Comparing volumes. • Developing visualization and spatial reasoning skills. • Using geometric models to solve problems. • Constructing a cube model from a drawing.	• Measuring volume by counting cubic units. • Recognizing that different shapes can have the same volume. • Estimating volume by building cube models for objects. • Comparing three-dimensional figures using volume and height. • Reporting volumes using numbers and units.	• Collecting and organizing data in a table.
Daily Practice and Problems	• Using math facts strategies to add (direct modeling, counting strategies, or reasoning from known facts). (C, D, E, F, H, J, K) • Practicing and assessing the addition facts in Group B.* (C, D, E, F, H, J) • Identifying odd or even numbers. (A) • Using a *100 Chart* to solve problems. (B) • Developing number sense for small numbers. (B) • Using related addition facts to subtract. (D) • Solving addition problems using multiples of 10. (E) • Using the strategies of making a ten and using a ten to add and subtract. (K) • Solving problems with missing parts. (K) • Dividing a collection of objects into groups of a given size and counting the leftovers. (G)	• Solving problems with missing parts. (K)	• Building cube models. (I)		• Interpreting bar graphs. (L)

*See the chart on page 11 in the Grade 1 Unit 11 *Unit Resource Guide* for a list of the facts in each group.

Problem Solving	Reasoning and Proof	Communication	Connections	Representation
• Using geometric models to solve problems.	• Recognizing that different shapes can have the same volume. • Developing spatial reasoning skills.	• Communicating mathematics verbally and in writing. • Reporting volumes using numbers and units.	• Connecting geometry and measurement. • Connecting mathematics to real-world situations: building models of classroom objects. • Connecting mathematics and language arts: reading a story about volume.	• Translating between different representations of shapes (three-dimensional drawings and cube models).
• Solving problems involving money. (E) • Solving problems involving volume. (I)	• Explaining mathematical reasoning using manipulatives. (A)	• Explaining math facts strategies. (C, D, F, H, J)		• Representing numbers using a *100 Chart.* (B) • Representing numbers using ten frames. (K)

	Number and Operations	Algebra	Geometry	Measurement	Data Analysis and Probability
Unit 13: Thinking About Addition and Subtraction **Lessons**	• Partitioning ten into two and three parts. • Solving addition and subtraction problems. • Representing doubles and halves using manipulatives, diagrams, and number sentences. • Using doubles to solve addition problems. • Making a ten to solve addition problems. • Using math facts strategies to add (direct modeling, counting strategies, or reasoning from known facts). • Representing odd and even numbers using manipulatives. • Identifying odd and even numbers.				
Daily Practice and Problems	• Using math facts strategies to add (direct modeling, counting strategies, or reasoning from known facts). (A, E, G, I, J, K, L, M, N, O, P) • Practicing and assessing the addition facts in Group C.* (A, E, I, J, K, L, N, P) • Developing number sense using part-part-whole relationships. (A, E, G, K) • Skip counting by twos, threes, fives, or tens. (B, D, F, H) • Writing addition and subtraction number sentences. (G, K) • Making a ten to solve addition problems. (G) • Representing doubles and halves using manipulatives, diagrams, or number sentences. (J) • Using the strategies of counting up and counting back to subtract. (K) • Using the strategies of counting all and counting on to add. (M, N) • Identifying odd or even numbers. (N) • Solving problems involving addition. (M)	• Exploring patterns in the *100 Chart*. (B, D, F, H) • Using number patterns to solve problems. (L, N) • Using part-part-whole representations. (A, E, G, K)	• Measuring volume by counting cubic units. (C) • Comparing three-dimensional figures using volume and height. (C)	• Measuring volume by counting cubic units. (C) • Comparing three-dimensional figures using volume and height. (C)	

*See the chart on page 11 in the Grade 1 Unit 11 *Unit Resource Guide* for a list of the facts in each group.

Problem Solving	Reasoning and Proof	Communication	Connections	Representation
• Solving addition and subtraction problems and communicating solution strategies. • Using doubles to solve addition problems. • Making a ten to solve addition problems. • Exploring different types of addition and subtraction problems.	• Solving addition and subtraction problems and explaining the reasoning.	• Communicating mathematics verbally and in writing. • Solving addition and subtraction problems and communicating solution strategies.	• Connecting mathematics to real-world situations: finding objects that come in pairs.	• Representing doubles and halves using manipulatives, diagrams, and number sentences. • Representing odd and even numbers using manipulatives.
• Problem solving using tens. (G) • Problem solving using addition. (M)	• Reasoning about even and odd numbers. (N) • Explaining math facts strategies. (I, P)	• Explaining math facts strategies. (I, P)		• Using part-part-whole representations. (A, E, G, K) • Representing halves and doubles using manipulatives. (J)

	Number and Operations	Algebra	Geometry	Measurement	Data Analysis and Probability
Unit 14: Exploring Multiplication and Division **Lessons**	• Representing multiplication and division situations using manipulatives and drawings. • Grouping and counting objects by twos, threes, and fives. • Creating stories for multiplication and division situations. • Solving multiplication and division problems.	• Making and interpreting bar graphs.			• Collecting, organizing, graphing, and analyzing data. • Making and interpreting bar graphs. • Using data to solve problems.
Daily Practice and Problems	• Using math facts strategies to add and subtract (direct modeling, counting strategies, or reasoning from known facts). (A, D, F, G, H, I, J) • Practicing and assessing the addition facts in Group D.* (A, D, F, G, H, J) • Solving multiplication and division problems. (B) • Developing number sense for two-digit numbers. (E) • Comparing two-digit numbers using more or less. (E) • Exploring fact families. (G)	• Solving addition and subtraction problems with missing parts. (F, H)			

*See the chart on page 11 in the Grade 1 Unit 11 *Unit Resource Guide* for a list of the facts in each group.

Problem Solving	Reasoning and Proof	Communication	Connections	Representation
• Creating stories for multiplication and division situations. • Solving multiplication and division problems and communicating solution strategies. • Using data to solve problems. • Communicating solution strategies verbally and in writing.	• Solving multiplication and division problems and explaining the reasoning.	• Communicating solution strategies verbally and in writing. • Creating stories for multiplication and division situations.	• Connecting mathematics and science to real-world situations: conducting a pet survey. • Using data to solve problems.	• Representing multiplication and division situations using manipulatives and drawings. • Making and interpreting bar graphs.
• Solving problems involving money. (C, F, I) • Solving multiplication and division problems. (B)		• Explaining math facts strategies. (A, D, G, H, J)		

	Number and Operations	Algebra	Geometry	Measurement	Data Analysis and Probability
Unit 15: Exploring 3-D Shapes **Lessons**			• Investigating properties of 3-dimensional shapes. • Identifying 3-dimensional shapes (cylinders, spheres, cubes, and prisms). • Describing 3-dimensional shapes using their properties. • Classifying 3-dimensional shapes using their properties. • Using geometric concepts and skills to solve problems.		
Daily Practice and Problems	• Using math facts strategies to add and subtract (direct modeling, counting strategies, or reasoning from known facts). (A, B, C, D, E, F, G, H, I, J) • Practicing and assessing the addition facts in Group E.* (C, E, F, H, I, J) • Exploring fact families. (I) • Using doubles and halves to solve problems. (E) • Developing number sense for two-digit numbers. (G) • Solving problems involving addition and subtraction. (B, D, F)				

*See the chart on page 11 in the Grade 1 Unit 11 *Unit Resource Guide* for a list of the facts in each group.

Problem Solving	Reasoning and Proof	Communication	Connections	Representation
• Using geometric concepts and skills to solve problems.	• Explaining the reasoning for classifying 3-dimensional shapes.	• Describing 3-dimensional shapes using their properties. • Explaining the reasoning for classifying 3-dimensional shapes.	• Connecting mathematics to real-world situations: identifying 3-dimensional shapes.	
• Solving problems involving money. (A) • Solving word problems involving addition and subtraction. (B, D, F)	• Explaining math facts strategies. (J)	• Explaining math facts strategies. (J)		

	Number and Operations	Algebra	Geometry	Measurement	Data Analysis and Probability
Unit 16: Collecting and Organizing Data **Lessons**	• Using tallies and symbols to represent numbers.	• Translating between graphs and real-world events. • Making and interpreting bar graphs.			• Using a survey to collect data. • Classifying items into categories. • Collecting, organizing, graphing, and analyzing data. • Making and interpreting bar graphs. • Using data to solve problems about daily food choices. • Translating between graphs and real-world events. • Using data to solve problems.
Daily Practice and Problems	• Using math facts strategies to add (direct modeling, counting strategies, or reasoning from known facts). (B, C, D, E, F, G, I) • Practicing and assessing the addition facts in Group F.* (C, E, G, I) • Grouping and counting objects by twos, fives, and tens. (A, H, J) • Exploring fact families. (E) • Dividing a collection of objects into groups of a given size and counting the leftovers. (A, H, J) • Using *100 Charts,* manipulatives, and number sentences to add and subtract. (B, D)				

*See the chart on page 11 in the Grade 1 Unit 11 *Unit Resource Guide* for a list of the facts in each group.

Problem Solving	Reasoning and Proof	Communication	Connections	Representation
• Using data to solve problems.	• Classifying items into categories.		• Connecting mathematics and science: conducting a nutrition survey. • Translating between graphs and real-world events. • Using data to solve problems.	• Using tallies and symbols to represent numbers. • Translating between graphs and real-world events. • Collecting, organizing, graphing, and analyzing data. • Making and interpreting bar graphs.
• Solving word problems involving addition and subtraction. (B, D, F)	• Explaining math facts strategies. (I)	• Explaining math facts strategies. (I) • Creating a story describing a mathematical situation. (F)		• Representing addition and subtraction with *100 Charts*, manipulatives, and number sentences. (B, D)

	Number and Operations	Algebra	Geometry	Measurement	Data Analysis and Probability
Unit 17: Moving Beyond 100 **Lessons**	• Representing numbers greater than 100 using manipulatives, pictures, symbols, and words. • Grouping and counting objects by hundreds, tens, and ones. • Solving addition problems using multiples of 10 and 100. • Using addition strategies with larger numbers.				
Daily Practice and Problems	• Using math facts strategies to add (direct modeling, counting strategies, and reasoning from known facts). (A, B, C, D, E, F, G, H, J) • Practicing and assessing the addition facts in Group G.* (A, C, D, F, H, J) • Solving problems involving addition and subtraction. (A, E, F) • Solving addition or subtraction problems using multiples of 10 and 100. (B, D) • Solving problems involving multiplication or division. (E, I) • Using the strategy of counting on to add. (G)				• Using data to solve problems. (F)

*See the chart on page 11 in the Grade 1 Unit 11 *Unit Resource Guide* for a list of the facts in each group.

Problem Solving	Reasoning and Proof	Communication	Connections	Representation
• Solving addition problems using multiples of 10 and 100.		• Representing numbers greater than 100 using manipulatives, drawings, symbols, and words.		• Representing numbers greater than 100 using manipulatives, drawings, symbols, and words.
• Solving problems involving addition and subtraction. (A, E, F) • Solving problems involving multiplication and division. (E, I) • Using data to solve problems. (F)		• Explaining math facts strategies. (B, C, G, H, J)		• Representing numbers with ten frames. (C) • Representing numbers with counters. (A, E, F, I)

	Number and Operations	Algebra	Geometry	Measurement	Data Analysis and Probability
Unit 18: Pieces, Parts, and Symmetry **Lessons**	• Exploring the part-whole relationship of fractions. • Representing fractions ($\frac{1}{2}$ and $\frac{1}{4}$) using manipulatives, drawings, symbols, and words. • Recognizing that fractional parts of the whole (halves and fourths) must have equal area. • Partitioning shapes into halves and fourths. • Partitioning sets of objects into halves, fourths, and other fractions.		• Identifying lines of symmetry.		
Daily Practice and Problems	• Using math facts strategies to add and subtract (direct modeling, counting strategies, or reasoning from known facts). (A, B, C, D, E, F, G, H, I) • Practicing the addition or related subtraction facts in Groups A, B, and C.* (A, B, C, D, E, G, H, I) • Solving addition or subtraction problems using multiples of 10 and 100. (B, H, K, L) • Using patterns to solve related addition problems. (F) • Solving problems involving addition and subtraction. (A, D, G, I) • Using doubles to solve addition problems. (F) • Counting objects by tens and ones. (K, L)	• Solving addition and subtraction problems with missing parts. (A, C, D)	• Identifying 3-dimensional shapes (cylinders, spheres, cubes, and prisms). (J)	• Exploring time concepts (days, weeks, months). (D)	• Interpreting a data table to solve problems. (G, I)

*See the chart on page 11 in the Grade 1 Unit 11 *Unit Resource Guide* for a list of the facts in each group.

Problem Solving	Reasoning and Proof	Communication	Connections	Representation
• Solving fraction puzzles.	• Solving fraction puzzles.	• Representing fractions ($\frac{1}{2}$ and $\frac{1}{4}$) using manipulatives, drawings, symbols, and words.		• Representing fractions ($\frac{1}{2}$ and $\frac{1}{4}$) using manipulatives, drawings, symbols, and words.
• Solving problems involving money. (E) • Solving addition and subtraction problems using math facts strategies. (A, D, G, I)			• Connecting mathematics with science. (G)	• Using part-part-whole representation. (A, D)

	Number and Operations	Algebra	Geometry	Measurement	Data Analysis and Probability
Unit 19: Measurement and Mapping **Lessons**	• Calculating the distance between two points on a map.		• Describing the location of an object using direction (left or right) and distance. • Locating an object on a map using direction (left or right) and distance. • Calculating the distance between two points on a map.	• Measuring length using nonstandard units (links).	• Recording information in a table.
Daily Practice and Problems	• Using math facts strategies to add (direct modeling, counting strategies, and reasoning from known facts). (A, B, C, D, E, H) • Practicing the addition or related subtraction facts in Groups D and E.* (A, B, C, D, E, H) • Solving addition or subtraction problems using multiples of 10 and 100. (B, D, F) • Representing doubles and halves using manipulatives. (G) • Solving problems involving addition and subtraction. (E, H) • Counting objects by tens and ones. (F)	• Using number patterns to solve problems. (B, C, D) • Solving problems with missing parts. (A)			• Using data to solve problems. (H)

*See the chart on page 11 in the Grade 1 Unit 11 *Unit Resource Guide* for a list of the facts in each group.

Problem Solving	Reasoning and Proof	Communication	Connections	Representation
		• Describing the location of an object using direction (left or right) and distance.	• Translating between a map and the real-world situation it represents.	• Describing the location of an object using direction (left or right) and distance. • Representing the location of an object using a map.
• Solving problems involving addition and subtraction. (E, H) • Using data to solve problems. (H) • Using patterns to solve problems. (B, C, D)				• Representing numbers with ten frames. (A, C) • Representing numbers with pictures. (F) • Representing doubles and halves using manipulatives. (G)

	Number and Operations	Algebra	Geometry	Measurement	Data Analysis and Probability
Unit 20: Looking Back at First Grade **Lessons**	• Representing numbers using drawings, manipulatives, and symbols. • Solving addition and subtraction problems. • Solving multiplication and division problems. • Using math facts strategies to add (direct modeling, counting strategies, and reasoning from known facts).	• Identifying and extending patterns.			• Using data to solve problems.
Daily Practice and Problems	• Using math facts strategies to add and subtract (direct modeling, counting strategies, and reasoning from known facts). (B, C, D, F, G, H) • Practicing the addition or related subtraction facts in Groups F and G.* (B, D, F, H) • Identifying odd or even numbers. (C) • Skip counting by fives or tens. (E) • Representing doubles and halves using manipulatives, diagrams, or number sentences. (G) • Comparing and ordering numbers. (I)	• Solving addition and subtraction problems with missing parts. (B, D, F, H)	• Identifying and describing 2-dimensional shapes using their properties (number of sides, length of sides, number of corners). (A) • Comparing areas. (I)	• Exploring time concepts (time of day, days, weeks, months). (J) • Comparing areas. (I)	• Interpreting a data table to solve problems. (C, I)

*See the chart on page 11 in the Grade 1 Unit 11 *Unit Resource Guide* for a list of the facts in each group.

Problem Solving	Reasoning and Proof	Communication	Connections	Representation
• Solving addition and subtraction problems and communicating solution strategies. • Solving multiplication and division problems and communicating solution strategies. • Using data to solve problems.	• Solving addition and subtraction problems and explaining the reasoning. • Solving multiplication and division problems and explaining the reasoning.	• Representing numbers using drawings, manipulatives, and symbols. • Solving addition and subtraction problems and communicating solution strategies. • Solving multiplication and division problems and communicating solution strategies.	• Using data to solve problems.	• Representing numbers using drawings, manipulatives, and symbols.
• Solving problems involving money. (G) • Solving problems using math facts strategies. (C, F, G, H) • Solving multistep problems. (F)				• Representing doubles and halves with ten frames and manipulatives. (G)

6

Math Facts and Whole-Number Operations

The Math Facts and Whole-Number Operations section outlines the *Math Trailblazers* approach to developing fluency with the math facts and whole-number operations.

Calculators are used as a tool for solving problems.

Math Facts and Whole-Number Operations

Work with whole numbers pervades the elementary mathematics curriculum. A major goal of *Math Trailblazers* is to prepare students to compute accurately, flexibly, and appropriately in all situations. Standard topics in arithmetic—acquisition of basic math facts and fluency with whole-number operations—are covered extensively.

In this section, we briefly describe our approach to developing fluency with the math facts and whole-number operations. Table 1 outlines the development of these two topics in Grades K–5. We also summarize below the fundamental characteristics of our work with whole numbers. More detailed information can be obtained from the following sources:

- Two TIMS Tutors in Section 9 of the *Teacher Implementation Guide: Arithmetic* and *Math Facts;* and
- Background sections and lesson guides from individual *Math Trailblazers* units.

Introduction to the Math Facts in *Math Trailblazers*

In developing our program for the math facts, we sought a careful balance between strategies and drill. This approach is based on a large body of research and is advocated by the NCTM *Principles and Standards for School Mathematics.* The research indicates that the methods used in the *Math Trailblazers* math facts program lead to more effective learning and better retention of the math facts and also helps develop essential math skills.

The *Math Trailblazers* program for teaching the math facts is characterized by these elements:

- *Early emphasis on problem solving.* Students first approach the basic facts as problems to be solved rather than as facts to be memorized. Students invent their own strategies to solve these problems or learn appropriate strategies from others through class discussion. Students' natural strategies, especially counting strategies, are explicitly encouraged. In this way, students learn that math is more than memorizing facts and rules that "you either get or you don't."
- *De-emphasis of rote work.* Fluency with the math facts is an important component of any student's mathematical learning. Research has shown that an overemphasis on memorization and the frequent administration of timed tests are counterproductive. We encourage the use of strategies to find facts, so students become confident they can find answers to fact problems that they do not immediately recall.
- *Gradual and systematic introduction of facts.* Students study the facts in small groups that can be solved using similar strategies. Students first work on simple strategies for easy facts and then progress to more sophisticated strategies and harder facts. By the end of the process, they gain fluency with all the required facts.

- *Ongoing practice.* Work on the math facts is distributed throughout the curriculum, especially in the Daily Practice and Problems (Grades 1–5), Home Practice (Grades 3–5), and games. This practice for fluency, however, takes place only after students have a conceptual understanding of the operations and have achieved proficiency with strategies for solving basic fact problems. Delaying practice in this way means that less practice is required to achieve fluency.

- *Appropriate assessment.* Teachers assess students' knowledge of the facts through observations as they work on activities, labs, and games as well as through the appropriate use of written tests and quizzes. Beginning in first grade, periodic, short quizzes in the Daily Practice and Problems naturally follow the study of small groups of facts organized around specific strategies. As self-assessment in Grades 3–5, each student records his or her progress on *Facts I Know* charts and determines which facts he or she needs to study. Inventory tests of all facts for each operation are used sparingly in Grades 2–5 (no more than twice per year) to assess students' progress with fact fluency. The goal of the math facts assessment program is to determine the degree to which students can find answers to fact problems quickly and accurately and whether they can retain this skill over time.

- *Multiyear approach.* In Grades 1 and 2, *Math Trailblazers* emphasizes strategies that lead to fluency with the addition and subtraction facts. In Grade 3, students gain fluency with the multiplication facts while reviewing the addition and subtraction facts. In Grade 4, students achieve fluency with the division facts and verify fluency with the multiplication facts. In Grade 5, the multiplication and division facts are systematically reviewed and assessed. This is outlined in Table 1.

- *Facts are not gatekeepers.* Students are not prevented from learning more complex mathematics because they do not perform well on fact tests. Use of strategies, calculators, and other math tools (e.g., manipulatives, hundreds charts, printed multiplication tables) allows students to continue to work on interesting problems and important mathematical concepts while they are still learning the facts.

Whole-Number Operations in *Math Trailblazers*

Math Trailblazers helps students develop efficient and accurate methods for computation with the four basic operations. The treatment of whole-number computation proceeds in several stages. The grade levels for the stages vary with the operation—full development of division, for example, comes long after addition—but the general pattern is similar for all the operations. Roughly speaking, the stages are:

- developing meaning for the operation,
- inventing procedures for solving problems, and
- becoming more efficient at carrying out procedures, all leading to
- developing mathematical power.

Developing mathematical power with an operation means that students understand *when* to apply the operation and *how* to use varied computational methods to solve problems, even complex or nonroutine problems.

With each of the operations, we seek a balance between conceptual understanding and procedural skill. Standard methods for solving problems are not introduced until students have developed good conceptual and procedural understandings. Research has shown that the too-early introduction of such procedures may short-circuit students' common sense, encouraging mechanical and uncritical behavior. As a result, formal instruction in some standard procedures is delayed slightly beyond the traditional time, but problems that would normally be solved by standard procedures are often introduced sooner than is customary. This forces students to use their prior knowledge to devise their own methods to solve the problems.

Students practice using the operations in activities, games, and laboratory investigations. More practice is provided in the Daily Practice and Problems in Grades 1–5 and in the Home Practice in Grades 3–5. Even after standard methods have been analyzed and practiced, students are still encouraged to solve problems in more than one way. Flexible thinking and mathematical power are our goals, not rote fluency with a handful of standard algorithms.

The *Math Trailblazers* approach to all mathematics topics promotes the coordinated development of both procedural skill and conceptual understanding. This is particularly apparent in our approach to computation.

The following table describes the development of math facts and whole-number operations in *Math Trailblazers*. The shaded portions of the table highlight development of the math facts program in each grade. Expectations for fluency with math facts are indicated in bold. The white portions of the table highlight development of the whole-number operations.

Grade	Addition	Subtraction	Multiplication	Division
K	Introduce concepts through problem solving and use of manipulatives.			
1	Develop strategies for addition facts. Solve addition problems in context.	Develop strategies for subtraction facts. Solve subtraction problems in context.	Develop concepts through problem solving and use of manipulatives.	
2	Continue use of addition facts in problems. Continue use of strategies for addition facts. **Assess for fluency with addition facts.** Continue solving addition problems in context. Introduce procedures for multidigit addition using manipulatives and paper and pencil.	Continue use of subtraction facts in problems. Continue use of strategies for subtraction facts. **Assess for fluency with subtraction facts.** Continue solving subtraction problems in context. Introduce procedures for multidigit subtraction using manipulatives and paper and pencil.	Continue concept development through problem solving and use of manipulatives.	
3	Diagnose and remediate with addition facts as needed. Develop procedures for multidigit addition using manipulatives and paper and pencil. Practice and apply multidigit addition in varied contexts.	Maintain fluency with subtraction facts through review and assessment. Develop procedures for multidigit subtraction using manipulatives and paper and pencil. Practice and apply multidigit subtraction in varied contexts.	Continue use of multiplication facts in problems. Develop strategies for multiplication facts. **Assess for fluency with multiplication facts.** Solve multiplication problems in context. Introduce paper-and-pencil multiplication (1-digit × 2-digits).	Continue use of division facts in problems. Develop strategies for division facts. Continue concept development. Solve division problems in context.
4	Diagnose and remediate with addition facts as needed. Practice and apply multidigit addition in varied contexts. Review paper-and-pencil procedures for multidigit addition.	Diagnose and remediate with subtraction facts as needed. Practice and apply multidigit subtraction in varied contexts. Review paper-and-pencil procedures for multidigit subtraction.	Maintain fluency with multiplication facts through review and assessment. Develop procedures for multiplication using manipulatives and paper and pencil (1-digit and 2-digit multipliers). Practice and apply multiplication in varied contexts.	Continue use of division facts in problems. Continue development of strategies for division facts. **Assess for fluency with division facts.** Solve division problems in context. Develop procedures for division using manipulatives and paper and pencil (1-digit divisors).
5	Diagnose and remediate with addition facts as needed. Practice and apply multidigit addition in varied contexts.	Diagnose and remediate with subtraction facts as needed. Practice and apply multidigit subtraction in varied contexts.	Maintain fluency with multiplication facts through review and assessment. Review paper-and-pencil procedures. Practice and apply multiplication in varied contexts.	Maintain fluency with division facts through review and assessment. Develop paper-and-pencil procedures (1-digit and 2-digit divisors). Practice and apply division in varied contexts.

Table 1: *Math Facts and Whole-Number Operations Overview*

Daily Practice and Problems Guide

The Daily Practice and Problems Guide explains the purpose
and use of the Daily Practice and Problems (DPP) within
the curriculum.

Students work cooperatively to solve a problem from the Daily Practice and Problems.

Daily Practice and Problems Guide

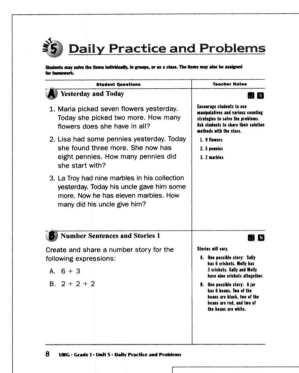

Figure 1: *Two pages from the DPP for Grade 1, Unit 5.*

Daily Practice and Problems

The Daily Practice and Problems (DPP) is a set of short exercises that provides ongoing review, practice, and study of math concepts and skills. These exercises are found in each unit in the *Unit Resource Guide* immediately preceding the lesson guides and on the *Teacher Resource CD.* The DPP should become a routine part of daily instruction since the problems serve several important functions in the curriculum:

- They develop concepts and skills such as number sense, telling time, and working with money throughout the year;
- They review topics from earlier units, presenting concepts in new contexts and linking ideas from unit to unit; and
- They provide a structure for systematic study of the basic math facts and practice in computation.

Two DPP items are included for each class session listed on the Unit Outline. Each item is composed of Student Questions and Teacher Notes as shown in Figure 1. The Teacher Notes often discuss possible problem-solving strategies or suggest which tools should be available to students, such as connecting cubes, calculators, or rulers. Eight icons designate the subject matter of the problems. See Figure 2.

The Scope and Sequence chart in Section 5 of the *Teacher Implementation Guide* lists the topics covered in the DPP in each unit. This chart correlates the items in the DPP to the National Council of Teachers of Mathematics *Principles and Standards for School Mathematics.* Teachers can use this chart to track the development of a particular standard throughout first grade and locate items on particular topics to use for review, extra practice, or enrichment. For example, by looking at the Number and Operations column, teachers can follow the sequence of items providing computation and facts practice. By looking at the Measurement column in the same way, teachers can find all the items that deal with telling time. For a specific description of the study and assessment of the math facts, see the TIMS Tutor: *Math Facts.*

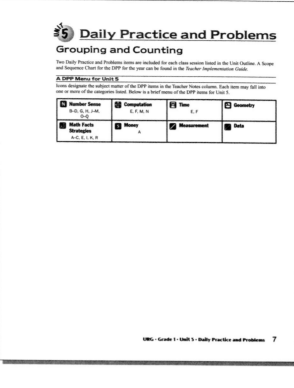

Figure 2: *DPP icons and DPP menu in the Daily Practice and Problems Guide.*

Eight icons designate the subject matter of each item:

N **Number Sense** (estimating, partitioning numbers, skip counting, etc.);

Math Facts Strategies (developing strategies for the addition and subtraction facts);

Computation (problems that may be solved using paper-and-pencil methods, estimation, mental math, or calculators);

$ **Money** (counting change, combining various coins, or estimating total cost);

Time (exploring time concepts including time of day, days, weeks, months, and using the calendar);

Measurement (measuring length, area, or volume);

Geometry (work with shapes, coordinates, or other geometric topics); and

Data (collecting, organizing, graphing, or analyzing data).

How to Use the Daily Practice and Problems

The Suggestions for Teaching the Lesson section and the At a Glance in most lessons provide suggestions on how and when to use each DPP item. These are only suggestions. The following provides further description on how to incorporate the DPP into your math instruction.

Assign one or two DPP items each day to present students with the review and practice they need. Most of the items are designed to be short, quick questions that need little instruction from the teacher. Students should be able to complete them independently. For many problems, it will be appropriate for students to work in pairs or groups. Some items, such as those that require the use of a manipulative, may take longer than five or ten minutes to complete. Some may extend a topic or provide extra practice. Others can be used as enrichment for those students who need less skill practice and are ready for more complex problems.

Teachers use the Daily Practice and Problems in many ways. Many problems can easily be written on the blackboard or displayed using an overhead projector. Items can also be photocopied or printed (without the teacher portion) from the *Teacher Resource CD* and distributed to students daily, or several items can be stapled together in a packet and distributed weekly. For many items (such as facts practice or mental arithmetic), it is appropriate for students to just write answers on scrap paper. For others (such as skip counting), students can respond orally. One way to establish routines is to have students use their math journals for any written responses. This will also preserve a record of their work. Teacher notes sometimes recommend conducting a discussion of students' problem-solving strategies. These discussions are an important part of the problem-solving process, but they need not be extensive since topics are revisited many times.

Students will use tools and manipulatives to solve problems in the DPP items. Teachers have found it helpful to create DPP kits and make them readily available to students. These kits contain beans or other counters, coins, blank ten frames, *100 Charts,* pattern blocks, calculators, and rulers. Ten frames and *100 Charts* are available in the Generic Section of the *Unit Resource Guide* File.

When to Use the Daily Practice and Problems

At the Beginning of Math Class. The DPP items can be used to begin class and focus students' attention on mathematics. Students immediately answer the questions and then the class can discuss the answers before they begin work on the current lesson. Alternatively, the teacher can assign the items at the beginning of a lesson and students can solve the problems as they have time during class. This is an especially effective method if students are collecting data for an experiment and have to take turns using equipment.

During Daily Routines. DPP items can be used as part of morning (or afternoon) routines that also include taking the roll, calendar work, language arts practice, or geography questions. A "Problem of the Day" can also be part of the daily routine in which the teacher presents students with an item which they can work on throughout the day or take home to complete for homework or as extra credit. For some items, it may be appropriate to ask students to describe their problem-solving process.

During Transition Times. Many items, especially practice with the math facts, can be used during transition times throughout the day. Possible times include when students have completed an assignment, when money or permission slips are being collected, when an activity is delayed, or when an activity ends earlier than expected.

As Homework or Assessment. Problems can also be assigned for homework or used for short assessments.

Assessment

The Assessment section details the philosophy, goals, and components of assessment in the curriculum.

A teacher and her students assess their work on a problem.

Assessment

PART I | Philosophy of the Assessment Program in *Math Trailblazers*

Assessment in *Math Trailblazers* is ongoing and reflects the program's content and goals. Throughout the program, assessment serves several purposes:

- It helps teachers learn about students' thinking and knowledge. This information is then used to guide instruction.
- It communicates the goals of instruction to students, parents, and others.
- It informs students, parents, and others about progress toward these goals.

The assessment program is built around two main principles: assessment should reflect the breadth and balance of the curriculum; and assessment activities should be valuable educational experiences.

Alignment with Goals

The National Council of Teachers of Mathematics (NCTM) *Principles and Standards for School Mathematics* describes the understanding, concepts, and skills students need to acquire. These principles and standards call for a mathematically rich curriculum for all students. The curriculum must teach a broad range of content and develop mathematical processes including problem solving, reasoning, and communication.

Math Trailblazers is designed to meet recommendations in the *Principles and Standards.* As such, the program requires significant shifts in emphases relative to a traditional program—changes in content, learning, teaching, evaluation, and expectations. The implications with regard to student assessment are also significant. We can no longer focus narrowly on the assessment of only isolated skills and procedures, using single sources of information at the end of a learning cycle. Instead, assessment needs to shift toward collecting information over the course of the year from a variety of sources, covering a wide range of mathematical content, and incorporating the rich problem-solving situations that are characteristic of the curriculum. The NCTM's *Principles and Standards for School Mathematics* describes this as follows:

> *Many assessment techniques can be used by mathematics teachers, including open-ended questions, constructed-response tasks, selected-response items, performance tasks, observations, conversations, journals, and portfolios.* (NCTM, 2000, p. 23)

Integral with Instruction

Assessment is an integral part of instruction. All assessment activities are valuable educational experiences that have their own merit. By making assessment both integral to instruction and reflective of the overall mathematical content of the curriculum, we communicate what we value in mathematics. Again, the NCTM *Principles and Standards* addresses this idea:

> *To ensure deep, high-quality learning for all students, assessment and instruction must be integrated so that assessment becomes a routine part of ongoing classroom activity rather than an interruption.* (NCTM, 2000, p. 23)

Our assessment program gives teachers frequent opportunities to assess student progress. Concepts and skills are assessed in many different ways but especially as they are used within the context of solving problems. Assessments are designed to elicit more than just an answer. In solving problems, students show their thinking and give a picture of their understanding of mathematical concepts, strategies, tools, and procedures.

Integrating assessment with instruction has significant implications for the structure of the assessment program. There is no separate assessment book; assessment activities and other components of the assessment program are fully integrated into units. Furthermore, because much of the curriculum's content is revisited many times in varying contexts, students are assessed many times on many concepts. This flavors both instruction and assessment. Teachers can focus on student progress since they know that there will be other opportunities to review and assess and thus do not expect mastery at every juncture. At the same time, students' mathematical progress is not put on hold until they pass any particular assessment.

Balanced Assessment

The assessment program reflects the curriculum's instruction in another important way: it is varied and balanced. The *Math Trailblazers* curriculum is balanced across several dimensions:

- **Math Content.** The program incorporates a broad range of mathematical content and procedures, and connections between different topics abound.
- **Communication.** Students are expected to communicate their mathematical work and represent mathematical ideas in many different ways, such as written and oral explanations, number sentences, tables, graphs, pictures, and models.

- **Student Groupings.** Students work individually, in pairs, and in small groups.
- **Length of Activities.** There are short activities (5–15 minutes), tasks that take a full class period, and longer investigations that take several days.
- **Amount of Teacher Direction.** Some activities involve substantial teacher direction; others are more student-directed.
- **Varied Contexts.** Mathematics is presented in a variety of contexts, such as laboratory experiments, real-life settings, word problems, and numerical problems.

Our assessment program is balanced in similar ways. A balanced assessment program gives each student an opportunity to demonstrate what he or she knows by allowing multiple approaches, covering a wide range of content, allowing access to tools when appropriate, varying the difficulty and pedagogy, and assessing within different kinds of contexts.

Using multiple sources of evidence improves the validity of judgments made about students' learning. With more than one source of information about students' progress, strengths in one source can compensate for weaknesses in others. It also helps teachers judge the consistency of students' mathematical work. (NCTM, 2000, p. 24)

Promoting Student Reflection

Assessment activities in *Math Trailblazers* do more than provide momentary snapshots of a student's progress. Students are often asked to revise work based upon commonly understood criteria for excellence. In Grades K–2, these criteria are communicated largely by the teachers. Beginning in Grade 3, the Student Rubrics provide an additional source of information to students about what is expected of them. As students become more involved in the assessment process, they become more reflective and can make constructive, critical judgments about their work and the work of others.

Components in Grades 1-5

Watching students grow intellectually throughout the course of the school year is one of the great satisfactions of teaching. The components of the assessment program provide teachers with the tools necessary to document students' progress over time as they acquire skills and concepts, develop their abilities to solve problems, and learn to communicate their thinking. While most components are included at all grade levels, the assessment program does vary from grade to grade based on the needs of the students.

All the materials provided to assess student learning are located in the units, either in the student materials or the *Unit Resource Guide.* Each unit contains assessment ideas and activities appropriate for the content and goals of the unit. Many components are also available in electronic form on the *Teacher Resource CD.* This section describes the following components:

Observational Assessment	***Written Assessments***
Assessment Indicators	Assessment Pages
Observational Assessment Record	Math Journals
Individual Assessment Record Sheet	Assessment in the
	Suggestions for Teaching
	the Lesson
	Assessment Lessons
	Assessment Labs
	Open-Response Problems
	Tests
	Assessment Units
	Portfolios
	Facts Assessment

Observational Assessment

Teachers have always assessed student learning through informal classroom observations, thus integrating instruction and assessment. The NCTM *Principles and Standards* confirms the importance of these observations.

Observations and conversations in the classroom can provide insights into students' thinking, and teachers can monitor changes in students' thinking and reasoning over time with reflective journals and portfolios. (NCTM, 2000, p. 24)

Teachers use the information gathered from classroom observations to guide instruction. While watching, questioning, and listening to students, they make moment-to-moment instructional decisions that change the direction and emphasis of the lesson. Teacher evaluation of student responses during a lesson will also affect the content of succeeding lessons.

Classroom observations can also be used to evaluate student achievement and monitor student progress. Skills such as using a graduated cylinder to measure volume, habits such as estimating regularly to check results, and behaviors such as working effectively within a group can best be assessed through observing students at work. Assessing students through observation is especially important in the primary grades, because students at this age can often communicate their thinking very well in a discussion, but sometimes cannot fully express the same ideas on paper. Also, what we assess becomes what we value. If we only assess written work, other important behaviors such as verbal communication will be neglected. Finding a manageable way to organize and record these observations is critical to an effective assessment program.

Two tools are included in each unit to help teachers organize and document informal assessments: Assessment Indicators and the *Observational Assessment Record*.

Assessment Indicators

The Background for each unit in Grades 1–5 lists several Assessment Indicators that orient teachers to important skills, behavior, and knowledge they should assess in the unit. See Figure 1.

Assessment Indicators

- Can students group and count objects by twos, fives, and tens?
- Can students divide a collection of objects into groups of a given size and count the leftovers?
- Can students collect, organize, graph, and analyze data?
- Can students identify the relationships among pennies, nickels, and dimes?

Figure 1: *Assessment Indicators from Grade 1 Unit 5*

Observational Assessment Record

An *Observational Assessment Record* similar to the one shown for Grade 1 Unit 5 in Figure 2 follows the Background in each unit. The Assessment Indicators for that unit are listed at the top of each sheet. Each indicator is identified with an icon. An additional line is provided for teachers to include their own ideas. Each sheet has 32 rows for student names with columns for recording observations and extra space for comments. It is not necessary to record an observation about each child in each column. The grid provides a snapshot of the class's understanding of the main concepts, procedures, and skills covered in the unit.

OBSERVATIONAL ASSESSMENT RECORD

(A1) Can students group and count objects by twos, fives, and tens?
(A2) Can students divide a collection of objects into groups of a given size and count the leftovers?
(A3) Can students collect and organize data in a table?
(A4) Can students identify the relationships among pennies, nickels, and dimes?
(A5) _____

Name	A1	A2	A3	A4	A5	Comments
1.						
2.						
3.						
4.						
5.						
6.						
7.						
8.						
9.						
10.						
11.						
12.						
13.						

URG · Grade 1 · Unit 5 · Observational Assessment Record   5

Figure 2: *Sample* Observational Assessment Record *from Grade 1 Unit 5*

In first and second grade, the icons are also placed in the At a Glance sections of the Lesson Guides to indicate which skills and concepts described in the Assessment Indicators might be assessed during that particular lesson. Figure 3 is a sample At a Glance section from Grade 1 Unit 5 Lesson 2. The use of the icon (A1) shows that during this lesson students can be assessed on their abilities to count objects by twos, fives, and tens.

Individual Assessment Record Sheets

Information from the *Observational Assessment Record* can be transferred to *Individual Assessment Record Sheets.* The *Individual Assessment Record Sheet* is located at the end of Part VI of this section and provides an organizational tool for compiling a year-long, anecdotal record for each child. Assessment Indicators for the entire year are listed by unit along with a line for comments as shown in Figure 4.

AT A GLANCE

Math Facts Strategies and Daily Practice and Problems

DPP item C practices partitioning numbers into two and three parts and writing addition number sentences. Item D practices skip counting by twos, fives, and tens. Items E and F involve adding on the calendar.

Part 1. Things That Come in Fives

1. Students think of objects that come in fives.
2. Students trace their hands and color in the outlines.
3. Display the tracings around the room as a guide for counting by fives and tens.

Part 2. Pennies and Nickels (A1) (A4)

1. Students skip count to twenty by fives using the *Penny Count* Transparency Master as a guide.
2. Show a different number of pennies on the transparency so that students can skip count by fives and ones.
3. Students estimate the number of pennies in a bag.
4. Students group the pennies into fives and leftovers.
5. Students count the pennies and discuss their counting strategies.
6. Students trade a nickel for each row of five pennies and count again.

Part 3. Pennies on Ten Frames (A1) (A4)

1. Students group pennies into tens on the *Ten Frames* Activity Page.
2. Students count the pennies and discuss counting strategies.
3. Students trade a nickel for each complete row on the ten frames.
4. Students count by fives and ones. Collect the nickels.
5. Students trade a dime for each complete ten frame.
6. Students count by tens and ones and discover that the sum is still the same.

Assessment

1. Give each student pair a bag filled with a different number of pennies. Ask students to arrange the pennies on the *Ten Frames* Activity Page and count them. Students share how they counted the pennies and other ways to count the total.
2. Use the Assessment Indicators (A1, A4) and the *Observational Asses*... *Record* to document students' abilities to skip count by fives and tens an... relationships among pen... ...s, and dimes.

Notes:

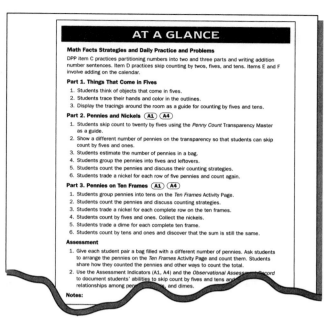

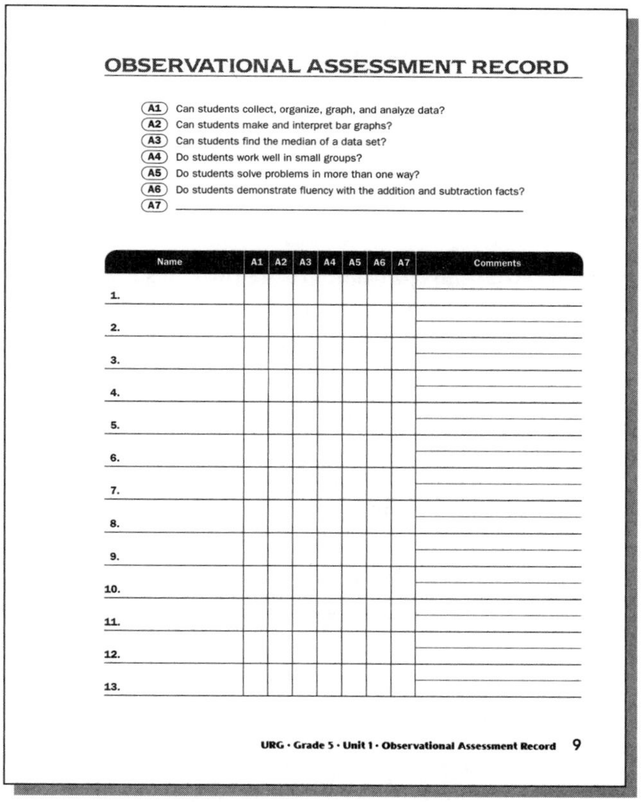

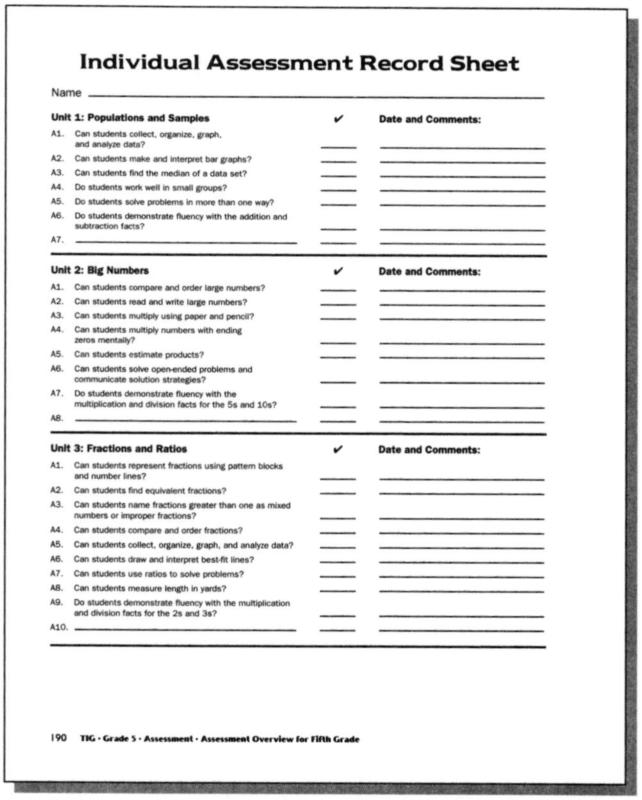

Figure 3: *Sample At a Glance from Grade 1 Unit 5 Lesson 2*

OBSERVATIONAL ASSESSMENT RECORD

(A1) Can students collect, organize, graph, and analyze data?
(A2) Can students make and interpret bar graphs?
(A3) Can students find the median of a data set?
(A4) Do students work well in small groups?
(A5) Do students solve problems in more than one way?
(A6) Do students demonstrate fluency with the addition and subtraction facts?
(A7) ____

Name	A1	A2	A3	A4	A5	A6	A7	Comments
1.								
2.								
3.								
4.								
5.								
6.								
7.								
8.								
9.								
10.								
11.								
12.								
13.								

URG • Grade 5 • Unit 1 • Observational Assessment Record 9

Individual Assessment Record Sheet

Name ____

Unit 1: Populations and Samples ✔ **Date and Comments:**

A1. Can students collect, organize, graph, and analyze data?
A2. Can students make and interpret bar graphs?
A3. Can students find the median of a data set?
A4. Do students work well in small groups?
A5. Do students solve problems in more than one way?
A6. Do students demonstrate fluency with the addition and subtraction facts?
A7. ____

Unit 2: Big Numbers ✔ **Date and Comments:**

A1. Can students compare and order large numbers?
A2. Can students read and write large numbers?
A3. Can students multiply using paper and pencil?
A4. Can students multiply numbers with ending zeros mentally?
A5. Can students estimate products?
A6. Can students solve open-ended problems and communicate solution strategies?
A7. Do students demonstrate fluency with the multiplication and division facts for the 5s and 10s?
A8. ____

Unit 3: Fractions and Ratios ✔ **Date and Comments:**

A1. Can students represent fractions using pattern blocks and number lines?
A2. Can students find equivalent fractions?
A3. Can students name fractions greater than one as mixed numbers or improper fractions?
A4. Can students compare and order fractions?
A5. Can students collect, organize, graph, and analyze data?
A6. Can students draw and interpret best-fit lines?
A7. Can students use ratios to solve problems?
A8. Can students measure length in yards?
A9. Do students demonstrate fluency with the multiplication and division facts for the 2s and 3s?
A10. ____

190 TIG • Grade 5 • Assessment • Assessment Overview for Fifth Grade

Figure 4: Observational Assessment Record *from Grade 5 Unit 1 and* Individual Assessment Record Sheet *from Grade 5*

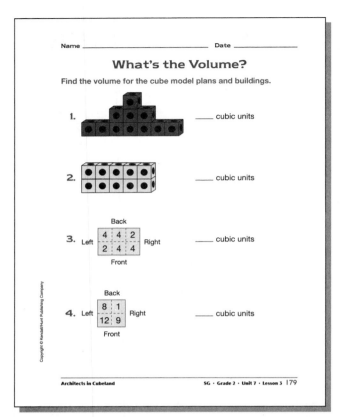

Figure 5: *Assessment Page from Grade 2 Unit 7*

Written Assessments

Assessment Pages

Many lessons in *Math Trailblazers* include short paper-and-pencil assessments that can be used to check skills or concepts developed in a unit. While some assessment pages can be used to assess students as they work in groups, often these pages can serve as quizzes to assess students individually. Checking student work gives both the teacher and student feedback on a student's current abilities. The *What's the Volume?* Assessment Page from Grade 2 Unit 7 is shown in Figure 5. Students must combine their arithmetic skills with their measurement skills to complete the page correctly.

Math Journals

Students' entries in their math journals are a rich source of assessment information. Journal Prompts, a regular feature in the lesson guides, elicit information about students' understanding of specific concepts. Figure 6 shows an example of a Journal Prompt in Grade 5 Unit 1 Lesson 3.

 Journal Prompt
A stream has an average depth of 1 meter. Can you wade across?

Figure 6: *A Journal Prompt from Grade 5 Unit 1 Lesson 3*

Figure 7: *A second-grade journal entry*

Regular journal writing provides teachers and parents with a means of documenting a student's growth in mathematical thinking, attitudes, and communication skills. (For information on math journals, see the TIMS Tutor: *Journals.*) Young children often begin by drawing pictures in their journals or combining pictures with a few words. The journal entry in Figure 7 is an early effort by Jayne, a second-grader, at communicating her thoughts about a math lesson on doubling. Jayne used six circles and six squares to show two examples of doubling three. She also wrote a short paragraph about the class:

> *Today my class did some math. and we did some writ (write) some math too! I like it!*

Suggestions for Teaching the Lesson: Assessment

The Assessment section of the Suggestions for Teaching the Lesson at the end of most lesson guides lists ideas for assessing the content of the lesson. The following components are often recommended as assessment: Assessment Pages, Journal Prompts, classroom observations corresponding to the Assessment Indicators, and appropriate questions from the student pages and Homework sections. The level of a student's response to these questions can also be recorded on the *Observational Assessment Record* or in a grade book. Figure 8 shows the Suggestions for Teaching the Lesson for Grade 1 Unit 6 Lesson 2, including Assessment.

Assessment Lessons

Some units include specially designed assessment lessons. These lessons are generally one of three types: assessment labs, open-response problems, or written tests composed of short items. Each type of lesson provides different kinds of information to teachers so that they can develop and document a complete picture of their students' progress toward the goals of the curriculum.

Assessment Labs

Two or three laboratory experiments in each grade have been designated as assessment labs. Teachers can use them to assess students' abilities to work with a group on an investigation that takes several days. Teachers can also observe students to see if they are confident enough to tackle new ideas and to use previously learned mathematics in new contexts. Working on projects such as these—problems requiring integration and application of many concepts and skills over a period of time—more closely resembles the work of mathematicians and scientists (as well as working adults in many occupations) than any other kind of work students do in school. Suggestions for evaluating labs are included in Part III.

Open-Response Problems

In these lessons, students are presented with a task that requires them to demonstrate their problem-solving skills individually or as they work in a group. Students are also assessed on their understanding of the mathematical content and their abilities to communicate their strategies. They must produce a product that allows teachers to examine their processes as well as their final answers. More than a few minutes are required to solve such a problem and students will often need a whole class period to find solutions and describe their strategies. To encourage students to give full explanations and improve their writing skills, teachers can comment on students' initial responses and ask them to make revisions. Part III includes rubrics for scoring student responses to these problems.

Suggestions for Teaching the Lesson

Math Facts Strategies

DPP item D practices addition math facts.

Homework and Practice

- The *Two Car Roll-off* Homework Page presents students with a visual representation of measuring the distance a car rolls with links. Students count the links and compare the distances.
- DPP item C practices addition in a measurement context. For DPP item E, students estimate lengths of objects. Item F reviews even and odd numbers. Item G practices partitioning numbers. Students divide groups of cookies among 4 people and count leftovers. Item H asks students to solve problems using skip counting.

Assessment

- The *Brian's Class* Assessment Page asks students to examine the data for a fictional class. **Questions 1–4** are similar to questions found in the class discussion while **Question 5** is a challenge.
- Use children's journal entries to assess whether students understand the connection between "fairness" and controlled variables.
- Use the *Observational Assessment Record* to record students' abilities to make and interpret bar graphs and also to solve problems using data involving length.

Figure 8: *Suggestions for Teaching the Lesson: Assessment from Grade 1 Unit 6 Lesson 2*

Class Party

Name _____ Date _____

Suppose there are 25 students in your class and you have $10 for a class party. Use the prices in the table to plan a party.

Tell how you would spend the money, and explain why you would spend it that way. Use as much of the $10 as you can, but do not plan to spend more than $10. (There is no tax.) Be sure your plan works for a class of 25.

Write your plan on another piece of paper. Be sure to explain how you solved the problem and how you made your decisions.

Item	Cost
pitcher of lemonade (10 servings)	$2.50
paper cups (package of 24)	69¢
ice cream bars	30¢
oatmeal cookies (package of 16)	99¢
bag of popcorn (30 servings)	$1.09
napkins (package of 50)	49¢

Assessment Blackline Master   URG · Grade 3 · Unit 10 · Lesson 3   45

Figure 9 shows Jayne's response to an open-response problem written at midyear of third grade. Jayne is the same student who wrote the journal entry shown in Figure 7. Compare her writing here with her paragraph from second grade and also with her work at the end of third grade on the Earning Money problem shown in Figure 19 in Part III. Comparing these three responses shows how she has developed her communication skills.

Tests

Tests that assess students' conceptual understanding and procedural skills are composed of short items that can be easily graded. There is a test in the final unit of both first and second grade. In third grade, there is a midyear and an end-of-year test. In fourth and fifth grades, there is a midterm test in both the fall and spring semesters in addition to a midyear and end-of-year test.

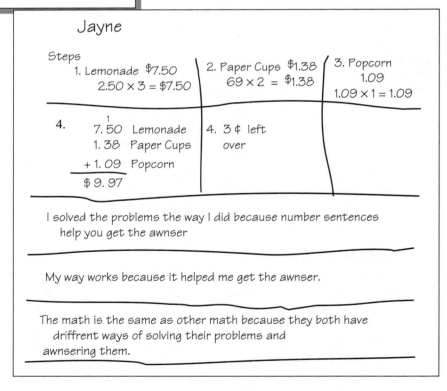

Figure 9: *Jayne's work for an open-response problem*

Assessment Units

In each grade, specific units are designated as assessment units. These units include lessons that emphasize assessment at the same time that content is reviewed and new material is introduced. Teachers can assess students' abilities to apply previously studied concepts in new contexts and their willingness to approach new mathematics.

Assessment units at the beginning of each grade provide opportunities to observe students and collect baseline data on students' mathematical knowledge. Teachers can use this information to plan instruction that meets students' needs and to begin the process of documenting students' mathematical growth over the course of the year. See the Assessment Overview in Part VI for specific information on the assessment units.

Portfolios

Portfolios are important tools for documenting students' growth throughout the year. They are collections of students' written work and teachers' anecdotal records. To provide a complete picture of a student's learning, a portfolio should include assessments that demonstrate the range of the child's abilities. Samples of student work on labs, open-response problems, assessment activity pages, and tests can be included along with samples of students' daily work. Work from the beginning through the end of the year will show students' growth over time. Certain lessons in the assessment units assist in this process and are especially appropriate for inclusion in portfolios. Refer to the TIMS Tutor: *Portfolios* for more information.

Facts Assessment

In *Math Trailblazers,* teachers assess students' knowledge of the facts through observations as they work on activities, labs, and games as well as through the appropriate use of quizzes and tests. Periodic, short quizzes in the Daily Practice and Problems naturally follow the study of small groups of facts organized around specific strategies. As self-assessment in third, fourth, and fifth grades, each student can record his or her progress on *Facts I Know* charts and determine which facts he or she needs to study. The goal of the math facts assessment program is to determine the degree to which students can find answers to fact problems quickly and accurately and whether they can retain this skill over time. For more information on teaching and assessing the math facts, see the TIMS Tutor: *Math Facts.*

PART III | Implementing the Assessment Program

Evaluating and reporting on a broad range of student achievement throughout the school year is a complex task. It is only practical if the assessment process is built into day-to-day instruction. The components of the assessment program are designed so that teachers can gather information about students as they are learning. This section outlines a plan for introducing the various components of the assessment program gradually during the first weeks of instruction and provides information on evaluating and scoring written work.

Getting Started

An assessment program that emphasizes the documentation of students' growth over time establishes a climate in which each child is valued for the knowledge and skills he or she brings to the classroom and in which each student is expected to make significant gains in mathematics. These are high expectations that also reflect reality. Students begin and end the school year with varying abilities, backgrounds, and accomplishments. Therefore, it is important to record what each student can do initially, as well as during the learning process, so that the teacher, student, and parents can fully appreciate progress throughout the year.

Begin Observational Assessments

Activities in the first two or three units of each grade provide many opportunities for observing students as they use mathematics. These observations provide a rich source of baseline information about students. For example, in Units 1–3 of first grade, students count objects in many contexts. By routinely observing four or five students during appropriate lessons, the teacher can make a record of those students who can count and those students who may need additional help. At the same time, all students are working on their counting skills as well as on related concepts such as comparing numbers and organizing data.

Unit 2 of third grade is also designated as an assessment unit. As part of this unit, students review strategies in order to maintain fluency with the subtraction facts. Students discuss strategies, play games, work with flash cards, assess themselves using *Facts I Know* charts, and use subtraction facts as part of a data collection activity. Observing students as they participate in each of these activities gives teachers information about students' knowledge of the facts and, more importantly, about students' abilities to use the facts to solve problems. Since students will continually use the facts in many activities as well as in the Daily Practice and Problems, the teacher need only record observations for a small number of students at a time. (For more information on assessment of the math facts, see the TIMS Tutor: *Math Facts.*)

Using the *Observational Assessment Record.* Before beginning
assessment observations, teachers need a system for recording short, anecdotal records. Such a system should allow recording of a broad range of evidence of students' behavior, attitudes, and understanding of mathematics and should make recording and retrieving information easy and convenient. The *Observational Assessment Record* and the Assessment Indicators help organize data from observations. Teachers can develop their own shorthand to denote satisfactory progress toward a goal or proficiency with a skill or concept.

In Grades 1–5, information from the *Observational Assessment Record* can be transferred to *Individual Assessment Record Sheets* to create a year-long anecdotal record of growth for each child. The *Individual Assessment Record Sheet* is located at the end of Part VI of this section. It can be copied and placed in each student's portfolio. The *Individual Assessment Record Sheet* is also available on the *Teacher Resource CD.* Teachers can use it to maintain records of each student's progress electronically.

As part of planning for a lesson, the teacher can choose one or two behaviors, concepts, or skills to check during class. The Assessment Indicators for each unit and the Assessment section in the Suggestions for Teaching the Lesson in the lesson guides can facilitate this process. The teacher should choose no more than four or five students to observe in a day. Additional students can be observed in succeeding lessons or units to provide further information about individual students' progress and the improvement of the class as a whole.

Figure 10 is an example of an *Observational Assessment Record* for Grade 1 Unit 1 that shows one possible scheme for recording classroom observations. Note that the teacher chose to observe students' abilities to work together as well as counting skills.

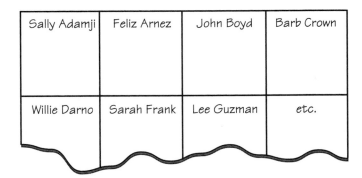

OBSERVATIONAL ASSESSMENT RECORD

The following questions may be used to assess your students' progress. It may be necessary to assess additional content.

A1 Can students count objects?
A2 Can students identify the number of a small group of objects without counting?
A3 Can students compare numbers using *more, less,* or *about the same*?
A4 Can students count on from a given number?
A5 Can students work cooperatively with a partner?
A6 _____

Name	A1	A2	A3	A4	A5	A6	Comments
1. Susie	9/2 Yes		9/2 to 15				Counted a row of students 1–10
2. Chan	9/2 No						Uses counting all.
3. Roosevelt	9/2 Yes						Counted blocks 1–15
4. Lee				9/1 Yes			DPP item C.
5. Kristen					9/3 Yes	9/3 Yes	Counted on from numbers less than 10 to 10. Helped David.
6. David					9/3 with help	9/3 Yes	Counted buttons 1–10. Worked well with Kristen.
7.							
8.							
9.							
10.							
11.							
12.							
13.							

URG · Grade 1 · Unit 1 · Observational Assessment Record 7

Figure 10: *Sample* Observational Assessment Record *for Grade 1 Unit 1*

Other suggestions from teachers for organizing anecdotal records are given below:

Student Grid. A teacher can make a grid that allows note-taking about all students on one piece of paper as shown in Figure 11. The grids include as many cells as there are students in the class, each cell labeled with a student's name. Observations are written in the cells. Like the *Observational Assessment Record,* this provides a view of the entire class's progress.

Sally Adamji	Feliz Arnez	John Boyd	Barb Crown
Willie Darno	Sarah Frank	Lee Guzman	etc.

Figure 11: *Student grid*

Flip Chart. A flip chart can be made by lining up index cards and taping them to a clipboard or a piece of heavy cardboard so that they overlap by all but a strip of about $\frac{1}{2}$ inch as shown in Figure 12. Students' names are written on the uncovered area of each card, so that the teacher can easily flip to a student's card and write a quick, dated note about the observation. As a card is filled, it can be removed to a card file or a student's portfolio and replaced with a new card.

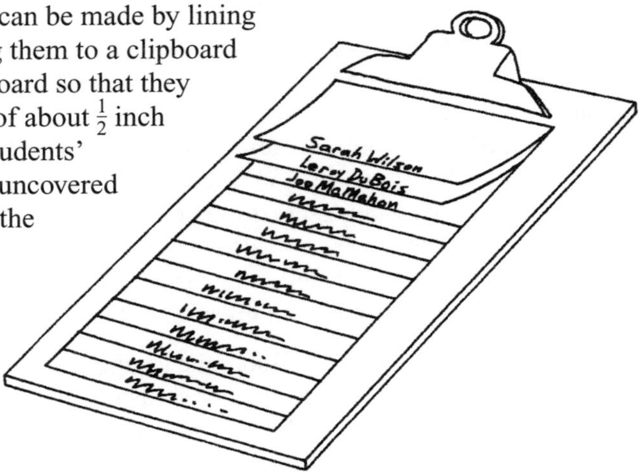

Figure 12: *Flip chart*

Flip Cards. A variation of the flip chart can be made by fastening together a set of index cards—one index card labeled for each student in the class. A binder ring is placed through a hole in a corner of each card.

Self-Adhesive Notes. Some teachers prefer to write their observations about individual students on self-adhesive notes, which are then attached to a sheet of paper in the student's portfolio. These notes have the advantage of being easily transferable, so that they can be grouped and regrouped by student, subject, day, etc.

Begin Math Journals

At the beginning of the year, math journals provide a safe place for students to start communicating their insights. By writing regularly in their journals, they gain the experience necessary to write more and learn to express themselves clearly. Students can write in response to journal prompts or record answers to questions from the *Student Guide* or Daily Practice and Problems. See the TIMS Tutor: *Journals* for more information on using journals to assess students.

Begin Portfolios

The TIMS Tutor: *Portfolios* recommends establishing portfolios by starting small with modest goals. This implies using portfolios to document progress in one or two specific areas such as communicating mathematically or collecting and analyzing data. One way to begin is to assign each student a collection folder so that early examples of student work can be saved. Later in the process, teachers can designate or students can select a smaller number of pieces that show evidence of growth in these areas.

It is important to choose examples of work from the beginning of the year so that a student's first efforts can be compared to later work. The earliest entries in the portfolio will most likely show results that are much less sophisticated than those that are added toward the end of the year. For example, to compare students' use of the TIMS Laboratory Method at the beginning of the year to their abilities to conduct an experiment at the end of the year, include a data table and a graph from an early lab in each student's portfolio. Good choices of initial labs to collect in portfolios include the following: In Grade 1, save students' weather graphs from Unit 2; in Grade 2, use the Button Sizer Graph from Unit 3; and in Grade 3, choose student work from the lab *Kind of Bean* in Unit 1 or the graph and write-up from *Spinning Differences* in Unit 2. At the beginning of Grade 4, include *Arm Span vs. Height* from Unit 1 and *Perimeter vs. Length* from Unit 2. In Grade 5, begin portfolios with the labs *Searching the Forest* from Unit 1 and *Distance vs. Time* from Unit 3.

Scoring Open-Response Problems

In *Math Trailblazers,* most lessons involve multiple mathematical topics, skills, and processes. Assessing student progress requires tools that allow students to respond using multiple approaches and that let teachers evaluate student communication and problem-solving strategies as well as mathematical knowledge.

TIMS Multidimensional Rubric

To assist teachers in evaluating student performance and in communicating progress to students and parents, we have developed a rubric—a scoring guide—for evaluating student work on open-response problems. The *TIMS Multidimensional Rubric* addresses three dimensions of mathematical learning: (i) knowing, (ii) solving, and (iii) telling. Using these three dimensions broadens the focus of assessment from the traditional emphasis on rote procedures to a more complete view of mathematics learning. The rubric outlines our criteria for excellence and provides an explicit indication of what we value in mathematics. Examples of using the rubric to score student work are included in lesson guides beginning in Grade 3. The ideas embodied in the rubric are generally applicable to younger children and can be modified for use in earlier grades. The rubric is displayed in Part V.

The three dimensions of mathematical understanding emphasized in the *TIMS Multidimensional Rubric* are described here briefly.

- *Solving.* This section focuses on students' understanding of a problem and their abilities to devise a plan for solving it, organize information, analyze results, and reflect on the mathematical implications of the problem.
- *Knowing.* This portion of the rubric examines students' comprehension of mathematical concepts and their abilities to apply procedures, rules, and facts to a given mathematical situation. This includes effective use of representations, such as written numbers, words, graphs, tables, or pictures, and the ability to make connections among different mathematical ideas.
- *Telling.* This part of the rubric stresses students' abilities to explain their problem-solving strategies, justify their solutions, use symbols and terminology correctly, and discuss connections among mathematical topics.

The *TIMS Multidimensional Rubric* specifies criteria for assigning scores on each of the three dimensions to one piece of student work. Level 4 is the highest and is intended to represent excellence in that particular dimension. A paper might earn, for example, a 3 in *Solving*, a 4 in *Knowing*, and a 3 in *Telling*. It is not necessary to assign a score for all three dimensions for every task. For many tasks, it may be more appropriate to give scores for only one or two dimensions.

Student Rubrics

Corresponding Student Rubrics for each dimension make the expectations of student performance clear. These rubrics provide students with goals as they solve problems, communicate their solutions, and revise their work. Students also use these rubrics as guides when assessing their own work. The student rubrics are introduced gradually in the *Student Guide* throughout the first semester of third, fourth, and fifth grades. They are included in lessons with open-response problems.

The Student Rubrics are shown in Figure 13.

The Student Rubrics are located in Appendices A, B, and C and on the inside backcover of the *Student Guides* for Grades 3–5. Blackline Masters of the Student Rubrics are included in Part V so teachers can make transparencies or use a copier to enlarge the rubrics to make classroom posters.

Student Rubric: Knowing

What is a rubric?

It tells me how to make sure I've done my best work!

In My Best Work in Mathematics:

- I show that I understand the ideas in the problem.
- I show the same mathematical ideas in different ways. I use pictures, tables, graphs, and sentences when they fit the problem.
- I show that I can use tools and rules correctly.
- I show that I can use the mathematical facts that apply to the problem.

TIG · Grade 1 · Assessment · Master Copies of Rubrics   173

Student Rubric: Solving

How does this rubric help you?

It helps me plan strategies, find solutions, and check my work when I solve problems.

In My Best Work in Mathematics:

- I read the problem carefully, make a good plan for solving it, and then carry out that plan.
- I use tools like graphs, pictures, tables, or number sentences to help me.
- I use ideas I know from somewhere else to help me solve a problem.
- I keep working on the problem until I find a good solution.
- I look back at my solution to see if my answer makes sense.
- I look back at my work to see what more I can learn from solving the problem.

174   TIG · Grade 1 · Assessment · Master Copies of Rubrics

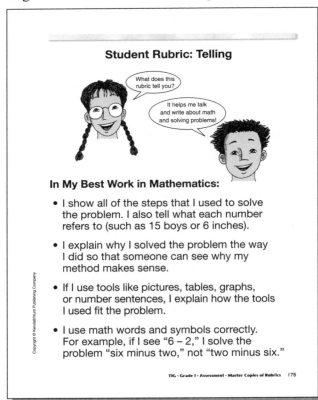

Student Rubric: Telling

What does this rubric tell you?

It helps me talk and write about math and solving problems!

In My Best Work in Mathematics:

- I show all of the steps that I used to solve the problem. I also tell what each number refers to (such as 15 boys or 6 inches).
- I explain why I solved the problem the way I did so that someone can see why my method makes sense.
- If I use tools like pictures, tables, graphs, or number sentences, I explain how the tools I used fit the problem.
- I use math words and symbols correctly. For example, if I see "6 − 2," I solve the problem "six minus two," not "two minus six."

TIG · Grade 1 · Assessment · Master Copies of Rubrics   175

Figure 13: *Student Rubrics:* Knowing, Solving, *and* Telling

Using the Rubrics: An Early Example

Using the student rubrics to inform students of your expectations as well as using the *TIMS Multidimensional Rubric* to score student work is a process that evolves throughout the year. For example, Grade 3 Unit 2 includes the first assessment lesson with an open-response problem. This is the students' first exposure to the student rubrics. The problem is shown in Figure 14.

To begin the lesson the class reads and discusses the problem. It is similar to the problem in an earlier lesson (Unit 2 Lesson 2 *Spinning Sums*), so students should be familiar with the procedures. They also read and discuss the Student Rubric: *Knowing*. The teacher may ask students what tools, rules, and mathematical facts apply to the problem. She explains that she will grade their work based on the rubric.

After students understand the problem, they work in groups to plan a strategy for solving the problem and to carry out their plans. Then students write paragraphs describing their problem-solving processes and their results. The teacher directs students either to write the paragraph with their groups or to write the paragraph individually. When students have completed their paragraphs, the teacher reviews their work and makes suggestions for improvement.

It is a good idea to make transparencies of exemplary work from previous years or the lesson guide. The teacher discusses the exemplary work with the class, comparing the work to the standards set forth in the rubric. Finally, students revise their work based on the teacher's comments. A student response with teacher comments is shown in Figure 15.

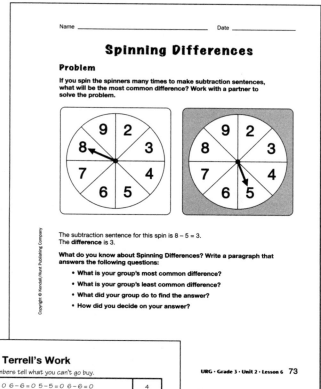

Figure 14: *Assessment lesson from Grade 3 Unit 2*

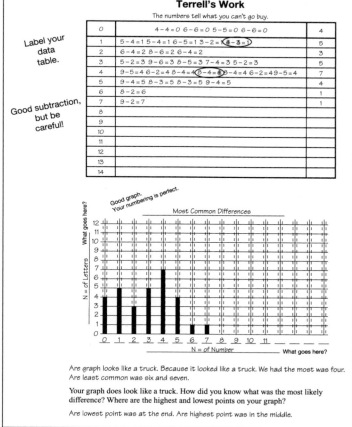

Figure 15: *A student response to a teacher's comments*

The teacher used the Knowing dimension of the *TIMS Multidimensional Rubric* to score students' work. The Lesson Guide provides questions specific to this problem to guide the teacher in the scoring. The questions provided for this problem are given below:

- Were the data table and graph appropriately labeled?
- Was the graph scaled properly?
- Were the bars correctly drawn?
- Were the subtraction sentences correct?
- Were the most common differences identified?

Many of the criteria in the rubric overlap. In addition, the student's data table, graph, and written paragraphs tell us about more than one component of the problem. Consequently, the score for a dimension will result from the compilation of all the evidence, not necessarily from an arithmetic average of scores in each cell of the rubric. Figure 16 shows the Knowing dimension of the *TIMS Multidimensional Rubric* with the teacher's notations after she scored Terrell's paper.

How would you score Terrell's work? Terrell's teacher decided that he earned a 3. He worked with his group using tools to spin the spinners 30 times, record the results in a table, and display the data in a graph. The bars are drawn correctly on the graph and the axes are scaled correctly. However, the incorrect labels on both the data table ("The numbers that tell what you can't go buy") and graph ("Most Common Differences" and "$N = $ of Letters") indicate that he was not clear on his goal for collecting data and therefore did not completely understand the problem's concepts and applications. The incorrect labels also show major errors translating between tables, graphs, and real situations, although he did correctly identify the most common and least common differences. The correct number sentences are evidence that he knows the subtraction facts. (See the Lesson Guide for *Spinning Differences* in Grade 3 Unit 2 for other examples of student work scored using the rubric.)

Knowing	Level 4	Level 3	Level 2	Level 1
Understands the task's mathematical concepts, their properties and applications...	Completely	Nearly completely	Partially	Not at all
Translates between words, pictures, symbols, tables, graphs, and real situations...	Readily and without errors	With minor errors	With major errors	Not at all
Uses tools (measuring devices, graphs, tables, calculators, etc.) and procedures...	Correctly and efficiently	Correctly or with minor errors	Incorrectly	Not at all
Uses knowledge of the facts of mathematics (geometry definitions, math facts, etc.)...	Correctly	With minor errors	With major errors	Not at all

Figure 16: *Scoring an open-response problem using one dimension of the* TIMS Multidimensional Rubric

Using the Rubrics: A Second Example

During the school year, students become familiar with all three of the student rubrics and use them as they solve problems. Depending on the problem, one or more of the rubrics may be used. The results of these assessments are often saved in portfolios to show students and parents progress over time. The problem in Figure 17 is posed to students in the final assessment unit of third grade.

Before students begin solving the problem, the class reads and discusses the problem. Students should understand that play money will be available to help solve the problem and that they will be asked how a calculator can be used to solve the problem. The teacher also reviews all three student rubrics and advises students that their work for this problem will be scored using all three dimensions.

Students use the tools available to them to find solutions and write about their strategies. The teacher may use samples of students' work to provide good examples for students to emulate. The teacher also comments on students' first drafts and students revise their work accordingly.

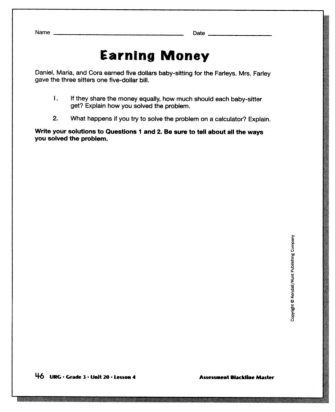

Figure 17: *An open-response problem from Grade 3 Unit 20*

Samples of two students' work are shown in Figures 18 and 19. Scores for both students for all three dimensions of the *TIMS Multidimensional Rubric* are discussed below. The teacher was guided by additional questions in the Lesson Guide which are specific to this problem and point out elements to consider while scoring.

The teacher gave Marco a 2 on Solving. Marco chose a legitimate problem-solving strategy—guess and check—but did not use it systematically or efficiently, nor did he organize his work. His work does show evidence that he persisted in the problem-solving process, but does not show that he

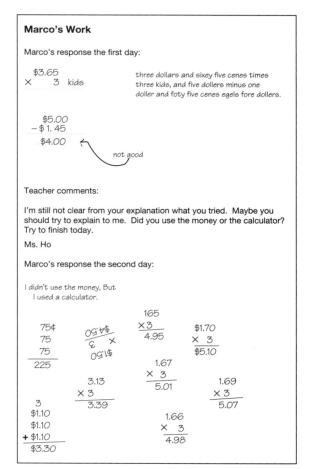

Figure 18: *Marco's work*

identified all the elements of the problem since he does not indicate that he knows that there will be money left over. He makes no connections to previously studied mathematics or previously solved problems.

On the Knowing dimension, the teacher gave Marco a 3 since he correctly used his knowledge of mathematics and he used appropriate tools (a calculator) and procedures (repeated addition and multiplication) to solve the problem. He did not demonstrate that he completely understood the nature of the task or show that he can translate between symbols and real situations since he did not calculate the amount of money that would be left over.

Marco received a 1 on the Telling dimension. His explanation was very short and totally unclear, with no supporting arguments. Since he did not identify which trial was successful, we are not even sure of his final answer. He used symbols to show his trials, but made no attempt to organize them. Appropriate terminology is not present.

A second sample of student work on the Earning Money problem is shown below:

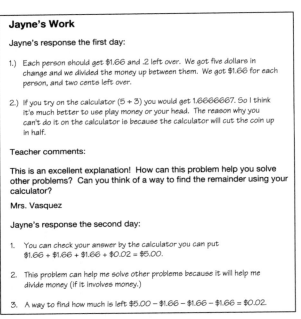

Jayne's Work

Jayne's response the first day:

1.) Each person should get $1.66 and .2 left over. We got five dollars in change and we divided the money up between them. We got $1.66 for each person, and two cents left over.

2.) If you try on the calculator (5 ÷ 3) you would get 1.6666667. So I think it's much better to use play money or your head. The reason why you can't do it on the calculator is because the calculator will cut the coin up in half.

Teacher comments:

This is an excellent explanation! How can this problem help you solve other problems? Can you think of a way to find the remainder using your calculator?

Mrs. Vasquez

Jayne's response the second day:

1. You can check your answer by the calculator you can put $1.66 + $1.66 + $1.66 + $0.02 = $5.00.

2. This problem can help me solve other problems because it will help me divide money (if it involves money.)

3. A way to find how much is left $5.00 − $1.66 − $1.66 − $1.66 = $0.02.

Figure 19: *Jayne's work*

Jayne's teacher gave her a score of 4 for Solving. She fully met the criteria in the rubric. She clearly identified the elements of the problem when she described the problem first as dividing the play money "up between them" and finding the amount left over and then as using a calculator to divide (5 ÷ 3) resulting in a repeating decimal. With prompting from the teacher, she looked for other strategies and found that she could use repeated addition and subtraction to find the remainder. All of her strategies are effective and they are presented in an organized fashion. Jayne's first conclusion that "you can't do it (find the remainder) on the calculator is because the calculator will cut the coin up in half" is insightful, although not quite correct mathematically. The use of both repeated addition and subtraction on the calculator to find the remainder shows that she made meaningful connections between the operations and that she was willing to persist in the problem-solving process.

Jayne also received a 4 in Knowing since she clearly understood the mathematical concepts of the problem. She readily translated the real situation into words when she described the process of dividing up the money and then translated words into symbols using correct addition, subtraction, and division sentences. The use of play money and a calculator is evidence that she can use tools correctly and efficiently and her calculations show that she can use the facts of mathematics correctly as well.

The teacher gave Jayne a score of 3 for the Telling dimension. Her explanations and responses were fairly complete and clear. However, we are not entirely sure how the group shared the money. Did they trade the dollars for quarters and then the quarters for dimes, etc., or were they able to make the process more efficient in some way? Her supporting arguments are sound, but they contain a few minor gaps. Did she use repeated subtraction or repeated addition first to find the remainder? Why did she choose these operations? She used many symbols and terms correctly. However, she reported that two cents were left over and wrote it first as ".2."

Like any new tool, using the rubric efficiently will require practice. As you begin to work with the rubric, we suggest that you work closely with other teachers. For example, you might score a half-dozen papers and ask one or more colleagues to score the same set; then compare and discuss the results, negotiating any differences. Repeating this process over the course of the year will help establish school-wide norms for applying the rubrics.

Using Assessment Observations, Math Journals, and Portfolios
The rubrics can be combined with other components of the assessment program to provide a more complete picture of students' skills at solving open-response problems. For example, to assess students' willingness to tackle new problems or work cooperatively in a group, teachers can observe students as they work on the problem or ask them to write in their journals about the process. For example, the Journal Prompt for the Earning Money problem concerns students' feelings about working in groups in math class. (See Figure 20.)

Journal Prompt
How did your group share the work on this problem? How do you feel about working with a group in math class?

Figure 20: *Journal prompt for Earning Money (Grade 3 Unit 20)*

Considerable growth in mathematical power is often evident when several write-ups of open-response problems from different times of the year are included in a student's portfolio. We can see growth in Jayne's problem-solving and communication skills when we look at her work on both the Class Party and Earning Money problems. (See Figure 9 in Part II and Figure 19.)

Evaluating Labs

Teachers have used the following ideas to evaluate student performance on labs:

Group Work

Students work in their groups to polish a lab write-up and turn in one completed lab for each group or to prepare an oral report to be presented to the class. They may include in their reports how the work was distributed among the members of the group. Students can also write a paragraph in their journals describing how each of the members functioned in the group and how the process can be improved.

Using the Multidimensional Rubric

Choose one or two important questions to score using one or more dimensions of the *TIMS Multidimensional Rubric*. Often suitable questions will be suggested in the Assessment section of the Suggestions for Teaching the Lesson in the Lesson Guide. These are usually open-response questions that ask students to make predictions or solve a problem using the data collected during the experiment.

Self-Assessment

Students can grade their own labs in class. This provides a forum for discussing the most important aspects of the lab.

Using a Point System

To grade a lab, teachers can assign a given number of points to each part of the lab and grade each part based on the criteria below. Teachers can also choose to grade only a portion of the lab such as the picture or the graph.

1. Drawing the Picture
   - Are the procedures and the materials clearly illustrated?
   - Are the variables labeled?
2. Collecting and Recording the Data
   - Are the data organized in a table?
   - Are the columns in the data table labeled correctly?
   - Are the data reasonable?
   - Are the correct units of measure included in the data table?
   - If applicable, did students average the data (find the median or mean) correctly?
3. Graphing the Data
   - Does the graph have a title?
   - Are the axes scaled correctly and labeled clearly? Labeling should be consistent with the picture and the data table and should include appropriate units of measure.
   - If it is a bar graph, are the bars drawn correctly?
   - If it is a point graph, are the points plotted correctly?
   - If the points suggest a straight line or a curve, did the student draw a best-fit line or fit a curve to the points?
   - Did the students show any interpolation or extrapolation on the graph?

4. Solving the Problems
   - Are the answers correct based on the data?
   - Did students use appropriate tools (calculators, rulers, graphs, etc.) correctly?
   - Are the answers, including the explanations, clear and complete?

References

Elementary Grades Assessment. *Balanced Assessment for the Mathematics Curriculum.* University of California. Dale Seymour Publications, White Plains, NY, 1999.

Lane, Suzanne. "The Conceptual Framework for the Development of a Mathematics Performance Assessment Instrument" in *Educational Measurement: Issues and Practice.* Vol. 12, Number 2. National Council on Measurement in Education, Washington, DC, 1993.

Mathematics Resource Guide for Fourth- and Eighth-Grade Teachers. Vermont Department of Education, Montpelier, VT, 1996.

Middle Grades Assessment. *Balanced Assessment for the Mathematics Curriculum.* University of California. Dale Seymour Publications, White Plains, NY, 2000.

Pellegrino, J. W., N. Chadowsky, and R. Glaser (Eds.) *Knowing What Students Know: The Science and Design of Educational Assessment.* National Research Council. National Academy Press, Washington, DC, 2001.

Performance Assessment in Mathematics: Approaches to Open-Ended Problems. Illinois State Board of Education, Springfield, IL, 1994.

Principles and Standards for School Mathematics. National Council of Teachers of Mathematics, Reston, VA, 2000.

Stenmark, J.K. (Ed.) *Mathematics Assessment: Myths, Models, Good Questions, and Practical Suggestions.* National Council of Teachers of Mathematics, Reston, VA, 1991.

PART IV

Master Copies of Rubrics

PART V

This section is composed of blackline masters of the *TIMS Multidimensional Rubric* and the three Student Rubrics: *Knowing, Solving,* and *Telling.* The Scoring Open-Response Problems section in Part III describes the rubrics and provides examples of their use in the curriculum. The *TIMS Multidimensional Rubric* is provided here so that teachers can use it as they score student work. The copies of the three student rubrics in this section can be used to make transparencies for the overhead projector or they can be enlarged to make posters for the classroom.

TIMS Multidimensional Rubric

Solving	Level 4	Level 3	Level 2	Level 1
Identifies the elements of the problem and their relationships to one another.	All major elements identified	Most elements identified	Some, but shows little understanding of relationships	Few or none
Uses problem-solving strategies which are . . .	Systematic, complete, efficient, and possibly elegant	Systematic and nearly complete, but not efficient	Incomplete or unsystematic	Not evident or inappropriate
Organizes relevant information . . .	Systematically and efficiently	Systematically, with minor errors	Unsystematically	Not at all
Relates the problem and solution to previously encountered mathematics and makes connections that are . . .	At length, elegant, and meaningful	Evident	Brief or logically unsound	Not evident
Persists in the problem solving process . . .	At length	Until a solution is reached	Briefly	Not at all
Looks back to examine the reasonableness of the solution and draws conclusions that are . . .	Insightful and comprehensive	Correct	Incorrect or logically unsound	Not present

Knowing	Level 4	Level 3	Level 2	Level 1
Understands the task's mathematical concepts, their properties and applications . . .	Completely	Nearly completely	Partially	Not at all
Translates between words, pictures, symbols, tables, graphs, and real situations . . .	Readily and without errors	With minor errors	With major errors	Not at all
Uses tools (measuring devices, graphs, tables, calculators, etc.) and procedures . . .	Correctly and efficiently	Correctly or with minor errors	Incorrectly	Not at all
Uses knowledge of the facts of mathematics (geometry definitions, math facts, etc.) . . .	Correctly	With minor errors	With major errors	Not at all

Telling	Level 4	Level 3	Level 2	Level 1
Includes response with an explanation and/or description which is . . .	Complete and clear	Fairly complete and clear	Perhaps ambiguous or unclear	Totally unclear or irrelevant
Presents supporting arguments which are . . .	Strong and sound	Logically sound, but may contain minor gaps	Incomplete or logically unsound	Not present
Uses pictures, symbols, tables, and graphs which are . . .	Correct and clearly relevant	Present with minor errors or somewhat irrelevant	Present with errors and/or irrelevant	Not present or completely inappropriate
Uses terminology . . .	Clearly and precisely	With minor errors	With major errors	Not at all

Student Rubric: Knowing

What is a rubric?

It tells me how to make sure I've done my best work!

In My Best Work in Mathematics:

- I show that I understand the ideas in the problem.

- I show the same mathematical ideas in different ways. I use pictures, tables, graphs, and sentences when they fit the problem.

- I show that I can use tools and rules correctly.

- I show that I can use the mathematical facts that apply to the problem.

Student Rubric: Solving

In My Best Work in Mathematics:

- I read the problem carefully, make a good plan for solving it, and then carry out that plan.

- I use tools like graphs, pictures, tables, or number sentences to help me.

- I use ideas I know from somewhere else to help me solve a problem.

- I keep working on the problem until I find a good solution.

- I look back at my solution to see if my answer makes sense.

- I look back at my work to see what more I can learn from solving the problem.

Student Rubric: Telling

In My Best Work in Mathematics:

- I show all of the steps that I used to solve the problem. I also tell what each number refers to (such as 15 boys or 6 inches).

- I explain why I solved the problem the way I did so that someone can see why my method makes sense.

- If I use tools like pictures, tables, graphs, or number sentences, I explain how the tools I used fit the problem.

- I use math words and symbols correctly. For example, if I see "6 – 2," I solve the problem "six minus two," not "two minus six."

PART VI

Assessment Overview for First Grade

The assessment overview includes short descriptions of the components in the assessment program followed by a table that lists each of the assessments in first grade. The table names the assessments in each unit and gives the lesson name and number, the type of assessment, and the location of the assessment within the unit.

Component Summary

Assessment Indicators: A list of important topics covered in a given unit. The Assessment Indicators help the teacher focus on important skills and behaviors that can be assessed.

Observational Assessment Record: A tool that helps teachers record student progress on the Assessment Indicators. Information about all students in the class can be recorded on the *Observational Assessment Record.* This provides a quick view of how both individual students and the class as a whole are progressing during the course of a unit. Student information can later be transferred to *Individual Assessment Record Sheets.*

Individual Assessment Record Sheet: A tool for tracking individual students' progress with the Assessment Indicators from all sixteen units.

Suggestions for Teaching the Lesson: Assessment: Suggested ways to assess student progress during a lesson are included as Assessment in the lesson guides. This section might highlight particular parts of an activity as appropriate for observations, direct teachers to an assessment page or activity, or suggest a journal prompt or homework questions for assessment.

Math Journals: As a part of the assessment for a lesson, students are sometimes asked to respond in their Math Journals to a specific question or prompt.

Assessment Pages: Short paper-and-pencil assessments that can be used to check skills or concepts developed in a unit. Some are designed for use in groups; others are for individual work.

Assessment Lessons: Specially designed lessons to gauge student progress. There are three basic types of assessment lessons: assessment labs, open-response problems, and written tests composed of short items.

Assessment Labs: Some laboratory experiments are designated as Assessment Labs. They are used to assess students' abilities to work in a group on an investigation that takes several days.

Assessment Units: Specific units in each grade that are designed to help teachers monitor student progress as part of the learning process.

Portfolios: Collections of students' written work and teachers' anecdotal records. Portfolios are used to document students' growth over time.

Assessment Component	Component Description	Location
Unit 1—Welcome to First Grade: A Baseline Assessment Unit		
Observational Assessment Record **Individual Assessment Record Sheet**	**Assessment Record** **Assessment Record**	**URG** **TIG**
Lesson 1—Look Around You	**Assessment Lesson**	**URG, AB**
Lesson 2—We're Counting on You! DPP Item G—Count On Counting at the Toy Store How Many Are There?	**Assessment Lesson** Assessment DPP Item Assessment Activity Page Assessment Activity Page	**URG, SG** URG SG SG
Lesson 3—The Train Game DPP Item I—Count On Again	**Assessment Game** Assessment DPP Item	**URG** URG
Lesson 4—More or Less DPP Item N—More or Less DPP Item P—Making a Train	**Assessment Lesson** Assessment DPP Item Assessment DPP Item	**URG, SG** URG URG
Unit 2—Exploring Shapes		
Observational Assessment Record **Individual Assessment Record Sheet**	**Assessment Record** **Assessment Record**	**URG** **TIG**
Lesson 2—Describing Shapes DPP Item H—More Than/Less Than One More Time Alike and Different 2	**Lesson** Assessment DPP Item Assessment Activity Page	**URG** URG SG
Lesson 4—How Many Does It Take? The Rocket	**Lesson** Assessment Activity Page	**URG** SG
Lesson 5—Mystery Figure DPP Item M—Sentences 5	**Lesson** Assessment DPP Item	**URG** URG
Lesson 6—Weather 1: Eye on the Sky DPP Item P—Alike and Different 2	**Lab** Assessment DPP Item	**URG** URG
Unit 3—Pennies, Pockets, and Parts		
Observational Assessment Record **Individual Assessment Record Sheet**	**Assessment Record** **Assessment Record**	**URG** **TIG**
Lesson 1—Favorite Colors DPP Item B—What Number?	**Lesson** Assessment DPP Item	**URG** URG
Lesson 2—Ten Frames What's My Sentence?	**Lesson** Assessment Activity Page	**URG** SG
Lesson 5—Pocket Parts Pockets	**Lesson** Assessment Activity Page	**URG** SG
Lesson 6—What's in That Pocket? DPP Item Y—Penny Problems 2 Nine Pennies Data Table	**Lesson** Assessment DPP Item Assessment Activity Page	**URG** URG SG

Assessment Component	Component Description	Location
Unit 4—Adding to Solve Problems		
Observational Assessment Record **Individual Assessment Record Sheet**	**Assessment Record** **Assessment Record**	**URG** **TIG**
Lesson 3—Parts and Wholes DPP Item E—Even or Odd 1? More Parts and Wholes	**Lesson** Assessment DPP Item Assessment Activity Page	**URG** URG URG
Lesson 4—Counting On to Add DPP Item H—Adding Trains DPP Item J—Parts and Wholes	**Lesson** Assessment DPP Item Assessment DPP Item	**URG** URG URG
Unit 5—Grouping and Counting		
Observational Assessment Record **Individual Assessment Record Sheet**	**Assessment Record** **Assessment Record**	**URG** **TIG**
Lesson 3—Sharing Cookies DPP Item H—Parts and Wholes 2	**Lesson** Assessment DPP Item	**URG** URG
Lesson 5—Colors DPP Item M—Sharing Stickers	**Lab** Assessment DPP Item	**URG** URG
Unit 6—Measurement: Length		
Observational Assessment Record **Individual Assessment Record Sheet**	**Assessment Record** **Assessment Record**	**URG** **TIG**
Lesson 1—Linking Up DPP Item A—Skip Counting with Leftovers	**Lesson** Assessment DPP Item	**URG** URG
Lesson 2—Rolling Along with Links Brian's Class	**Lab** Assessment Activity Page	**URG** SG
Lesson 4—Using Unusual Units DPP Item M—Nickels and Dimes	**Lesson** Assessment DPP Item	**URG** URG
Lesson 5—Delightful Dachshunds Comparing Links and Cubes	**Lesson** Assessment Activity Page	**URG** SG
Lesson 6—Give 'em an Inch Could Be or Crazy?	**Lesson** Assessment Activity Page	**URG** SG
Unit 7—Patterns and Designs		
Observational Assessment Record **Individual Assessment Record Sheet**	**Assessment Record** **Assessment Record**	**URG** **TIG**
Lesson 2—Pick Apart a Pattern Twins	**Lesson** Assessment Activity Page	**URG** SG
Lesson 3—Name Patterns Names and Grids	**Lesson** Assessment Activity Page	**URG** SG
Lesson 4—Pattern Block Symmetry Tree	**Lesson** Assessment Activity Page	**URG** SG

Assessment Component	Component Description	Location
Unit 8—Subtracting to Solve Problems		
Observational Assessment Record **Individual Assessment Record Sheet**	**Assessment Record** **Assessment Record**	**URG** **TIG**
Lesson 2—Our Own Stories DPP Item D—Share and Share Alike	**Assessment Lesson** Assessment DPP Item	**URG** URG
Unit 9—Grouping by Tens		
Observational Assessment Record **Individual Assessment Record Sheet**	**Assessment Record** **Assessment Record**	**URG** **TIG**
Lesson 2—More or Less Than 100? DPP Item D—How Many in the Bag?	**Lesson** Assessment DPP Item	**URG** URG
Lesson 3—Spin for Beans DPP Item F—Groups of 10 and Leftovers	**Game** Assessment DPP Item	**URG** URG
Lesson 5—The *100 Chart* Target Numbers	**Lesson** Assessment Activity Page	**URG** URG
Lesson 7—Numbers in the News Journal Prompt	**Lesson** Assessment Prompt	**URG** URG
Lesson 8—Full of Beans DPP Item S—Naming Numbers Maria and José's Graph	**Lab** Assessment DPP Item Assessment Activity Page	**URG** URG SG
Unit 10—Measurement: Area		
Observational Assessment Record **Individual Assessment Record Sheet**	**Assessment Record** **Assessment Record**	**URG** **TIG**
Lesson 2—Goldilocks and the Three Rectangles Journal Prompt	**Lesson** Assessment Prompt	**URG** URG
Lesson 3—How Much Area? Tiles 3	**Lesson** Assessment Activity Page	**URG** SG
Lesson 5—Unit Designs Which Two?	**Lesson** Assessment Activity Pages	**URG** SG
Unit 11—Looking at 100		
Observational Assessment Record **Individual Assessment Record Sheet**	**Assessment Record** **Assessment Record**	**URG** **TIG**
Lesson 4—Arrow Dynamics DPP Item L—Addition Facts 3 Follow the Arrows	**Game** Assessment DPP Item Assessment Activity Page	**URG** URG SG
Lesson 5—How Long Is 100? DPP Item N—Addition Facts 4	**Lesson** Assessment DPP Item	**URG** URG
Lesson 6—Weather 2: Winter Skies Winter Weather	**Lab** Assessment Activity Page	**URG** SG
Lesson 8—Maria's Marble Mart Journal Prompt	**Assessment Lesson** Assessment Prompt	**URG, SG** URG

Assessment Component	Component Description	Location
Unit 12—Cubes and Volume		
Observational Assessment Record **Individual Assessment Record Sheet**	**Assessment Record** **Assessment Record**	**URG** **TIG**
Lesson 3—TIMS Towers DPP Item H—You Can Add DPP Item J—You Can Add Again TIMS Radio Tower Journal Prompt	**Lesson** Assessment DPP Item Assessment DPP Item Assessment Activity Page Assessment Prompt	**URG** URG URG SG URG
Lesson 4—A World of Cubic Animals Comparing Ruffy and the Snake	**Lesson** Assessment Activity Page	**URG** SG
Unit 13—Thinking About Addition and Subtraction		
Observational Assessment Record **Individual Assessment Record Sheet**	**Assessment Record** **Assessment Record**	**URG** **TIG**
Lesson 2—Seeing Doubles Doubles Problems	**Lesson** Assessment Activity Pages	**URG** SG
Lesson 4—Odd and Even Revisited Journal Prompt	**Lesson** Assessment Prompt	**URG** URG
Lesson 5—Problem Solving DPP Item P—Addition Facts 2 Recipe for Peanut Butter, Jelly, and Banana Sandwiches How Many?	**Lesson** Assessment DPP Item Assessment Activity Page Assessment Activity Page	**URG** URG SG SG
Unit 14—Exploring Multiplication and Division		
Observational Assessment Record **Individual Assessment Record Sheet**	**Assessment Record** **Assessment Record**	**URG** **TIG**
Lesson 2—Pets Room 222's Pets Graph More Pet Problems	**Lab** Assessment Activity Page Assessment Activity Page	**URG** SG SG
Lesson 3—Problems That Will Knock Your Socks Off! DPP Item J—Addition Facts 2 Basil the Basset Hound	**Lesson** Assessment DPP Item Assessment Activity Page	**URG** URG SG
Unit 15—Exploring 3-D Shapes		
Observational Assessment Record **Individual Assessment Record Sheet**	**Assessment Record** **Assessment Record**	**URG** **TIG**
Lesson 3—Looking at Prisms Find the Shapes 3-D Shapes	**Lesson** Assessment Activity Page Assessment Activity Pages	**URG** SG SG
Lesson 4—In the Shapes Kitchen DPP Item J—Addition Facts 2	**Lesson** Assessment DPP Item	**URG** URG

Assessment Component	Component Description	Location
Unit 16—Collecting and Organizing Data		
Observational Assessment Record **Individual Assessment Record Sheet**	**Assessment Record** **Assessment Record**	**URG** **TIG**
Lesson 3—Healthy Kids DPP Item I—Math Facts 2 David's and Cindy's Food	**Lab** Assessment DPP Item Assessment Activity Pages	**URG** URG SG
Unit 17—Moving Beyond 100		
Observational Assessment Record **Individual Assessment Record Sheet**	**Assessment Record** **Assessment Record**	**URG** **TIG**
Lesson 2—Our Class in Tensland Terry in Tensland	**Lesson** Assessment Activity Page	**URG** SG
Lesson 3—Counting One Hundred Seventy-two DPP Item H—Money Math Facts 1 Pumpkin Patch	**Lesson** Assessment DPP Item Assessment Activity Pages	**URG** URG SG
Lesson 4—Adding Hundreds DPP Item J—Money Math Facts 2	**Lesson** Assessment DPP Item	**URG** URG
Unit 18—Pieces, Parts, and Symmetry		
Observational Assessment Record **Individual Assessment Record Sheet**	**Assessment Record** **Assessment Record**	**URG** **TIG**
Lesson 1—Fold and Color Halves and Fourths	**Lesson** Assessment Activity Page	**URG** SG
Lesson 2—Equal and Unequal Halves and Fourths	**Lesson** Assessment Activity Page	**URG** URG
Lesson 3—Fraction Puzzles Which Shape Is It?	**Lesson** Assessment Activity Page	**URG** SG
Lesson 4—A Class Full of Fractions Drawing Fractions	**Lesson** Assessment Activity Pages	**URG** SG
Lesson 5—Fraction Finale DPP Item I—Tegan's Chores Pieces of Eighths	**Lesson** Assessment DPP Item Assessment Activity Page	**URG** URG SG
Unit 19—Measurement and Mapping		
Observational Assessment Record **Individual Assessment Record Sheet**	**Assessment Record** **Assessment Record**	**URG** **TIG**
Lesson 2—Mr. Origin Left/Right DPP Item E—Adding Bears Vanessa Finds Her Money	**Lab** Assessment DPP Item Assessment Activity Page	**URG** URG SG
Unit 20—Looking Back at First Grade		
Observational Assessment Record **Individual Assessment Record Sheet**	**Assessment Record** **Assessment Record**	**URG** **TIG**
Lesson 2—End-of-Year Test End-of-Year Test	**Assessment Lesson** Assessment Test Pages	**URG** URG

Individual Assessment Record Sheet

Name _____

Unit 1: Welcome to First Grade: A Baseline Assessment Unit	✔	Date and Comments:

A1. Can students count objects? _____ _____

A2. Can students identify the number of a small group of objects without counting? _____ _____

A3. Can students compare numbers using *more, less,* or *about the same?* _____ _____

A4. Can students count on from a given number? _____ _____

A5. _____ _____ _____

A6. _____ _____ _____

Unit 2: Exploring Shapes	✔	Date and Comments:

A1. Can students identify 2-dimensional shapes? _____ _____

A2. What 2-dimensional shapes can students draw? _____ _____

A3. Can students describe 2-dimensional shapes using their properties (number of sides, length of sides, and number of corners)? _____ _____

A4. Can students partition shapes in different ways? _____ _____

A5. Can students use a calendar to measure the passage of time? _____ _____

A6. _____ _____ _____

Unit 3: Pennies, Pockets, and Parts	✔	Date and Comments:

A1. Can students identify a number represented on a ten frame? _____ _____

A2. Can students translate between representations of numbers (ten frames, tallies, manipulatives, and symbols)? _____ _____

A3. Can students count on to solve addition problems? _____ _____

A4. Can students partition a number into two and three parts? _____ _____

A5. Can students solve addition problems and explain their reasoning? _____ _____

A6. Can students use manipulatives to solve problems? _____ _____

A7. _____ _____ _____

Name _____

Unit 4: Adding to Solve Problems   ✔   **Date and Comments:**

A1. Can students write number sentences for addition situations? _____ _____

A2. Can students partition numbers into two and three parts and represent them with number sentences? _____ _____

A3. Can students solve addition problems and explain their reasoning? _____ _____

A4. Can students count on to solve addition problems? _____ _____

A5. Can students create a story for an addition number sentence? _____ _____

A6. Can students identify odd and even numbers? _____ _____

A7. Can students use a calendar to measure the passage of time? _____ _____

A8. _____ _____ _____

Unit 5: Grouping and Counting   ✔   **Date and Comments:**

A1. Can students group and count objects by twos, fives, and tens? _____ _____

A2. Can students divide a collection of objects into groups of a given size and count the leftovers? _____ _____

A3. Can students collect and organize data in a table? _____ _____

A4. Can students identify the relationships among pennies, nickels, and dimes? _____ _____

A5. _____ _____ _____

Unit 6: Measurement: Length   ✔   **Date and Comments:**

A1. Can students predict and measure length using nonstandard units? _____ _____

A2. Do students report length using numbers and units? _____ _____

A3. Can students make and interpret bar graphs? _____ _____

A4. Can students use data to solve problems involving length? _____ _____

A5. Can students group and count objects by fives and ones? _____ _____

A6. _____ _____ _____

Unit 7: Patterns and Designs   ✔   **Date and Comments:**

A1. Can students identify and describe patterns? _____ _____

A2. Can students represent patterns using manipulatives, words, and symbols? _____ _____

A3. Can students extend patterns? _____ _____

A4. Can students use symmetry to solve problems? _____ _____

A5. _____ _____ _____

A6. _____ _____ _____

Name _____

Unit 8: Subtracting to Solve Problems   ✔   **Date and Comments:**

A1. Can students write number sentences for subtraction
     situations?   _____   _____

A2. Can students create a story for a subtraction number
     sentence?   _____   _____

A3. Can students represent subtraction situations using
     whole-part-part language?   _____   _____

A4. Can students count up or count back to solve subtraction
     problems?   _____   _____

A5. Can students solve subtraction problems and explain their
     reasoning?   _____   _____

A6. _____   _____   _____

Unit 9: Grouping by Tens   ✔   **Date and Comments:**

A1. Can students group and count objects by tens and ones?   _____   _____

A2. Can students count objects by twos, fives, and tens?   _____   _____

A3. Can students describe a number in relation to
     other numbers?   _____   _____

A4. Can students measure length using nonstandard
     units (links)?   _____   _____

A5. Can students make and interpret bar graphs?   _____   _____

A6. Can students use data to solve problems involving volume? _____   _____

A7. Can students represent two-digit numbers using
     manipulatives, ten frames, and *100 Charts*?   _____   _____

A8. _____   _____   _____

Unit 10: Measurement: Area   ✔   **Date and Comments:**

A1. Can students measure length in inches?   _____   _____

A2. Can students estimate area by covering shapes with
     nonstandard units?   _____   _____

A3. Can students measure area by covering shapes with
     square inches and half-square inches?   _____   _____

A4. Do students recognize that different shapes can have the
     same area?   _____   _____

A5. Do students report areas using numbers and units?   _____   _____

A6. Can students collect and organize data in a table?   _____   _____

A7. _____   _____   _____

Name _____

Unit 11: Looking at 100   ✔   **Date and Comments:**

A1. Can students group and count objects by fives and tens? _____ _____

A2. Can students solve addition and subtraction problems using multiples of five and ten? _____ _____

A3. Can students partition 100 into groups of tens? _____ _____

A4. Can students represent numbers using ten frames, *100 Charts,* manipulatives, and number sentences? _____ _____

A5. Can students find the value of a collection of nickels, dimes, and quarters? _____ _____

A6. Can students use a calendar to measure the passage of time? _____ _____

A7. Do students use math facts strategies to add (direct modeling, counting strategies, or reasoning from known facts)? _____ _____

A8. _____ _____ _____

Unit 12: Cubes and Volume   ✔   **Date and Comments:**

A1. Can students measure volume by counting cubic units? _____ _____

A2. Can students sort and classify cube models using volume, area of the base, and height? _____ _____

A3. Do students recognize that different shapes can have the same volume? _____ _____

A4. Can students construct a cube model from a drawing? _____ _____

A5. Do students report volumes using numbers and units? _____ _____

A6. Do students use math facts strategies to add (direct modeling, counting strategies, or reasoning from known facts)? _____ _____

A7. _____ _____ _____

Unit 13: Thinking About Addition and Subtraction   ✔   **Date and Comments:**

A1. Can students partition ten into two and three parts? _____ _____

A2. Can students solve addition and subtraction problems and explain their reasoning? _____ _____

A3. Can students identify even and odd numbers? _____ _____

A4. Can students use doubles to solve addition problems? _____ _____

A5. Can students make a ten to solve addition problems? _____ _____

A6. Do students use math facts strategies to add (direct modeling, counting strategies, or reasoning from known facts)? _____ _____

A7. _____ _____ _____

Name _____

Unit 14: Exploring Multiplication and Division   ✔   **Date and Comments:**

A1. Can students represent multiplication and division situations using manipulatives or drawings?   _____   _____

A2. Can students create stories for multiplication and division situations?   _____   _____

A3. Can students solve multiplication and division problems and explain their reasoning verbally?   _____   _____

A4. Can students make and interpret bar graphs?   _____   _____

A5. Can students use data to solve problems?   _____   _____

A6. Do students use math facts strategies to add (direct modeling, counting strategies, or reasoning from known facts)?   _____   _____

A7. _____   _____   _____

Unit 15: Exploring 3-D Shapes   ✔   **Date and Comments:**

A1. Can students identify 3-dimensional shapes (cylinders, spheres, and prisms)?   _____   _____

A2. Can students describe 3-dimensional shapes using their properties?   _____   _____

A3. Can students classify 3-dimensional objects using their properties and explain their reasoning?   _____   _____

A4. Do students use math facts strategies to add (direct modeling, counting strategies, or reasoning from known facts)?   _____   _____

A5. _____   _____   _____

Unit 16: Collecting and Organizing Data   ✔   **Date and Comments:**

A1. Can students collect and organize data in a table?   _____   _____

A2. Can students make and interpret bar graphs?   _____   _____

A3. Can students use data to solve problems?   _____   _____

A4. Do students use math fact strategies to add (direct modeling, counting strategies, or reasoning from known facts)?   _____   _____

A5. _____   _____   _____

Unit 17: Moving Beyond 100   ✔   **Date and Comments:**

A1. Can students represent numbers greater than 100 using manipulatives, symbols, and words?   _____   _____

A2. Can students group and count objects by hundreds, tens, and ones?   _____   _____

A3. Can students solve addition problems using multiples of ten and 100?   _____   _____

A4. Do students use math facts strategies to add (direct modeling, counting strategies, or reasoning from known facts)?   _____   _____

A5. _____   _____   _____

Name _____

Unit 18: Pieces, Parts, and Symmetry   ✔   Date and Comments:

A1.   Can students represent and describe fractions ($\frac{1}{2}$ and $\frac{1}{4}$) using manipulatives, drawings, and symbols?   _____   _____

A2.   Do students recognize that fractional parts of a whole (halves and fourths) must have equal areas?   _____   _____

A3.   Can students partition shapes into halves and fourths?   _____   _____

A4.   Can students partition sets of objects into fractional parts?   _____   _____

A5.   Can students use math facts strategies to add (direct modeling, counting strategies, or reasoning from known facts)?   _____   _____

A6.   _____   _____   _____

Unit 19: Measurement and Mapping   ✔   Date and Comments:

A1.   Can students describe the location of an object relative to Mr. Origin using direction (left or right) and distance?   _____   _____

A2.   Can students measure length using nonstandard units (links)?   _____   _____

A3.   Can students locate objects on a map using direction (left or right) and distance?   _____   _____

A4.   Do students use math facts strategies to add (direct modeling, counting strategies, or reasoning from known facts)?   _____   _____

A5.   _____   _____   _____

Unit 20: Looking Back at First Grade   ✔   Date and Comments:

A1.   Can students solve addition and subtraction problems and explain their reasoning?   _____   _____

A2.   Can students solve multiplication and division problems and explain their reasoning?   _____   _____

A3.   Can students identify and extend patterns?   _____   _____

A4.   Can students use data to solve problems?   _____   _____

A5.   Do students use math facts strategies to add (direct modeling, counting strategies, or reasoning from known facts)?   _____   _____

A6.   _____   _____   _____

Additional Comments:

TIMS Tutors

The TIMS Tutors section provides an in-depth exploration of the mathematical concepts and ideas behind *Math Trailblazers*.

Students use a graduated cylinder to find the volume of small objects.

Table of Contents

TIMS Tutors

Arithmetic

Introduction

The last 40 years have seen many changes in elementary school mathematics. For many people, "mathematics" is synonymous with "arithmetic." But today, while reasonable people can still debate the proper content of an elementary mathematics curriculum, nearly all parties can agree that a curriculum focused largely on rote arithmetic will not meet the needs of students who will graduate from high school in the twenty-first century.

Much more than just arithmetic is now expected—geometry, probability, statistics, measurement, graphing, even algebra. Technology is dramatically changing the world, making it hard to imagine what our children will need to know in 20 or 40 more years, but also ensuring that many of the skills that were critical 40 years ago are less essential. Despite recent advances in psychology, educational research, and curriculum design, we are far from resolving all the uncertainties of the elementary school mathematics curriculum. A few things, however, do seem to be clear:

- The school mathematics curriculum can and must be more rigorous.
- Arithmetic is only one piece, albeit an important one, of a broad mathematics curriculum.
- We need to do better at helping children connect marks on paper and the real world. Too many children and adults fail to use common sense when they are dealing with mathematical symbolism. Discussing mathematics and integrating subject matter may help students make these connections.
- As we correct for the overemphasis on skills in the traditional mathematics curriculum, we should avoid over-correcting. Problem solving requires both procedural skill and conceptual understanding. As William Brownell (1956) noted during a previous period of reform, "In objecting to the emphasis on drill prevalent not so long ago, we may have failed to point out that practice for proficiency in skills has its place too." In *Math Trailblazers,* we consistently seek a balance between conceptual understanding and procedural skill.

The National Council of Teachers of Mathematics' (NCTM) *Principles and Standards for School Mathematics* advocates learning mathematics with understanding. "In recent decades, psychological and educational research on the learning of complex subjects such as mathematics has solidly established the important role of conceptual understanding in the knowledge and activity of persons who are proficient. Being proficient in a complex domain such as mathematics entails the ability to use knowledge flexibly, applying what is learned in one setting appropriately in another. One of the most robust findings of research is that conceptual understanding is an important component of proficiency, along with factual knowledge and procedural facility" (Bransford, Brown, and Cocking, 1999). The alliance of factual knowledge, procedural proficiency, and conceptual understanding makes all three components usable in powerful ways. Students who memorize facts or procedures without understanding often are not sure when or how to use what they know, and such learning is often quite fragile (Bransford, Brown, and Cocking, 1999; NCTM, 2000).

Several arguments can be made in support of the NCTM position. One is that the computational proficiency of American students comes at too high a cost. The hundreds of hours devoted to arithmetic computation in elementary school leave too little time for other important topics. The traditional rote approach to computation undermines higher-level thinking: children learn that mathematics is blindly following rules, not thinking.

Another argument for shifting away from the traditional arithmetic curriculum is that technology has altered the role of paper-and-pencil calculation. As noted in the NCTM *Principles and Standards,* ". . . most of the arithmetic and algebraic procedures long viewed as the heart of the school mathematics curriculum can now be performed with handheld calculators. Thus, more attention can now be given to understanding the number concepts and the modeling procedures used in solving problems." (NCTM, 2000) More practical topics—probability and statistics, geometry, measurement, mental computation and estimation—deserve more attention.

A final and most important argument in favor of the changes recommended by the NCTM is that new approaches to instruction in arithmetic are more effective in helping students learn both appropriate calculation skills and how to apply those skills in solving problems. These new approaches build on students' own knowledge and intuitive methods and engage their common sense. This more meaningful approach helps students to be efficient and flexible in their computation and can reduce, though not eliminate, the amount of practice required. Thus, a greater emphasis on conceptual understanding can lead to better procedural skills and problem-solving abilities (Brown & Burton, 1978; Skemp, 1978; Hiebert, 1984; Van Lehn, 1986; Carpenter, 1986; Baroody and Ginsburg, 1986; Good, Mulryan, and McCaslin, 1992; Hiebert, 1999; National Research Council; 2001).

A final and most important argument in favor of the changes recommended by the NCTM is that new approaches to instruction in arithmetic are more effective in helping students learn both appropriate calculation skills and how to apply those skills in solving problems.

Numeration and Place Value

Numeration in kindergarten emphasizes developing oral counting skills, making one-to-one correspondence between objects and numbers, developing the concept of cardinality, discovering patterns in our number system, and writing numbers. Students in Grade 1 continue to develop these skills and concepts. They take part in activities that help them become familiar with the structure of the number system.

In kindergarten and Grade 1, students practice their counting skills. They learn to count past 100 by ones, twos, fives, and tens. They count forward and backward from any given number. They group objects for counting.

Students use counting to solve addition and subtraction problems. They learn to write numbers up to and beyond 100. Beginning in kindergarten, a ten frame is frequently used as a visual organizer. (See Figure 1.) The *100 Chart* is introduced and used for a variety of purposes, including solving problems and studying patterns. Students partition, or break apart, numbers in several ways ($25 = 20 + 5$, $25 = 10 + 10 + 5$, and so on). These activities help children develop number sense that allows them to use numbers flexibly.

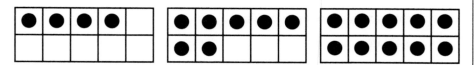

Figure 1: *Sample ten frame*

While formal study of place value is thus not a focus in kindergarten or Grade 1, the multiple grouping and counting experiences described above provide children with a foundation for building an intuitive sense for the meaning of place value.

Work with counting continues in Grade 2, especially skip counting and counting backwards. Place value is explored in the context of counting and grouping by tens. Children continue to count and group everyday objects such as buttons or peanuts. They use connecting cubes to represent these objects and often group the cubes by tens. Later, base-ten pieces represent these same objects, thus linking the base-ten representations with quantities of actual objects.

Numbers well into the hundreds are explored. Counting is still used for problem solving, but more elaborate procedures may be employed. For example, a student may solve $885 - 255$ by counting up, first by hundreds (355, 455, 555, 655, 755, 855) and then by tens (865, 875, 885), yielding 630 as the answer.

More elaborate partitions of numbers are investigated in Grade 2. Particularly important are partitions in which every part is a single digit times 1, 10, 100, or 1000: $359 = 300 + 50 + 9$ and so on. Attention is also given to partitioning numbers in more than one way:

$$359 = 300 + 50 + 9$$
$$= 200 + 150 + 9$$
$$= 100 + 250 + 9$$

This work with multiple partitioning is closely related to multidigit addition and subtraction. One way to think about addition and subtraction—indeed, one way to think about much of elementary mathematics—is as procedures for renaming numbers in more convenient forms. For example, $563 + 13$ is a number that we usually rename as 576. $875 \div 25$ is another number, renamable as 35 when it suits our purposes.

In Grade 3, more formal study of place value takes place. Students work in varied contexts that involve numbers through the thousands. For example, students draw an outline of a coat and determine how many square centimeters of material are required to make the coat. The use of contexts such as that example encourages students to associate quantities of actual objects with representations of the quantities using base-ten pieces and with the numerals that represent them. Most of this work is closely connected with investigations of addition and subtraction of multidigit numbers. Indeed, a good reason for studying computational algorithms is that they provide a context for learning about place value.

In Grade 4, large numbers up to the millions are studied and used in various contexts. Continued efforts are made to connect the numbers with actual quantities. For example, the class creates its own base-ten pieces for large numbers—pieces we call super skinnies (10,000), super flats (100,000), and megabits (1,000,000). (See Figure 2.)

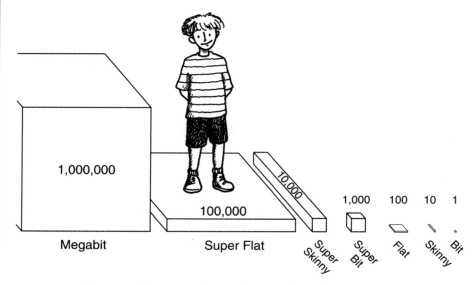

Figure 2: *Base-ten pieces for small and large numbers*

Once the basics of the base-ten place value system for whole numbers have been reviewed and established, the system is extended to include decimals beginning in third grade. In Grade 4, the ten-for-one trading rules and other aspects of our number system are extended to the right of the decimal point for the first time.

In Grade 5, the number system is extended to even larger numbers. The story of Archimedes' attempt to calculate the number of grains of sand that would fill the observed universe introduces students to numbers far beyond what we encounter in everyday life. With the use of scientific calculators in Grade 5, scientific notation for large numbers is needed and is introduced.

Basic Number Facts

In developing the math facts program, we sought a careful balance between strategies and drill. This approach is based on a large body of research and advocated by the NCTM *Principles and Standards for School Mathematics.* The research indicates that the methods used in the *Math Trailblazers* math facts program lead to more effective learning and better retention of the math facts and also helps develop essential math skills.

The *Math Trailblazers* program for teaching the math facts is characterized by these elements:

- *Early emphasis on problem solving.* Students first approach the basic facts as problems to be solved rather than as facts to be memorized. Students invent their own strategies to solve these problems or learn appropriate strategies from others through class discussion. Students' natural strategies, especially counting strategies, are explicitly encouraged. In this way, students learn that math is more than memorizing facts and rules that "you either get or you don't."

- *De-emphasis of rote work.* Fluency with the math facts is an important component of any student's mathematical learning. Research has shown that an overemphasis on memorization and the frequent administration of timed tests are counterproductive. (National Research Council, 2001). We encourage the use of strategies to find facts, so students become confident they can find answers to fact problems that they do not immediately recall.

- *Gradual and systematic introduction of facts.* Students study the facts in small groups that can be solved using similar strategies. Students first work on simple strategies for easy facts and then progress to more sophisticated strategies and harder facts. By the end of the process, they gain fluency with all the required facts.

- *Ongoing practice.* Work on the math facts is distributed throughout the curriculum, especially in the Daily Practice and Problems, Home Practice, and games. This practice for fluency, however, takes place only after students have a conceptual understanding of the operations and have achieved proficiency with strategies for solving basic fact problems. Delaying practice in this way means that less practice is required to achieve fluency.

- *Appropriate assessment.* Teachers assess students' knowledge of the facts through observations as they work on activities, labs, and games as well as through the appropriate use of written tests and quizzes. Beginning in first grade, periodic, short quizzes in the Daily Practice and Problems naturally follow the study of small groups of facts organized around specific strategies. As self-assessment in Grades 2–5, each student records his or her progress on *Facts I Know* charts and determines which facts he or she needs to study. Inventory tests of all facts for each operation are used sparingly in Grades 2–5 (no more than twice per year) to assess students' progress with fact fluency. The goal of the math facts assessment program is to determine the degree to which students can find answers to fact problems quickly and accurately and whether they can retain this skill over time.

- *Multiyear approach.* In Grades 1 and 2, *Math Trailblazers* emphasizes strategies that lead to fluency with the addition and subtraction facts. In Grade 3, students gain fluency with the multiplication facts while reviewing the addition and subtraction facts. In Grade 4, students achieve fluency with the division facts and verify fluency with the multiplication facts. In Grade 5, the multiplication and division facts are systematically reviewed and assessed. This is outlined in Table 1.
- *Facts are not gatekeepers.* Students are not prevented from learning more complex mathematics because they do not perform well on fact tests. Use of strategies, calculators, and other math tools (e.g., manipulatives, hundreds charts, printed multiplication tables) allows students to continue to work on interesting problems and important mathematical concepts while they are still learning the facts.

The *Math Trailblazers* approach to the math facts is discussed more fully in the TIMS Tutor: *Math Facts* located in this section of the *Teacher Implementation Guide.*

Concepts of Whole-Number Operations

Concepts and Skills

Over the past 150 years, numerous attempts have been made to teach mathematics meaningfully rather than by rote. Unfortunately, as Lauren Resnick points out in *Syntax and Semantics in Learning to Subtract,* ". . . the conceptual teaching methods of the past were inadequate to the extent that they taught concepts instead of procedures and left it entirely to students to discover how computational procedures could be derived from the basic structure of the number and numeration system." (1987, p. 136)

Many educators have long recognized, however, that there is no real conflict between skills and concepts. (Whitehead, 1929; Dewey, 1938; Brownell, 1956; May, 1995; National Research Council, 2001) New conceptual understandings are built on existing skills and concepts; these new understandings in turn support the further development of skills and concepts. Thomas Carpenter describes the relationship in this way: ". . . It is an iterative process. Procedures are taught that can be supported by existing conceptual knowledge, and the conceptual knowledge base is extended to provide a basis for developing more advanced concepts. At every point during instruction, procedures are taught that can be connected to existing conceptual knowledge." (1986, p. 130) This integration of concepts and skills underlies our work with arithmetic in *Math Trailblazers.*

Subtraction in Grades K to 5

To illustrate how concepts and skills are balanced in *Math Trailblazers,* we outline in this section how one operation—subtraction—is developed with whole numbers in Grades K–4. Though the details may differ for the other operations, the same general approach described here with subtraction applies to all four arithmetic operations.

In kindergarten and Grade 1 of *Math Trailblazers,* students solve a variety of problems involving subtraction of numbers up to and even beyond 100. These problems are based on hands-on classroom activities and realistic situations from children's experiences. Different subtraction problem types are represented, including take-away, comparison, part-whole, and missing addend problems. (See the TIMS Tutor: *Word Problems* for a discussion of these and other problem types.)

Students in even the earliest grades are thus faced with problems for which they have no ready solution methods, problems that in the traditional view are beyond their ability. They do, however, have much prior knowledge that is relevant. They have their common sense—their conceptual knowledge of the problem situations. They know, for example, that if Grace begins with 50 marbles and loses 17, then she must end with fewer than 50 marbles. Young students also have considerable procedural knowledge, including various kinds of counting skills: ordinary counting, counting on, counting back, and skip counting by twos, fives, and tens. Students have tools they can use in solving the problems. These include connecting cubes, links, *100 Charts,* ten frames, other manipulatives, paper and pencil, calculators, and number lines. Researchers note that initial work with any operation should involve classroom activities that use real-world or imaginary contexts, manipulatives, or drawings that highlight the attributes of the numbers and operations. (Carpenter et al., 1998; Fuson and Briars, 1990, Hiebert et al., 1997) This research further emphasizes the importance of long-term use of the manipulatives and of linking the manipulatives with written notation.

On one side, then, are hard problems involving many types of subtraction. On the other side are the kindergartners and first-graders, with their common sense, their counting skills, and tools. Traditionally, word problems and other applications involving subtraction (and other operations) were introduced only after students had extensive practice with a subtraction algorithm. Research on students' learning of addition and subtraction (Carpenter et al., 1998) strongly suggests that it is more effective to have students solve and pose word problems and other context-based problems (such as problems in the laboratory investigations in *Math Trailblazers*) before they learn formal, paper-and-pencil procedures for subtraction. As the students apply their resources to solve the problems, they build their conceptual and procedural understanding of subtraction. They devise methods for solving the problems; they make records of their work; they discuss their methods with their teacher and classmates. Their new knowledge about subtraction is closely linked to their prior knowledge, especially their out-of-school knowledge and their counting skills. (Baroody and Ginsburg, 1986)

The teacher comments on students' methods and may show students how to use conventional symbols to describe their work, but the teacher makes no attempt to standardize students' methods. Any method that yields a correct result is acceptable—as long as it makes sense. The goal is to encourage students to apply their prior knowledge to problems they encounter and to let students know that their intuitive methods are valid.

As the students apply their resources to solve the problems, they build their conceptual and procedural understanding of subtraction. They devise methods for solving the problems; they make records of their work; they discuss their methods with their teacher and classmates.

First grade focuses on various strategies that can be used to solve single-digit subtraction problems. For example, a problem like 9 − 3 can be solved by counting back 3 from 9: 8, 7, 6. This work aims not at achieving fluency with the subtraction facts, but rather at building conceptual understanding of subtraction and procedural skill with various strategies. (See the TIMS Tutor: *Math Facts.*)

In the beginning of Grade 2, the problem-solving approach to subtraction continues. Problems with numbers up to 1000 are introduced, but again no standard solution method is taught at this point. Students devise their own ways to solve the problems, drawing on their prior knowledge of the problem situations and the number system, and share their thinking with the class.

The strategies approach to the subtraction facts continues in Grade 2. As students' fluency with the addition facts and simple subtraction facts increases, more sophisticated strategies become feasible. For example, a child may solve 14 − 6 by reasoning that "to take away 6 from 14, I first can take away 4, which leaves 10. Then I take away 2 more, which equals 8." These new strategies, sometimes called derived fact strategies or reasoning from known facts, illustrate how new knowledge builds on prior skills.

Later in Grade 2, systematic work begins on paper-and-pencil methods for subtracting two-digit numbers. Students solve two-digit subtraction problems using their own methods and record their solutions on paper. The class examines and discusses the various procedures that students devise. At this time, if no student introduces a standard subtraction algorithm, then the teacher does so, explaining that it is a subtraction method that many people use. The standard method is examined and discussed, just as the invented methods were. Students who do not have an effective method of their own are urged to adopt the standard method.

Problems that require borrowing are included from the beginning. Though this differs markedly from traditional approaches, we view it as important in developing a sound conception of subtraction algorithms. Giving children only multidigit problems that do not involve borrowing encourages the development of a rote and faulty algorithm that may not carry over into problems that require borrowing.

By the beginning of Grade 3, students have a strong conceptual understanding of subtraction and significant experience devising procedures to solve subtraction problems with numbers up to 1000. They also have some experience with standard and invented paper-and-pencil algorithms for solving two-digit subtraction problems. In Grade 3, this prior knowledge is extended in a systematic examination of paper-and-pencil methods for multidigit subtraction.

This work begins with a series of multidigit subtraction problems that students solve in various ways. Many of these problems are set in a whimsical context, the TIMS Candy Company, a business that uses base-ten pieces to keep track of its production and sales. Other problems are based on student-collected data, such as a reading survey.

Giving children only multidigit problems that do not involve borrowing encourages the development of a rote and faulty algorithm that may not carry over into problems that require borrowing.

As in Grade 2, the class discusses and compares the several methods students use to solve these problems. Again, any method that yields correct results is acceptable, but now a greater emphasis is given to methods that are efficient and compact. This work leads to a close examination of one particular subtraction algorithm. (See Figure 3.) Students solve several problems with base-ten pieces and with this standard algorithm, making connections between actions with the manipulatives and steps in the algorithm. After a thorough analysis of the algorithm, including a comparison of the standard algorithm and other methods, students are given opportunities to practice the algorithm or other methods of their choice.

$$
\begin{array}{r}
\overset{3}{}\overset{16}{} \\
7\ \cancel{4}\ \cancel{0} \\
-\ 4\ 3\ 9 \\
\hline
3\ 0\ 7
\end{array}
$$

Figure 3: *A standard subtraction algorithm*

Practice in paper-and-pencil methods for multidigit subtraction is distributed throughout Grades 3 and 4. Students encounter sets of problems that encourage them to look at each problem and choose an efficient method for solving the problem. For many of these problems, a standard algorithm will be the most efficient choice. For other problems, students can use mental math or counting strategies. For example, students should identify the problem $4001 - 3998$ as a problem that can easily be solved by counting up three from 3998 to 4001.

By the beginning of Grade 4, basic work with whole number subtraction is complete. Students have a firm conceptual understanding of subtraction and they have a diverse repertoire of methods that they can use to solve subtraction problems. Work in Grade 4 is designed to maintain and extend these skills and understandings. Fluency with the subtraction facts is verified and remediation is provided for students who need it. In the laboratory experiments and other work, students solve a wide variety of subtraction problems using methods of their own choosing. The Daily Practice and Problems and Home Practice include distributed practice in paper-and-pencil subtraction so that those skills do not deteriorate.

In Grade 5 students continue to use subtraction in activities and labs. As in earlier grades, they are encouraged to decide when it is appropriate to use paper and pencil, calculators, or estimation. A review of subtraction modeled with base-ten pieces is included for students who have not used *Math Trailblazers* in previous grades. Distributed practice is provided in the Daily Practice and Problems and the Home Practice. Fluency with the subtraction facts is assessed in the first unit, and remediation is provided in the Addition and Subtraction Math Facts Review section in the *Facts Resource Guide.*

Whole-Number Computation in *Math Trailblazers*

Many other topics in *Math Trailblazers*—addition, multiplication, division, fractions, and decimals—are treated in ways similar to that sketched for subtraction above. In all these areas, we seek a balance between conceptual understanding and procedural skill. For all operations, standard methods for solving problems are not introduced until students have developed good conceptual and procedural understandings—the too-early introduction of such procedures may short-circuit students' common sense, encouraging mechanical and uncritical behavior. (Brownell & Chazall, 1935; Resnick & Omanson, 1987; Rathmell & Huinker, 1989; Perry, 1991; Hiebert, 1999)

Grade	Addition	Subtraction	Multiplication	Division
K	• concepts of the operation	• concepts of the operation	• concepts of the operation	• concepts of the operation
1	• concepts of the operation • informal methods	• concepts of the operation • informal methods	• concepts of the operation	• concepts of the operation
2	• concepts of the operation • invented algorithms • standard methods for small numbers	• concepts of the operation • invented algorithms • standard methods for small numbers	• concepts of the operation • informal methods	• concepts of the operation • informal methods
3	• invented algorithms • standard methods for larger numbers	• invented algorithms • standard methods for larger numbers	• concepts of the operation • invented algorithms • standard methods for small numbers	• concepts of the operation
4	• review, practice, apply, and extend	• review, practice, apply, and extend	• invented algorithms • standard methods for larger numbers	• invented algorithms • standard methods for larger numbers
5	• review, practice, apply, and extend	• review, practice, apply, and extend	• review, practice, apply, and extend	• standard methods for larger numbers

Table 1: *Whole-number operations scope and sequence*

Even after standard methods have been analyzed and practiced, students are still encouraged to solve problems in more than one way. Flexible thinking and mathematical power are our goals, not rote fluency with a handful of standard algorithms.

Varieties of Computation

There is much more to computation than the standard paper-and-pencil algorithms for adding, subtracting, multiplying, and dividing. These algorithms are good for obtaining exact answers with simple technology, but, depending on the resources available and the result desired, there are many other kinds of computation. For example, if you are in a supermarket check-out line with several items and you find only $10 in your wallet, then a quick judgment whether you have sufficient funds is desirable. In this case, a rough mental estimate of the total cost of your purchases is what you want. If you are planning an addition to your house, however, different computational demands must be met. The situation is more complex than the supermarket checkout, and the penalty for making a mistake is more severe, so greater care must be taken. You will want more resources—paper and pencil, a calculator, time to work, perhaps a computer spreadsheet—and you will probably want rather precise estimates for the cost of various alternative designs for the addition.

A well-rounded mathematics program should prepare students to compute accurately, flexibly, and appropriately in all situations. Figure 4 shows a classification of computational situations using two criteria, the result desired and the resources available. Although you may want to move some of the questions to other cells or insert your own examples, these six categories of computation indicate the scope required of a complete mathematics curriculum (Coburn, 1989).

Even after standard methods have been analyzed and practiced, students are still encouraged to solve problems in more than one way.

Resources Available

	Paper & Pencil	Machine	Mental
Exact	How many students are in the three third grades at my school?	How much will my monthly payment be on my car loan?	How much baking soda do I need if I am tripling a recipe that calls for 2 teaspoons?
Approximate	What is my share of the national debt?	House remodeling: Which design(s) can I afford?	Supermarket checkout: Do I have enough money for these items?

Result Desired

Figure 4: *Six varieties of computation*

The TIMS Philosophy: Meaning, Invention, Efficiency, Power

The treatment of computation in *Math Trailblazers* proceeds in several stages. The grade levels for the stages vary with the operation—ideas of division, for example, develop long after addition—but the general pattern is similar for all the operations. Roughly speaking, the stages are

- developing meaning for the operation,
- inventing procedures for solving problems, and
- becoming more efficient at carrying out procedures, all leading to
- developing mathematical power.

Developing mathematical power with an operation means that students understand *when* to apply the operation and *how* to use varied computational methods to solve problems, even complex or nonroutine problems.

The goal of the first stage is to help students understand the meaning of the operation. Most of the work involves solving problems, writing or telling "stories" that involve operations, and sharing solution strategies. These methods typically involve a great deal of mental arithmetic and creative thinking. The use of manipulatives, pictures, and counting is encouraged at this stage. Discussing these informal methods helps develop students' understanding of the operation.

In the next stage, the focus shifts from developing the concept of the operation to devising and analyzing procedures to carry out the operation. At this stage, students "invent" methods for carrying out the operation, explaining, discussing, and comparing their procedures. Multiple solution strategies—mental, paper and pencil, manipulative, calculator—are encouraged, and parallels between various methods are explored. There is evidence that this "invented algorithms" approach enhances students' number and operation sense and problem-solving abilities (Madell, 1985; Sawada, 1985; Kamii, Lewis & Jones, 1991; Burns, 1992; Kamii, Lewis & Livingston, 1993; Porter & Carroll, 1995; Carroll & Porter, 1997). Inventing their own methods helps make mathematics meaningful for children by connecting school mathematics to their own ways of thinking. The expectation that mathematics should make sense is reinforced.

In the third stage, a standard algorithm for the operation is introduced. This algorithm is not presented as the one, true, and official way to solve problems, but rather as yet another procedure to be examined. The algorithms used in *Math Trailblazers* are not all identical to the traditional ones taught in school. The addition and subtraction algorithms are only a little different, but the procedures for multiplication and division are considerably different. (See Figures 5 and 6.)

$$
\begin{array}{r}
5\ 8 \\
\times\ 3\ 6 \\
\hline
4\ 8 \\
3\ 0\ 0 \\
2\ 4\ 0 \\
1\ 5\ 0\ 0 \\
\hline
2\ 0\ 8\ 8
\end{array}
$$

Figure 5: *All-partials multiplication*

```
           1  9 R 31
      3 2)6  3  9
         -3  2  0    10
          3  1  9
         -1  6  0     5
          1  5  9
         -   9  6     3
             6  3
         -   3  2     1
             3  1 | 19
```

Figure 6: *A division algorithm*

These alternative algorithms for multiplication and division have been chosen for several reasons. First, they are easier to learn than the traditional methods. Second, they are more transparent, revealing what is actually happening. Third, they provide practice in multiplying by numbers ending in zero, an important skill for estimation. Finally, even though they are less efficient than the traditional algorithms, they are good enough for most purposes—any problem that is awkward to solve by these methods should probably be done by machine anyway.

Students who have no reliable method of their own are urged to adopt the standard algorithm. However, even after a standard algorithm for an operation has been introduced and analyzed, alternative methods are still accepted, even encouraged, for students who are comfortable with them. In particular, the standard algorithm is very inefficient with some problems. For example, students using *Math Trailblazers* should be able to compute 40×30 mentally to get 1200. Using the standard algorithm here would be inefficient. Or consider $16,000 - 5$. Using a standard algorithm to solve this problem is tedious and often results in errors.

In the last stage, students achieve mathematical power through the mastery of procedures that solve entire classes of problems: efficient and reliable computational algorithms. This procedural fluency, moreover, is based on solid conceptual understandings so that it can be applied flexibly to solve problems. These procedures become part of the students' base of prior knowledge—on which they can build more advanced conceptual and procedural understandings.

Fractions and Decimals

The approach to fractions and decimals in *Math Trailblazers* parallels that for whole numbers. At first, the focus is on developing concepts and meanings for fractions and decimals. Next comes a period in which students invent procedures for solving problems, connecting school mathematics to their own informal methods and common sense. Finally, formal procedures are investigated, not as substitutes for common sense, but as more efficient methods for achieving desired results.

Fraction Meanings

One of the problems with fractions is that they are so useful. Consider some of the meanings for $\frac{1}{2}$:

- half of a cookie (a part-whole fraction)
- $1 \div 2$ (division)
- one cup water to two cups flour (a ratio, sometimes written 1:2)
- $\frac{1}{2}$ mile (a measurement)
- the point midway between 0 and 1 (the name of a point on a number line)
- the square root of $\frac{1}{4}$ (a pure number)
- the chance a fair coin will land heads up (a probability)

Because the same notation can mean so many different things, children and even adults sometimes become confused and may manipulate fraction symbols haphazardly, often with unfortunate results. A better approach develops sound meanings for the symbols before focusing on how to manipulate them (Mack, 1990).

Part-Whole Fractions

Early fraction work focuses on part-whole fractions. Many fractions in daily life are part-whole fractions, so even young children are familiar with terms like one-half and three-fourths in part-whole contexts. Also, many key ideas about fractions are well illustrated in part-whole situations.

There are two concepts that are fundamental in understanding part-whole fractions: knowing what the whole is and understanding what a part is in relation to the whole. For example, to understand the statement, "Last night I ate three-fourths of a carton of ice cream," requires knowing what the whole is. Just how big a carton of ice cream was it? One must also understand that the parts into which the whole is divided must be equal—they should have the same area or mass or number, etc. A way to make this clear to children is to talk about "fair shares."

The whole in a part-whole fraction can be either a single thing (e.g., a pizza) or a collection (e.g., a class of students). When the whole is a collection, then counting is generally used to make fair shares; when the unit is a single thing, the fairness of the shares depends on some measurable quantity. Half of one pizza is different from half of three pizzas. Often, area is the variable that must be equally allocated among the parts; such a situation may be called an area model for fractions.

Symbols and Referents

A key idea in the *Math Trailblazers* approach to fractions is that fractions should be represented in several ways and that students should be able to make connections between those representations. The fraction two-thirds, for example, can be expressed in words, symbols, pictures, or real objects (Figure 7).

Because the same notation can mean so many different things, children and even adults sometimes become confused and may manipulate fraction symbols haphazardly, often with unfortunate results. A better approach develops sound meanings for the symbols before focusing on how to manipulate them.

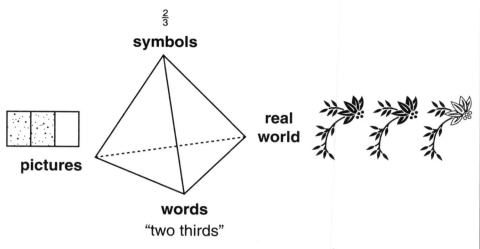

$\frac{2}{3}$

symbols

pictures

real world

words

"two thirds"

Figure 7: *Representations of $\frac{2}{3}$*

The ability to move freely between these several representations is an essential component of the mathematical understanding of fractions (Lesh, Post & Behr, 1987). Especially important are connections between fraction symbols and the real-world situations to which those fractions refer. Given symbols for a fraction, can the student draw an illustrative picture or tell a story? Can students explain the relationship between a group of five girls and two boys and the fraction $\frac{5}{7}$?

Math Trailblazers makes extensive use of manipulatives in teaching fractions in all grades. Pictures, pattern blocks, geoboards, paper folding, and number lines are among many tools used to promote students' conceptual understanding of fractions. When paper-and-pencil procedures for adding, subtracting, multiplying, and dividing fractions are introduced in Grades 4 and 5, they are always linked closely with other representations of fractions, such as manipulatives or pictures.

Decimals

Decimals are treated in two ways in *Math Trailblazers:* first, as another way to write certain common fractions—those with denominators that are powers of ten—and second, as an extension of the whole number place value system. Similar to the coverage of other topics in *Math Trailblazers,* considerable attention is placed upon developing a solid conceptual foundation about decimals before formal, paper-and-pencil operations are introduced. Students with strong conceptual understandings of decimals learn procedures more easily and can apply those procedures to problem situations more effectively

> *The ability to move freely between these several representations is an essential component of the mathematical understanding of fractions. Especially important are connections between fraction symbols and the real-world situations to which these fractions refer.*

(Ball, 1993; Behr & Post, 1992; Hiebert, Wearne & Taber, 1991; Lesh, Post & Behr, 1987). Connections between fractions (common fractions) and decimals (decimal fractions) are stressed throughout.

As with work with whole numbers and fractions, work with decimal fractions includes extensive work with manipulatives. Often these models are used to make strong connections between fractions, decimals, and percents. Figures 8 and 9 show two examples of tools used in Grade 5 lessons on decimals. These representations create visual images of the decimal fractions and link those images with students' previous work with fractions and percent.

Figure 8: *Interlocking centiwheel disks model $\frac{1}{4}$, 0.25, and 25%.*

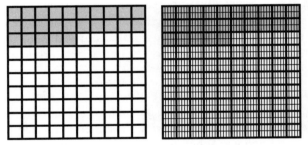

Figure 9: $\frac{25}{100} = 0.25$ and $\frac{250}{1000} = 0.250$

A Developmental Approach

Kindergarten fraction work emphasizes the idea that the fractional parts of a whole must be the same size. Work with symbols is not emphasized.

Fraction work in Grades 1–3 of *Math Trailblazers* focuses primarily on establishing links between symbols and referents for part-whole fractions. Children learn to make connections between marks on paper and the real world. Concepts of the unit—identifying the unit, knowing how the size of the unit affects the value of the fraction, appreciating the importance of fair shares—are also explored (Figure 10). Decimals are treated primarily as an alternative notation for certain fractions, and some attention is given to the interpretation of decimals that appear on calculators. Real-world situations, especially fair sharing, and area models predominate.

If  is $\frac{1}{3}$,

then what is one whole?

Figure 10: *A concept-of-unit exercise*

In Grade 3, students continue to develop concepts of the unit, but they begin to use more varied models. Children explore the relative size of fractions, especially with respect to the benchmark numbers 0, $\frac{1}{2}$, and 1. They also study equivalent fractions in Grade 3. Fractions are represented with a variety of manipulatives—paper folding, pattern blocks, geoboards. Collections of objects are divided to represent fractions.

Decimals are investigated more extensively in Grade 3, again being treated as a kind of fraction. Decimals in metric length measurement and on number lines are investigated. Base-ten pieces are used to create concrete and visual representations of decimal fractions. Translating between common fractions and decimals is again stressed.

In Grade 4, work on operations with fractions and decimals begins, but standard procedures are not taught. As discussed above, modeling concepts and procedures with manipulatives is intended to establish a basis for more algorithmic work in Grade 5. In fourth grade, students solve problems involving addition and subtraction, largely with the aid of manipulatives and other fraction models.

Operations with fractions and decimals include more than simply the four arithmetic operations. Putting fractions and decimals in order by size, renaming the same number in several equivalent forms, and estimating sums, differences, and so on, are all operations that can be carried out with fractions and decimals. Again, manipulatives, such as pattern blocks and base-ten pieces, are used to develop conceptual understanding and provide a concrete representation of the symbols.

In Grade 5, paper-and-pencil procedures for addition, subtraction, and multiplication of fractions and decimals are explored, including use of common denominators and reducing. Repeating decimals are introduced. Students also use calculators to rename fractions as decimals for comparing and ordering common fractions.

Many contexts are used to reinforce students' understanding of fraction and decimal concepts. For example, in a Grade 5 laboratory investigation, *Comparing Lives of Animals and Soap Bubbles,* students collect data about the "life spans" of soap bubbles. As they analyze the data, they convert the data first to a fractional quantity, then to the equivalent decimal fraction. Making these connections between mathematical concepts and with real-world situations helps students make sense of the mathematics they are learning.

Conclusion

Our goal in developing *Math Trailblazers* has been to create a balanced program that will promote the coordinated development of both procedural skill and conceptual understanding. Students will connect school mathematics with intuitive knowledge and informal procedures. They will use a variety of techniques and manipulatives for modeling the mathematical ideas. In doing so, students will not only develop skills and concepts, but will be able to use those skills and concepts to solve problems.

References

Ball, D. "Halves, Pieces, and Twoths: Constructing and Using Representational Contexts in Teaching Fractions." In T.P. Carpenter, E. Fennema, and T.A. Romberg (Eds.), *Rational Numbers: An Integration of Research.* pp. 157–195. Lawrence Erlbaum Associates, Hillsdale, NJ, 1993.

Baroody, A.J., and H.P. Ginsburg. "The Relationship between Initial Meaning and Mechanical Knowledge of Arithmetic." In J. Hiebert (ed.), *Conceptual and Procedural Knowledge: The Case of Mathematics.* Lawrence Erlbaum Associates, Hillsdale, NJ, 1986.

Behr, M.J., and T.R. Post. "Teaching Rational Number and Decimal Concepts." In *Teaching Mathematics in Grades K–8: Research Based Methods.* Allyn and Bacon, Boston, MA, 1992.

Bransford, J.D., A.L. Brown, and R.R. Cocking, eds. *How People Learn: Brain, Mind, Experience, and School.* National Academy Press, Washington, DC, 1999.

Brown, J.S., and R.R. Burton. "Diagnostic Models for Procedural Bugs in Basic Mathematical Skills." *Cognitive Science,* 2, pp. 155–192, 1978.

Brownell, W.A., and C.B. Chazal. "The Effects of Premature Drill in Third-Grade Arithmetic." *Journal of Educational Research,* 29 (1), 1935.

Brownell, W.A. "Meaning and Skill—Maintaining the Balance." *Arithmetic Teacher,* 34 (8), pp. 18–25, (Original work published in 1956), 1987.

Carpenter, T.P. "Conceptual Knowledge as a Foundation for Procedural Knowledge." In J. Hiebert (ed.), *Conceptual and Procedural Knowledge: The Case of Mathematics.* Lawrence Erlbaum Associates, Hillsdale, NJ, 1986.

Carpenter, T.P., E. Fennema, and M.L. Franke. *Cognitively Guided Instruction: Building the Primary Mathematics Curriculum on Children's Informal Mathematical Knowledge.* A paper presented at the annual meeting of the American Educational Research Association, San Francisco, CA, April 1992.

Carpenter, T.P., M.L. Franke, V.R. Jacobs, E. Fennema, and S.B. Empson. "A Longitudinal Study of Invention and Understanding in Children's Multidigit Addition and Subtraction." *Journal for Research in Mathematics Education,* 29, pp. 3–20, 1998.

Carroll, W., and D. Porter. "Invented Algorithms: Helping Students to Develop and Use Meaningful Mathematical Procedures." *Teaching Children Mathematics,* pp. 370–374, March 1997.

Coburn, T.G. "The Role of Computation in the Changing Mathematics Curriculum." In P.R. Trafton (ed.), *New Directions for Elementary School Mathematics.* National Council of Teachers of Mathematics, Reston, VA, 1989.

Dewey, J. *Experience and Education.* Macmillan, New York, 1938.

Finn, C. E., Jr. "What if those Math Standards Are Wrong?" *Education Week,* 20 January 1993.

Fuson, K.C., and D.J. Briars. "Using a Base-Ten Blocks Learning/Teaching Approach for First- and Second-Grade Place-Value and Multidigit Addition and Subtraction." *Journal for Research in Mathematics Education,* 21, pp. 180–206, 1990.

Good, T. L., C. Mulryan, and M. McCaslin. "Grouping for Instruction in Mathematics: A Call for Programmatic Research on Small-Group Processes." In D.A. Grouws (ed.), *Handbook of Research on Mathematics Teaching and Learning: A Project of the National Council of Teachers of Mathematics* (Chapter 9). Macmillan, New York, 1992.

Hiebert, J. "Children's Mathematical Learning: The Struggle to Link Form and Understanding." *Elementary School Journal,* 84 (5), pp. 497–513, 1984.

Hiebert, J. "A Theory of Developing Competence with Written Mathematical Symbols." *Educational Studies in Mathematics,* 19, pp. 333–355, 1988.

Hiebert, J. "Relationships between Research and the NCTM Standards." *Journal for Research in Mathematics Education,* 30 (1), pp. 3–19, 1999.

Hiebert, J. and D. Wearne. "Procedures over Concepts: The Acquisition of Decimal Number Knowledge." In J. Hiebert (Ed.), *Conceptual and Procedural Knowledge: The Case of Mathematics.* Lawrence Erlbaum Associates, Hillsdale, NJ, 1986.

Hiebert, J., D. Wearne, and S. Taber. "Fourth Graders' Gradual Construction of Decimal Fractions during Instruction Using Different Physical Representations." *Elementary School Journal,* 91 (4), pp. 321–341, 1991.

Hiebert, J., T. Carpenter, E. Fennema, K.C. Fuson, D. Wearne, H. Murray, A. Oliver, and H. Piet. *Making Sense: Teaching and Learning Mathematics with Understanding.* Heinemann, Portsmouth, NH, 1997.

Kamii, C., B.A. Lewis, and S. Jones. "Reform in Primary Mathematics Education: A Constructivist View." *Educational Horizons,* 70 (1), pp. 19–26, 1991.

Kamii, C., B.A. Lewis, and S.J. Livingston, "Primary Arithmetic: Children Inventing Their Own Procedures." *Arithmetic Teacher,* 41 (4), pp. 200–203, 1993.

Lesh, R., T. Post, and M. Behr. "Representations and Translations among Representations in Mathematics Learning and Problem Solving." C. Janvier, ed., *Problems of Representation in the Teaching and Learning of Mathematics.* Lawrence Erlbaum Associates, Hillsdale, NJ, 1987.

McKnight, C.C., F.J Crosswhite, J.A. Dossey, E. Kifer, J.O. Swafford, K.J. Travers, and T.J. Cooney. *The Underachieving Curriculum: Assessing U.S. School Mathematics from an International Perspective.* Stipes, Champaign, IL, 1987.

Mack, N.K. "Learning Fractions with Understanding: Building on Informal Knowledge." *Journal for Research in Mathematics Education,* 21 (1), pp. 16–32, 1990.

Madell, R. "Children's Natural Processes." *Arithmetic Teacher,* 32 (7), pp. 20–22, 1985.

Mathews, J. "Psst, Kid, Wanna Buy a Used Math Book? They're Old-Fashioned and a Bit Tedious, but John Saxon's Books are Hot Stuff in the Education Underground." *Newsweek,* 121, pp. 62–63, 1993.

May, L. "Reflections on Teaching Mathematics Today." *Illinois Mathematics Teacher,* 46 (3), pp. 5–8, 1995.

Principles and Standards for School Mathematics. National Council of Teachers of Mathematics, Reston, VA, 2000.

National Research Council. *Adding It Up: Helping Children Learn Mathematics.* National Academy Press, Washington, DC, 2001.

Perry, M. "Learning and Transfer: Instructional Conditions and Conceptual Change." *Cognitive Development,* 6, pp. 449–468, 1991.

Porter, D., and W. Carroll. "Invented Algorithms: Some Examples from Primary Classrooms." *Illinois Mathematics Teacher,* pp. 6–12, April 1995.

Press, M. "Drill and Practice Add Up." *San Jose Mercury News,* 27 February 1995.

Rathmell, E.C., and D.M. Huinker. "Using 'Part-Whole' Language to Help Children Represent and Solve Word Problems." In P.R. Trafton (ed.), *New Directions for Elementary School Mathematics,* pp. 99–110. National Council of Teachers of Mathematics, Reston, VA, 1989.

Resnick, L.B. "Syntax and Semantics in Learning to Subtract." In R. Glaser (ed.), *Advances in Instructional Psychology* (Vol. 3). Lawrence Erlbaum Associates, Hillsdale, NJ, 1987.

Resnick, L.B., and S.F. Omanson. "Learning to Understand Arithmetic." In *Advances in Instructional Psychology* (Vol. 3). Lawrence Erlbaum Associates, Hillsdale, NJ, 1987.

Resnick, L.B., S. Lesgold, and V. Bill. *From Protoquantities to Number Sense.* A paper prepared for the Psychology of Mathematics Education Conference, Oaxtapec, Mexico, 1990.

Sawada, D. "Mathematical Symbols: Insight through Invention." *Arithmetic Teacher,* 32 (6), pp. 20–22, 1985.

Shuard, H. "CAN: Calculator Use in the Primary Grades in England and Wales." In J. T. Fey (ed.), Calculators in Mathematics Education, Reston, VA, 1992.

Skemp, R.R. "Relational Understanding and Instrumental Understanding." *Arithmetic Teacher,* 26 (3), pp. 9–15, 1978.

Swart, W.L. "Some Findings on Conceptual Development of Computational Skills." *Arithmetic Teacher* 32 (5), pp. 36–38, 1985.

Usiskin, Z. "Paper-and-Pencil Skills in a Calculator/Computer Age." *UCSMP Newsletter,* 16, pp. 7–14, 1994.

Van Lehn, K. "Arithmetic Procedures Are Induced from Examples." In J. Hiebert (ed.), *Conceptual and Procedural Knowledge: The Case of Mathematics.* Lawrence Erlbaum Associates, Hillsdale, NJ, 1986.

Whitehead, A.N. "The Rhythmic Claims of Freedom and Discipline." In *The Aims of Education and Other Essays.* Macmillan, New York, 1929.

Averages

Introduction

"Average" is one of those words that mean different things to different people. Baseball players talk about their batting averages. A teacher might confide to a colleague that "Jim is just an average student." At the university, students always want to know what the class average is on an exam. Sometimes you hear the statement that the temperature will be about average for this time of year. When someone asks you how you feel, you may reply, "Just average." In everyday usage, "average" is a word that can be anything from a synonym for "typical," "normal," or "usual," to a number derived according to some formula or rule. This TIMS Tutor lays out some of the different numerical meanings of "average" and explains some of the importance of averages in mathematics and science.

The Mean—A Wage Dispute

In his wonderful little book, *How to Lie with Statistics,* Darrell Huff gives the example of a factory owner and his workers who are arguing over wages. There are 25 workers including the owner. The owner pays himself $45,000. The others make $15,000, $10,000, $10,000, $5700, $5000, $5000, $5000, $3700, $3700, $3700, $3700, $3000, $2000, $2000, $2000, $2000, $2000, $2000, $2000, $2000, $2000, $2000, $2000, and $2000. The owner says the average wage is $5700 but the workers claim the average wage is only $3000. Even though prices have gone way up since Huff wrote his book 50 years ago, the discrepancy is clear: there is a big disagreement over what people are being paid, let alone what they should be paid.

So, what's going on here? Who's right, the owner or the workers? Both! The factory owner's average is the (arithmetic) mean; the workers' average is the median. There are other averages too, such as the **mode** (the number or value that occurs most often in a data set). However, in *Math Trailblazers,* we primarily use the mean and/or the median when finding average values. These two averages will be the focus of our discussion in this tutor.

Usually when people use the term "average," they are referring to the **mean.** This is the familiar add-up-all-the-numbers-and-divide average you learned in school. The mean has many useful properties that make it beloved by schoolteachers, statisticians, and scientists alike. Consider finding the average height of all the children in a class. Data for 23 children from a third-grade class is shown in Figure 1.

The mean height of these 23 children is

$$<H> = \frac{\text{sum of heights}}{\text{number of children}}$$

$$= \frac{(133 + 136 + ... + 129 + 134) \text{ cm}}{23}$$

$$= \frac{3064 \text{ cm}}{23}$$

$$= 133.2 \text{ cm}$$

Name	H Height (in cm)
Karina	133
Federico	136
Ramon	135
Kiela	127
Aesha	126
Bravlia	128
Zuzia	133
Anthony	139
Iorta	146
Cordeli	135
Mary	137
Gennice	124

Name	H Height (in cm)
Curtis	139
Brian C	125
David	135
Anna	141
Brian M	131
Adriana	137
Boberto	134
Lucas	131
Gennifer	129
Amber	129
Nathan	134

Figure 1: *Data from a third-grade class*

For scientists, the mean is often the first number they calculate when looking at a data sample.

Although no child may have this mean height, it gives everyone a point of departure for making comparisons. For scientists, the mean is often the first number they calculate when looking at a data sample.

There is another way to interpret the mean height of this class. This may seem strange, but consider the following situation. Suppose you walk into another class and find 23 students all to be exactly the same height. The mean is clearly that height. If the mean height of this new class and the mean in our class are the same, then the sum of the heights of the children is the same. That is, imagine making two stacks of the children, one for our class and one for the new class. Stack the children one on top of another. Then the two stacks would be the same height. So, if two class means are the same and the number of children in each class is the same, then the sums of the heights in the classes are the same, even if the individual heights that make the sums are vastly different.

Statisticians like the mean because it is often the "best" estimate of an unknown quantity like a length, an area, or a mass. For example, suppose you are trying to measure the mass of a large steel sphere. You have an unbiased balance, and you know that you need to take repeated readings to get an accurate measurement. So, suppose you make eleven measurements and find the sphere's mass to be 129 gm, 133 gm, 132 gm, 130 gm, 128 gm, 129 gm, 130 gm, 131 gm, 130 gm, 129 gm, and 131 gm. Then

$$\frac{(129 + 133 + \ldots + 130 + 129 + 131) \text{ gm}}{11}$$

$$= \frac{1432 \text{ gm}}{11}$$

$$= 130 \text{ gm}$$

This is the best estimate of the "true" mass of the sphere, given these measurements. (Notice that the quotient above is actually equal to 130.18181818 . . . gm. However, since our original measurements are to the nearest gram, it makes sense to give the average only to the nearest gram.)

Similar situations arise all the time in everyday life. Our factory owner is using the mean. He computes the average wage by adding up everyone's salary (including his big fat one) and dividing by the total number of workers:

$$\frac{\$142,500}{25} = \$5,700$$

As one final example, suppose Marty scores 85, 84, 86, 87, 84, 87, 85, 85, 83, and 85 on 10 rounds of golf and Ellen scores 83, 83, 95, 97, 81, 83, 82, 84, 96, and 84. Then Marty's mean score is

$$= \frac{85 + 84 + 86 + 87 + 84 + 87 + 85 + 85 + 83 + 85}{10}$$

$$= 85.1$$

and Ellen's mean score is

$$= \frac{83 + 83 + 95 + 97 + 81 + 83 + 82 + 84 + 96 + 84}{10}$$

$$= 86.8$$

So, it would appear that Marty is a better golfer than Ellen. (In golf, a lower score is a better score.)

But anyone who plays golf and bets will notice that if Marty and Ellen played 10 rounds against each other and scored as above, then Marty would win three times and Ellen would win seven times. And the workers in the factory still feel underpaid, despite that nice mean salary. So, to get some perspective on what is happening here, let's look at another average, the median.

The Median

The **median** is the number in the middle. That is, roughly speaking, the median splits a set of numbers into two halves: one half is less than the median; the other half is more than the median. So, to find the median, rank the numbers from smallest to largest and take the one in the middle.

Suppose, for example, you want to find the median selling price of homes in your town. You go to the town office and find that 15 homes have been sold in the last six months. The selling prices, in rank order, were $67,000, $78,000, $82,000, $85,000, $92,000, $97,000, $112,000, $118,000, $125,000, $132,000, $133,000, $139,000, $167,000, $175,000, and $186,000. The median price was $118,000: seven houses sold for less than $118,000 and seven houses sold for more than $118,000.

When there is an even number of values, then the median can be a little harder to find. Say only 14 of the homes above to have been sold. Suppose that the highest-priced house, the one costing $186,000, went unsold. What is the new median? Counting up seven from the $67,000 house, we end up at the $112,000. Counting down seven from the $175,000 house, we end up at $118,000. The 7th house from the bottom is not the 7th house from the top! What to do? Easy. Go halfway between the two numbers closest to the middle. Halfway between $112,000 and $118,000. That comes out to be $115,000. So the median price of the 14 homes that sold would be $115,000.

Going back to our factory workers' example, there were 25 employees including the owner. The thirteenth salary (from the top or from the bottom) is $3000: there are 12 employees who make less than $3000, and 12 who make more than $3000. So, the median salary is $3000.

Sometimes the median is a better average to use than the mean. One common situation where the median may be preferred is when there are extreme values. In such cases, the mean can give a distorted picture of the "average" because the extreme values tend to "pull" the mean away from where the typical values are. Statisticians say the median is more "robust" than the mean; that is, the median is less affected by extreme values than the mean. This is why the factory workers prefer the median: it gives a truer picture of what a typical worker earns than the mean, which is pulled up by the owner's big salary.

The median offers some insight into our golfing example, too. Marty's (ranked) golf scores were 83, 84, 84, 85, 85, 85, 85, 86, 87, and 87. The two numbers in the middle are 85 and 85, so Marty's median score is 85. Ellen's scores were 81, 82, 83, 83, 83, 84, 84, 95, 96, and 97. The two numbers in the middle are 83 and 84, so Ellen's median score is 83.5. Thus, using medians, Ellen is a slightly better golfer, on average. Every few rounds she has a high score, but her typical score is better than Marty's typical score, so she usually wins.

Obviously, the median has several advantages with respect to the mean: it is less affected by extreme values; it requires little computation; it can be a better indicator of what is typical. You will want to be flexible, sometimes using the mean, sometimes using the median.

*The **median** is the number in the middle. That is, roughly speaking, the median splits a set of numbers into two halves: one half is less than the median; the other half is more than the median.*

One common situation where the median may be preferred is when there are extreme values. In such cases, the mean can give a distorted picture of the "average" because the extreme values tend to "pull" the mean away from where the typical values are.

The Mode

The **mode** of a set of data is the number that appears most often. For example, in Ellen's golf scores above, the number that appears most often is 83. In our first example from *How to Lie with Statistics,* we considered the example of a factory owner and his 25 workers who are arguing over wages. The owner pays himself $45,000. The others make $15,000, $10,000, $10,000, $5700, $5000, $5000, $5000, $3700, $3700, $3700, $3700, $3000, $2000, $2000, $2000, $2000, $2000, $2000, $2000, $2000, $2000, $2000, $2000, and $2000. To present their best argument, the workers could have argued that the modal salary was $2,000, since 12 workers had that salary.

Making Sense of Measures of Central Tendency

The median, mean, and mode are all "measures of central tendency." They each tell us something about the way the information in the data set clusters. Of course, when we replace a whole data set with one number, we lose a lot of information. Depending on the nature of the data set, the mean, median, or mode may or may not provide us with useful information. These measures of central tendency are most useful when the data clusters around some value.

Averaging in the *Math Trailblazers* Classroom

So how are averages used in *Math Trailblazers?* Suppose you have second-grade students who collected the data shown in Figure 2 for the TIMS Laboratory Investigation, *Rolling Along in Centimeters.* There are three experimental values for each car, and the students need some measure of the middle that fairly represents their data for each car. In this case, the median is a perfectly respectable average.

T Type of Car	D Distance (in $\frac{cm}{unit}$)			
	Trial 1	Trial 2	Trial 3	Median
Red	83	93	86	
Blue	44	44	43	
Orange	39	53	46	
Black	194	199	189	

Figure 2: *Data from* Rolling Along in Centimeters

One way to get a median from data like this is illustrated in Figure 3. The students cross out the largest and smallest numbers in each row and use the one that is left as their average value. Finding the median value of the three trials does not require young children to do any arithmetic and conceptually illustrates quite nicely the idea of an average representing a middle value.

T Type of Car	D Distance (in cm/unit)			
	Trial 1	Trial 2	Trial 3	Median
Red	~~85~~	~~95~~	(86)	86
Blue	~~44~~	(44)	~~45~~	44
Orange	~~39~~	~~55~~	(46)	46
Black	(194)	~~189~~	~~188~~	194

Figure 3: *Finding the median*

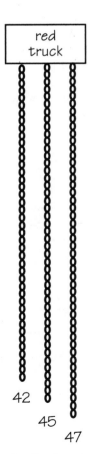

red truck

42
45
47

Figure 4: *Finding the median in* Rolling Along with Links

Finding the median can be illustrated more concretely by using links (or string, adding machine tape, etc.) to create "lengths" that match the actual distance that the cars roll each time. At the end of three rolls, the students will have three lengths of links that each represent the distance a car rolled in a trial.

This is illustrated in Figure 4. The median value can then be found by comparing the lengths and discarding the shortest and longest; the remaining length represents the median. A process somewhat like this is used in the first-grade experiment *Rolling Along with Links*.

In fourth grade, students begin finding the mean as well as the median. Again the concepts are introduced concretely. For example, students find the median value for several towers of cubes by lining them up from shortest to tallest and selecting the tower in the middle. This is illustrated in Figures 5a and 5b. Figure 6 illustrates the case when there is an even number of trials. To find the median here, students have to find the halfway point between the two middle towers.

Figures 5a and 5b: *Finding the median with cubes*

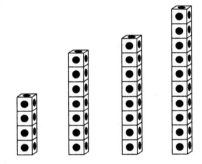

Figure 6: *The median number of cubes is $7\frac{1}{2}$.*

Cubes are also used when introducing the mean. For example, suppose students begin with the same five towers that are illustrated in Figure 5a. They first estimate the mean by figuring out a way to "even out the towers," as illustrated in Figure 7. The mean, to the nearest whole cube, is ten cubes. In this manner, the concept of the mean as a representative measure is stressed rather than focusing purely on the arithmetic procedure. Students then learn to calculate the mean using numerical values.

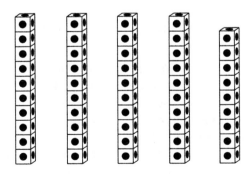

Figure 7: *Estimating the mean by "evening out" towers of cubes*

Students will often use calculators to calculate the mean of a data set. For example, the mean distance for the red car in Figure 2, when found by calculator, is:

$$\frac{(83 + 93 + 86) \text{ cm}}{3} = 87.333333 \text{ cm}$$

This is an example of too much of a good thing. In this case, the calculator gives many more digits than are meaningful. The students have to determine an appropriate level of significance. Keep in mind that our goal is to get a reasonable number to use as an average. Here, the original measurements were made to the nearest cm, so it makes sense to also report the mean value also to the nearest cm.

Why Average?

Finding the average is a critical step in a *Math Trailblazers* experiment. It is an important step from raw data to understanding. Errors are inevitable when measurements are made, and averaging is one way to detect and control error. If a group of students makes the same measurement three times and gets 67 cm, 64 cm, and 84 cm, they should notice that the 84 cm is way off. They can detect their error and redo that measurement.

When we carry out a measurement, many factors prevent us from getting an exact answer. First, is the precision of our measuring tools. A meterstick can measure only to the nearest tenth of a centimeter. When we measure the area of an irregular figure by counting square centimeters, we have to estimate the area of the fraction pieces of square centimeters, etc. In addition, when we perform an experiment, we might get somewhat different measurements each time we perform the experiment. If we drop a ball from a height of 100 centimeters and try to measure how high it bounces, we will get different answers each time we drop the ball. This is due to the difficulty in controlling variables (can we be sure we dropped the ball exactly the same way each time?) and the difficulty in measuring how high a moving object bounces. Nevertheless, if students are careful and practice measuring, they should get answers that are reasonably close. Even when all the measurements are close, the average minimizes error. If the measurements are 67 cm, 64 cm, and 67 cm, then the mean, 66 cm, is a more accurate prediction of future measurements than any of the actual measurements.

Another function of averaging is to aggregate raw data. Unlike computers, people cannot handle too many numbers at once. If I tell you the income of every child in a school, then you will be overwhelmed by numbers. If I tell you the median income of children in the school, you know less but probably understand more. The situation in a typical *Math Trailblazers* experiment is similar. From 12 actual measurements in *Rolling Along in Centimeters,* we cut down to four medians that are then used to display the data in a graph.

References

Huff, Darrell. *How to Lie with Statistics.* W.W. Norton & Co., New York, 1954.

Johnson, Robert. *Elementary Statistics,* 3rd ed., Wadsworth, Inc., Belmont, CA, 1980.

Estimation, Accuracy, and Error

For many people, one of the most attractive aspects of mathematics is that it is exact. The story problems that we worked on in our youth were reassuring (or terrifying) in the certainty of their answers. If one potato weighs 2 pounds, then 100 potatoes weigh 200 pounds. The only problem is that the real world is not so exact. One potato does not weigh exactly 2 pounds and 100 potatoes probably do not weigh 200 pounds. In this tutor, we discuss ways we deal mathematically with situations where exactness is not called for (when we estimate) or impossible (when we measure within a certain degree of accuracy).

Virtually all mathematics educators agree that estimation should be an important part of any elementary curriculum. Unlike content areas such as number and operation and geometry, there is very little traditional curriculum on estimation as well as some disagreement about exactly what is meant by estimation. Some mathematicians and educators make a distinction between estimation and approximation, but there is no generally agreed definition of these terms. This tutor provides a general overview of the concept of estimation and discusses some of the more common strategies and applications. For a more exhaustive treatment of estimation, we recommend the NCTM yearbook (1986).

What Is Estimation?

According to *Webster's Ninth New Collegiate Dictionary,* **to estimate** means to judge tentatively or approximately the value, worth, or significance of something. Alternatively, it means to calculate approximately. **An estimate** is a general calculation of size, value, etc., especially an *approximate* computation of the probable cost of a piece of work. This leads one to ask for the definition of **approximate.** The dictionary states that approximate means located close together, or nearly correct or exact. Moreover, **an approximation** is an *estimate,* guess, or mathematical result that is close in value but not the same as a desired quantity.

Leaving aside the fact that these definitions appear to be circular (an estimate is an approximation and an approximation is an estimate), the dictionary does give us a general idea of what these words mean. As with most words, these words have several meanings and their exact meaning is determined by the particular context in which they are used. In particular, these words are used in a variety of ways in mathematics. You should first note that unlike most mathematical concepts, estimate and approximate do not have precise definitions. What does it mean for two numbers to be "near in position, close together?" Is 5 close to 10? Is 1250 close to 1300? Is 1000 close to 3000? It's hard to say. In spite of our inability to precisely define closeness, we shall see that the varied uses of estimation are an important ingredient in mathematical problem solving.

Pedagogical Aspects of Estimation

In her survey article, "Estimation and Number Sense," Judith Threadgill-Sowder (1992) points out that

> *Good estimators are flexible in their thinking, and they use a variety of strategies. They demonstrate a deep understanding of number and operations, and they continually draw upon that understanding. Poor estimators seem to be bound, with only slight variations, to one strategy—that of applying algorithms more suitable for finding an exact answer. Poor estimators have only a vague notion of the nature and purpose of estimation; they believe it to be inferior to exact calculation (Morgan, 1988) and equate it with guessing.*

It follows from this view of estimation that teaching estimation is a complex task. Rather than being a simple skill that follows a few basic rules, estimation requires a variety of strategies. Rather than being a separate subject, estimation is a habit of mind that is carried out in the course of many mathematical activities. Thus, there are few lessons in the *Math Trailblazers* curriculum that are devoted solely to estimation, while there are many lessons that offer opportunities for estimation. While estimation is not a simple skill, there are a number of simple skills, such as rounding and mental multiplication, that are extremely useful when doing estimation.

Students often have difficulty with estimation because they are uncomfortable about having more than one correct answer. They want to know "the right answer" and dislike being told "that's a good estimate." So it is the task of the teacher to keep reminding students of the purpose of estimation and that different strategies can result in different correct answers. The laboratory experiments in *Math Trailblazers* help students develop an appreciation of the approximate nature of measurement and the fact that some problems can have more than one solution.

To help organize our thoughts about estimation, we will break the uses of estimation in the elementary mathematics curriculum into four major categories:

1. Estimating the result of a calculation (in particular, addition, subtraction, multiplication, and division) to see if the answer is reasonable.
2. Measurement error, experimental error, and predictions.
3. Estimating the magnitude of a measurement; for example, the height of a building, the area of a wall, the volume of a jar, or the weight of a person.
4. Estimating how many; for example, the number of peanuts in a jar, the number of students in a school, the number of people at a concert.

Good estimators are flexible in their thinking, and they use a variety of strategies. They demonstrate a deep understanding of number and operations, and they continually draw upon that understanding.

It is the task of the teacher to keep reminding students of the purpose of estimation and that different strategies can result in different correct answers.

Estimating the Results of a Calculation

Two of the primary reasons for estimating the results of a calculation are:

1. To check that the exact answer is (possibly) correct. The estimation can be done either before or after the calculation. Getting an answer that is far from your estimate indicates that the calculation is incorrect. On the other hand, an estimate that is close to the calculation does not guarantee that it is correct.
2. As a substitute for the exact answer. In many situations an exact answer is not needed and may not even make sense.

We will discuss a few of the more common strategies that are used to estimate the results of a calculation. Undoubtedly, you and your students will find other good strategies.

Addition and Subtraction

For the purposes of estimation, the most important digits in a number are the ones to the left, i.e., the leading digits. When estimating a sum or difference, one strategy that can usually be carried out mentally is to look at the first one or two *place-value columns*. For example, here are some statistics on the New England states from a 1987 almanac:

	Population (1984)	Area (sq mi)
Maine	1,164,000	33,215
New Hampshire	998,000	9304
Vermont	535,000	9609
Massachusetts	5,822,000	8257
Rhode Island	968,000	1214
Connecticut	3,174,000	5009

When estimating a sum or difference, one strategy that can usually be carried out mentally is to look at the first one or two place-value columns.

If we wanted to estimate the total population of New Hampshire and Vermont using "front end estimation," we could look at the first column on the left. In this case, it is the hundred thousands column. Adding the 9 and the 5 we get 14, which tells us that the sum is approximately 14 hundred thousands; in other words, one million, four hundred thousand. In fact, the first two digits of the sum must be either 14 or 15 (depending on whether or not there is any carrying when we do the addition algorithm). You can have your estimate be 1,400,000 or you can look at the next digits to see if there is likely to be any carrying. In this case, the digits in the ten thousands column are 9 and 3, so there will be carrying. Thus, 1,500,000 is an even better estimate. Of course, the whole point of estimation is to get a quick, approximate answer. If you start looking at too many digits, you might as well find the exact answer.

A second quick method for this estimate is to think that the population of New Hampshire is approximately 1 million and that of Vermont is about $\frac{1}{2}$ million, so the total is about 1.5 million. Since the "exact" answer is 1,533,000, an estimate of 1.5 million is only off by about 2%. A more rule-bound approach that said, "round off the nearest million" would give us 1 million plus 1 million which is 2 million. This is not a very close estimate (it's about 30% off). In fact, there is no simple rule that gives a good estimate in all situations. A rule that often gives good results is "round each number to one significant digit and then add." (A whole number has one significant digit if all the digits after the first one are equal to zero.) That's what we did in this case, rounding 1,164,000 to 1,000,000 and 535,000 to 500,000.

The same strategies can be applied to estimate the results of subtraction calculations. For example, if we wanted to know how much larger the population of New Hampshire was than the population of Vermont, we could round each population to one significant digit, and subtract 500,000 from 1 million to get 500,000. Rounding to the nearest million definitely doesn't work in this problem, since both populations round to 1 million, and we would get the nonsensical estimate that there are no more people in New Hampshire than there are in Vermont! It should be noted that looking at the difference between two numbers is not always the best way of comparing them. If we wanted to compare the populations of New Hampshire and Vermont, it might be better to look at the ratio of their populations and say that New Hampshire has twice the population of Vermont.

The fact that the population figures are rounded off to the nearest thousand in the table is an acknowledgment that census figures themselves are estimates. In this case, there are two reasons that the data is not exact. Population data for the U.S. is based on census data. Since the population of the United States is so large and not everyone cooperates with the census takers, it is impossible to count everyone in the country. The population is also a moving target. Every day, tens of thousands of people are born or die. Finally, the figures for 1984 population are obtained by starting with the 1980 figures and extrapolating based on assumptions about the rate of population growth. Since many factors affecting population growth change, it is highly unlikely that predictions for population would be very accurate.

Rounding is also one effective strategy for mentally estimating the sum of a series of numbers. For example, to find the total population of New England from the individual state populations above, you might round the numbers in the population column to the nearest half million, namely 1, 1, $\frac{1}{2}$, 6, 1, and 3 million. Adding these mentally gives $12\frac{1}{2}$ million, which is pretty close to the actual total of 12,661,000 people. Try to estimate the total area of New England, mentally. The exact answer is 66,608 square miles.

Note that these are not the only strategies for estimating the sum or difference of several numbers. For example, if you wanted to purchase items that cost $3.79, $4.19, $2.23, and $6.49, you might want to add the dollars mentally $(3 + 4 + 2 + 6 = 15)$ and then round the cents to the nearest quarter, i.e., 79 cents is about 75 cents, etc. This way, you see you need about $1.75 more (or 7 quarters). So, the total is pretty close to $16.75.

Multiplication: Rounding and Mental Math

The most basic technique for estimating the result of a multiplication problem is to replace (if necessary) the original numbers in the problem with other numbers which permit us to do the calculation mentally, or rapidly with paper and pencil. For example, if you wanted to know the number of minutes in a day, you would have to multiply 24 hours by 60 minutes per hour. Finding 24×60 is too hard for most people to do mentally, but 25×60 can be done by many fourth- and fifth-graders. Now, 25×60 is the same as $25 \times 6 \times 10$, and 25×6 is 150. (Think of 6 quarters being a dollar-fifty. Most of us are pretty

The most basic technique for estimating the result of a multiplication problem is to replace (if necessary) the original numbers in the problem with other numbers which permit us to do the calculation mentally . . .

good at calculating with multiples of 5, 10, and 25, since we have had a lot of practice doing mental arithmetic with money.) Finally, if 6×25 is 150, then $6 \times 25 \times 10$ is 1500. This is a pretty good estimate for 24×60. Note that we repeatedly used the commutative property of multiplication—i.e., the order in which we multiply several numbers does not affect the result. An alternative estimate for 24×60 can be obtained by rounding off 24 to 20 and multiplying 20 by 60 to get approximately 1200 minutes in a day. This estimate is not as close, but it may suffice for many purposes.

A basic skill that is fundamental to being able to estimate in multiplication and division situations is being able to multiply and divide by ten and powers of ten (100, 1000, etc.). Thus, as early as third grade in *Math Trailblazers*, we observe the pattern that multiplying a whole number by 10 amounts to adding the digit 0 to the right of the number, i.e., $10 \times 57 = 570$, $10 \times 365 = 3650$, etc. Similarly, multiplying by 100 amounts to adding two 0 digits to the right, etc. When we start to work with decimals, we observe that multiplying a decimal by 10 amounts to moving the decimal point to the right one place. For example, $10 \times 45.76 = 457.6$. This is really the same pattern we see with whole numbers, since $10 \times 57.0 = 570$, etc.

Another fundamental process in the examples above was finding convenient numbers that were close to the numbers we started with. Here, convenient means numbers with which we can calculate mentally. For example, we rounded 24 to 25, since multiples of 25 are easy to figure out. Often, the convenient numbers are what we call round numbers. For example, when we used our second strategy to estimate 24×60, we rounded 24 to the nearest 10, which gave us 20. All this means is that 20 is the multiple of 10 that is nearest to 24 (since 24 is between 20 and 30 but is closer to 20).

Rounding

Traditionally, students have been taught a lot of rules about rounding, but they often are not able to apply them successfully since they did not understand the purpose of rounding, nor did they have a good understanding of place value. When we are doing mental estimation, we frequently want to round a number in the hundreds to the nearest hundred, a number in the thousands to the nearest thousand, etc. For example, 457 rounded to the nearest hundred is 500, while 447 rounded to the nearest hundred is 400. That's because both numbers are between 400 and 500, and 457 is closer to 500 and 447 is closer to 400. Now 450 is exactly halfway between 400 and 500, so it is not obvious how to round 450 to the nearest hundred. Strictly speaking, it does not make sense to talk about **the** nearest hundred in this situation, since 450 is 50 away from 400 and 50 away from 500. In the context of estimation, this means that you can use either 400 or 500 as an estimate for 450. For example, if we wanted to estimate 450×321, we could say $400 \times 300 = 120,000$ is an estimate for the answer. This estimate is certainly smaller than the actual answer, since 400 is less than 450 and 300 is less than 321. On the other hand, $500 \times 300 = 150,000$, which is probably bigger than the actual answer. So the answer is probably between 120,000 and 150,000 (it's actually 144,450).

It used to be taught that numbers halfway between should always be rounded up, but there is really no reason for doing so. In general, the choice is determined by the context in which the rounding takes place and the reason you are rounding. For example, if you want to make sure you have enough money to purchase the items in your grocery cart, it is probably best to make a conservative estimate and round items that cost $12.50 up to $13. Banks have another solution to rounding off halves. They round 4.5 cents to 4 cents if they're calculating money they owe you and round 4.5 cents to 5 cents if they're calculating money you owe them.

Division

It may be surprising to realize that the operation we need to estimate most frequently in daily life is division. This results from the fact that many of the decisions we have to make are based on proportional reasoning. How many miles per gallon is your car getting? Which brand of cereal is the least expensive? (One costs $2.65 for 14 oz and the other costs $3.55 for 24 oz.) All these can be easily answered with a calculator, but we often have to make decisions when we do not have a calculator handy. More significantly, students often perform the wrong calculations on the calculator. Letting students first solve their problem using convenient numbers allows them to focus on the essential parts of the problem, without being distracted by a lot of digits and a lot of mechanical manipulations. Once they have found a reasonable solution strategy, they can return to solve the original messy problem.

The easiest problems to deal with are ones that can be turned into a problem that requires dividing by a power of 10. Dividing by 10 is the inverse of multiplying by 10. Thus, we can divide by 10 mentally by moving the decimal point one place to the left. For example, $\frac{279}{10} = 27.9$, $\frac{456.2}{10} = 45.62$, etc. Similarly, we can divide by 100 by moving the decimal point two places to the left. When dividing a whole number by 10, we get a fairly good estimate for the result by just dropping the ones digit. For example, $\frac{279}{10}$ is approximately 27. Note that the estimate we get in this way is always smaller than the exact answer.

One method for estimating the results of a division problem is to replace each number by a suitable nearby convenient number and then carry out the first step in the division algorithm. The rounding is chosen in such a way as to make the division easy. For example, suppose we wanted to estimate the population density of Maine in 1987. The data in Table 1 tells us that the density is 1,164,000 people ÷ 33,215 square miles. We can round off the divisor to 30,000 square miles and round off the dividend to 1,000,000 people. To estimate 1,000,000 ÷ 30,000, we can ask what times 30,000 gives 1,000,000. Multiplying 30,000 by 10 gives 300,000 and multiplying this by 3.3 gets us near 1,000,000. So, our estimate is about 33. Another method would be to replace the divisor and dividend with nearby convenient numbers. For example, 33,215 is near 30,000 and 1,164,000 is close to 1,200,000. We chose this pair of numbers because 12 is divisible by 3. So, our estimate now amounts to 1,200,000 people ÷ 30,000 square miles. Again, we see we need to multiply 30,000 by 40 to get 1,200,000. So, 40 people per square mile is a reasonable estimate for the population density of Maine. Putting the numbers back into the context of the problem is important for checking any result.

It may be surprising to realize that the operation we need to estimate most frequently in daily life is division. This results from the fact that many of the decisions we have to make are based on proportional reasoning.

A powerful technique for estimating the result of a division problem is to consider the division as a ratio. For example, suppose you had traveled 637 miles and used 22 gallons of gas. To find miles per gallon, divide 22 into 637. Write the ratio 637 miles/22 gallons. Rounding 637 to 600 and 22 to 20 we get

$$\frac{637 \text{ mi}}{22 \text{ gal}} \approx \frac{600 \text{ mi}}{20 \text{ gal}}$$

Note that we have used the symbol $\approx$ instead of the equal sign. This symbol means "approximately equal." Now, we can simplify the ratio $\frac{600}{20}$ by dividing both numerator and denominator by 10. So

$$\frac{600 \text{ mi}}{20 \text{ gal}} = \frac{60 \text{ mi}}{2 \text{ gal}}$$

and dividing numerator and denominator by 2 gives us

$$\frac{60 \text{ mi}}{2 \text{ gal}} = \frac{30 \text{ mi}}{1 \text{ gal}}$$

Putting this all together, we get 637 mi/22 gal $\approx$ 30 mi/1 gal; in other words, our estimate is 30 miles per gallon.

A note on canceling. Many people learned to simplify ratios by "canceling" the same thing in the numerator and the denominator. You might be tempted to say that when we wrote 600 mi/20 gal $\approx$ 60 mi/2 gal, we "canceled a 0" in the numerator and the denominator. Unfortunately, this can lead to some bad habits. For example, can you cancel the fives in $\frac{875}{25}$ to get $\frac{87}{2}$, or cancel the fives in $(X + 5)/(Y + 5)$ to get X/Y? You had better not, since this amounts to subtracting the 5 from the numerator and denominator and this results in a fraction that is not equal to the one we started with.

$$\frac{875}{25} \neq \frac{87}{2}$$

$$\frac{X + 5}{Y + 5} \neq \frac{X}{Y}$$

So, canceling does not always result in an equal ratio. For this reason, we always say exactly what we are doing, dividing numerator and denominator by the same number, rather than using the word "cancel."

Here are some examples of estimation in a division context:

Example 1: Estimate the quotient $\frac{80,000}{30}$. This is approximately $\frac{8000}{3}$, which is between $\frac{7500}{3}$ and $\frac{9000}{3}$, i.e., between 2500 and 3000. Note that if we estimated $\frac{80,000}{30}$ by replacing 30 with 40 (since 40 goes into 80,000 evenly) we get $\frac{80,000}{40} = \frac{8000}{4} = 2000$, which is not as good as our previous estimate. This might be a little surprising, since we only made a change of 10 in replacing 30 by 40. But what is important here is not the size of the change (10), but the relative size of the change (10 out of 30 is 33%).

A powerful technique for estimating the result of a division problem is to consider the division as a ratio.

Here are some additional examples of estimation in a division context. See if you can follow the reasoning in these estimates. Can you make an estimate in a different way?

$$\frac{6206}{8271} \approx \frac{6000}{8000} = \frac{6}{8} = \frac{3}{4} = 0.75$$

$$\frac{78,221}{987} \approx \frac{80,000}{1000} = 80$$

$$\frac{77,921}{289} \approx \frac{75,000}{250} = \frac{7500}{25} = 300$$

$$\frac{828}{38,765} \approx \frac{800}{40,000} = \frac{8}{400} = \frac{2}{100} = .02$$

Measurement Error, Experimental Error, and Predictions

The theme of this tutor is the way in which "inexactness" is dealt with in real-world mathematics. One class of situations that involve inexactness is that which involves measurement error or experimental error. **Measurement error** is the unavoidable error that occurs due to the limitations inherent to any measurement instrument. Any measurement in the real world is an approximation. It is not really possible to guarantee that an object is exactly 1 meter long since any measuring instrument has a limit to its accuracy. For example, our centimeter ruler can only measure to the nearest tenth of a centimeter and the two-pan balance usually used in *Math Trailblazers* can only measure mass to the nearest gram. **Experimental error** is the variation in measurement that results from the inability to control extraneous variables in an experiment.

These two types of error are closely related. Let's consider three examples of measurement in real-world contexts to get some idea of the meaning of measurement and experimental error:

Example 1: A student is selected from the class and every student measures the circumference of her head to the nearest tenth of a centimeter. Most students get between 47 and 49 centimeters. One student gets 37.4 centimeters.

Example 2: Students drop a ball from a height of 80 centimeters three times to see how high it bounces. They get 41 centimeters, 45 centimeters, and 44 centimeters.

Example 3: Students measure the volume of a marble using a graduated cylinder. Most students get either 7 or 8 cubic centimeters. Two students get 67 cubic centimeters.

Example 4: A student finds that the mass of one blue pattern block is 11 grams. She predicts that 2 blue pattern blocks will have a mass of 22 grams and 4 blue pattern blocks will have a mass of 44 grams. When she checks her results, she finds that 2 pattern blocks do have a mass of 22 grams, but 4 pattern blocks have a mass of 42 grams.

Measurement error is the unavoidable error that occurs due to the limitations inherent to any measurement instrument. . . . Experimental error is the variation in measurement that results from the inability to control extraneous variables in an experiment.

Errors vs. Mistakes

In Examples 1, 2, and 3, there were repeated measurements of the same thing that produced seemingly different answers. The fact that most students obtained slightly different answers in Example 1 is due to slight variations in how they performed the measurement—where they placed the tape measure, how tight they held it, etc. All these measurements are "close" to each other (see below for a discussion of "what's close?"). However, the student whose measurement was 37.4 centimeters probably made a *mistake* such as reading the tape measure incorrectly or placing the tape measure in the wrong position. In mathematics, we try to distinguish between the words "error" and "mistake." Of course, "mistake" is one of the common meanings of "error." *Webster's New World Dictionary of the American Language* gives as its first definition of the word "error," "the state of believing what is untrue, incorrect, or wrong." However, in the current context, "error" has a different meaning. This is the fifth definition given for "error" in that dictionary, namely "the difference between a computed or estimated result and the actual value as in mathematics." The dictionary goes on to explain that "error implies deviation from truth, accuracy, correctness, right, [while] mistake suggests an error resulting from carelessness, inattention, misunderstanding, etc." Most of the measurements in Example 1 involved some measurement error, but those measurements were correct. However, the student who measured 37.4 centimeters must have made a mistake. In this case, the teacher would help the student find the reason for the mistake and then repeat the measurement correctly.

In Example 2, it is not surprising that repeating the activity, i.e., dropping the ball from 80 centimeters, results in a different measurement. It's pretty hard to measure how high the ball bounces, since the ball does not stop at the height of its bounce and wait for you to measure its distance from the floor. Also, there can be slight variations caused by different parts of the ball being "bouncier" or different spots on the floor being "bouncier." This is a typical example of the experimental error that results from the inability to control all the fixed variables in an experiment. (See the TIMS Tutor: *The TIMS Laboratory Method.* Fixed Variables in Controlled Experiments.)

In Example 3, students used a graduated cylinder to measure the volume by displacement. Two students forgot to subtract the volume of the water in the cylinder, so they obtained measurements that were very different from the others. This is a clear example of a mistake. The actual volume of the marble was between 7 and 8 cubic centimeters.

Reducing Experimental Error

In Examples 1 through 3, we have seen that repeating a measurement does not always give the same answer. To get more reliable and accurate results, scientists often repeat a measurement several times and then take the average of all the measurements. The "average" that we use in this situation can be either the mean or the median. (See the TIMS Tutor: *Averages.*) In Example 2, we can take the median of the three measurements and say that dropping the ball from 80 centimeters results in a bounce height of 44 centimeters. We could also use the mean, in which case the bounce height would be nearly the same—approximately 43 centimeters.

In mathematics, we try to distinguish between the words "error" and "mistake."

To get more reliable and accurate results, scientists often repeat a measurement several times and then take the average of all the measurements.

In many experiments, we have another way of minimizing experimental error. If the data points plotted on a graph appear close to a straight line, we find a best-fit line that is close to all the data points. (See the TIMS Tutor: *The TIMS Laboratory Method.*) Using the best-fit line is a way of averaging out the experimental error. In *Math Trailblazers*, we draw a best-fit line "by eye," using a transparent ruler. In addition to averaging out the error, these lines help scientists and mathematicians make predictions based upon the patterns in the data. Scientists, mathematicians, and statisticians use a variety of sophisticated methods to find best-fit lines for data, but the "eyeball" method is pretty good for making approximate predictions. One example of an activity where both averaging and best-fit lines are used to minimize experimental error is the *Math Trailblazers* fourth-grade lab, *The Bouncing Ball*. In this lab, students drop a ball from heights of 40, 80, and 120 cm and record their data in a data table. (See Figure 1.) Note that the ball was dropped three times from each height. When the data is graphed, we can see that the data points lie close to a straight line. In Figure 2, we see an estimated best-fit line drawn by a student. For further information, see the TIMS Tutor: *The TIMS Laboratory Method,* Point Graphs: Fitting Lines and Curves.

Tennis Ball

D Drop Height in cm	B Bounce Height in cm			
	Trial 1	Trial 2	Trial 3	Average
40	27	22	21	22
80	50	40	43	43
120	72	62	68	68

Figure 1: The Bouncing Ball *data table*

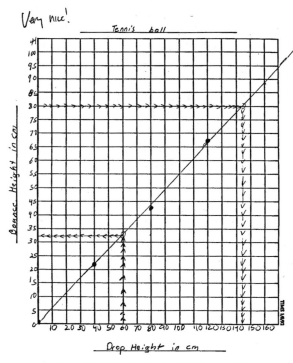

Very nice!

Tennis ball

Bounce Height in cm

Drop Height in cm

Figure 2: The Bouncing Ball *graph*

What's Close?

Recall that the notions of approximation and estimation involved the notion of finding a number that is close to a desired number. But how do we decide what is close? The most fundamental idea about closeness is that it is a **relative** idea. For example, suppose two merchants are selling the same item and the prices differ by $1. Are the prices close? If the merchant were selling cars that cost around $30,000, you would not make your decision based on a $1 difference in price. On the other hand, if you could buy a cup of coffee in one restaurant for $1 and it cost $2 at another restaurant, you might go out of your way for the $1 coffee (provided the quality was not vastly different). Why are these two choices for coffee significantly different? Because one brand costs twice as much as the other! This leads us to the fundamental idea for discussing closeness: when comparing closeness of numbers or measurements, we should look at the **ratio** of the two numbers, rather than the difference. The only problem with this approach is that the concept of ratio is difficult to understand fully. Developing this concept requires time and exposure to many experiences. We deal with this problem in two ways. First, instead of using ratios, we use a related concept—percent. Second, instead of calculating specific percentages (another difficult concept), we make comparisons to certain benchmark percentages, such as 10%. Using 10% as a benchmark for closeness, we see that $1 is not close to $2 since $2 is more than 10% bigger than $1 (in fact, it's 100% bigger). On the other hand, if we compare $30,000 and $30,001 we see that the difference, $1, is a lot less than 10% of $30,000.

> The most fundamental idea about closeness is that it is a **relative** idea.

In Example 1 above, the example in which many students measured the head circumference of one person, all the measurements fell between 47 and 49 centimeters. A rough estimate for 10% of these numbers is 4 cm. Now the difference between 47 cm and 49 cm is 2 cm, so there is clearly less than 10% variation between the largest and smallest measurement. We can safely say that these measurements are "close." On the other hand, the student who got 37.5 cm was almost 10 cm less than 47 cm. This is nowhere close to being within 10% of the other measurements, so we should suspect that there is a mistake in that measurement. In Example 2, students took three measurements of the bounce height of a ball—41 cm, 45 cm, and 44 cm. Again, the variation is less than 10%. Finally, in Example 3, when students were measuring the volume of a marble, most obtained a value between 7 cc and 8 cc, while a few measured 67 cc. Now, 10% of 7 or 8 cc is less than 1 cc, so the students who measured 67 cc are nowhere close to the others. It should be pointed out that in situations such as Example 3, we do not decide who had the correct measurements by taking a majority vote. While the majority is usually right, it is not always right. The different results are a warning flag telling us to seek out the reasons for the discrepancies. Someone is making a mistake, but we can only find out who is making the mistake by looking more closely. Once the mistake is found, then we discard the incorrect information.

The 10 Percent Solution

It's natural to ask why we use 10% as a standard of closeness. We have a variety of reasons:

1. It's easy to find 10% of a number, or at least to estimate it. Just divide by 10. For whole numbers bigger than 10, the simplest estimate for 10% is obtained by dropping the last digit. Thus 10% of 187 is about 18 (it's between 18 and 19) and 10% of 5623 is about 562.
2. In many of the hands-on experiments we do in *Math Trailblazers*, 10% is about the accuracy we can expect from students using the equipment they have, while 10% accuracy is still good enough for seeing the patterns in the data on graphs.
3. Psychologically, 10% is near the limit of our visual estimating ability. For example, if a person sees two drawings in sequence, one of which is an enlargement of the other, in most cases that person will have difficulty distinguishing pictures that are less than 10% different in size, but will be able to distinguish figures that are much more than 10% different in size. Of course, this 10% borderline is not exact, and the point at which different people will be able to make distinctions is different.

Estimating the Magnitude of a Measurement

The basic measurement variables in the *Math Trailblazers* curriculum are length, area, volume, mass, and time. While much of the discussion that follows will apply to any type of measurement, it is a good idea to keep these few variables in mind. The examples given in this section will use these five variables.

There are two important types of knowledge that are used in many measurement estimation exercises. First, you need to know the measurements of some objects to use as a reference point. Second, you must know how to estimate unknown measurements by comparison with things you know. Very often this will involve some kind of proportional reasoning. The first type of knowledge is gained from experience. Therefore, students should have a wide variety of hands-on experiences as well as knowledge gained from external sources. For example, students should know the height of an average adult in English and metric systems ($5\frac{1}{2}$–6 feet, 160–185 cm), the length of their feet, and the width of their hands. We would hope that students have a general idea of the width of the continental U.S. from east to west (3000 miles) and from north to south (1000 miles). These facts can be used to make other estimates. For example, what is the area of the U.S.? The continental U.S. looks as though it would fit in a rectangle that is 3000 miles long and 1000 miles wide. This gives us an estimate of 3 million square miles. The actual area is close to 3.6 million square miles. To estimate the height of a three-story building (Figure 3), we could first estimate the height of one floor. Looking at an adult standing in the room, we might estimate that the distance from floor to ceiling is twice the height of the person. If the person is about 6 feet tall, then we get an estimate of 12 feet from floor to ceiling. If there are three floors, then the total height of the building is approximately $3 \times 12 = 36$ feet high.

Figure 3: *Estimating the height of a three-story building*

Accuracy and Precision

The accuracy required in a measurement depends on the use we are going to make of the measurement. By its very nature, any measurement we make in the real world is an estimation. What does it mean to say that a sheet of paper is 21.6 cm wide? How does one find this out? One way is to put the 0 cm mark on the ruler even with the left-hand edge of the paper and see that the right-hand edge of the paper is even with the 22.6 cm mark. If the paper is really 22.61 cm wide, we could not tell this with our ruler, which is only divided into tenths of a centimeter. So the measurements we make are really estimates that are accurate to the nearest tenth of a centimeter. Measuring the width of a piece of paper to an accuracy of more than a tenth of a centimeter would probably not make sense, since the sides cannot be perfectly even and measuring the width in different places would give different answers (like 22.613 cm and 22.615 cm). In any case, a measurement of 22.6 cm is probably more than sufficient for our purpose.

By its very nature, any measurement we make in the real world is an estimation.

Dealing with Decimal Digits

One important fact to note is that in the course of solving a problem we can end up with a number that has many digits, most of which do not make sense in the real world (although they make mathematical sense). For example, suppose we wanted to share 16 ounces of orange juice among three students. When I divide 16 by 3 on my calculator, I get 5.3333333333. It makes no sense at all to say that we should give each student 5.3333333333 ounces of juice, since, with the tools we have, we cannot measure more accurately than to the nearest tenth of an ounce. In fact, when we say that we want to share 16 ounces of orange juice, we do not mean that we have exactly 16 ounces of juice. Unless we were using unusually sensitive measuring instruments, it would only make sense to say that we would give each student 5.3 ounces or $5\frac{1}{3}$ ounces of juice. Although 5.3 and $5\frac{1}{3}$ are not equal, they are approximately equal in this context.

Estimating "How Many"

In this type of estimation, we estimate the number of objects in some collection. It could be the number of trees in the United States, the number of students that will be in a school district next year, or the number of beans in a jar. This class of problems has a lot in common with the estimation problems we have already discussed. Many problems that require estimating "how many" are similar to estimating a measurement in that they involve knowing how many objects there are in some known set and then comparing the unknown with the known. Here are some examples:

Example 1: Students are asked to estimate the number of peanuts in a jar. If the students have not had any previous experience with peanuts or jars, this is not really an estimate, but rather a guess. The answers will vary widely because students do not have any idea of what the answer might be and no strategies to use to get a sensible answer. A more reasonable exercise is to give them a small jar and have them count how many peanuts can fit in the jar. If they are now given a larger jar, they should be able to make a sensible estimate by comparing the large jar to the small one. How many large jars would they think fit in the small jar? If the small jar holds 10 peanuts and it appears that 12 small jars fit in the large one, what is a reasonable estimate for the number of peanuts that fit in the large jar?

Example 2: How many students are in your school? The reference set here can be the number of students in a class. Students should know how many students are in their class. They should also be able to estimate the number of classes in the school. This gives an estimate for the number of students in the school (using multiplication).

Example 3: How many total hours of television were watched by all the children in the school? We can find the *exact* answer by asking every student how much they watched and then adding the number of hours. The answer can be *estimated* using a very important technique called sampling. Take a survey of some of the children in the school (say one class or two students in each class) and then scale up.

Example 4: We have a picture of the crowd at a basketball game. How can we determine the number of people at the game? It would be tedious to count the number of people in the picture. We could draw a square on the picture and count the number of people in that square. Then multiply that result by the number of such squares needed to cover the crowd. Figure 4 from the *Math Trailblazers* fourth-grade curriculum shows a picture used to pose a similar problem.

Figure 4: *Picture of a basketball game crowd*

Example 5: Will more people vote for Fred or Amy in the next election? This is another example of a kind of problem that frequently occurs in the real world. The common technique for estimating the answer is to take a sample of the voters and use the sample to predict the results for the whole population. For example, if 40% of the sample says they will vote for Fred and 60% says they will vote for Amy, we might predict that Amy will win. We might even predict that Fred will get 40% of the vote and Amy 60%. We know from real life that predictions like this are not always accurate. Some things that affect the accuracy of such estimates are the size of the sample (compared to the whole population) and the randomness of the sample (how well the sample represents the whole population).

Example 6: How many households are there in the U.S.? We can only make this estimate if we know enough facts about the population of the U.S. We know that the population of the U.S. is about 250 million people and that the average family has 2.3 children. If we think that some households have only one person, while others have several generations living together, we might say that the average household size is about 4 or 5 people. Using a household size of 5 for our estimate (since 5 goes evenly into 25) we get a figure of 50 million households.

The best way to become a good estimator is to estimate.

Conclusion

We hope that this tutor gives you an overview of the way estimation is treated in the *Math Trailblazers* curriculum. Naturally, it could not deal with all the types of estimation situations and all kinds of estimation strategies. The best way to become a good estimator is to estimate. The best way for children to learn to be good estimators is to be given meaningful situations that require estimation and to be given the opportunity to discuss their strategies with others. As with all mathematics instruction, the teacher plays a valuable role by moderating discourse and by adding new strategies when appropriate.

References

Schoen, Harold L., and Marilyn J. Zweng (eds.). *Estimation and Mental Computation—1986 Yearbook.* National Council of Teachers of Mathematics, Reston, VA, 1986.

Sowder, J., "Estimation and Number Sense," in *Handbook of Research on Mathematics Teaching and Learning.* Douglas A. Grouws (ed.). Macmillan Publishing Co., New York, 1992.

Threadgill-Sowder, J. "Computational Estimation Procedures of School Children." *Journal of Educational Research,* 77 (6), 1984.

Webster's Ninth New Collegiate Dictionary. Merriam-Webster, Inc., Springfield, MA, 1990.

Functions

Introduction

Function is one of those words with a mathematical meaning that is not the same as the everyday meaning. In everyday life, a function can be an important celebration, a role someone or something has, or the purpose for something. In mathematics and science, a function is a special and very important kind of relationship between variables. Discovering functional relationships between variables is what science is all about.

Three Blind Men and an Elephant. There is a story about three blind men who encounter an elephant. The first comes up against one of the elephant's legs and says, "An elephant is like a tree." The second touches the side of the elephant and says, "No, no. An elephant is like a wall." The third blind man finds the elephant's trunk and claims, "You're both wrong. An elephant is like a big snake."

Each blind man has some notion of what an elephant is. The story doesn't tell whether they eventually resolve their differences and come to a proper understanding of elephants; we can only hope so. Our approach to functions will be similar: We will begin with three different views of functions. This, we hope, will lead to a fuller and more proper understanding of functions.

Tables

Many functions are displayed as tables. For example, consider this data table from the experiment *Mass vs. Number*, shown in Figure 1.

N Number of <u>Erasers</u>	M Mass (in gm)
1	39 gm
2	79 gm
4	158 gm

Figure 1: Mass vs. Number *data table*

This table displays a functional relationship between the variables N and M. For each value of N we have a value of M; we say that the mass is a function of the number of erasers. That is, if we know what N is, then we can find M. This is the essence of a function: knowing one variable's value enables us to find the corresponding value of the other variable. In this example, the data has a distinctive pattern: within experimental error, doubling one variable causes the other to double. *N* and *M* are said to be (directly) proportional.

Many of the functions we encounter in everyday life come to us as tables. Stock tables, for example, can be thought of as functions: one variable is the company, the other is the closing price. If you know the company, you can look up the price. Almanacs are filled with tables of information, most of which can be thought of as functions: one variable is the name of the country, the other is the population, and so on. The sports pages are filled with tabular functions of team standings and individual statistics.

Many functions come to us first as tables, and some, like batting averages or almanac information, are normally given only as tables. Tables of numbers, however, can be very difficult to understand. Patterns in the data can go undetected—patterns that might help us better understand the function. One of the best ways to get a handle on patterns is to make a visual image of the data in the form of a graph.

Graphs

If a picture is worth a thousand words, a graph is worth a billion numbers. The graph of the *Mass vs. Number* data, seen in Figure 2, is a good example.

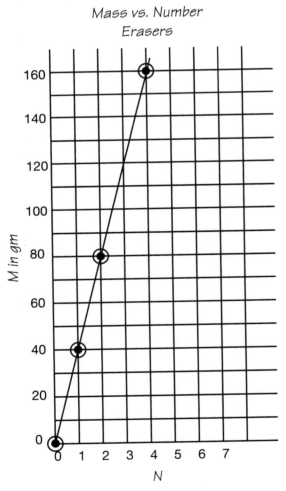

Figure 2: *Graph of* Mass vs. Number *data*

The key thing about this graph is that the data points lie on a straight line through (0,0). This confirms that N and M are proportional: we can fit a straight line through (0,0) if and only if the variables are proportional. Many other types of functions besides direct proportion are characterized by their graphs.

Often, experimental error obscures the nature of the relationship between the variables until the data is plotted. Like taking multiple measurements and averaging, graphing the data and fitting a curve can help control error. With error minimized, the true nature of the relationship between the variables may become clearer. Stock analysts graph their data to spot trends in order to make predictions (and money); such trends are unlikely to be noticed in the stock tables. Scientists graph their data almost as soon as they get it because the graph is so much more likely to be revealing than the raw data.

The graph is a crucial step on the road from the concrete apparatus to formal understanding. Sometimes, this formal understanding can be distilled in a few symbols, as in a formula.

Formulas

A more abstract way to consider a function is as a formula. In our *Mass vs. Number* example, we can exploit the fact that when variables are proportional, their ratio is constant. The value of this constant ratio is the slope of the best-fit line. So,

$$\frac{M}{N} = \frac{39.5 \text{ gm}}{1 \text{ eraser}} .$$

This can be rewritten to give a formula for M as a function of N:

$$M = \frac{39.5 \text{ gm}}{1 \text{ eraser}} \times N$$

Such formulas are very useful when they can be found. When we do manage to obtain a formula, it allows us to solve problems quickly and accurately. We can also use formulas to ascend to higher levels of abstraction. This movement to ever greater abstraction and generality is the driving force behind much of science and mathematics.

The graph is a crucial step on the road from the concrete apparatus to formal understanding.

G Number of Generations	A Number of Ancestors
1	2
2	4
3	8
4	16

Figure 3: *Ancestors data table*

Often students are not able to understand formulas, but they are, nevertheless, able to continue a pattern in a data table or devise a rule that works. For example, the pattern in the table shown in Figure 3 is easy to extend. Five generations back, you have 32 ancestors: each further generation doubles the number of ancestors (ignoring the inevitable overlap). Extending patterns like this is a first step towards formulas. Later, the students may be able to give a rule for a data table. For example, consider the table in Figure 4, the number of fence posts needed for a given length of fence.

L Length of Fence in _feet_	N Number of Fence Posts
10	2
20	3
30	4
40	5

Figure 4: *Fence posts data table*

The rule may be stated: the number of fence posts is just one more than $\frac{1}{10}$ the number of feet in the fence.

$$N = \frac{L}{10} + 1$$

It is not much harder for us to express this sentence as a formula, but this type of expression may be confusing to a third-grader. Often, a rule stated in ordinary language is more accessible.

Formulas are the most powerful way of looking at functions but are often not appropriate for elementary school students. The great temptation is to drive on to formulas as quickly as possible. This sometimes leads to quick gains, but over the long run it is often problematic. Pushing formulas at children is like building a house of cards: students need to build a conceptual foundation by handling apparatus, gathering data, and graphing and analyzing it. Only after the students have developed an understanding of the relationship of the variables is it proper to distill that understanding into a formula. Extending patterns and figuring out rules are excellent alternatives for younger students moving towards higher levels of abstraction.

What Is a Function?

A **function** is a special kind of relationship between variables that can often be expressed as a data table, graph, or formula. One of the variables is the manipulated (or independent) variable; the other is the responding (or dependent) variable.

But not every relationship is a function. The main requirement for a relationship to be a function is that for each value of the manipulated variable, there is only one value of the responding variable. For example, suppose the manipulated variable is the edge length of a cube and the responding variable is the surface area. Then, for each given edge length there is exactly one surface area: if the edge is 3 cm, then the surface area is 54 sq cm, and so on. Or consider the manipulated variable to be the company and the responding variable to be the closing price: each stock has exactly one closing price each day. Notice that many stocks may have the same closing price; that's okay. The requirement says only that each value of the manipulated variable must have exactly one value of the responding variable. Values of the responding variable may repeat, and often do.

. . . not every relationship is a function. The main requirement for a relationship to be a function is that for each value of the manipulated variable, there is only one value of the responding variable.

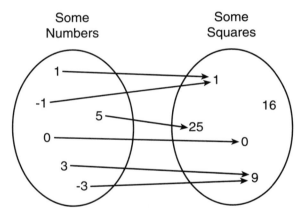

Figure 5: *Map of a squaring function*

One way to visualize this requirement is to think about functions as mappings. Figure 5 shows a map of a squaring function.

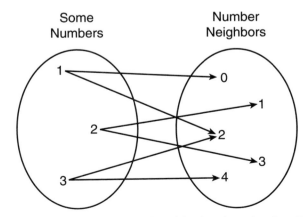

Figure 6: *Map of a relationship that is not a function*

Every number has exactly one square; this corresponds to the single arrow leaving each number on the left above. Notice that more than one arrow can end at a single number; the requirement is only that exactly one arrow leave each of the starting numbers. The mapping in Figure 6 is not a function because two arrows leave each number.

But you may object, saying that when we do experiments we often have several different values of the responding variable for each value of the manipulated variable. Isn't there a functional relationship between variables like the drop height and the bounce height in *The Bouncing Ball?* In a word, yes. But with real data, things get more complicated. Experimental error creeps in; there are other uncontrolled variables; there is uncertainty inherent in all our measurements. One useful way to think about the situation is to suppose there is some "true" value of the responding variable that we cannot measure exactly. So, instead we measure the responding variable several times and then take the average as our best estimate of the true value.[1] Then we have a function: for each value of the manipulated variable there is exactly one *true* value of the responding variable. The only trouble is, in most real-world situations, we usually don't know what that true value is.

Mathematicians have precise and abstract definitions of function. We could go on and on describing more precisely the requirements a relationship must have to be a function. We could spell out the meanings of technical terms having to do with functions—terms like *domain, range, one-to-one, many-to-one,* and so on. For most purposes, however, thinking about functions in the terms outlined above is enough.

Functions in the Classroom

The concept of a function is a powerful one for organizing and extending mathematical ideas. From time to time, we have activities that deal with functions, for example, *Function Machines* in second grade. The best approach to functions, however, is just doing the *Math Trailblazers* lessons. As your students do TIMS Laboratory Investigations and other activities, they will move naturally from the apparatus to the data table, graph, and questions. Much of the data analysis is designed to help the children see how changes in one of these correspond to changes in the others. Thus, in each experiment the students will deal with specific functions in several guises and will gain facility in moving between different representations of functions. This is the best possible preparation for the explicit study of functions later in high school and beyond.

As your students do TIMS Laboratory Investigations and other activities, they will move naturally from the apparatus to the data table, graph, and questions. Much of the data analysis is designed to help the children see how changes in one of these correspond to changes in the others. . . . This is the best possible preparation for the explicit study of functions later in high school and beyond.

[1] See the TIMS Tutor: *Averages.*

Journals

We at TIMS embrace the idea of writing across the curriculum. We see helping students to write better as part of every teacher's job.

By writing in mathematics and science class, students improve their communication skills and develop their subject-matter understanding. Writing about mathematics and science helps students consolidate ideas, see connections between school and life, and think more abstractly.

Another reason to have students write about mathematics and science lessons is so that you can gain insight into how those lessons are being received and what the students are learning. Collecting and saving students' writing is also an excellent way to document long-term student progress.

We have tried several ways to incorporate writing into *Math Trailblazers*. We often ask for students to write a short or extended answer to a question and we may also ask students to explain how they obtained their solutions. Students may be asked to write about problems they have solved in cooperative groups.

Journals can be another effective way to use writing in mathematics and science. Typically, a journal is a small, bound book in which students write regularly. The writing can be in response to various prompts, or it can be rather undirected. Because each student can respond at his or her own level and rate, journal writing is accessible to all students.

The teacher reads students' journals regularly, possibly responding in writing to what the students have written. Usually journal writing is not corrected for grammar, spelling, and punctuation—the focus is on the content of the writing rather than on the form.

The physical form of the journal is not important. A cloth-covered bound book, a spiral notebook, or even several sheets of paper stapled together will work just fine.

Journal Prompts

We urge you to have your students write regularly, every day or at least every week. Start with short periods and gradually extend the amount of time. When a student fills up one journal, give him or her another. Students will also enjoy reading their writing aloud and discussing it.

The writing your students do in their journals should take a variety of forms. Here are some suggestions for assignments ranging from highly structured to rather open-ended.

Sentence Completion

Give part of a sentence and ask students to complete it (Azzolino, 1990). For example, you might ask students to complete sentences like these:

> "A shape is symmetric when . . ."
> "Today we learned . . ."
> "Before you use an equal-arm balance it's important to . . ."

A variation of this activity is to give one or more complete sentences and then to ask students to continue.

Explanations of Procedures

Ask your students to explain how to measure the area of a leaf, how to use an equal-arm balance, how to add two three-digit numbers, or how to make a graph of some data. An explanation of an entire procedure or only of certain steps may be required.

Answers to Specific Questions

Sometimes you may pose a specific question about a lesson. For example, ask students to describe the shape of the graph for a certain experiment and to explain why the graph has that shape. Many *Math Trailblazers* lessons include questions that require some writing; these questions can be answered in the journals.

A question to ask sometimes is, "How did working in your group turn out?" You may get valuable information that can help you improve the dynamics of your small groups.

Descriptions of Solutions

There are usually many ways to solve a mathematics problem; it is often worth exploring multiple solutions. To correct the common misconception that there is usually only one way to solve a problem, students need to learn that the process of problem solving is often as important as the answer. In *Math Trailblazers,* they see connections by comparing different solutions. They learn that mathematics makes sense because their own ideas are validated. They are exposed to advanced ideas through other students' solutions, but without undue stress if they fail to understand those advanced ideas.

One way to encourage multiple solutions is to ask students to write about how they solved a problem. Ask them to describe all the ways they were able to solve a problem or to describe a single way in depth. Ask them to write about failed solutions or what they did when they got stuck. Such assignments will encourage students to see such efforts not as failures but as periodic by-products of the problem-solving process.

Definitions

Ask students to define a key concept like area or volume. You may be surprised at some of the answers you get.

Advice to Adventure Book Characters

Often the characters in the *Adventure Books* and other activities encounter problems that yield to the techniques the students have been learning in the labs and activities. You might stop part way through an Adventure Book story and ask your students to write some advice, perhaps in the form of a letter, to the hero. When you finish the book, compare what the hero actually did with students' advice.

Reactions

Ask your students what they liked or didn't like about a certain lab, activity, or adventure book. Or, ask what they learned or what confused them.

Word Banks

Supply a list of words or phrases and ask students to use those words in a piece of writing (Azzolino, 1990). For example, you might supply the following words, "ten, hundred, thousand, less than, seven, more than, nine."

Problems

Students enjoy writing their own problems. Ask them to write another problem like a given problem; to write an addition, subtraction, or sharing problem; to write a number riddle; or to make up any problem that students in the class would find interesting to solve.

Free Writing

Other times, simply tell students to write whatever they want about a certain lesson.

Some Tips for Getting Started

- Start with brief periods of writing and gradually extend the amount of time.
- Encourage pictures, data tables, graphs, number sentences, and other mathematical and scientific forms of communication.
- Vary the prompt. Sometimes be very specific; other times make the assignment more open-ended.
- Do not worry about grammar, spelling, and punctuation. Focus on content.

One way to encourage multiple solutions is to ask students to write about how they solved a problem. Ask them to describe all the ways they were able to solve a problem or to describe a single way in depth. You might even ask them to write about failed solutions or what they did when they got stuck.

Conclusion

The name of our project—TIMS (Teaching Integrated Mathematics and Science)—expresses our conviction that the teaching of mathematics and science should be integrated. But we also feel strongly that integration should not stop there; language arts and social studies can and should be integrated with mathematics and science. Journals are one way to use writing in mathematics and science. Reading and writing are too important to be confined to language arts lessons.

References

Azzolino, A. "Writing as a Tool for Teaching Mathematics: The Silent Revolution." In *Teaching and Learning Mathematics in the 1990s: 1990 Yearbook.* T.J. Cooney and C.R. Hirsch, Eds. National Council of Teachers of Mathematics, Reston, VA, 1990.

Burns, Marilyn, and Robyn Sibley. "Incorporating Writing into Math Class." *So You Have to Teach Math? Sound Advice for K–6 Teachers.* Math Solutions Publications, Sausalito, CA, 2000.

Countryman, Joan. *Writing to Learn Mathematics.* Heinemann, Portsmouth, NH, 1992.

Math Facts

Students need to learn the math facts. Estimation, mental arithmetic, checking the reasonableness of results, and paper-and-pencil calculations require the ability to give quick, accurate responses when using basic facts. The question is not if students should learn the math facts, but how. Which teaching methods are most efficient and effective? To answer this question, the authors of *Math Trailblazers* drew upon educational research and their own classroom experiences to develop a comprehensive plan for teaching the math facts.

Philosophy

The goal of the *Math Trailblazers* math facts strand is for students to learn the basic facts efficiently, gain fluency with their use, and retain that fluency over time. A large body of research supports an approach that is built on a foundation of work with strategies and concepts. This not only leads to more effective learning and better retention, it also leads to development of mental math skills. Therefore, the teaching and assessment of the basic facts in *Math Trailblazers* is characterized by the following elements:

- *Early emphasis on problem solving.* Students first approach the basic facts as problems to be solved rather than as facts to be memorized. Students invent their own strategies to solve these problems or learn appropriate strategies from others through class discussion. Students' natural strategies, especially counting strategies, are explicitly encouraged. In this way, students learn that math is more than memorizing facts and rules that "you either get or you don't."

- *De-emphasis of rote work.* Fluency with the math facts is an important component of any student's mathematical learning. Research has shown that an overemphasis on memorization and the frequent administration of timed tests are counterproductive. Both of these can produce undesirable results (Isaacs and Carroll, 1999; Van de Walle, 2001; National Research Council, 2001). We encourage the use of strategies to find facts, so students become confident they can find answers to fact problems that they do not immediately recall.

- *Gradual and systematic introduction of facts.* Students study the facts in small groups that can be solved using similar strategies. Students first work on simple strategies for easy facts and then progress to more sophisticated strategies and harder facts. By the end of the process, they gain fluency with all required facts.

- *Ongoing practice.* Work on the math facts is distributed throughout the curriculum, especially in the Daily Practice and Problems (DPP), Home Practice, and games. This practice for fluency, however, takes place only after students have a conceptual understanding of the operations and have achieved proficiency with strategies for solving basic fact problems. Delaying practice in this way means that less practice is required to achieve fluency.

- *Appropriate assessment.* Teachers assess students' knowledge of the facts through observations as they work on activities, labs, and games as well as through the appropriate use of written tests and quizzes. Beginning in first grade, periodic, short quizzes in the DPP naturally follow the study of small groups of facts organized around specific strategies. As self-assessment in Grades 3–5, each student records his or her progress on *Facts I Know* charts and determines which facts he or she needs to study. Inventory tests of all facts for each operation are used sparingly in Grades 2–5 (no more than twice per year) to assess students' progress with fact fluency. The goal of the math facts assessment program is to determine the degree to which students can find answers to fact problems quickly and accurately and whether they can retain this skill over time.

- *Multiyear approach.* In Grades 1 and 2, *Math Trailblazers* emphasizes strategies that lead to fluency with the addition and subtraction facts. In Grade 3, students gain fluency with the multiplication facts while reviewing the addition and subtraction facts. In Grade 4, students achieve fluency with the division facts and verify fluency with the multiplication facts. In Grade 5, the multiplication and division facts are systematically reviewed and assessed.

- *Facts are not gatekeepers.* Students are not prevented from learning more complex mathematics because they do not perform well on fact tests. Use of strategies, calculators, and other math tools (e.g., manipulatives, hundred charts, printed multiplication tables) allows students to continue to work on interesting problems while they are still learning the facts.

Expectations by Grade Level

The following goals for the math facts are consistent with the recommendations in the National Council of Teachers of Mathematics *Principles and Standards for School Mathematics:*

- In kindergarten, students use manipulatives and invent their own strategies to solve addition and subtraction problems.
- By the end of first grade, all students can solve all basic addition and subtraction problems using some strategy. Fluency is not emphasized; strategies are. Some work with beginning concepts of multiplication takes place.
- In second grade, learning efficient strategies for addition and especially subtraction continues to be emphasized. Work with multiplication concepts continues. By the end of the year, students are expected to demonstrate fluency with all the addition and subtraction facts.
- In third grade, students review the subtraction facts. They develop efficient strategies for learning the multiplication facts and demonstrate fluency with the multiplication facts.
- In fourth grade, students review the multiplication facts and develop strategies for the division facts. By the end of year, we expect fluency with all the division facts.
- In fifth grade, students review the multiplication and division facts and are expected to maintain fluency with all the facts.

This is summarized in the following chart:

Grade	Addition	Subtraction	Multiplication	Division
K	• invented strategies	• invented strategies		
1	• strategies	• strategies		
2	• strategies • practice leading to fluency	• strategies • practice leading to fluency		
3	• review and practice	• review and practice	• strategies • practice leading to fluency	
4	• assessment and remediation as required	• assessment and remediation as required	• review and practice	• strategies • practice leading to fluency
5	• assessment and remediation as required	• assessment and remediation as required	• review and practice	• review and practice

Table 1: *Math Facts Scope and Sequence*

Strategies for Learning the Facts

Students are encouraged to learn the math facts by first employing a variety of strategies. Concepts and skills are learned more easily and are retained longer if they are meaningful. By first concentrating on concepts and strategies, we increase retention and reduce the amount of time necessary for rote memorization. Researchers note that over time, students develop techniques that are increasingly sophisticated and efficient. Experience with the strategies provides a basis for understanding the operation involved and for gaining fluency with the facts. In this section, we describe possible strategies for learning the addition, subtraction, multiplication, and division facts. The strategies for each operation are listed roughly in order of increasing sophistication.

Strategies for Addition Facts

Common strategies include counting all, counting on, doubles, making or using 10, and reasoning from known facts.

Counting All

This is a particularly straightforward strategy. For example, to solve $7 + 8$, the student gets 7 of something and 8 of something and counts how many there are altogether. The "something" could be beans or chips or marks on paper. In any case, the student counts all the objects to find the sum. This is perhaps not a very efficient method, but it is effective, especially for small numbers, and is usually well understood by the student.

Counting On

This is a natural strategy, particularly for adding 1, 2, or 3. Counters such as beans or chips may or may not be used. As an example with counters, consider 8 + 3. The student gets 8 beans, and then 3 more, but instead of counting the first 8 again, she simply counts the 3 added beans: "9, 10, 11."

Even if counters are not used, finger gestures can help keep track of how many more have been counted on. For example, to solve 8 + 3, the student counts "9, 10, 11," holding up a finger each time a number word is said; when three fingers are up, the last word said is the answer.

Doubles

Facts such as 4 + 4 = 8 are easier to remember than facts with two different addends. Some visual imagery can help, too: two hands for 5 + 5, a carton of eggs for 6 + 6, a calendar for 7 + 7, and so on.

Making a 10

Facts with a sum of 10, such as 7 + 3 and 6 + 4, are also easier to remember than other facts. Ten frames can create visual images of making a 10. For example, 8 is shown in a ten frame like the one in Figure 1:

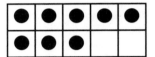

Figure 1: *A ten frame*

This visual imagery helps students remember, for example, that 8 + 2 = 10.

Using a 10

Students who are comfortable partitioning and combining small numbers can use that knowledge to find the sums of larger numbers. In particular, there are many strategies that involve using the number 10. For example, to find 9 + 7, we can decompose 7 into 1 + 6 and then 9 + 7 = 9 + 1 + 6 = 10 + 6 = 16. Similarly, 8 + 7 = 8 + 2 + 5 = 10 + 5 = 15.

Reasoning from Known Facts

If you know what 7 + 7 is, then 7 + 8 is not much harder: it's just 1 more. So, the "near doubles" can be derived from knowing the doubles.

Strategies for Subtraction Facts

Common strategies for subtraction include using counters, counting up, counting back, using 10, and reasoning from related addition and subtraction facts.

Using Counters

This method consists of modeling the problem with counters like beans or chips. For example, to solve 8 − 3, the student gets 8 beans, removes 3 beans, and counts the remaining beans to find the difference. As with using the addition strategy "counting all," this is a relatively straightforward strategy that may not be efficient but has the great advantage of usually being well understood by the student.

Counting Up

The student starts at the lower number and counts on to the higher number, perhaps using fingers to keep track of how many numbers are counted. For example, to solve $8 - 5$, the student wants to know how to get from 5 to 8 and counts up 3 numbers: 6, 7, 8. So, $8 - 5 = 3$.

Figure 2: *Counting up*

Counting Back

Counting back works best for subtracting 1, 2, or 3. For larger numbers, it is probably best to count up. For example, to solve $9 - 2$, the student counts back 2 numbers: 8, 7. So, $9 - 2 = 7$.

$$9 - 2 = 7 \qquad 9 \quad 8 \quad 7$$

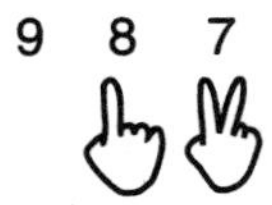

Figure 3: *Counting back*

Using a 10

Students follow the pattern they find when subtracting 10, e.g., $17 - 10 = 7$ and $13 - 10 = 3$, to learn close facts, e.g., $17 - 9 = 8$ and $13 - 9 = 4$. Since $17 - 9$ will be 1 more than $17 - 10$, they can reason that the answer will be 8, or $7 + 1$.

Making a 10

Knowing the addition facts which have a sum of 10, e.g., $6 + 4 = 10$, can be helpful in finding differences from 10, e.g., $10 - 6 = 4$ and $10 - 4 = 6$. Students can use ten frames to visualize these problems as shown in Figure 4. These facts can then also be used to find close facts, such as $11 - 4 = 7$.

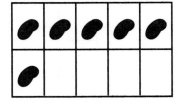

$$10 - 4 = 6$$

Figure 4: *Using a ten frame*

Using Doubles

The addition doubles, e.g., $8 + 8 = 16$ and $6 + 6 = 12$, can be used to learn the subtraction "half-doubles" as well: $16 - 8 = 8$ and $12 - 6 = 6$. These facts can then be used to figure out close facts, such as $13 - 6 = 7$ and $15 - 8 = 7$.

Reasoning from Related Addition and Subtraction Facts

Knowing that $8 + 7 = 15$ would seem to be of some help in solving $15 - 7$. Unfortunately, however, knowing related addition facts may not be so helpful to younger or less mathematically mature students. Nevertheless, reasoning from known facts is a powerful strategy for those who can apply it and should be encouraged.

Strategies for Multiplication Facts

Common strategies for multiplication include skip counting, counting up or down from a known fact, doubling, breaking a product into the sum of known products, and using patterns.

Skip Counting

Students begin skip counting and solving problems informally that involve multiplicative situations in first grade. By the time formal work with the multiplication facts is begun in third grade, they should be fairly proficient with skip counting. This strategy is particularly useful for facts such as the 2s, 3s, 5s, and 10s, for which skip counting is easy.

Counting Up or Down from a Known Fact

This strategy involves skip counting forwards once or twice from a known fact. For example, if a child knows that 5×5 is 25, then this can be used to solve 6×5 (5 more) or 4×5 (5 less). Some children use this for harder facts. For 7×6, they can use the fact that $5 \times 6 = 30$ as a starting point and then count on by sixes to 42.

Doubling

Some children use doubling relationships to help them with multiplication facts involving 4, 6, and 8. For example, 4×7 is twice as much as 2×7. Since $2 \times 7 = 14$, it follows that 4×7 is 28. Since 3×8 is 24, it follows that 6×8 is 48.

Breaking a Product into the Sum of Known Products

A fact like 7×8 can be broken into the sum $5 \times 8 + 2 \times 8$ since $7 = 5 + 2$. (See Figure 5.) The previous two strategies are special cases of this more general strategy.

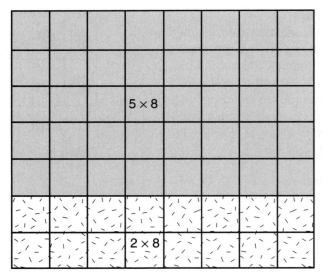

$$7 \times 8 =$$
$$5 \times 8 + 2 \times 8 =$$
$$40 + 16 = 56$$

Figure 5: *Breaking up 7 × 8*

Patterns

A. Perhaps the best-known examples of patterns are the nines patterns:

1. When the nines products are listed in a column, as shown below, it is easy to see that the digits in the tens place count up by one (0, 1, 2, 3, . . .) and that the digits in the ones place count down by one (9, 8, 7, . . .).

   9
   18
   27
   36
   45
   54
   63
   72
   81

2. The sums of the two digits in each of the nines products above are all equal to nine. For example, the sum of the digits in 36 is $3 + 6 = 9$; the sum of the digits in 72 is $7 + 2 = 9$. Adding the digits of a number to see whether they add up to nine can be a strategy in remembering a nines fact. For example, a student might think, "Let me see, does 9×6 equal 54 or 56? It must be 54 since $5 + 4$ is 9, but $5 + 6$ is not 9."

3. The digit in the tens place in a nines fact is one less than the number being multiplied. For example, $4 \times 9 = 36$, and 3 is one less than 4. This can be combined with the previous pattern to derive nines facts. For example, 3×9 is in the twenties. Since $2 + 7$ is 9, 3×9 must be 27.

4. Nines can easily be computed using the counting down strategy. Nine times a digit is the same as 10 times the digit, minus the digit. For example, 9×6 is $10 \times 6 - 6 = 54$

B. Other patterns.

   There are other patterns that can be useful in remembering other special facts:

1. 0 times a number equals 0.

2. 1 times a number equals the number.

3. 2 times a number is double the number.

4. 5 times a number ends in 0 or 5; even numbers times 5 end in 0 and odd numbers times five end in 5.

5. 10 times a number is the same number with a 0 on the end.

Sequencing the Study of Multiplication Facts

In kindergarten, children solve word problems involving multiplication situations. Beginning in first grade, the curriculum develops a conceptual foundation for multiplication through a variety of multiplication models, including repeated addition, the array model, and the number-line model. Fluency with the multiplication facts is expected by the end of third grade. Strategies are often introduced in specific, third-grade lessons. Practice is continued in subsequent lessons and especially in the Daily Practice and Problems and Home Practice. We do not introduce the multiplication facts in the order in which they are traditionally taught (first learning the 2s, then the

3s, then the 4s, etc.). Rather, we emphasize thinking strategies for the facts, introducing fact-groups in the following order:

2s, 3s, 5s, and 10s. The 2s, 3s, 5s, and 10s are easily solved using skip counting.

Square numbers such as $3 \times 3 = 9$, $4 \times 4 = 16$, and $5 \times 5 = 25$. These are introduced by arranging tiles into square arrays.

Nines. Students explore patterns for nines.

Last six facts. After students have learned the facts listed above and their turn-around facts ($9 \times 6 = 6 \times 9$), there are only six more facts to learn: 4×6, 4×7, 4×8, 6×7, 6×8, and 7×8.

Strategies for the Division Facts

The main strategy for learning the division facts is to think of the related multiplication fact. Therefore, students review the multiplication facts and develop fluency with the division facts by working with fact families. (Fact families are groups of related facts. An example of a fact family is $3 \times 4 = 12$, $4 \times 3 = 12$, $12 \div 3 = 4$, and $12 \div 4 = 3$.)

Using the Right Strategy

Different strategies appeal to different students. Students should not feel overburdened with the need to determine which is the "correct" strategy for a given fact. We do not intend to give them a new layer of things to learn. For example, when asked to explain a strategy for a fact, a student may say, "I've used it so much that now I just remember it." "Just remembering" is obviously an efficient strategy. The purpose of suggesting and discussing various strategies is to give students other, perhaps helpful, ways of learning the facts and to give them the confidence to think problems through when necessary. Students should have the opportunity to choose the strategies that work best for them or to invent their own.

Math Facts Lessons

The *Math Trailblazers* math facts program pervades most of the curriculum's components. Work with math facts can be found in different kinds of lessons. These are described in this section.

Figure 6: *Discussing fact strategies*

Everyday Work

As students work on problems in the labs and activities, they should be encouraged to use and to discuss various strategies for solving math facts problems. A number of important goals can best be reached through such discussions.

One goal is to legitimize all valid strategies, even those that may be less efficient. When students see their intuitive methods recognized and validated, they tend to perceive mathematical knowledge as continuous with everyday knowledge and common sense. We thus hope to avoid the unfortunate tendency of many students to separate their knowledge of mathematics from their knowledge of the real world.

By discussing strategies as they arise in context, students and teachers can explore how the strategies work and can verify that they are being used properly. Students should come to realize that a fact strategy that gives wrong answers is not very useful.

A second goal of our approach is to encourage students to communicate mathematical ideas. There are several reasons to stress communication: Students can learn from one another; communicating a method requires higher orders of thinking than simply applying that method; and skill at communicating is important in itself. We are social creatures. Mathematics and science are social endeavors in which communication is crucial.

A third goal of encouraging discussions of various methods is to give the teacher opportunities to learn about how students think. Knowing more about students' thinking helps the teacher ask better questions and plan more effective lessons.

Strategy Lessons

We feel that occasionally it is appropriate for lessons to focus on certain strategies that are developmentally appropriate for most students. Our plan is to begin with simple strategies that should be accessible to all students and to progress gradually to more complex forms of reasoning. For example, in the fall of first grade, we have several lessons that stress counting on to solve certain addition problems. Later, we explicitly introduce making a 10 and other, more sophisticated, strategies.

In general, you should expect your students to come up with effective strategies on their own. Our strategy lessons are intended to explore how and why various strategies work and also to codify and organize the strategies the students invent. They are not meant to dictate the only appropriate strategy for a given problem or to discourage students from using strategies they understand and like. They should be seen as opportunities to discuss strategies that may be appropriate for many students and to encourage their wider use.

Practice

Our ultimate goal is to produce students who can think mathematically, who can solve problems and deal easily with quantified information, and who enjoy mathematics and are not afraid of it. It is easier to do all of the above if one has fluency with the basic math facts. Practice strengthens students' abilities to use strategies and moves students towards fluency with the facts. Practice that follows instruction that stresses the use of strategies has been shown to improve

As students work on problems in the labs and activities, they should be encouraged to use and to discuss various strategies for solving math facts problems.

Our ultimate goal is to produce students who can think mathematically, who can solve problems and deal easily with quantified information, and who enjoy mathematics and are not afraid of it. It is easier to do all of the above if one has fluency with the basic math facts.

students' fluency with the math facts. We recommend, and have incorporated into the curriculum, the following practice to gain this fluency.

Practice in Context

The primary practice of math facts will arise naturally for the students as they participate in the labs and other activities in the curriculum. These labs and activities offer many opportunities to practice addition, subtraction, multiplication, and division in a meaningful way. The lessons involve the student visually with drawings and patterns, auditorily through discussion, and tactilely through the use of many tools such as manipulatives and calculators.

Pages of problems on the basic facts are not only unnecessary, they can be counterproductive. Students may come to regard mathematics as mostly memorization and may perceive it as meaningless and unconnected to their everyday lives.

Structured Practice

Student-friendly, structured practice is built into the curriculum, especially in the DPP, Home Practice, and games. One small group of related math facts is presented to the students at a time. The practice of groups of facts is carefully distributed throughout the year. A small set of facts grouped in a meaningful way leads students to develop strategies such as adding doubles, counting back, or using a 10 for dealing with a particular situation. Furthermore, a small set of facts is a manageable amount to learn and remember.

Beginning in the second half of first grade and continuing through fifth grade, a small group of facts to be studied in a unit is introduced in the DPP. Through DPP items, students practice the facts and take a short assessment. Beginning in second grade, students use flash cards for additional practice with specific groups of facts. Facts are also practiced in many word problems in the DPP, Home Practice, and individual lessons. These problems allow students to focus on other interesting mathematical ideas as they also gain more fact practice.

Games

A variety of games are included in the curriculum, both in the lessons and in the DPP items of many units. A summary of the games used in a particular grade can be found in Section 12. Once students learn the rules of the games, they should play them periodically in class and at home for homework. Games provide an opportunity to encourage family involvement in the math program. When a game is assigned for homework, a note can be sent home with a place for the family members to sign, affirming that they played the game with their student.

Figure 7: *Playing a game*

Use of Calculators

The relationship between knowing the math facts and the use of calculators is an interesting one. Using a multiplication table or a calculator when necessary to find a fact helps promote familiarity and reinforces the math facts. Students soon figure out that it is quicker and more efficient to know the basic facts than to have to use these tools. The use of calculators also requires excellent estimation skills so that one can easily check for errors in calculator computations. Rather than eliminating the need for fluency with the facts, successful calculator use for solving complex problems depends on fact knowledge.

When to Practice

Practicing small groups of facts often for short periods of time is more effective than practicing many facts less often for long periods of time. For example, practicing 8 to 10 subtraction facts for 5 minutes several times a week is better than practicing all the subtraction facts for half an hour once a week. Good times for practicing the facts for 5 or 10 minutes during the school day include the beginning of the day, the beginning of math class, when students have completed an assignment, when an impending activity is delayed, or when an activity ends earlier than expected. Practicing small groups of facts at home involves parents in the process and frees class time for more interesting mathematics.

Practicing small groups of facts often for short periods of time is more effective than practicing many facts less often for long periods of time.

Assessment

Throughout the curriculum, teachers assess students' knowledge of the facts through observations as they work on activities, labs, and games. In Grades 3–5, students can use their *Facts I Know* charts to record their own progress in learning the facts. This type of self-assessment is very important in helping each student to become responsible for his or her own learning. Students are able to personalize their study of facts and not waste valuable time studying facts they already know.

In the second half of first grade, a sequence of facts assessments is provided in the Daily Practice and Problems. A more comprehensive facts assessment program begins in second grade. This program assesses students' progress in learning the facts, as outlined in the Expectations by Grade Level section of this tutor. As students develop strategies for a given group of facts, short quizzes accompany the practice. Students know which facts will be tested, focus practice in class and at home on those facts, then take the quiz. As they take the quiz, they use one color pencil to write answers before a given time limit, then use another color to complete the problems they need more time to answer. Students then use their *Facts I Know* charts to make a record of those facts they answered quickly, those facts they answered correctly but with less efficient strategies, and those facts they did not know at all. Using this information, students can concentrate their efforts on gaining fluency with those facts they answered correctly, but not quickly. They also know to develop strategies for those facts they could not answer at all. In this way, the number of facts studied at any one time becomes more manageable, practice becomes more meaningful, and the process less intimidating.

Tests of all the facts for any operation have a very limited role. They are used no more than two times a year to show growth over time and should not be given daily or weekly. Since we rarely, if ever, need to recall 100 facts at one time in everyday life, overemphasizing tests of all the facts reinforces the notion that math is nothing more than rote memorization and has no connection to the real world. Quizzes of small numbers of facts are as effective and not as threatening. They give students, parents, and teachers the information needed to continue learning and practicing efficiently. With an assessment approach based on strategies and the use of small groups of facts, students can see mathematics as connected to their own thinking and gain confidence in their mathematical abilities.

Conclusion

Research provides clear indications for curriculum developers and teachers about the design of effective math facts instruction. These recommendations formed the foundation of the *Math Trailblazers* math facts program. Developing strategies for learning the facts (rather than relying on rote memorization), distributing practice of small groups of facts, applying math facts in interesting problems, and using an appropriate assessment program— all are consistent with recommendations from current research. It is an instructional approach that encourages students to make sense of the mathematics they are learning. The resulting program will add efficiency and effectiveness to your students' learning of the math facts.

References

Ashlock, R.B., and C.A. Washbon. "Games: Practice Activities for the Basic Facts." In M.N. Suydam and R.E. Reys (eds.), *Developing Computational Skills: 1978 Yearbook.* National Council of Teachers of Mathematics, Reston, VA, 1978.

Beattie, L.D. "Children's Strategies for Solving Subtraction-Fact Combinations." *Arithmetic Teacher,* 27 (1), pp. 14–15, 1979.

Brownell, W.A., and C.B. Chazal. "The Effects of Premature Drill in Third-Grade Arithmetic." *Journal of Educational Research,* 29 (1), 1935.

Carpenter, T.P., and J.M. Moser. "The Acquisition of Addition and Subtraction Concepts in Grades One through Three." *Journal for Research in Mathematics Education,* 15 (3), pp. 179–202, 1984.

Cook, C.J., and J.A. Dossey. "Basic Fact Thinking Strategies for Multiplication—Revisited." *Journal for Research in Mathematics Education,* 13 (3), pp. 163–171, 1982.

Davis, E.J. "Suggestions for Teaching the Basic Facts of Arithmetic." In M.N. Suydam and R.E. Reys (eds.), *Developing Computational Skills: 1978 Yearbook.* National Council of Teachers of Mathematics, Reston, VA, 1978.

Fuson, K.C. "Teaching Addition, Subtraction, and Place-Value Concepts." In L. Wirszup and R. Streit (eds.), *Proceedings of the UCSMP International Conference on Mathematics Education: Developments in School Mathematics Education Around the World: Applications-Oriented Curricula and Technology-Supported Learning for All Students.* National Council of Teachers of Mathematics, Reston, VA, 1987.

Fuson, K.C., and G.B. Willis. "Subtracting by Counting Up: More Evidence." *Journal for Research in Mathematics Education,* 19 (5), pp. 402–420, 1988.

Fuson, K.C., J.W. Stigler, and K. Bartsch. "Grade Placement of Addition and Subtraction Topics in Japan, Mainland China, the Soviet Union, Taiwan, and the United States." *Journal for Research in Mathematics Education,* 19 (5), pp. 449–456, 1988.

Greer, B. "Multiplication and Division as Models of Situations." In D.A. Grouws (ed.), *Handbook of Research on Mathematics Teaching and Learning: A Project of the National Council of Teachers of Mathematics* (Chapter 13). Macmillan, New York, 1992.

Hiebert, James. "Relationships between Research and the NCTM Standards." *Journal for Research in Mathematics Education,* 30 January, pp. 3–19, 1999.

Isaacs, A.C., and W.M. Carroll. "Strategies for Basic Facts Instruction." *Teaching Children Mathematics,* 5 May, pp. 508–515, 1999.

Kouba, V.L., C.A. Brown, T.P. Carpenter, M.M. Lindquist, E.A. Silver, and J.O. Swafford. "Results of the Fourth NAEP Assessment of Mathematics: Number, Operations, and Word Problems." *Arithmetic Teacher,* 35 (8), pp. 14–19, 1988.

Myers, A.C., and C.A. Thornton. "The Learning-Disabled Child—Learning the Basic Facts." *Arithmetic Teacher,* 25 (3), pp. 46–50, 1977.

National Research Council. *Adding It Up: Helping Children Learn Mathematics.* National Academy Press, Washington, DC, 2001.

Principles and Standards for School Mathematics. National Council of Teachers of Mathematics, Reston, VA, 2000.

Rathmell, E.C. "Using Thinking Strategies to Teach the Basic Facts." In M.N. Suydam and R.E. Reys (eds.), *Developing Computational Skills: 1978 Yearbook.* National Council of Teachers of Mathematics, Reston, VA, 1978.

Rathmell, E.C., and P.R. Trafton. "Whole Number Computation." In J.N. Payne (ed.), *Mathematics for the Young Child.* National Council of Teachers of Mathematics, Reston, VA, 1990.

Swart, W.L. "Some Findings on Conceptual Development of Computational Skills." *Arithmetic Teacher,* 32 (5), pp. 36–38, 1985.

Thornton, C.A. "Doubles Up—Easy!" *Arithmetic Teacher,* 29 (8), p. 20, 1982.

Thornton, C.A. "Emphasizing Thinking Strategies in Basic Fact Instruction." *Journal for Research in Mathematics Education,* 9 (3), pp. 214–227, 1978.

Thornton, C.A. "Solution Strategies: Subtraction Number Facts." *Educational Studies in Mathematics,* 21 (1), pp. 241–263, 1990.

Thornton, C.A. "Strategies for the Basic Facts." In J.N. Payne (ed.), *Mathematics for the Young Child.* National Council of Teachers of Mathematics, Reston, VA, 1990.

Thornton, C.A., and P.J. Smith. "Action Research: Strategies for Learning Subtraction Facts." *Arithmetic Teacher,* 35 (8), pp. 8–12, 1988.

Van de Walle, J. *Elementary and Middle School Mathematics: Teaching Developmentally.* Addison Wesley, New York, 2001.

Portfolios

A portfolio is a purposeful collection of a student's work that provides evidence of the student's skills, understandings, or attitudes. If the portfolio includes work collected over time, then it may also reflect the student's growth.

This tutor outlines reasons portfolios may be useful and provides some guidance for getting started and going further. A bibliography includes suggestions for additional reading.

Why Portfolios?

Portfolios can help teachers:

- better assess student learning;
- foster student autonomy;
- communicate the goals of instruction to students and parents; and
- improve their own teaching.

Student Assessment

Since a portfolio contains direct samples of student work, it may, for certain purposes, be superior to indirect indicators like grades. For example, an actual graph shows a student's skill at graphing better than a grade; and the juxtaposition of two graphs, one from September and the other from January, documents learning over time much more accurately than two grades could ever do.

Many outcomes that are hard to assess by more conventional methods—communication, reasoning, problem solving, confidence, perseverance, flexibility, and so on—can be assessed using portfolios. Portfolios can help teachers learn more about how students think and track the development of that thinking.

Student Autonomy

Portfolios can encourage students to assess their own learning. Students become more self-directed and motivated by examining and reflecting on their own work and the work of their peers.

Many outcomes that are hard to assess by more conventional methods . . . can be assessed using portfolios. Portfolios can help teachers learn more about how students think and track the development of that thinking.

Communication

Concrete examples of student work reveal much that cannot be easily conveyed in grades or comments. Parents and others can see for themselves progress and achievement.

The examples of student work in a portfolio also convey the content and goals of the curriculum in a specific way that complements the generalities of curriculum philosophies and scope and sequence charts. Portfolios focus on the work students actually do, not on ideology or wishful thinking. Communication between students and their parents, teachers, and peers can be enhanced by having particular examples to discuss.

Portfolios can help establish public norms for mathematics achievement. When assessment focuses on tests and grades, then a narrow conception of what is valuable in mathematics is communicated. When assessment is more broadly based, then a broader vision of mathematics is promoted.

Improvement of Instruction

Student portfolios can be useful both for making instructional decisions and for evaluating and improving instruction.

Certainly, better understanding of how students think and feel can help teachers make better decisions about directions for future instruction. But portfolios can also help teachers improve their teaching more generally. Portfolios can facilitate discussions with professional colleagues about different approaches to the same topic; they can reflect the range of instructional opportunities being offered; and they can indicate the use of manipulatives, group work, and technology in an implemented curriculum.

Student portfolios might be included in a Teaching Portfolio that a teacher can use for self-evaluation. One's own teaching can be refined by collecting and examining several years of student portfolios. Some of the benefits that portfolios promise for students—collegiality, establishment of public norms, improvement of higher-level skills—may thus become available to teachers.

Getting Started

The beginnings of all things are small.

—Cicero

There is no single right way to do portfolios.

There is no single right way to do portfolios. The suggestions offered below have worked for others and may work for you, but you should expect to learn by trial and error and to have to rely on your own judgment. If you have used portfolios for writing or some other subject, then your experience will be invaluable. If you possibly can, work with a colleague as you implement portfolios for the first time.

Starting small, with modest goals, is a good idea. For example, you may organize your portfolio program around one well-defined area that is hard to assess by more traditional methods. For instance, choose one of the following areas as a theme for the portfolios:

- measurement,
- graphing,

- drawing pictures and diagrams, or
- communication of solution methods.

Besides starting small, start early so that you have a baseline of student attitudes and achievement. Before and after comparisons are useful, but are impossible without early samples. All materials in a portfolio must be dated.

A box with a file folder for each child's work is a simple way to get started. If the box is easily accessible, then the portfolios are more likely to fit into classroom routines. Anticipate the need for more room as items are added to the portfolios.

What goes in the portfolios is a key question. Figure 1 shows some kinds of materials that might be included in a portfolio, although clearly no real portfolio will have such a wild collection. Figure 2 is a table of contents for a possible third-grade portfolio.

You might aim for balance in the selection of materials: group vs. individual assignments; short problems vs. longer projects; real life vs. purely mathematical problems; on-demand vs. no-deadline tasks; attitude vs. skill vs. concept-oriented work; and so on. The number of pieces should not be so few that there is not enough evidence about important outcomes, nor so many that there is no judgment about what is important or worthwhile. About eight to ten pieces might be enough for a semester.

How to pick what to put in the portfolios must also be decided. We suggest that the selection of items be made by the students subject to constraints imposed by the teacher. These constraints might range from compelling that particular items be included, to requiring that items be chosen to meet certain criteria, to allowing complete freedom of choice by students. The amount of latitude allowed by the teacher will depend on his or her class and goals. Younger children, for example, usually need more direction. Putting fewer constraints on what goes in the portfolios may foster student autonomy, but may result in portfolios with few overlapping items so that comparisons between students are difficult, or may even yield useless collections of random scraps.

The number of pieces should not be so few that there is not enough evidence about important outcomes, nor so many that there is no judgment about what is important or worthwhile. About eight to ten pieces might be enough for a semester.

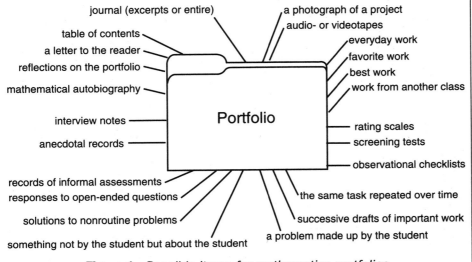

Figure 1: *Possible items for mathematics portfolios*

One way to organize the selection process is to have two folders for each child—a collection folder and the portfolio proper. Then, from time to time (once every several weeks or so), the collection folder can be harvested and a few select items added to the portfolio. At the same time, the portfolio can also be weeded so that the total number of items does not become too large. This selection can be done by students in small groups or pairs subject to teacher constraints as described above. The items remaining in the collection folder can be kept there or sent home.

Eight to ten well-chosen and chronologically arranged pieces of work can be most useful. You will have specific examples that communicate at parent conference time what your curriculum is and how your students are progressing; you will have a sampling of the products of your instruction so that you can critically examine your teaching; and your students will be confronted with a cross section of their own work so that they can attain greater self-awareness and autonomy. You have accomplished much even if your portfolios are no more than this.

Going Further

There are, however, other things that you might want to try as you gain experience with portfolios, especially if you are working with older students. Periodic reviews of the portfolios, writing about the portfolios, and assessing the portfolios are worth considering.

Jarrett's Portfolio • Table of Contents		
Item	**Description**	**Date**
Letter to Reader	My letter tells what my portfolio shows about my math work this semester.	9/22
Journal	A few times a week we write about math in our journals. Mine has 35 pages so far!	
Spinning Differences	I used a spinner to make subtraction problems and then graphed how many times I got each difference.	9/27
The Better "Picker Upper"	I used water to make spots on different kinds of paper towels. Then I counted square cm to find the areas of the spots.	10/25
Joe the Goldfish	Joe needed a raincoat and I figured out how much cloth he would need to make it.	11/1
Palindromes	A palindrome is a number that is the same frontwards and backwards. I used addition to make numbers into palindromes.	11/10
Lemonade Stand	This was the first line graph I ever made.	11/15
Mass vs. Number	I measured the mass of different numbers of marbles. Then I made a line graph and used it to make some predictions.	12/5
Stencilrama	This was my favorite. We made stencils out of index cards and then used the stencils to make designs. We had to figure out how many times we would have to move the stencil to make a border around the bulletin board.	1/15

Figure 2: *Sample third-grade portfolio with an emphasis on graphing*

Portfolio Review

Most teachers will be hard-pressed to find time to meet with individual students to review portfolios. Whole-class discussion and peer consultations, however, can accomplish many of the same goals.

For example, ask students to look through their collection folders for their best graphs to be added to their portfolios. First, through whole-class discussion, help students identify characteristics of a good graph. Then in small groups or pairs, students can examine their collections to pick out the best graphs. This opportunity for students to examine one another's work can help establish public norms for excellence.

Portfolio Writing

Asking students to write about the contents of their portfolios encourages reflection and self-assessment. This writing can take a variety of forms.

The most basic writing is a table of contents with the name of each piece, a brief description, and the date it was completed. Students can also include who chose the piece and why, who worked on the piece, and what was learned or liked or hard about the piece.

You might ask students to write a letter to the reader of the portfolio. The letter can identify favorite pieces and explain why they are favorites, or best work, or work that shows the most progress. The letter might point out what the portfolio reveals about the student as a learner of mathematics.

Assessing the Portfolios

You should not feel that you must assess the portfolios. The work included in them, after all, has most likely been graded already, and the collection is itself a direct indicator of achievement and attitude, a direct indicator that may be sufficient for your purposes.

Assessing the portfolios, however, can have advantages, especially if you are working with older students. For one, it shows that you care about the portfolios and so communicates to the students that they should take them seriously. It can also model processes you want students to apply in peer- and self-assessment of the portfolios.

If you do intend to grade the portfolios, you should make your expectations known to the students in advance. The establishment of such public criteria for excellence, like the TIMS Student Rubrics, will help students know what they should aim for so that their work can be better focused. You might concentrate on how well the portfolios are organized—table of contents, correct chronological order, completeness, etc.—or on the quality of the reflective writing about the portfolio. You may encourage a balanced selection of items, documentation of improvement over time, clarity of communication, accuracy of self-assessment, neatness, or something else. As long as your criteria are known to the students and so long as you have the time to do it, such grading can be useful.

Conclusion

Portfolios will not solve all the problems of mathematics education. And there are some costs for using them. Using portfolios as part of an assessment program will certainly take extra time and can be difficult, especially at first. Getting students to reflect on their own learning is particularly hard. But despite such pitfalls, portfolios offer great promise for improving your teaching and your students' learning. The basic idea is simple: collect, select, reflect.

References

Crowley, Mary L. "Student Mathematics Portfolio: More Than a Display Case." *Mathematics Teacher,* 86 (7), pp. 544–547, 1993.

Kuhs, Therese. "Portfolio Assessment: Making It Work for the First Time." *Mathematics Teacher,* 87 (5), pp. 332–335, 1994.

Lambdin, Diana V., and Vicki L. Walker. "Planning for Classroom Portfolio Assessment." *Arithmetic Teacher,* 41 (6), pp. 318–324, 1994.

Mumme, Judith. *Portfolio Assessment in Mathematics.* (A publication of the California Mathematics Project.) University of California, Santa Barbara, CA, 1990.

Stenmark, Jean Kerr, ed. *Mathematics Assessment: Myths, Models, Good Questions, and Practical Suggestions.* National Council of Teachers of Mathematics, Reston, VA, 1991.

Word Problems

In fact, word problems should not just be integrated into the mathematics curriculum; they should form the basis of the curriculum.

—CARPENTER, FENNEMA, AND PETERSON, 1987

Although word problems are not the basis of the *Math Trailblazers* curriculum, we do agree that students should confront a wide variety of challenging word problems and exercises. Word problems can highlight applications of the mathematics students are learning. They can introduce, motivate, and develop new mathematics in meaningful contexts.

This tutor provides a summary for teachers of research and background information about word problems. It outlines the theoretical and practical frameworks that underlie the extensive use of word problems in *Math Trailblazers*.

Problem Representations

Problems are presented to us in different ways. Sometimes a problem arises from a real situation; other times we have problems given in words, pictures, or symbols. These different ways are sometimes called modes of representation.

Real Situations

Consider this problem: "Jessica and Meri Joy baked 36 cookies. Then, Meri Joy dropped 12 cookies on the floor. How many were left?" Now this problem has a basis in reality: Jessica and Meri Joy are the daughters of two members of the *Math Trailblazers* development team; they really did bake cookies; some cookies really were dropped and spoiled. Note that Meri Joy and Jessica could answer the question simply by counting the cookies that were not dropped.

Such real-life situations are the most concrete level of problem representation. People rarely go wrong when they solve such problems. (Resnick, 1987)

Concrete Model

If, however, some time has passed and the cookies are no longer at hand, we can still ask and answer the question. One way is to get some beans and to pretend they are cookies. To solve the problem, we can count out 36 beans, separate 12, and count how many remain.

This use of beans to represent cookies is one step up the ladder of abstraction: a concrete model represents a real situation. Good evidence exists that even kindergarten students can handle complex problems that are represented by concrete models. (Carpenter, Ansell, Franke, Fennema, and Weisbeck, 1993)

Figure 1: *Twelve of 36 cookies dropped*

Pictures

Another way to approach the problem is via pictures. Each cookie can be represented by a circle. We can solve the problem by drawing 36 circles, crossing out 12, and counting those left.

This sort of pictorial representation is often useful in mathematics and science. Even when the picture does not lead immediately to a solution, it often helps us understand the problem situation and starts us on the road to a solution.

Verbal Representations

Most school problems are stated in words. This is often necessary (How else could our cookie problem have been presented in this essay?) and builds on a well-developed set of skills your students have—their language skills.

Language is the first and most powerful symbol system we learn. The recent emphasis on discourse and communication in learning is based at least in part on a recognition of the importance of language in human thought.

Symbols

We can also represent Jessica and Meri Joy's cookies in symbols:

$$36 - 12 = \Box$$

Such symbolic representations are abstract and powerful. Much of the explosive growth of mathematics in the last 400 years is due to the invention of more efficient symbol systems.

Unfortunately, for too many students, mathematical symbolism is a code they never crack. Such students do not see the marks on paper as meaningful or related to the real world in any way. Instead, they see the marks as part of an arcane game.

When writing number sentences, it is important to use units. Of course, constantly writing the units can be tedious. One compromise is to omit the units in the middle of a sequence of symbolic representations, but to be sure to include them at the beginning and again at the end.

Even when the picture does not lead immediately to a solution, it often helps us understand the problem situation and starts us on the road to a solution.

We want students to learn to write, read, and understand mathematical symbolism, especially number sentences. Here, word problems can be particularly useful. The situations in many word problems are straightforward enough that the corresponding number sentences are simple.

Usually, several number sentences are appropriate for each problem. Consider, for example, the following problem: "Janice had 9 stickers. Then her mother gave her some more. Then Janice had 16 stickers. How many stickers did Janice's mother give her?"

An adult might see this as a subtraction problem and write

$$16 - 9 = 7 \hspace{4cm} \text{(a)}$$
or
$$16 - 9 = \square \hspace{4cm} \text{(b)}$$

These number sentences are in the normal or "canonical" form. That is, the known quantities are on the left-hand side of the equals sign and the unknown or the answer is on the right-hand side.

Many students, however, write something like

$$9 + \square = 16 \hspace{4cm} \text{(c)}$$
or
$$9 + 7 = 16 \hspace{4cm} \text{(d)}$$

These "non-canonical" forms reflect the students' way of thinking about the problem: Janice had 9 stickers, then she got some more, and then she had 16 stickers. Often a student who writes (c) or (d) will solve the problem by counting on from 9 to 16 rather than by subtracting 9 from 16. We consider these non-canonical number sentences to be as correct as the canonical forms. They can also be more understandable for the students.

Translations between Representations

So we have a hierarchy of levels of representation: real objects, physical models, pictures, words, symbols.

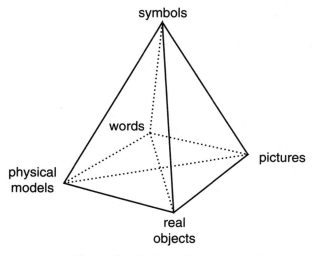

Figure 2: *Modes of representation*

Recent cognitive theory indicates that the ability to translate from one representation to another is a crucial part of conceptual understanding and problem-solving skill. . . . Our goal is to have students create mental "two-way streets" between symbols, words, concrete models, pictures, and real situations.

But perhaps "hierarchy of levels" is not quite the right phrase; it may be better to consider that there are a number of different modes of representation, each of which has certain strengths and weaknesses. Recent cognitive theory indicates that the ability to translate from one representation to another is a crucial part of conceptual understanding and problem-solving skill. Being able to connect symbols with real referents, for example, permits one to understand symbolic manipulations and results in terms of real situations. Earlier, we saw how translating a problem from a real or verbal presentation to a concrete model could yield a solution by an elementary method.

Unfortunately, too much instruction in mathematics focuses exclusively on symbols. While symbolic representations are compact and powerful, they cannot stand alone. Our goal is to have students create mental "two-way streets" between symbols, words, concrete models, pictures, and real situations. Word problems are an excellent vehicle for reaching this goal.

Solving Problems

One view of problem solving is that the most critical step is developing the right representation: when we see the problem in the correct light, then the solution is obvious. Of course, the right representation for me might not be right for you. Accordingly, just as multiple representations should be part of the mathematics curriculum, so should multiple solutions. Estimation and attention to the reasonableness of results must also be part of instruction in problem solving.

Multiple Solutions

Many students think the main thing in mathematics is to get the right answer. Incorrect or partial answers are seen as failures, and re-solving a problem in a different way is considered futile.

On the contrary, much can be learned by solving problems in several ways. When different methods yield the same answer, students gain confidence both in the answer and in the various methods. This can be particularly useful for students learning more abstract and powerful methods: if a more powerful method gives the same answer as a more familiar method, then the powerful method is more likely to be understood and trusted.

Students can also see connections within mathematics by comparing the points of view that generate different solutions to a problem. Making such connections is a key goal of the National Council of Teachers of Mathematics *Principles and Standards for School Mathematics* (NCTM, 2000). If students share their solution methods, then not only do they learn new methods from one another, but they also learn to communicate mathematically, another *Principles and Standards* goal.

Even incorrect or partial answers can be useful. Wrong answers are almost always the result of an honest attempt by the student to get the problem right. Examining and discussing wrong answers and the procedures that generated them can make students' thinking explicit so that misconceptions can be identified and cleared up.

Sometimes a partial answer is the best we can reasonably hope for. In fact, many practical problems are impossible or prohibitively expensive to solve exactly. In some real situations, a partial answer may be all that is required.

A partial solution may be based on an idea that can be modified or extended to yield a complete solution. If a problem is hard, then making progress towards an answer is perfectly respectable, and certainly far better than giving up.

One way to get the most out of partial solutions is to encourage students to talk and write about the problem even if they cannot solve it. This will also help students stay with difficult problems longer.

Estimation

A common reason for estimating is that an exact answer is not necessary. If we have $5 and want to buy milk, bread, and eggs, a quick estimate will tell us if we have enough money. Sometimes an estimate must serve because an exact answer is impossible or impractical to obtain. The exact number of piano tuners who live in Chicago, for example, can only be estimated.

Another reason to estimate an answer is to verify the accuracy of a result obtained in some other way. This is especially important in our age of computing machines—if we do not have some idea what the answer should be, then we may be at a loss to know whether the answer the machine gives us is reasonable.

A less commonly recognized reason to make an estimate is as a step on the way to an exact answer. As one of our favorite teachers used to say, "Never solve a problem until you know the answer." We think he meant that finding an approximate answer can be helpful in the search for the exact answer. By estimating an answer, we come to understand the problem better.

Learning to estimate builds number sense and encourages students to rely on their common sense rather than on rote procedures. Making a good estimate requires a flexible combination of common sense, experience, rules of thumb, and specific knowledge. Estimation is a high-level skill that takes a long time to develop. Estimation is, accordingly, built into *Math Trailblazers* from the beginning.

Reasonableness of Results

How often have you seen a student's paper with patently absurd answers? Such answers indicate that the student is not working at a meaningful level. Rather some procedures—half-understood, half-remembered—have been carried out and something has been produced, but the relationship of that product to the problem at hand is far from clear. No connection exists in the student's mind between the real situation and the symbolic manipulations.

Looking back when an answer is obtained, mapping the result of symbolic or other manipulations back onto the original problem statement, is a crucial part of the problem-solving process. George Polya, in his famous book *How to Solve It* (1957), included looking back as one of four basic steps in solving a problem. (Polya's other steps are to understand the problem; to make a plan to solve the problem; and to carry out the plan.)

When students look back at a solution, they should assess whether it is reasonable and correct. They can also look for ways to improve the solution, simplify it, or generalize it. By comparing their solution to other solutions, they can obtain further evidence of correctness and they have an opportunity to make connections between different approaches.

Addition and Subtraction Problem Types

Children typically use many varied methods to solve word problems. This, in part, is related to the fact that there is an underlying variety of problem types. The different problem types have been explored extensively by educational researchers in the last 20 years or so. Several different examples are discussed here. Additional discussion about the methods children use to solve problems can be found in the TIMS Tutor: *Math Facts*.

Students should have experience solving many different types of word problems. It is important to note, however, that in discussing the different problem types, we are not suggesting a new level of material for children to learn, i.e., we do not expect nor want children to have to learn about the different types of problems as a study in and of itself. Rather, we discuss the diversity in problem types so that teachers recognize that this variety exists and subsequently are better prepared to present their students with a rich and varied collection of word problems.

Thomas Carpenter and his colleagues (Carpenter, Fennema, and Peterson, 1987; Carpenter, Carey, and Kouba, 1990; Carpenter, et al., 1999) have devised a classification scheme for problems that most adults would solve by simple addition or subtraction. They identify four general types of situations that give rise to 11 different kinds of addition or subtraction problems. (Other researchers have devised similar schemes. See, for example, Riley, Greeno, and Heller, 1983, and Rathmell and Huinker, 1989.)

Join Situations

Carpenter begins with "join" situations. Here, something is joined to a beginning quantity so that a new quantity results. We think of these situations like this:

$$start + change = result$$

If the result is unknown, then we have an addition situation. Otherwise, we have a subtraction situation. Children often have more difficulty with problems in which the start is unknown than those in which the change is unknown.

Join/Result Unknown
Erick had 8 action figures. Then his father gave him 3 new ones. How many did he have then?

Join/Change Unknown
Janice had 9 stickers. Then her mother gave her some more. Then Janice had 16 stickers. How many stickers did Janice's mother give her?

Join/Start Unknown
Maria had some pennies. Then she found 3 more. Then she had 12 pennies. How many pennies did Maria have at first?

Separate Situations

Adults most often think of these situations as take-away problems:

$$start - change = result$$

If the result or change is unknown, then we have a subtraction (or take-away) situation. Otherwise, we have an addition situation.

Separate/Result Unknown

Thomas had 8 cookies. Then he ate 6. How many cookies did he have left?

Separate/Change Unknown

Leah had 12 dolls. Then she gave some of her dolls away. Then she had 7 dolls left. How many dolls did Leah give away?

Separate/Start Unknown

Michael had some marbles. He lost 5 of his marbles. Then he had 7 marbles. How many marbles did Michael have at first?

Part-Whole Situations

Carpenter's third category is part-whole. Here, a single whole is broken into two parts:

$$part + part = whole$$

This is similar to the join situation. The difference is that part-whole situations are static, the two parts coexisting from the beginning, whereas in join situations, two things are put together to form a new whole.

If the whole is unknown in a part-whole situation, then we have an addition situation. Otherwise, we have a subtraction situation.

Part-Whole/Whole Unknown

Ian has some action figures. He has 8 good guys and 3 bad guys. How many action figures does Ian have altogether?

Part-Whole/Part Unknown

There are 14 children who live in Clayton's building. Five of the children are boys. How many girls live in Clayton's building?

Compare Situations

Carpenter's last category is "compare." Here, two independent quantities are being compared:

$$q1 - q2 = difference$$

If the difference or q2 is unknown, then we subtract. If q1 is unknown, we add.

Compare/Difference Unknown

Samantha has $14. Kristin has $5. How much more money does Samantha have?

Compare/Q2 Unknown

Jason has 13 crayons. Angela has 6 fewer than Jason. How many crayons does Angela have?

Compare/Q1 Unknown

Lamar has some markers. Robin has 15 markers. Robin has 7 fewer markers than Lamar has. How many markers does Lamar have?

Compare problems seem to be the hardest for children to solve. The other three types—join, separate, and part-whole—all involve a whole with parts in situations that are either static or dynamic. In compare problems, on the other hand, there is no whole. Rather, there are two independent quantities and a difference between them.

Need for Diversity in Problem Types

Traditionally, just two of these 11 kinds of problems have dominated American elementary mathematics textbooks, a dominance that contrasts sharply with customary practice abroad (Stigler, Fuson, Ham, & Kim, 1986; Fuson, Stigler, & Bartsch, 1988). These favored problem types, moreover, are the easiest to solve. Most of the subtraction problems are take-away situations (separate/result unknown). Most of the addition problems are join/result unknown. By presenting such a limited variety of problems, these texts give students a wrong impression about what addition and subtraction are. Carpenter's four situations—join, separate, part-whole, and compare—and the various types of problems reflect a much wider conception of addition and subtraction. In *Math Trailblazers*, we present this full range of addition and subtraction problems beginning in the earliest grades.

Diversity in Strategies

The description of the various problem types identified addition and subtraction situations. However, students may approach the problems in different ways. For example, while adults may immediately subtract when they encounter a take-away situation (8 cookies − 6 cookies = 2 cookies) some children may choose to use an addition strategy and count up. (Thomas ate 6 cookies and he has 2 left. Two more than 6 is 8 cookies.) Both are valid strategies.

Types of Multiplication and Division Problems

Researchers who have studied multiplication and division have identified different types of multiplication and division problems. While students do not need to be able to identify these different types of problems by name, it is important that they encounter and solve them. The different types of multiplication and division problems are outlined below.

Problems Involving a Number of Equivalent Sets

These sets can be groups of objects, arrays, or jumps on the number line. An example: Ask a class of 20 students to stand in a group. Instruct them to break into teams of four.

Using this situation, three different questions emerge. One question is interpreted as a multiplication problem, the other two as division problems.

Traditionally, just two of these 11 kinds of problems have dominated American elementary mathematics textbooks, a dominance that contrasts sharply with customary practice abroad. . . . These favored problem types, moreover, are the easiest to solve.

The Unknown Is the Total Number in All the Groups

If there are 5 teams with 4 members on each team, how many players are there in all? There are two known factors and a missing product. Using established knowledge, students often interpret this correctly as a repeated addition problem ($4 + 4 + 4 + 4 + 4 = 20$). Through classroom experiences with many such problems, they can connect the repeated addition sentence to a multiplication sentence ($5 \times 4 = 20$).

The Unknown Is the Number of Groups

Twenty members of a class are divided into teams of four members each. How many teams are there? The problem gives the total number in all the groups and the measure or size of each group. This aspect of division is called *measurement division.*

The Unknown Is the Number in Each Group

Twenty members of a class are divided equally into five teams. How many students are on each team? The problem gives the total number of students and the number of partitions or groups. This aspect of division is known as *partitive division.*

Jumps on a number line and arrays provide additional experience with the multiplication and division of equivalent sets. Successive jumps of equal size on a number line provide a model for multiplication as repeated addition and division as repeated subtraction. In *Math Trailblazers*, we model this situation using mythical creatures called "mathhoppers." For example, a $+2$ mathhopper starts at 0 and hops 4 times. On what number will it land? (8)

An array is a group of objects arranged in rows and columns. For example, a candy box that contains 5 rows with 6 pieces in each row is a 5×6 array. One virtue of the array model is that it makes it very clear that $5 \times 6 = 6 \times 5$. The box can be rotated 90 degrees to form a 6×5 array. Another advantage is that it creates a visual image for both multiplication and division problems.

Problems Involving Scale Factors

This type of problem is often found in TIMS Laboratory Investigations. For example, after students have rolled three different cars down a ramp, they might be asked if one car rolled three times as far as another. Similarly, when finding the mass of objects, they may be asked if the mass of one object is one-half the mass of another object.

A Cartesian Product

This problem involves two sets of objects (such as shirts and pants) which must be joined into pairs (shirt-and-pant sets). The answer for this type of problem then becomes the number of unique pairs that can be formed from these two sets. While this type of problem is difficult for young children, they are able to solve it using manipulatives and diagrams.

Experiences with many types of problems should provide a strong conceptual foundation not only for multiplication and division, but for fractions, ratios, and proportional reasoning as well.

Problem Contexts

Most word problems in *Math Trailblazers* are embedded in a larger context; this is often an advantage since situational problems are more meaningful to the students than abstract problems. Sometimes, however, providing a context is constraining or distracting. Also, problems may come to us without context; often, we have to provide extra information to make sense of a problem. Accordingly, in an attempt to provide a balance between problems embedded in situations and problems that are self-contained, we often provide free-standing word problems.

Teaching Word Problems

A variety of approaches to teaching word problems can be useful and stimulating. Here are several:

Whole Class, Then Small Groups

First, present a sample problem to your whole class. Discuss the problem and ask students to estimate the answer. Also ask students to explain how they made their estimates. Neither the estimates nor the explanations are likely to be very good, but this is only the beginning.

Next, ask students to solve the problem in groups of two or three students. Tell them you want (1) an answer for the problem, (2) an explanation of how the answer was obtained, and (3) a number sentence for the problem.

Require students who need help to seek it first from other students in their groups. Clearly, this is beneficial for the students who need the help, but those who give the help also benefit since they must make explicit what they may understand only implicitly. You will also be freed up since your students will be helping one another instead of depending so much on you.

As the students work, move among them, listening to the strategies various groups are using. Use your judgment about what questions to ask and how much help to give, but try to restrain yourself. It will often be better if students struggle on their own and find a solution themselves.

When the groups have answers, reconvene the whole class and ask students to explain their solutions and number sentences for the problem. Be sure they assess the reasonableness and correctness of their results. During these discussions, emphasize that every student is responsible for understanding his or her group's solution. One way to accomplish this is to call on random students to explain each group's work.

Encourage students to solve problems in more than one way by accepting only novel solutions during class discussions. Thus, students will be motivated to search for multiple solutions in order to be able to contribute to the class discussion.

Small Groups, Then Whole Class

As your students gain experience, you can abbreviate or eliminate the whole-class introduction to the problem. Again, a whole-class discussion of solutions is appropriate.

Individual Work, Then Small Groups

Another approach is for students to work individually first and then to come together in pairs or small groups to compare solutions. Then, the small-group solutions can be shared with other groups during a class discussion.

Other Suggestions

Find some word problems appropriate for homework or for individual seatwork. Other problems may be so hard that no student is able to solve them; such problems can be used for whole-class investigations. You may use certain problems to introduce new mathematics like multiplication and division. An interesting problem can be used as an "opener" when students arrive or when math class begins.

TIMS Tips

- If students cannot solve a problem, ask them to describe the problem and to restate it in their own words or ask them to draw a picture. This may lead to a better understanding of the problem and then to a solution.
- Do only a few problems at a time. Distributed practice will be more effective than bunched practice.
- Vary the format: individual, small group, whole class, homework.
- Be sure to discuss multiple solution strategies. Compare and contrast strategies, and point out advantages of each, but accept all correct strategies.
- Discuss several number sentences for each problem. Ask students to explain how a given number sentence fits the problem situation.
- Ask students to explain why the answers they have are reasonable.
- Provide manipulatives and calculators to each group. Just having them available in the room may not be enough—these resources should be immediately at hand.

Conclusion

As your students work word problems and share solutions, they will be applying mathematics they already know and learning new mathematics. Word problems deserve a prominent place in your mathematics lessons.

References

Carpenter, T.P., E. Fennema, M.L. Franke, L. Levi, and S.E. Empson. *Children's Mathematics: Cognitively Guided Instruction.* Heinemann, Westport, CT, 1999.

Carpenter, T.P., E. Fennema, and P. Peterson. "Cognitively Guided Instruction: The Application of Cognitive and Instructional Science to Mathematics Curriculum Development." In *Developments in School Mathematics Education Around the World,* I. Wirszup and R. Streit, eds. National Council of Teachers of Mathematics, Reston, VA, 1987.

Carpenter, T.P., D. Carey, and V. Kouba. "A Problem-Solving Approach to the Operations." In *Mathematics for the Young Child,* J.N. Payne, ed. National Council of Teachers of Mathematics, Reston, VA, 1990.

Carpenter, T.P., E. Ansell, M.L. Franke, E. Fennema, and L. Weisbeck. "Models of Problem Solving: A Study of Fourth Grade Children's Problem-Solving Processes." *Journal for Research in Mathematics Education,* 24 (5), pp. 428–441, 1993.

Fuson, K.C., J.W. Stigler, and K. Bartsch. "Grade Placement of Addition and Subtraction Topics in Japan, Mainland China, the Soviet Union, Taiwan, and the United States." *Journal for Research in Mathematics Education,* 19 (5), pp. 449–456, 1988.

National Council of Teachers of Mathematics. *Principles and Standards for School Mathematics.* National Council of Teachers of Mathematics, Reston, VA, 2000.

Polya, G. *How to Solve It.* Princeton University Press, Princeton, NJ, 1957.

Rathmell, E.C. and D.M. Huinker. "Using Part-Whole Language to Help Children Represent and Solve Word Problems." In *New Directions for Elementary School Mathematics,* P.R. Trafton, ed. National Council of Teachers of Mathematics, Reston, VA, 1989.

Resnick, L.B. "Presidential Address: Learning In School and Out." *Educational Researcher,* 16 (9), pp. 13–20, 1987.

Riley, M.S., J.G. Greeno, and J.I. Heller. "Development of Children's Problem-Solving Ability in Arithmetic." In *The Development of Mathematical Thinking,* H.P. Ginsburg, ed. Academic Press, New York, 1983.

Stigler, J.W., K.C. Fuson, M. Ham, and M.S. Kim. "An Analysis of Addition and Subtraction Word Problems in American and Soviet Elementary Mathematics Textbooks." *Cognition and Instruction,* 3 (3), pp. 153–171, 1986.

The TIMS Laboratory Method

Math Trailblazers is a comprehensive mathematics program that incorporates many important scientific ideas. Scientific concepts often provide contexts for developing and practicing math concepts and skills. The tools and processes of science are integral to mathematical problem solving throughout the curriculum.

This tutor expands upon the *Math Trailblazers* connection with science. It outlines the Teaching Integrated Math and Science (TIMS) Project's view of science and describes the TIMS Laboratory Method, a version of the scientific method. This method forms a framework throughout the curriculum for students to explore science in much the way scientists work.

PART I | The TIMS View of Science

Traditionally, school science has focused on the results of science. Students learn about parts of the body, types of rocks, the solar system, evolution, and so on. Knowing basic facts of science is seen as part of being educated, today more than ever. However, the facts of science, important and interesting as they are, do not alone comprise a comprehensive and balanced science curriculum.

The great educator and philosopher John Dewey expressed this idea almost 100 years ago. In 1910, he wrote:

> *At times, it seems as if the educational availability of science were breaking down because of its sheer mass. There is at once so much of science and so many sciences that educators oscillate, helpless, between arbitrary selection and teaching a little of everything.*
>
> *Visit schools where they have taken nature study conscientiously. This school moves with zealous bustle from leaves to flowers, from flowers to minerals, from minerals to stars, from stars to the raw materials of industry, thence back to leaves and stones.*
>
> *Thus,. . . science teaching has suffered because science has been so frequently presented just as so much ready-made knowledge, so much subject-matter of fact and law, rather than as the effective method of inquiry into any subject-matter.*

Surely if there is any knowledge which is of most worth it is knowledge of the ways by which anything is entitled to be called knowledge instead of being mere opinion or guess-work or dogma.

Such knowledge ... is not information, but a mode of intelligent practise, an habitual disposition of mind.

In 1996, the National Research Council (NRC) published the *National Science Education Standards* for K–12 science education. Among the many recommendations of the NRC document is a direction for decreased emphasis on teaching scientific facts and information, and increased emphasis on teaching for understanding of scientific concepts and developing abilities of inquiry. The NRC *Standards* state:

Emphasizing active science learning means shifting away from teachers presenting information and covering science topics. The perceived need to include all the topics, vocabulary, and information in textbooks is in direct conflict with the central goal of having students learn scientific knowledge with understanding.

These points of view underlie the TIMS approach to science. If we were to describe the TIMS approach in the most concise way possible, we would choose two words, *variable* and *experiment.* The essence of modern science, as it is practiced by scientists, is to understand the relationships among variables. Out of the great sea of variables we have selected those that we feel are fundamental to the understanding of all areas of science, namely: length, area, volume, mass, and time. These variables might be considered the fundamental vocabulary of science. They are integral to the everyday work of biologists, chemists, physicists, astronomers, and earth scientists. The more that a child has explored these variables, the greater will be his or her command of scientific language and the more complete will be his or her ability to take up the adventure of science.

We have therefore made these variables the focus of experiments and activities in Grades K through 5 of *Math Trailblazers.* Explorations in kindergarten are conceptual in nature. As the curriculum progresses through the grades, students revisit the variables many times in increasingly more sophisticated ways. In Grade 5, students are able to move on to compound variables such as density and velocity, which involve two of the basic variables. For example, density involves both mass and volume while velocity involves both length and time. To understand these compound variables, it is important that students are first familiar with the more basic variables. Through repeated investigation of the variables in different contexts, fundamental science concepts and skills become generalized.

> *If we were to describe the TIMS approach in the most concise way possible, we would choose two words, variable and experiment.*

PART II — Variables in Scientific Experiments

A **variable** is a quantity that may assume any one of a set of values. The variable is the heart and soul of science because the variable is to scientific investigation what the word is to language—its foundation and the basis of its structure. All experiments center around at least two variables, and the ability to measure these variables satisfactorily will determine the success or failure of the experiment.

Variables and Values

Variables fall into two broad categories: categorical and numerical. Would you say that the color of a person's hair is a categorical or a numerical variable? Would you say that the height of a person is a categorical or numerical variable? A **numerical variable** is one that may assume a numerical set of values. In contrast, a **categorical variable** is one which does not assume numerical values.

Color, then, which can take on values such as red, blue, or yellow, is a categorical variable. Other categorical variables are shape, kind of object, and type of material of which the object is made. In each case, you have the broad classification, the variable, and then the values the variable can assume.

The simplest kind of numerical variable is the number of objects in a set. For example, if we were studying the number of students who came to class each day, the variable would be "Number of Students," and the possible values of the variable would be 0 students, 1 student, 2 students, etc. A second category of numerical variable is those involving measurement. The basic measurement variables stressed in *Math Trailblazers* are length, area, volume, mass, and time. The values for these variables are what we measure during the course of an experiment. For example, if we are investigating the variable length, the values might be the number of meters, centimeters, millimeters, or other appropriate unit of length. When the variable is area, the values might be the number of square centimeters. Or if volume is the variable, the value might be the number of cubic centimeters, and so on. The variable is the broad classification; the **values** for the variable describe what we are counting or measuring for that variable.

One point in studying variables that will take repeated practice for your students to master is the regular use of units of measure. In science, we never deal with numbers without understanding what their units are. For example, say that we tell you that Mary dropped a ball from a height of 30. A question your students will learn to ask is, "Thirty what?" Was it 30 centimeters, 30 feet, or 30 miles? The name after the number 30 is what we call the unit of measure, and every variable has a set of them. $5 + 4 = 9$ can be meaningless unless we know 5 of what. 5 apples $+$ 4 apples $=$ 9 apples, but 5 apples $+$ 4 pears does not equal either 9 apples or 9 pears. The sum is equal to 9 pieces of fruit. Invariably, children will give you the numerical value of the variable and leave off its unit. Learning to use units is merely a matter of discipline; that is, using them correctly so often that you feel uncomfortable when you either forget them or use them incorrectly. Developing this discipline in your students will help them later in their schooling as they examine more complicated scientific concepts.

Manipulated and Responding Variables in Controlled Experiments

In an experiment, a scientist tries to find a relationship between two variables. Where possible, the experimenter chooses ahead of time the values of one of the variables. This variable is called the **manipulated variable.** The values of the second variable are determined by the results of the experiment— something that the experimenter does not know ahead of time. We shall call the variable whose values result from the experiment, the **responding variable.**

For example, consider the following situation from a fourth-grade experiment, *The Bouncing Ball.* In this experiment, children study how high a ball bounces. They drop a ball from various heights and measure how high it bounces. As the experimenters, they decide what drop heights they want to use in the experiment, say 40 cm, 80 cm, and 120 cm. The drop height is the manipulated variable. But the height to which the ball bounces can only be determined after you drop the ball. It is not known ahead of time. So, the bounce height is the responding variable.

Or, say that you fill a plastic jar with different-colored blocks and that you have chosen red, yellow, and blue as the colors of your blocks. You then ask a child to reach in and pull out as many pieces as he or she can in one grab, sort the blocks by color, and count them. Color is the manipulated variable in this experiment. The number of each color that he or she pulls out is the responding variable. You choose the values of the colors that go in but you have no choice over the number of each color that comes out.

Beginning in the first grade of *Math Trailblazers*, the experimental variables are identified in all laboratory experiments. This is an essential part of conducting any scientific experiment. It is not until fourth grade, however, that we introduce the formal terms "manipulated" and "responding."

Note that in *Math Trailblazers*, we have elected to use the terms "manipulated" and "responding" to describe experimental variables. We have found manipulated and responding to be less abstract for children (and adults) and easier to understand than the more commonly used terms for variables, "independent" and "dependent."

Fixed Variables in Controlled Experiments

Experiments often have more than two variables. In an ideal experiment, more easily realized in the laboratory than in the real world, a scientist focuses on only two variables—the ones we have called manipulated and responding—and strives to hold all others constant. If too many variables change simultaneously in an experiment, obtaining meaningful results can be difficult or impossible.

Consider a laboratory experiment done in second grade, *Rolling Along in Centimeters.* Students roll different kinds of cars down a ramp and use metersticks to measure the distance each car rolls. Here, the "type of car" is the manipulated variable and the distance each car rolls is the responding variable. The height of the ramp, the starting line, the floor onto which the cars roll, and the method for releasing the car are all held constant each time a car is rolled down the ramp. We refer to these as the **fixed variables** (or controlled variables) in the experiment. Children intuitively understand this as "keeping things fair" while the data are collected during the course of the experiment.

In many situations, some of the variables in an experiment are hidden; that is, they are not immediately obvious, although changing them will greatly alter the results of your experiment. Consider an experiment in which you collect data on the kinds of pets owned by each child in the classroom. The kind of pet is the manipulated variable and the number of each kind of pet is the

In an ideal experiment, more easily realized in the laboratory than in the real world, a scientist focuses on only two variables—the ones we have called manipulated and responding—and strives to hold all others constant. If too many variables change simultaneously in an experiment, obtaining meaningful results can be difficult or impossible.

responding variable. If you think about it, you can see that your results depend upon where the pet owners live—in a high rise or a single-family house, in the city or a farm community, and even in which country. Thus the variable, "location," can drastically change the results.

One of the reasons cancer research is so difficult is because there are so many variables which are either difficult or impossible to control (such as environmental factors, personality traits, multitudinous viruses) that it is hard to pinpoint the variables that might be the cause of cancer. It is the complexity of biological and sociological systems that makes doing repeatable experiments in these areas very difficult.

Nonetheless, children can learn how to deal with simple physical systems where three or four variables are present. They should learn how to recognize the different variables involved and understand the importance of controlling all but two—the manipulated and the responding variable.

The TIMS Laboratory Method   PART III

Throughout *Math Trailblazers*, children carry out quantitative investigations in which they explore the relationships between variables. Each investigation is carried out with the same general format, which we call the TIMS Laboratory Method. One may call this our version of the scientific method. There are four phases: beginning the investigation and drawing the picture, collecting and organizing the data, graphing the data, and analyzing the experimental results. We discuss these four phases below, illustrating our discussion with references to *The Bouncing Ball* experiment described above and to *Marshmallows and Containers,* a second-grade experiment in which children study the number of marshmallows that fit into different-sized jars.

Phase 1: Beginning the Investigation and Drawing the Picture

Most investigations begin with a question. The question does not have to be momentous, but it must be meaningful to children. If the question connects in some authentic way with their experience, children will need no flashy inducements to want to find the answer. This is illustrated in the following classroom anecdote involving *Marshmallows and Containers*.

> *As class begins, students sit together in groups of three. Each group has three different containers: a margarine tub, a 100 cc graduated cylinder, and a small paper cup. The teacher shows the class a bag of miniature marshmallows and asks, "Which container will hold the most marshmallows? Why do you think so?"*
>
> *The teacher encourages the groups to discuss their predictions and explanations and to record their ideas in their journals. When the groups report to the class, many groups think that the graduated cylinder will hold the most because it is the tallest. One boy explains that he thinks the cylinder holds the most because even if he could stretch the plastic in the bowl so it was tall like the cylinder, it still would not be as tall and would not hold as much. Other groups choose the tub because it is fatter than the other containers.*

The teacher then asks, "How could you find out which container holds the most marshmallows?" This question leads naturally to an experiment: The students will fill each of the containers with marshmallows, count them, and record the numbers in a data table.

Once a suitable question has been posed—and posing such questions is far from trivial—then variables related to the question must be identified. *Marshmallows and Containers* examines the kind of container and the number of marshmallows. The size of the marshmallows and the method for packing the marshmallows into the jars is held fixed. In *The Bouncing Ball*, students measure the drop heights and bounce heights of a ball, while holding fixed the type of ball, the floor onto which the ball is dropped, and the method for dropping the ball.

Through class discussion, the original question has been refined into a precise query about the relationship between two variables. These variables become defined well enough so that the children know how to gather information about them. Drawing a picture is an excellent way to summarize and communicate this beginning phase, and also to plan what is to come.

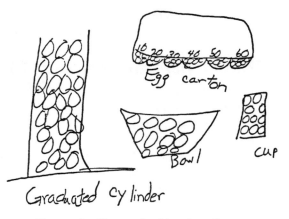

Figure 1: *Picture for* Marshmallows and Containers

Scientists often make sketches in experimental situations. In the TIMS Laboratory Method, drawing pictures helps children understand and organize what they are to do. A sketch gives the child time to think, to see relationships between variables, to place diverse relationships in a compact form, and to "explain" the experiment or problem to someone at a glance. Pictures also help teachers assess whether students are ready to proceed. Figure 1

Figure 2: *Picture for* The Bouncing Ball

shows one student's picture for *Marshmallows and Containers*. The picture indicates the student's understanding of the experimental variables and the procedure. Note that the student is using an egg carton to make groups of 10 when counting marshmallows. Figure 2 shows a picture from *Bouncing Ball*, indicating the manipulated and responding variables (the drop height and the bounce height) and the procedure for the experiment. The students who drew these pictures are ready to go on to the next step, gathering data.

Phase 2: Collecting and Organizing the Data

In Phase 2 of the TIMS Laboratory Method, children gather the data and organize it in a table. To illustrate, we return to our classroom anecdote involving *Marshmallows and Containers:*

On the next day, the children use their pictures to review the experiment before beginning the data collection. Each group receives a two-column data table, fills in the column headings, and writes the names (or draws pictures) of the containers in the first column. The teacher emphasizes the need for accuracy in counting, and the children discuss various methods for grouping and counting the marshmallows. As the students begin to collect the data, the teacher circulates among the groups, coaching and assessing.

After the children complete their data tables (Figure 3), the teacher leads a discussion in which the groups compare their results. This discussion centers on whether the groups' results are reasonable or not. Most groups report about 130 marshmallows in the graduated cylinder. Students agree that numbers close to 130, but not exactly 130, are acceptable. Based on this discussion, a group that had recorded only 110 marshmallows for the cylinder decides to refill the cylinder and count again.

Container	N Number of Marshmallows
Graduated cylinder	133
cup	121
bowl	181

Figure 3: *Data table from* Marshmallows and Containers

Tennis Ball				
D Drop Height in cm	B Bounce Height in cm			
	Trial 1	Trial 2	Trial 3	Average
40	27	22	21	22
80	50	40	43	43
120	72	62	68	68

Figure 4: *Data table from* The Bouncing Ball

Figure 3 shows a student's data table for *Marshmallows and Containers.* Figure 4 is a student's data table from *The Bouncing Ball.* The name of a variable, including units if appropriate, heads each column.

When creating data tables, scientists and mathematicians generally place the manipulated variable in the left column and the responding variable in the right column. Since the values for the manipulated variable are chosen by the experimenter before the experiment begins, the first column of the data table can be filled out prior to the experiment. Values of the responding variable can only be filled in as the experiment is conducted.

Data tables are tools for organizing data. In a real laboratory experiment, scientists have to record the data clearly and correctly the first time, during the experiment. It has to be recorded in such a way that not only you can read it, but also your colleagues and even a stranger. A story is told about the Nobel Prize-winner James Watson, who helped discover DNA. His teacher at Indiana University was asked if he suspected that Watson might go on to great things when he graduated. Yes, he answered. Watson would go far. Why? The teacher replied that although Watson did not take great care of his personal appearance, and his desk was a mess, he kept a neat notebook. That is a lesson that even young children can understand.

The data table is also useful in controlling error and identifying patterns. Children can detect blunders when a measurement deviates too much from established patterns (as in the *Marshmallows and Containers* anecdote above), and they can control inevitable measurement error by averaging several trials.

Note that in *The Bouncing Ball* lab, the students performed three trials for each measurement. In other words, to answer the question of how high does the ball bounce when dropped from 40 centimeters, they dropped the ball three times from 40 centimeters and recorded the bounce height, in this case (Figure 4), 27, 22, and 21 centimeters. The students then take the average (they used the median for the average) bounce height for their value of the bounce height. This is done to minimize the effect of measurement and experiential error on the experiment. (See the TIMS Tutors: *Averages* and *Estimation, Accuracy, and Error.*)

Phase 3: Graphing the Data

Graphing is the heart of scientific analysis. Graphs are powerful communication tools that create a picture of the data and "tell its story." They allow you to compare, predict, and infer. If there is a pattern in the relationship between the variables, you are more likely to see it clearly in a graph. Being able to read a graph and produce a graph from data should be a major goal of school science. Graphing cuts across many disciplines: biology, chemistry, sociology, and economics. Students using *Math Trailblazers* work extensively with graphs from kindergarten on.

Bar Graphs vs. Point Graphs

In *Math Trailblazers*, data are mostly graphed as either a bar graph or a point graph; these two types of graphs will thus be the focus of our discussion in this section. Since a graph is a visual representation of the relationship between variables, the type of graph used depends upon the types of variables studied in the experiment.

When both variables are numerical, a point graph is often (though not always) appropriate. In *The Bouncing Ball*, for example, both variables—the drop height and the bounce height—are numerical. Since the values for these variables are numbers and are not discrete—that is, there are values between the data points that make sense, such as 52.5 cm—it is possible to use points and lines on the graph instead of bars to represent the data. Drawing a line or a curve makes sense only when the variables are numerical and there is a pattern in the data. Figure 5 shows a student's graph from *The Bouncing Ball*.

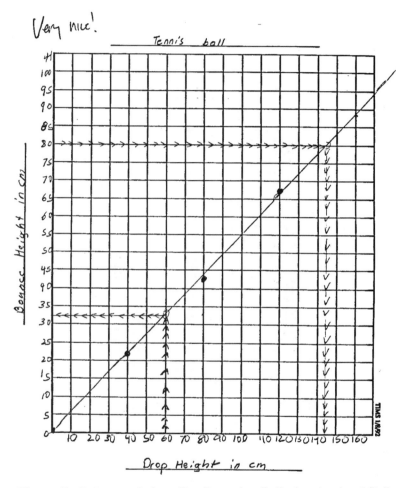

Figure 5: *Point graph from* The Bouncing Ball *showing best-fit lines, interpolation, and extrapolation*

Point graphs are introduced in *Math Trailblazers* in third grade and are used to represent a variety of different mathematical situations as well as to display data from laboratory experiments.

A bar graph is usually best when one of the variables is categorical (qualitative). In *Marshmallows and Containers,* for example, the type of container is a categorical variable and the number of marshmallows is numerical. Figure 6 shows the graph for *Marshmallows and Containers.* There are no values that make sense between the types of containers. Thus it does not make sense to connect them on the graph with a line. A bar graph, therefore, is appropriate for these kinds of situations.

A bar graph is usually best when one of the variables is categorical (qualitative).

Although point graphs are most often used when both experimental variables are numerical, that is not always the case. For example, in the experiment *First Names* from third grade, students collect data about the number of letters in the first names of students in the class. The two primary variables in this experiment are the number of letters (the manipulated variable) and the number of names (the responding variable). A graph for the experiment is shown in Figure 7. While both the variables in this experiment are numerical, they are also discrete—that is, it is not meaningful to speak of $6\frac{1}{2}$ letters in a name or $3\frac{1}{4}$ people who have that number of letters in their names. Thus, we can see why a point graph, in which values between the data points are represented, would not be appropriate in this case. Instead, the data is best represented on a bar graph.

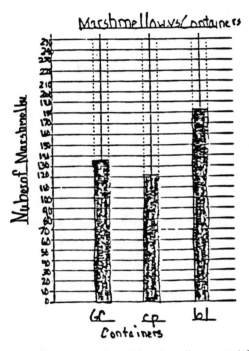

Figure 6: *Bar graph from* Marshmallows and Containers

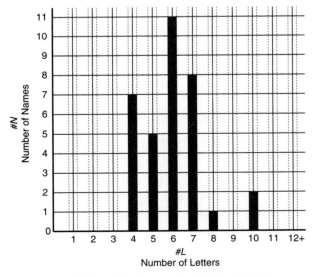

Figure 7: *Graph from* First Names

Labeling the Axes

With most types of data, it is conventional in science to place the manipulated variable along the horizontal axis and the responding variable along the vertical axis. The horizontal axis is labeled with a word or letter describing the manipulated variable and the vertical axis with a word or letter describing the responding variable. In Figure 7, for example, the horizontal axis—the manipulated variable—is labeled "#L, Number of Letters" and the vertical axis—the responding variable—is labeled "#N, Number of Names."

Once the axes are in place, the children can label the axes with the values for each variable. In the case of the *Marshmallows and Containers* in Figure 6, the student wrote in labels to represent the different kinds of containers.

With most types of data, it is conventional in science to place the manipulated variable along the horizontal axis and the responding variable along the vertical axis.

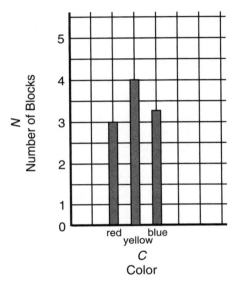

Figure 8: *Common errors in labeling the axes*

A common error in labeling axes is illustrated in Figure 8. This graph shows irregular spacing on both axes. The vertical axis in Figure 8 is incorrect with one space between 0 and 1 and two spaces between the other numbers. Technically, the categorical variables displayed on the horizontal axis do not have to be equally spaced, but it is a good idea to get your students into the habit of spacing their bars across the axis in regularly spaced intervals. This is because when dealing with numerical data, the values *must* be equally spaced.

Scaling the axes for numerical data requires an analysis of the range of the data and comparing it with the number of available intervals on your particular graph paper. Scaling by ones, two, fives, tens, or other numbers might be appropriate depending upon the data for a particular experiment. What is essential, however, is that the intervals are all equal along a given axis. Students will learn that it is best to determine the appropriate interval ahead of time. Otherwise they will end up plotting their initial data points and later discovering that other points will not fit on the graph.

In most cases, the scale on the horizontal axis is independent of the scale on the vertical axis. Students should number the axes in ways that make sense for the data. For example, the horizontal axis in *The Bouncing Ball* graph

(Figure 5) is scaled by tens but the vertical axis is scaled by fives. One exception to this is when making scale maps. Here, using different scales for the different axes would create a distorted image and make it difficult to find distances on the map.

As scientists do, students using the TIMS Laboratory Investigations often use their graphs to make predictions about physical phenomena. When making point graphs, therefore, we often encourage students to scale their axes to allow room for extrapolation. (See the section below entitled *Predictions from Point Graphs: Interpolation and Extrapolation* for information about extrapolation.)

Bar Graphs in *Math Trailblazers*

As early as kindergarten, students using *Math Trailblazers* work on graphing concepts, including making and interpreting simple graphs. A quick way to make bar graphs of classroom data is to place self-adhesive notes on a labeled graph. An example of this with *First Names* is illustrated in Figure 9. In this graph, each student placed a self-adhesive note with the data for his or her name on the graph. The data are clearly represented. The one-to-one correspondence between data points and the number of students in the class is particularly apparent in this type of graph, which we use primarily in kindergarten, first, and second grades.

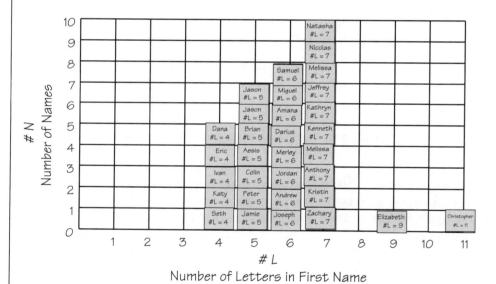

Figure 9: First Names *graph using self-adhesive notes*

In first grade, we introduce a graphing protocol that is different in *Math Trailblazers* than in some other programs. When making bar graphs, we encourage students to create their bars along the vertical lines in the graph rather than in the spaces between the lines. (See Figures 6, 7, and 9.) This does not affect the data or the reading of the graph. Rather it prepares students for making point graphs, where data points are plotted at the intersection of lines extending from the horizontal and vertical axes.

To assist students with this, we have created a special graph paper for making bar graphs. A version of this graph paper is shown in Figure 10. The dark vertical grid lines across the page are where the data for the manipulated variable is plotted. These lines are surrounded on both sides by a pair of dashed guide lines. Students make bars by coloring in the space on either side of the dark vertical lines. The result is a straight bar that is centered along a vertical line. The values for the manipulated variable are indicated on the horizontal axis directly below each bar.

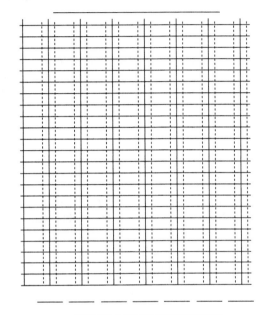

Figure 10: *TIMS bar graph paper*

The benefit of making bar graphs in this manner is most apparent in third grade as students make the transition to creating point graphs. To simplify students' initial attempt at creating a point graph, they first graph a data set as a bar graph and then convert the bar graph to a point graph. This is shown in Figure 11.

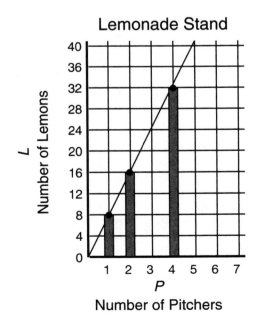

Figure 11: *Transition from bar graphs to point graphs in third grade*

Point Graphs: Fitting Lines and Curves

With point graphs, the data are plotted at the junction of the values of each variable. Once the data are plotted, we look for patterns. If the data points form a line or close to a line, we try to fit a line through the points. If the data form a curve, we try to fit a smooth curve through the points.

Figure 11 shows a graph in which the data points lie exactly on a straight line. Fitting a line to these data points is simply a matter of laying down a ruler and connecting the points.

For most experiments, we cannot expect the data to be so precise. In these experiments, the data may lie close to, but not exactly on a straight line. The "zigzags" in the data are due to experimental error. (See the TIMS Tutor: *Estimation, Accuracy, and Error.*) To average the error, one fits a line which comes as close to the data points as possible even though the line may not pass through any of these points. To assure a good fit, you would like as many points above the curve as below. You do not want to force the line through two points while missing the third by a mile. It is better to miss them all but come close to all than be too far from any one point.

As shown on *The Bouncing Ball* graph in Figure 5, a line can be fit to the data points, not by using some complicated statistical procedure, but simply "by eye." The student uses a clear ruler or a thread and moves it around until it fits the data points as closely as possible. This best-fit line is useful for minimizing error and making predictions.

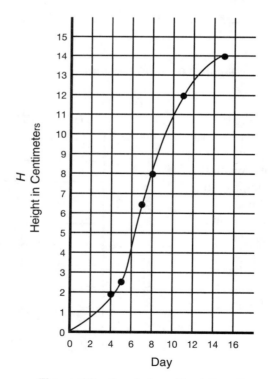

Figure 12: *Graph from* Plant Growth

Of course, not all experimental relationships result in data that yields straight lines on graphs. In *Math Trailblazers*, we also explore data that exhibits other kinds of patterns. Figure 12 shows the graph from a fourth-grade experiment, *Plant Growth,* where the data shows a pattern, but not a straight line.

When you can fit a smooth curve through the data points, you have uncovered one of nature's secrets—that the variables are related, that there is a predictable pattern to the data. We are then not restricted only to our specific data points, but can now use the pattern to predict what the value of the responding variable will be for any value of the manipulated variable.

Predictions from Point Graphs: Interpolation and Extrapolation

A major goal of mathematics and science is to find patterns in data and to use the patterns to make predictions. Interpolating and extrapolating on a point graph are two ways to do this.

Using the graph to find data points that lie between those in your data table is called **interpolation.** *Inter* means between or among. The simplest situation is when the pattern of data points produces a straight line. In the graph in Figure 5, the student interpolated to predict that a ball dropped from 60 cm would bounce about 32 cm. Note that in Figure 5 the student showed how she made her interpolation by starting at 60 cm on the horizontal axis, drawing a line (with arrows) up to the best-fit line, and then drawing a horizontal line to find the corresponding value of the bounce height—about 32 cm.

Extrapolation is an attempt to predict information beyond the last data point. *Extra* means outside or beyond. To extrapolate, we must extend the line into a region where there is no data. You can do this easily by laying a ruler on the straight line, extending the line, and reading off your prediction. In Figure 5, the student extrapolated to predict that a ball that bounced 80 cm was dropped from a height of about 144 cm. Here, the student began with values on the vertical axis (the bounce height) and predicted a value on the horizontal axis (the drop height). It is possible to interpolate and extrapolate in either of two directions: from values on the horizontal axis to values on the vertical axis or vice versa.

Having used these techniques to make predictions, it is important to have the children check their predictions experimentally and see how close their new data comes to the curve. This is one of the joys of science—to see that nature is often regular and predictable and that you can make predictions that come true! Checking predictions, though time-consuming, is worthwhile because it reinforces connections between mathematical abstractions and the real world.

A major goal of mathematics and science is to find patterns in data and to use the patterns to make predictions. Interpolating and extrapolating on a point graph are two ways to do this.

Phase 4: Analyzing the Data

After making the graph, students have explored the relationship between the variables in four ways: with the physical materials, in the picture, in the data table, and in the graph. The last phase of the TIMS Laboratory Method is the analysis of the entire situation, where students explore the relationship quantitatively and represent it symbolically (i.e., with numbers).

A major goal of mathematics and science is to find patterns in data and to use the patterns to make predictions. Interpolating and extrapolating on a point graph are two ways to do this.

One way to structure this analysis is to ask a series of questions. The questions usually begin on the literal level: *Did the tallest container hold the most marshmallows? How high did the tennis ball bounce when dropped from 60 cm?* More demanding questions require prediction: *How many marshmallows would two bowls hold? If a ball bounced to 45 cm, what height was it dropped from?* Asking what would happen if one of the fixed variables is changed can build a broader understanding of the situation: *What would happen if we used large instead of miniature marshmallows? What would happen if we used a Super ball instead of a tennis ball?* This quantitative analysis of the data is one place in *Math Trailblazers* where students regularly practice and reinforce arithmetic and other math skills.

The end of the investigation may be a completely satisfying answer to the original question, but, more often than not, the end is another question that can lead to further investigations. *Marshmallows and Containers,* for example, might lead to an investigation of the liquid capacities of other short and tall containers. After an initial experiment with tennis balls in *The Bouncing Ball,* children carry out an investigation using another type of ball and compare the results from the two experiments.

Picture, Table, Graph, and Questions: Putting It Together

Each of the four phases described above may require one or more class periods. In addition, time may be spent becoming familiar with the equipment at the beginning and on further experiments at the end. Thus, a lab is an extended activity that may last a week or even longer. This is much longer than a typical mathematics or science lesson, but there are significant benefits.

First, the four phases simplify the scientific method enough for children to use, but not so much that it fails to resemble what scientists do. Identifying variables, drawing pictures, measuring, organizing data in tables, graphing data, and looking for patterns are part of many scientists' work. Students are thus inducted via this method into the authentic practice of science.

The method fosters children's sense-making. Children handle numbers they have generated themselves by counting or measuring, numbers that are thus meaningful to them. As they deal with experimental error, they develop number sense and estimation skills. As they look for patterns in their tables and graphs, they make sense of the numbers before them. Arithmetic in context is more understandable.

The approach is multimodal, which has benefits for both individual students and heterogeneous groups of students. The multiple representations of relationships between the variables permit problems to be solved in more than one way, allowing different students to approach the same content in ways they understand. The container that holds the most marshmallows, for example, can be found from the graph, from the data table, or from the marshmallows themselves. A prediction about a bounce height might be obtained by extrapolating on the graph or by extending patterns in the data table, and can then be verified using the apparatus. Students can compare these various approaches, thus helping them make connections within mathematics as well as between the informal mathematics of their everyday experience and more formal mathematics.

Identifying variables, drawing pictures, measuring, organizing data in tables, graphing data, and looking for patterns are part of many scientists' work. Students are thus inducted via this method into the authentic practice of science.

Mathematics in Context

Two principles underlie the TIMS Laboratory Method. First, an investigation should begin within the children's own experiences. Children use objects from their everyday lives to investigate a familiar situation. Children's everyday knowledge, like a scientist's theory, provides a framework for interpreting the results of the investigation. Without that framework, the investigation would remain hollow and meaningless.

The second principle is that an investigation should also transcend children's everyday experiences. The exploration must go somewhere; it must lead the children both to a better understanding of the immediate situation and to improved skills, understandings, habits, and attitudes. The concepts can then be extended and transferred to new contexts.

Balancing these principles requires teacher judgment. The key is to enable students to follow their own ideas, but with the intention that those ideas will lead somewhere. How much scaffolding to provide, how much to guide students in directions that are fruitful rather than sterile, must be decided by the teacher in context. The goal is that students should advance not only in skill and understanding, but also in autonomy and perseverance. Just how much structure to provide along the way is perhaps a teacher's most important and difficult job.

The TIMS Laboratory Method helps children connect their everyday experiences with formal mathematics. As they investigate everyday situations quantitatively, children handle variables, explore relationships between variables, master a few powerful techniques for representing these relationships, and use these multiple representations to generate a wide variety of problem solutions. By beginning and ending in familiar situations, the abstractions of mathematics are linked to children's everyday knowledge. As students master this method, they become increasingly autonomous and flexible in its application. Then we can truly say they understand the fundamentals of *doing* science.

References

Archambault, Reginald D. (ed.), *John Dewey on Education: Selected Writings.* Modern Library, 1964.

Bruner, Jerome S. "The Course of Cognitive Growth." *American Psychologist* 19 (1), pp. 1–15, 1964.

Dewey, John. "Science as Subject-Matter and as Method." *Science* 31 (787), pp. 121–7, January 28, 1910.

Goldberg, Howard, and F. David Boulanger. "Science for Elementary School Teachers: A Quantitative Approach." *American Journal of Physics* 49 (2), pp. 120–124, 1981.

Goldberg, Howard, and Philip Wagreich. "Focus on Integrating Science and Math." *Science and Children* 2 (5), pp. 22–24, 1989.

Goldberg, Howard, and Philip Wagreich. "A Model Integrated Mathematics and Science Program for the Elementary School." *International Journal of Educational Research* 14 (2), pp. 193–214, 1990.

Hiebert, James. "A Theory of Developing Competence with Written Mathematical Symbols." *Educational Studies in Mathematics* 19, pp. 333–355, 1988.

Isaacs, Andrew C., and Catherine Randall Kelso. "Pictures, Tables, Graphs, and Questions: Statistical Processes." *Teaching Children Mathematics* 2 (6), pp. 340–345, 1996.

Isaacs, Andrew C., Philip Wagreich, and Martin Gartzman. "The Quest for Integration: School Mathematics and Science." *American Journal of Education* 106 (1), pp. 179–206, 1997.

Lesh, Richard, Thomas Post, and Merlyn Behr. "Representations and Translations among Representation in Mathematics Learning and Problem Solving." In C. Janvier (ed.), *Problems of Representation in the Teaching and Learning of Mathematics.* Lawrence Erlbaum Associates, Hillsdale, NJ, 1987.

National Research Council. *National Science Education Standards.* National Academy Press, Washington, DC, 1996.

Silver, Edward. "Using Conceptual and Procedural Knowledge: A Focus on Relationships." In J. Hiebert (ed.), *Conceptual and Procedural Knowledge: The Case of Mathematics.* Lawrence Erlbaum Associates, Hillsdale, NJ, 1986.

The Concept of Length

Units

In dealing with scientific problems, we must often know such things as the location of an object, the distance between objects, how tall or wide an object is, or how fast it is moving. Central to all these ideas is the concept of length. In this tutor, we shall examine the various disguises in which length can appear.

First, however, we must note the messy problem of units. The kinds of units chosen for length were for a long time quite arbitrary. The cubit, used by several ancient civilizations, was the length of a forearm between the tip of the middle finger and the elbow. The fathom was the width of a Viking sailor's embrace. (Fathom that!)

The foot was a convenient length defined as the length of a person's foot. Of course, everyone has a different-sized foot, so if we want to use, say, the king's foot as a standard, we will have to mark it permanently; we cannot very well lug the king around! Since the king is the ruler of the land, it was both rational and proper to call this marker a ruler as well. To show students the chaos caused by not having a standard length, have them measure the length of their desks in cubits or the width of the room in feet with each child using his or her own body measurements. You will have as many different values as measurers.

Nonstandard Units

At first, we have the children measure length using nonstandard units, often links. A link is shown in Figure 1 along with a chain of links. The measurement of the object shown is $4\frac{1}{2}$ links. The reasons we go to links are: (1) to make counting the unit length easy and (2) to keep the numbers manageable. Rather than dealing with hundreds of cm, we can count 50 links. And to count a link is easy since they are so large.

By alternating link colors (2 reds, 2 whites, 2 reds, etc.), one can make the counting even easier by skip counting by 2s. If you want to have the children skip count by 5s, then have a chain with 5 blues, 5 yellows, 5 blues, etc.

With links, it is also easy to round off to $\frac{1}{2}$ link as shown in Figure 1. If the edge we are measuring is near the middle, then the length is $4\frac{1}{2}$ links. If shorter, then the length is 4 links; if longer, the length is 5 links.

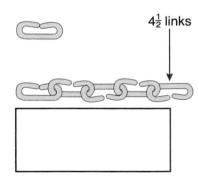

Figure 1: *Links*

The Metric System

Of course, links are not a commonly used standard of measure. In the United States, it is feet. Unfortunately, many objects are smaller than a foot. This means one must subdivide the standard unit. For some miserable reason, the smaller unit, the inch, is $\frac{1}{12}$ of a foot. Who likes to divide by 12? So, the French scientific community at the time of the French Revolution (c. 1790) chose as the standard unit of length a distance that they called a meter. It was chosen so that 10^7 (10 million) metersticks laid end to end would just fit between the North Pole and the equator, as shown in Figure 2. A platinum-iridium rod was constructed with two marks a meter apart and stored in a vault near Paris. Every meterstick, albeit indirectly, comes from this standard. Having defined the meter, the French were smart enough to define all subsequent subdivisions of the meter as integral powers of ten. The foot is divided into $\frac{1}{12}$s and $\frac{1}{48}$s, and other equally horrible numbers; for the meter, the divisions are $\frac{1}{10}$s, $\frac{1}{100}$s, and $\frac{1}{1000}$s. We shall now explore this point further.

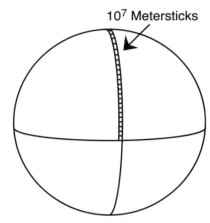

... the French scientific community at the time of the French Revolution (c. 1790) chose as the standard unit of length a distance that they called a meter. It was chosen so that 10^7 (10 million) metersticks laid end to end would just fit between the North Pole and the equator ...

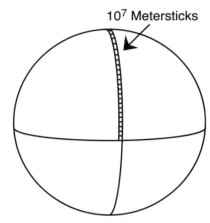

Figure 2: *Metersticks from the North Pole to the equator*

For measuring ordinary objects in the classroom, the meter is divided into three other units; the millimeter, the centimeter, and the decimeter (although the latter is rarely used). Without being specific as to the size of each unit, we can order them using the greater than (>) or less than (<) sign. Starting with the smallest, we have:

$$1 \text{ millimeter} < 1 \text{ centimeter} < 1 \text{ decimeter} < 1 \text{ meter}.$$

Reversing the order and starting with the largest, we have:

$$1 \text{ meter} > 1 \text{ decimeter} > 1 \text{ centimeter} > 1 \text{ millimeter}.$$

It is important that students know at least this much before going on to more exact relations.

The key to the subdivision of the meter is the prefix *milli*. Milli is related to the word mile. Mile was the distance it took a Roman soldier to step off 1000 paces, a pace being two steps. Since an average pace is approximately 5 feet (try it and see), a mile would be approximately 5000 feet. The crucial point is the number 1000 as related to the word mile. Milli is the prefix for "$\frac{1}{1000}$ of." Thus, a millimeter is one-thousandth of a meter. There are 1000 millimeters in a meter just as there are 1000 paces in a mile. In each case, we have a subunit that is one-thousandth of the main unit. The word mile is to remind us that there are 1000 paces in a mile. The word millimeter is to remind us that there are 1000 millimeters in a meter. One should try to picture this in one's mind. Millimeters are tiny; it takes a lot of them to make up any macroscopic length. (By macroscopic, we are referring to something one can see unaided versus microscopic where one would need a magnifying glass or microscope to see it.) On the other hand, because a meter is large, a millimeter is usually a fraction of most lengths one would measure in the lab. Thus, it is reasonable that a third-grader knows how to measure the length of his thumb as 3 cm or 30 mm, but not as 0.03 m.

How are mm, cm, dm, and m related? Let's start with the smallest and see how many mm are in a cm, a dm, and a meter.

  1 centimeter contains 10 mm;
  1 decimeter contains 100 mm;
  1 meter contains 1000 mm.

Based on these relationships, we should be able to figure out how many centimeters are in a decimeter or in a meter. Here, however, the French have made it easy for us; the prefix for each word gives the answer away. *Centi* stands for 100th and *deci* stands for one-tenth. Thus one centimeter is one-hundredth of a meter; there are 100 cm in a meter. A decimeter is one-tenth of a meter; there are 10 dm in a meter. What this boils down to then is the following:

  1 decimeter contains 10 cm;
  1 meter contains 100 cm;
  1 meter contains 10 dm.

Everything depends upon the size of the meter. Once that is fixed (by our rod in Paris), the sizes of all other metric units are determined.

Measuring Length

The simplest way to get started in the metric system is to count, using a meterstick, the number of mm or cm (and if they do not equal fractions, dm or meters) in a given length. Say we measure the width of the sheet of paper in cm. Then depending upon the accuracy of the meterstick (a cheap one could be off a bit) and the judgment of the student, one can see that there are between 21 and 22 cm across the page. If you stick to cm, then for students who are not yet comfortable with fractions or decimals, this is all you can say. As they begin to learn decimals, the children can determine the width as 21.6 cm. However, you can get still better accuracy even without decimals by going to mm instead of cm. Here, all one has to be able to do is count beyond 100. Thus, the width is 216 mm. In fact, one of the neat things about the metric system is that you can always choose a set of units to obtain almost any accuracy you want without going to fractions or decimals. On the other hand, you can purposely choose units that will give decimal or fractional answers. As we just saw, in cm units, the width of the page is a decimal, 21.6 cm. We could have asked for the width in meters. Since the width is less than a meter, we are dealing with fractions. In this case, the width is 0.216 meters or roughly $\frac{1}{5}$ of a meter. Clearly, there is great potential in the metric system for teaching math and linking this to scientific measurement.

With regard to addition, when adding numbers they must always have the same units. For example:

(a) 5 cm + 6 m = ? This is a "no-no"; the units are mixed.

(b) 5 cm + 600 cm = 605 cm. This is okay—we are adding the same units.

(c) 8 mm + 50 cm = ? We should convert the cm to mm and get:

(d) 8 mm + 500 mm = 508 mm.

Thus, if we ask a student to measure the length of his arm by separately measuring his hand (say in mm), his lower arm (say in cm), his upper arm (say in decimeters), and then adding them, he will first have to convert to a set of consistent units that he or she can handle. If you do not choose to have the students work with fractions, the students can change the units to millimeters as shown above. If you want to give the students a chance to work on decimal fractions, they can change the units to centimeters.

$$.8 + 50 \text{ cm} = 50.8 \text{ cm}$$

This brings us to another point—how to use a ruler. At first it seems quite apparent: just place the end of the ruler at the end of the object and read the length directly (Figure 3). However, a better test of whether students really understand how to use a ruler as well as a test of their ability to subtract is to place the object in the center of the ruler. Clearly, the length of the object should not depend upon its position vis-a-vis the ruler, but we have found that many young people (and even a few at our university) have trouble understanding how to find the length in the latter case.

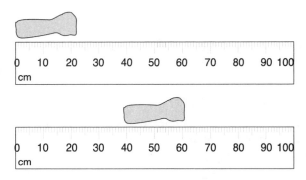

Figure 3: *How to use a ruler*

Since we do not always have a ruler handy, a few "natural" rulers might be fun to discuss and use. For example, say the length of a person's upper thumb from knuckle to tip is generally about 3 cm while his spread-out fingers span about 20 cm, as shown in Figure 4. Either can now be used to measure the length of an object. Of course, there is the foot, a convenient measure for stepping off distances. This person's foot, without his shoes, is 23 cm or about 9 inches. Anyway, you should have the children measure a few objects using natural rulers and have them compare their results with that of a meterstick.

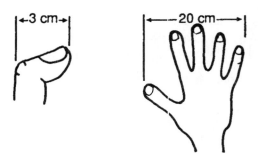

Figure 4: *Natural rulers*

The Concept of Area

Defining Area

The area of a shape or object can be defined in everyday words as the "amount of stuff" needed to cover the shape. Common uses of the concept of area are finding the amount of tile needed to cover a floor, the amount of wallpaper needed to cover a wall, and the amount of paint needed to cover a ceiling. Areas of different objects can often be compared directly, without measurement. For example, if one piece of carpet completely covers another, we know the top piece has more area.

Just as with length, in order to measure area we need a unit of measure. Many different units have been used throughout history. The acre is still used as a measure of land area, along with square miles. The square inch, square foot, and square yard are area units in the English system. For example, square yards is the unit of area measure for carpeting in the United States. Most of the world and all scientists use the metric system. For the classroom, the most frequent metric unit of area is the square centimeter. It is defined as the amount of flat surface within a square that is 1 cm on a side. This is illustrated in Figure 1.

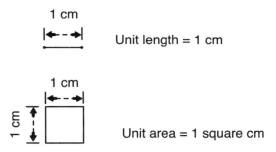

Figure 1: *Units of length and area*

A note on terminology: Scientists often use the term "centimeters squared" in place of "square centimeters." This may be due to the fact that one way of writing the symbol for square centimeters is cm^2. We prefer to use sq cm for square centimeters. On occasion, the use of cm^2 can confuse students. Since 7 squared is 49, they may reason that 7 centimeters squared is 49 square centimeters. Unfortunately, the symbols $7\ cm^2$ and $(7\ cm)^2$ sound the same when spoken, if you say cm^2 as "centimeters squared." For that reason, we stick to "square centimeters" and sq cm.

Measuring Area by Counting Square Centimeters—Part I

One way to find an area is to count the number of sq cm needed to cover a surface. To count the number of sq cm, you can construct unit squares within the desired area. For example, the rectangle in Figure 2 is 3 cm wide and 4 cm high. You can find its area by completing the following steps.

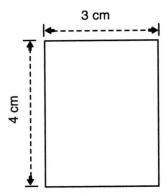

Figure 2: *A rectangle*

1. Draw a grid of lines so that each square in the grid is 1 cm on a side. (Figure 3.)

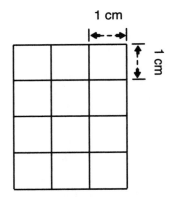

Figure 3: *A rectangle tiled with centimeter squares*

2. Count the number of sq cm enclosed in the rectangle. (Figure 4.)

1	2	3
4	5	6
7	8	9
10	11	12

Figure 4: *Counting square centimeters*

There are 12 sq cm in a rectangle that is 3 cm wide and 4 cm high. So the area of the rectangle is 12 sq cm.

Why Not Use Length × Width?

You may be wondering why we did not use the formula *length* × *width* to find the area of the rectangle. After all, $4 \times 3 = 12$. The formula works. Indeed, the reason the formula works is precisely because the rectangle can be represented by an ordered array of squares, 3 squares in each row and 4 rows of 3 squares each.

In any ordered array, you can count the total number of elements by multiplying the number of rows by the number of columns. Figure 5 shows 24 apples arrayed in 6 rows. Instead of counting each apple, we take advantage of the array and multiply 4×6 to obtain 24 apples. Using the length times width formula does give the area of a rectangle, but we delay teaching the formula for two reasons. First, we want students to build a mental image of the concept of area. Premature use of the formula for area of rectangles leads to rote use of the formula without understanding. In particular, many students are led to believe that the definition of area is length times width and that this formula works for any shape. While there are formulas for the areas of rectangles, circles, and other geometric shapes, there is no formula for the area of a leaf!

Premature use of the formula for area of rectangles leads to rote use of the formula without understanding. In particular, many students are led to believe that the definition of area is length times width and that this formula works for any shape.

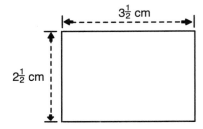

Figure 5: *An array of apples*

Furthermore, using the formula can be harder than counting square centimeters when the sides of the rectangle are not whole numbers.

For example, what is the area of the rectangle, $3\frac{1}{2}$ cm wide and $2\frac{1}{2}$ cm high, shown in Figure 6? We asked a group of sixth-graders to find the area of this rectangle. Even though the students knew the length × width formula, 80% could not find the area. They were not able to multiply fractions. It is likely that these students would have been able to find the area by counting sq cm, as we shall see in the next section.

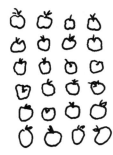

Figure 6: *Another rectangle*

Counting Square Centimeters–Part II

In Figure 7, we have set up the square cm grid. To keep track of the sq cm, we first number the whole square centimeters. There are six whole sq cm in the rectangle. Next, we turn to the fractions of sq cm. Students can manipulate sq cm pieces of paper to complete the task. The two half sq cm on the right make up the seventh sq cm and so both are numbered 7. The two half sq cm along the bottom make up the eighth sq cm and are numbered 8. One half sq cm and one fourth square cm make up the remaining areas. The area is $8\frac{3}{4}$ sq cm.

1	2	3	7
4	5	6	7
8	8	$\frac{1}{2}$	$\frac{1}{4}$

Figure 7: *Whole and part centimeter squares*

Most students can count squares to find area—no multiplication is necessary. But what if there is no "order" to the figure? The shape in Figure 8 has no unique length or width; the formula *length* × *width* does not apply. The only way to find the area is to count the number of sq cm contained within the boundary of the figure.

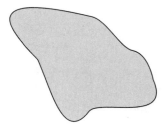

Figure 8: *A blob*

First, construct a sq cm grid to fit over the shape of Figure 8. It's often easier if the horizontal and vertical boundary of the grid each touch the figure at one point. The grid should extend beyond the figure. The completed grid would look similar to the grid in Figure 9.

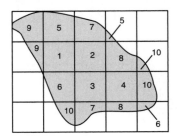

Figure 9: *Finding area by counting centimeter squares*

Next, count and number the whole sq cm. There are four. Now estimate which fractions of grid squares add together to form one square centimeter. For example, square centimeter number 5 is a big piece upper left and a little piece farther to the right. Number 6 is two pieces, a big piece on the left and a smaller piece in the lower right corner. Square centimeter number 7 is two pieces, each around a half square cm. Square centimeter 8 is made up of a $\frac{3}{4}$ and $\frac{1}{4}$ square cm piece. So is square centimeter 9. Three pieces make up square centimeter 10, two half square cm pieces and a smaller piece to the right.

Now, all of the shape is covered and counted in square centimeters. The shape has an area of about 10 square cm. While the method does not give an exact area, the result is usually close. And, the primary benefit of this method is that students will have the opportunity to "see" area, aiding their understanding of this important mathematical concept.

Surface Area

Often, students who understand area quite well seem to have difficulty with the notion of surface area. One problem may be that they have been led to believe that area and surface area are two different things. This is not surprising, since we use two different words. However, area and surface area are identical; a measure of the number of sq cm (or square units) needed to cover an object. Customarily, the term "surface area" is usually used for three-dimensional shapes and "area" for two-dimensional shapes.

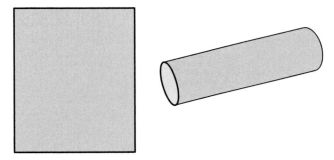

Figure 10: *Paper flat and rolled*

To measure the surface area of a three-dimensional object, we count the number of square centimeters needed to cover it, just as with flat shapes. In some cases, this is easy as in the case of a rectangular box (since it is made up of flat pieces). Another easy example can be made by taking a sheet of flat paper and rolling it to make a cylinder (Figure 10). As long as the edges do not overlap, the surface area of the outside of the cylinder will be the same as the flat piece of paper. Another way to find the area of a cylinder is to cover it with one square centimeter "stamps." As with flat shapes, you may need some fractional pieces. With more complex shapes, like a sphere, it is hard to get an exact measurement of the surface area, but we can approximate the surface area by covering the object with square centimeters or smaller squares.

The Concept of Volume

Defining Volume

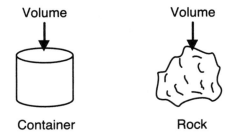

Figure 1: *Two meanings of volume*

Figure 1 shows a container and a rock. The space that the container surrounds (and is occupied by air) and the space that the rock takes up (and is occupied by elements such as oxygen, silicon, and aluminum) are both called **volume.**[1] The concept of volume is tricky. Two objects (like our container and rock) might occupy the same volume but might contain totally different amounts of matter. Children often confuse the amount of matter, which we call mass, with the space occupied, which we now know is volume. Thus children tell us that a "heavy" object has more volume than a "light" object even though the latter may actually occupy more space. Indeed, volume is so oversimplified in the elementary schools that many eighth-graders we asked thought of volume as length $\times$ width $\times$ height, no matter what the shape of the object. Others told us that volume was length squared. Misconceptions such as these are a result of a curriculum that emphasizes memorization of formulas without attention to the conceptual foundations of volume.

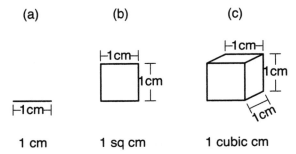

Figure 2: *Units of length, area, and volume*

---

[1]Sometimes, the space inside a container is called the capacity of the container. For simplicity, we prefer to use one term, volume, to denote both "space inside" and "space occupied."

Units

As with length and area, if we wish to measure volume, we need to decide on a unit of measure. In the metric system, the metric unit of length is the centimeter (Figure 2a), and the unit of area is the square centimeter (the extent of the plane surface that is bounded by a square 1 cm on a side) (Figure 2b), so it is not unreasonable that we take as our unit of volume the space occupied within a cube that is 1 cm on a side (Figure 2c). The volume occupied by such a cube is defined as 1 cubic centimeter whether that volume is occupied by a solid object (Figure 3a) or by empty space (Figure 3b).

(a)   (b)

Figure 3: *Full and empty cubic centimeter*

Unlike area, it is very hard to divide an object up and count cubic cm. We can't trace the volume the way we trace areas on square cm paper. In theory we could slice it up into 1 cubic cm pieces, but this process will destroy the object. Therefore, learning to understand and measure volume can be more difficult than understanding and measuring area.

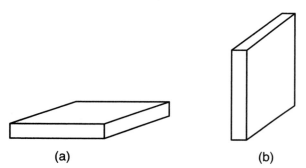

(a)   (b)

Figure 4: *Flat vs. tall shapes*

In everyday life, we are accustomed to a variety of other units of volume measure. Gallons, quarts, pints, and fluid ounces are one set of units, usually used to measure the capacity of a container. Cubic feet and cubic inches are also frequently used. For example, in the United States, air conditioners are often rated on the volume of space they can cool, measured in cubic feet. The remainder of this tutor uses metric units of measure, but many of the same underlying ideas apply to any system of measure.

Problem of Dimensionality

Another great difficulty in understanding volume is that the concept deals with three dimensions. As Piaget pointed out, it is much easier, and therefore usual, for a child to focus on one dimension. They will decide that a tall object has lots of volume because they only focus on the height and fail to take into account the other two dimensions to make a proper estimate. In Figure 4, the two objects have the same volume, but because (a) is flat and (b) is upright, young children will tell you that (b) has the greater volume.

Volume is an extremely important scientific variable. The way it is related to area and to mass and the manner in which it may change with time are all intrinsic to every area of scientific investigation. It is well worth our time to do a good job on volume.

Measuring Volume—Early Activities

Kindergarten students explore volume by filling containers with rice, water, pasta, sand, or beans. Another way to deal with volume in the primary grades is to have the children make figures out of a set of cubes. In first and second grade, we usually use connecting cubes that are about $\frac{3}{4}$-inch on a side. At the end of second grade, we start using standard centimeter linking cubes. For example, you can give each child 10 cubes and ask him or her to make a figure whose volume is 10 cubic units. You will get a variety of shapes, all of which have the same volume. This will begin to impress upon the children the idea that many different shapes can have the same volume.

Another centimeter cube activity to build the children's understanding at this level involves building shapes with different volumes. Give each child a few (3–10) centimeter cubes. Have each child make a shape with his or her centimeter cubes. Then have the children sort themselves into groups according to the volume of their shapes.

You can bring in some simple solid shapes, like a piece of chalk, a match box, a pile of washers, etc., and have the children make figures out of cubic units that approximate the volume (size and shape) of these objects. In this way, they can estimate the volume of the original object by keeping track of the number of cubic cm they used. An example is given in Figure 5 of a marking pen and cubic cms linked together to make a shape of approximately the same volume.

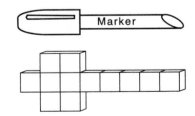

Figure 5: *A marker and a cm cube model*

Another great difficulty in understanding volume is that the concept deals with three dimensions. As Piaget pointed out, it is much easier, and therefore usual, for a child to focus on one dimension. They will decide that a tall object has lots of volume because they only focus on the height and fail to take into account the other two dimensions to make a proper estimate.

The next step would be for you to make several cube models and have the children count the number of unit cubes in each one. Pictures of three typical models, each a bit more complex than the previous, are given in Figures 6a, b, and c. There are two potential problems here. The children may confuse surface area and volume and count the faces of the cubes calling each face a cubic cm. A subtle problem, exemplified by Figure 6c, is when there are one or more "hidden" cubic centimeters buried inside the figure.

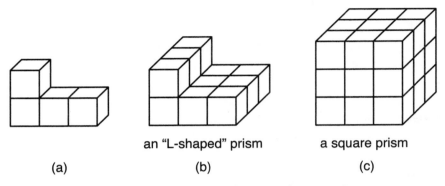

(a)   an "L-shaped" prism   a square prism
(a)   (b)   (c)

Figure 6: *Shapes made from centimeter cubes*

A very basic problem is learning to count the cubic centimeters properly. It is relatively easy to pick up 12 cubic centimeters, make a figure, and say the volume is 12 cc. It is quite another to hold a centimeter cube figure like that in Figure 6b, turn it over, and keep track of all the centimeters. We want the children to learn to be systematic, look for patterns, and use simple addition and multiplication to count the cubes. For example, Figure 6a is easy since it is only 4 cc. Figure 6b is made up of three layers, each of which is exactly like Figure 6a. Your students can then use addition to see that the volume is 4 cc + 4 cc + 4 cc, or use multiplication, 3 × 4 cc. Likewise in Figure 6c, it would be difficult to find and keep track of each cubic cm. A systematic approach allows the children to solve the problem easily. There are 9 cc in the top layer, and there are three layers; therefore the volume is

9 cc + 9 cc + 9 cc = 27 cc.

Note that Figures 6b and 6c are labeled as prisms. This means they are made of a number of identical layers. Figure 6b has three "L-shaped" layers and 6c has three "square-shaped" layers. It is important to know that these are prisms. Otherwise, there might be some hidden cubes behind the object that we cannot see, or there might be missing cubes "inside" the object.

A more difficult skill is finding the volume of an object directly from a perspective drawing, without actually building the object. This kind of spatial visualization skill can be developed by first having students build cube models from pictures. Students as early as first grade can build simple models from pictures. As the models get more complex, this task can become quite difficult. One important subtlety is that pictures such as 6b and 6c do not give enough information to reconstruct the model. For example, there

We want the children to learn to be systematic, look for patterns, and use simple addition and multiplication to count the cubic cm.

might be some unexpected cubes hidden behind the model in Figure 6c (see Figure 7).

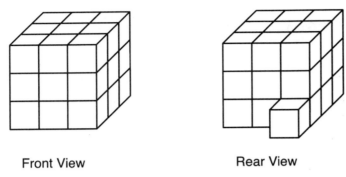

Front View   Rear View

Figure 7: *Front and rear views of Figure 6c*

For example, in Figure 7 we see what appears to be a $3 \times 3 \times 3$ cm cube from the front, but when we view the model from the rear, we see there is an "extra" cube stuck on.

Finally, and hardest of all, you can ask the children to try to draw a figure with a given number of cubic centimeters. It is very hard for anyone to draw a cube, and a figure with several cubic centimeters is harder still. Nevertheless, it is worth a try since doing so will help them improve their spatial perception and will force them to think in three dimensions.

Let's review the four steps we have just described:

1. Make figures out of a given number of centimeter cubes.
2. Count cubic centimeters in a cube model.
3. Count cubic centimeters in the drawing of a cube model—usually prisms.
4. Draw a figure with a given number of cubic centimeters.

This discussion covers volumes of objects made from cubes. The most important tool, however, for determining volume will be the graduated cylinder which we will discuss in the section after next. But first we want to talk about how the volume of prisms can be calculated.

Calculating Volume—An Upper Grade Exercise

The volume of a rectangular prism made of cubic centimeters can be found using multiplication. The number of cubic centimeters in the top layer is just the product of 3×6 since there are 3 rows of 6 cubic cm (see Figure 8). Thus, in each layer there are 18 cc. Because there are 5 layers, the total number of cubic centimeters is 5×18 cc = 90 cc. As often written in math books, this type of counting is expressed as

$$V = l \times w \times h.$$

You should interpret this as the number of cubic cm in the top layer (given by the value of $l \times w$) times the number of layers (given by the value of h).

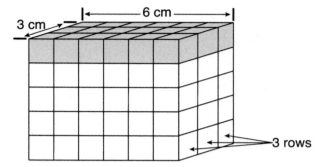

Figure 8: *A rectangular prism*

If the top layer is not rectangular but the figure is a right solid (sides perpendicular to top and bottom), then we can still find the volume by the above technique. The formula *length* $\times$ *width* $\times$ *height* will no longer work since the layers are not rectangular. However, since each horizontal slice has the same shape (see Figure 9), all we have to do is find the number of cubic cm in the top layer and multiply this by the number of layers. To find the number of cubic centimeters in the top layer, we have to find the number of square centimeters in the top surface, since each square centimeter of the surface is attached to a cubic centimeter in the top layer. Thus, if in Figure 9 by counting square cm we find that there are 22 sq cm on the top surface, then there must be 22 cubic cm in the top layer and in each subsequent layer. The total volume, then, is:

$$\frac{22 \text{ cubic cm}}{1 \text{ layer}} \times 5 \text{ layers} = 110 \text{ cubic cm}$$

for the object shown in Figure 9. As a general formula we have:

$$V = A \times h,$$

where the area A of the top tells us the number of cc in the top layer, and the value of h tells us the number of layers. The children should not just memorize each formula. They should understand what is behind the formulas.

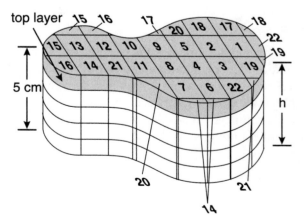

Figure 9: *A right solid*

When using a formula like $l \times w \times h$, the old bugaboo of units reappears. Since l, w, and h are all measured in centimeters, it is tempting to say that the units of volume are centimeters cubed written as $(cm)^3$. And indeed this is what is often done in scientific texts. Yes, it's technically correct to write $(cm)^3$ or cm^3, but again it can be misleading for children just as "centimeter squared" can be misleading for area. If we say a volume is 7 centimeters cubed, is that $(7\ cm)^3 = 343$ cc? We can avoid this confusion by writing what we mean; that the volume is 7 cubic centimeters or 7 cc.

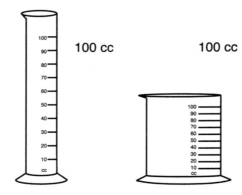

Figure 10: *Graduated cylinders*

Clearly, the ability to calculate volume is rather limited to certain special shapes. An irregularly shaped container or object will require a different approach.

A Volume Measurer: The Graduated Cylinder

We have seen that a ruler which is calibrated in cm can be used to measure length. There is no comparably simple device for measuring area, but there is one for measuring volume. It is the graduated cylinder calibrated in cubic centimeters. Two graduated cylinders are shown in Figure 10. They can be made of glass or Pyrex, both of which are breakable, or plastic, which is not. The cylinder most suitable for classroom use would be calibrated in 1 cc, 5 cc, or 10 cc divisions and have a capacity of 100 to 150 cc. When filled with a liquid (usually water) or a fluid substance like sand or salt, one can read the volume of the material off the side of the graduated cylinder. One cannot use this device to directly measure the volume of a number of marbles since the marbles piled in the cylinder will leave an unknown volume of air spaces between them. This is illustrated in Figure 11b. As we shall see in the next section, we can find the volume of solid objects like marbles by the method of displacement. The rest of this section will discuss using the graduated cylinder for finding the volume of liquid, particularly water.

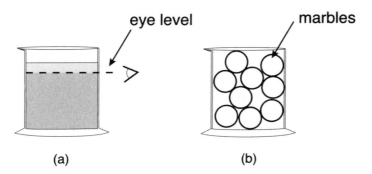

Figure 11: *Liquid and marbles in graduated cylinder*

To read the volume of water in a graduated cylinder, your eyes must be level with the liquid, as shown in Figure 11a. Since water is pulled up at the sides of the cylinder into a curved surface called a meniscus, one must measure the water level at the center of the cylinder. This is done by using the lower of the two lines that one sees (Figure 12) when looking at the water from the side. The top line is due to the pulled up water and should be ignored. (This phenomenon tends to be more pronounced when using glass rather than plastic graduated cylinders.)

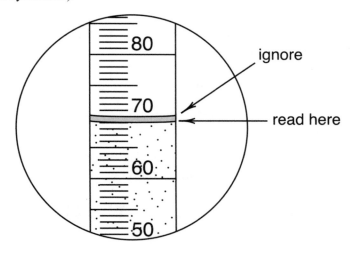

Figure 12: *The meniscus*

One must be careful about what one puts into a graduated cylinder. A tall, narrow one will generally have 1 cc divisions and thus can be used for accurate measurements. The trouble is, that because it is narrow, only small objects can be used. Many a time a student has misjudged the size of an object and found it stuck in the narrow cylinder never to come out again.

Chalk off one cylinder. A good general size that we like is one about 4 cm in diameter with a 150 cc capacity and made of plastic. The divisions are usually 5 or 10 cc. We shall discuss in the next section how to use a "big" graduated cylinder to measure the volume of small objects.

Many graduated cylinders that you purchase will have several different scales along the sides. This is due to the diversity of units for liquid measurements. Many cylinders will have a scale for fluid ounces and another for milliliters. The metric unit of volume is the milliliter, which is defined to be 1 cubic cm:

$$1 \text{ ml} = 1 \text{ cc.}$$

The liter is often encountered in daily life (for example, soda bottles are often 1 or 2 liters). It is exactly 1000 ml.

One of the first exercises the children can do with a graduated cylinder is simply to fill the cylinder to a specified level—10 cc, for example. An eyedropper is handy for getting the volume exactly right, since by pouring one usually overshoots or undershoots the mark. Whatever the divisions of the cylinder are, choose some volumes that fall right on a major division and some that fall between divisions, where the children will have to interpolate. An example is shown in Figure 13 for a cylinder with 10 cc divisions.

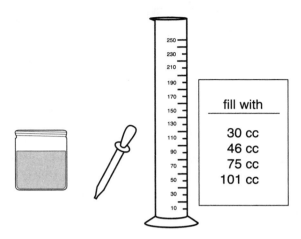

Figure 13: *A graduated cylinder exercise*

Once the second- or third-graders are good at reading the scale, they can use the graduated cylinder to find the capacity or volume of a set of three jars (Figure 14). You should build up a collection of jars of all shapes and volumes, from small baby food jars, through peanut butter containers, to large coffee jars. Exotic shapes are nice. To find the volume of a jar, one can either fill the jar to the brim and then keep pouring the water into the graduated cylinder, or one can keep filling the graduated cylinder and pour the water into the jar until it is filled. Either way, the children have to keep track of the number of times the graduated cylinder is filled and the total volume of water accumulated this way. This activity appears as a lesson called *Fill 'er Up* in third grade.

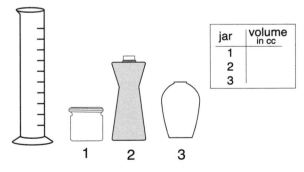

Figure 14: *A capacity exercise*

Volume Measurement by Displacement

How would you measure the volume of a small rock? This problem is dealt with in lessons on volume beginning in Grade 2. The technique is illustrated in Figure 15. First, you fill the graduated cylinder with a convenient amount of water, for example, 40 cc rather than 43 cc. Then you place the rock in the graduated cylinder without losing any water (there must be enough water in the cylinder initially to cover the object). You then read the new volume V. Since the volume of water V_{water} stays constant, the volume V is due to the water plus the rock. The rock displaces, or pushes aside, its volume in water and the water level rises. Thus, we have:

$$V_{rock} = V - V_{water}.$$

For example, in Figure 15 the volume of the rock is 22 cc. Note that subtraction is easier if you start with a multiple of ten for the volume of water. The technique works for any solid object no matter what its shape. To start with, then, the children should be asked to find the volume of a wide variety of objects, some spheres, cubes, rocks, coins, washers, etc.

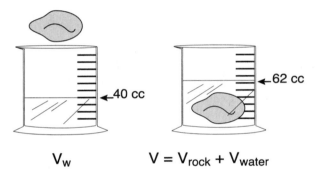

$$V_w \qquad\qquad V = V_{rock} + V_{water}$$

Figure 15: *Volume by displacement*

But what if the object is too big to fit into the graduated cylinder? If a bigger graduated cylinder isn't handy, then you can use your graduated cylinder to calibrate a large jar, and then away you go. One word of warning: When you place a large object in a graduated cylinder or jar, a considerable amount of water may splash out, even though you are very careful. You can get around this by placing the object in the graduated cylinder first and then pouring in a known amount of water V_w, and then read $V = V_{rock} + V_{water}$ off the scale. An alternative method is to find a large container and fill it with water to the brim. When the object is carefully placed in the container, it overflows, and the volume of the overflow liquid is equal to the volume of the object. If you catch all the overflow liquid in a second container, you can then use a graduated cylinder to find the volume of that liquid.

Finding the volume of small objects is also a problem, since the object may be so small you can't see the water level rise. Of course, you can always use a smaller graduated cylinder, one with 1 cc divisions instead of 5 or 10 cc divisions. The trouble is that sometimes even 1 cc per division is too large. The only way out is to measure the volume of several of the small objects at once (Figure 16b). (The volume of the several objects are identical.) For example, suppose you have 10 identical objects. To find the volume of one object, subtract the volume of the water and divide by 10. In this fashion, the children can find the volume of small washers, paper clips, pins, etc. Using 10 objects is a good idea since it is easy to divide by 10.

Too big   Too small

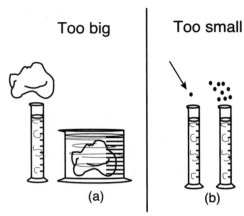

(a)   (b)

Figure 16: *Finding volumes of large or small objects*

Obtaining Accurate Results

A few words about accuracy are appropriate here. Most of the time you have to interpolate between divisions in order to read the volume. This usually leads to a reading error of about 20% of the value between the scale marks. Thus, if your graduated cylinder has 10 cc divisions, you might expect an error (i.e., children will get readings that differ) by up to 2 cc. This is illustrated in Figure 17a. If the object has raised the water level several divisions, then this 20% per division uncertainty is not a serious problem. For example, our rock changed the water level from 40 cc to 62 cc. If a reading error is up to 2 cc, then three children who read the same graduated cylinder might read 62 cc, but possibly 61 cc or 63 cc (if they are careful; maybe even more if they are not). But the volume of the rock is 62 cc − 40 cc = 22 cc for one child, but 23 cc for another, and 21 cc for the third. Thus we have a spread in reading of about 2 parts in 22 or 10%. A bigger rock, with a volume of, say, 46 cc would still have the same reading error of 2 cc, but its volume error would only be 2 parts in 46 or about 5%.

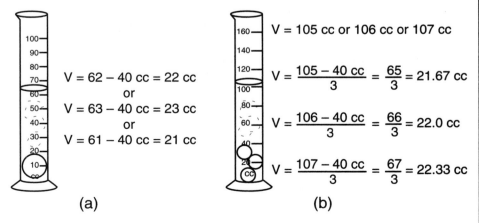

(a)   (b)

Figure 17: *Measurement error*

A good rule of thumb is that your reading will not be accurate unless the object raises the water level by more than one division. There are two ways to achieve this. One, use a narrow graduated cylinder, or two, use several identical objects if they are available. In the case of the latter, you find the volume of one object by dividing by the number of identical objects, as we did above for very small objects. For example, three objects would still produce a reading error of 2 cc but a volume error of only 2 cc/3 = 0.67 cc. This is illustrated in Figure 17b where three marbles give a volume spread of only 0.67 cc in 22 cc or 3%, compared to 10% for one marble. Of course, this would not work for finding the volume of a rock, since it would be difficult to find three identical rocks.

If the object floats, you have to push it under in order to measure its volume. In this situation, what is important is how you push it under. If you use your finger, then what you measure is the volume of the object plus the volume of your submerged finger. Since the volume of your finger may be comparable to the volume of the object, this is clearly not a good idea. What you need is a pusher whose volume is much less than the volume of the object. A straightened paper clip or a pin will do (Figure 18).

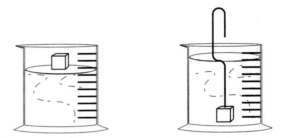

Figure 18: *Finding the volume of something that floats*

Two Misconceptions

Early on, the children should come to grips with two important ideas concerning volume:

1. The volume of an object is independent of the material it is made of.
2. The volume of an object does not change when its shape changes.[2]

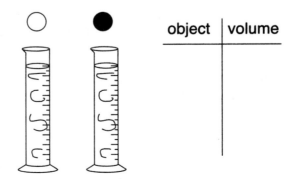

Figure 19: *Volume vs. material*

---

[2]Usually. See later discussion.

As to the first point, you can study spheres of the same volume but made of a wide variety of materials (steel, lucite, glass, even wood). The children should discover that their volumes are the same. As illustrated in Figure 19, students can fill two identical cylinders to the same level with water, carefully place both objects in, and see that the volume displaced is the same. Initially, many children will say that the heavier object has more volume and that the water will go up higher in its graduated cylinder. They are confusing mass and volume. If you take a clay cube and mash it into a thin disk, many children will say that the disk has less volume than the cube. Here they confuse one dimension, thinness, with volume: they mistakenly assume all thin objects have a small volume. Again, using the graduated cylinder the child can see that the volumes are the same (Figure 20). They can make all kinds of shapes out of a single piece of clay and determine that they all have the same volume. Indeed, the only way that they can change its volume is to tear off a piece.

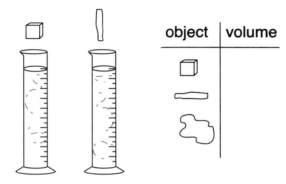

Figure 20: *Volume vs. shape*

The Concept of Mass

Defining Mass

Mass is one of the most difficult variables to understand. It is also one of the most important. Length, area, and volume have straightforward definitions. The volume of an object, for example, is defined as a measure of the space it occupies. Does mass have a similar straightforward definition? In a sense it does and in a sense it does not. Basically, **mass** is a measure of the quantity of matter in an object. That is its simple definition. Unfortunately, that begs the question. One can ask, what is matter, and we are back to where we started. So we have to look more closely at mass. And that is where things get difficult. Mass is defined through what it *does,* and this sets it apart from length, area, and volume. Moreover, mass does two things which means, in a sense, it has two definitions.

One of the things that mass does is absolutely crucial for the existence of our universe. Mass is the cause of the force of gravity. Without mass, there would be no gravity, and without gravity, matter would not have clumped into galaxies and stars and us. Since mass causes gravity, we can define mass through the pull of gravity—the greater the pull, the greater the mass an object has.

The other thing that mass does has to do with the motion of an object. All other variables being equal, the mass of an object determines how much the velocity of an object will *change* when subject to a given force. In layman's terms, the larger the mass of an object, the harder you have to push to change its speed. Since we are not ready to study motion, we will not discuss the details of this aspect of mass. Nevertheless, we might note that it was Einstein's contemplation of both properties of mass (gravity and motion) that led him to his general theory of relativity.

Figure 1: *Dropping two objects*

One way, then, to determine which of two objects has more mass is to determine which one is pulled on more strongly by the Earth's gravitational force. One possible way to do this is to drop two objects, as shown in Figure 1, and see which reaches the ground first. You might suppose, since the more mass an object has, the bigger the force of gravity, that the more massive object would fall faster and reach the ground first. If you do this exercise, however (as Galileo did), you will find that

*Basically, **mass** is a measure of the quantity of matter in an object.*

both objects reach the ground at the same time! What went wrong? Well, we are breaking one of our cardinal rules, which is keeping variables fixed. When the objects fall, we not only have gravity pulling on them, but their velocity is changing as well. Therefore, both definitions of mass are involved and the overall effect is no longer obvious. It appears that in some way the effects cancel!

So we need a way of measuring the pull of gravity (i.e., using definition 1) without having the object move (i.e., eliminating definition 2). As we shall see in the next section, we can do this with an equal arm balance.

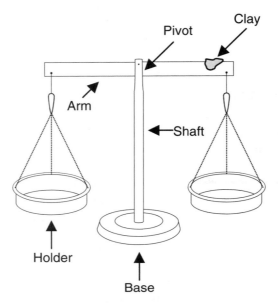

Figure 2: *A balance*

Equal Arm Balance

The equal arm balance is the key to our operational definition of mass for children. If two objects balance, they have the same mass. If the arm tilts to one side, the object in the lower of the two pans has more mass than the object in the other pan.

Basically, the equal arm balance is a stick that is pivoted at its center and has two holders that are mounted on at points which are equidistant from the pivot (hence the name equal arm balance). Figure 2 pictures a balance that we often use in *Math Trailblazers*. It is quite sturdy and accurate enough for use in the elementary classroom. The tall wooden shaft and long arms of the balance make it very useful in a variety of balancing experiments. If you would like to make your own, you can use a block of wood (Figure 3a) or a book to hold the pivot rod (Figure 3b). A ruler can act as the arm and the bottom of paper cups as pans. These latter pieces can be attached to the arm with string and paper clips.

The equal arm balance is the key to our operational definition of mass for children. If two objects balance, they have the same mass. If the arm tilts to one side, the object in the lower of the two pans has more mass than the object in the other pan.

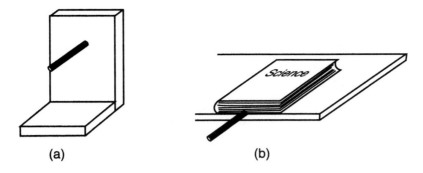

(a)   (b)

Figure 3: *Making a balance*

Once you have put your equal arm balance together, it must be zeroed. That is, the arm must be level before any masses are added. You can do this by adding small pieces of clay to one end of the arm, as shown in Figure 2, until it is level. We suggest that you do this once for each balance and then have the children check to see that it is level before and during each experiment.

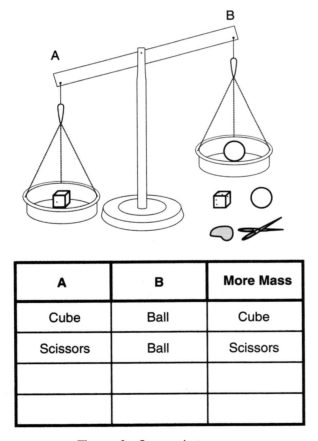

A	B	More Mass
Cube	Ball	Cube
Scissors	Ball	Scissors

Figure 4: *Comparing masses*

We are now ready to find out which of two objects, A or B, has greater mass. One is placed in each pan. Since the object with more mass will experience the bigger gravitational pull, the balance will tilt either one way or the other. If A has more mass it will tilt to the left, as shown in Figure 4, while if B has more mass it will tilt to the right. If the masses in the pans are equal, the pull of gravity on both is the same and the balance will remain level. One word of caution, though: If the masses are the same and the arm is tilted when the masses are placed on the balance, then the ruler will often remain tilted. Thus, to be sure, bring the arm back to level and see if it remains there.

One of the first exercises you can do with children in kindergarten through second grade is to have them compare, two at a time, the masses of a wide variety of objects. Then they should order the objects from the most massive to the least massive (see *Putting Masses in Order* in Grade 2 Unit 10). A washer, connecting cube, small scissors, steel ball, etc., can be used. Notice that the equal arm balance does away with the motion definition of mass since the balance is at rest when the measurement is made. Thus, the equal arm balance allows us to relate the object's mass directly to the pull of gravity.

Measuring Mass: The Mass Standard

The above is fine for comparing masses, but how do we measure *the* mass of an object? In other words, how do we assign a number to the mass of our object? Just as when we measure length, area, and volume, we need to decide on a unit. Say that we take as our standard masses a set of identical washers (paper clips would do as well). Let's call the mass of each washer 1 *ugh*. Then, if our object is balanced by 4 washers, its mass is 4 ughs, as shown in Figure 5. If the mass of the object is between 4 and 5 ughs, then the balance will not level out but tilt one way for 4 washers and the other way for 5. In this way, the child can assign unique masses to a wide range of objects. Clearly, the smaller the washer, the more accurately one can determine the mass of an object.

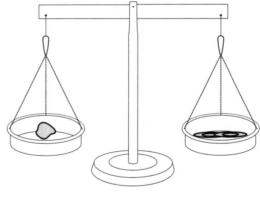

But washers are not a very satisfactory standard. The washers in your class may not have the same mass as those used in another school in your district, much less in another city or another country. What we need is a universal standard that is accepted by the entire scientific community. This problem was recognized by scientists a long time ago and was resolved when the Paris Academy of Sciences submitted a report to

Object	Number of Washers	Mass in ughs
Ball	4	4
Cube	2	2

Figure 5: *Measuring masses*

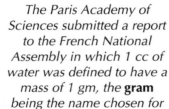

*The Paris Academy of Sciences submitted a report to the French National Assembly in which 1 cc of water was defined to have a mass of 1 gm, the **gram** being the name chosen for the unit of mass.*

the French National Assembly in which 1 cc of water was defined to have a mass of 1 gm, the **gram** being the name chosen for the unit of mass. Then, using this definition, a platinum cylinder was made and declared to be the standard for 1000 grams. In 1875, an international treaty was signed by most "civilized" nations which established an International Bureau of Weights and Measures in Sevres, France, near Paris. The international prototype kilogram, made of platinum iridium alloy, is kept there. If you want your own kilogram, you have to go to Paris with an equal arm balance and some material and hack away at the material until it balances the platinum iridium standard. The National Bureau of Standards in Washington, DC, has an accurately constructed copy as do other governments throughout the world.

For small measurements, one needs a mass that is smaller than a kilogram, just as one needs a length that is smaller than a meter. The gram, like the centimeter, is perfect for this. Most objects that you will deal with in the elementary school science program will have masses between 1 and 100 grams. Masses are commercially available, usually in 1-, 5-, 10-, 20-, 50-, 100-, 200-, 500-, and 1000-gram pieces. It might be a good idea to have one good set of very accurate standard masses for your school (locked in a closet marked "Paris," of course), but they are expensive. For general classroom use, there are less expensive sets of plastic masses available. However, since the plastic masses may not be as accurate, you may wish to compare them to a good set of standard masses or find their mass using a triple beam balance or other accurate scales.

The cheapest standard mass is a nickel. It has a mass very close to 5 grams! But alas, a dime does not have a mass of 10 grams. There are two ways to get around having to buy sets of expensive standard masses.

To determine the mass of a small object, measure the mass of several of the objects and then divide the total mass by the number of objects. For example, if it turns out that 10 small objects balance a 5-gram piece, then each object will have a mass of 0.5 grams. (5 grams ÷ 10 objects = 0.5 grams per object.)

If you go to a hardware store and make a pest of yourself—bring your equal arm balance—you can usually find washers that have "nice" masses, like 1, 2, 5, 8 grams, etc. Figure 6 shows such a collection that can be used as standard masses. Once you have the washers, you can give each child several of each and a lot of objects whose mass you want them to determine. A good data table is a big help since you want to keep track of the number of

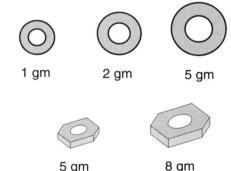

Object	Number of Standard Masses				Mass in gm
	1 gm	2 gm	5 gm	8 gm	
Plastic Cylinder	3	1	2	2	31

Figure 6: *Using washers as standard masses*

different washers it takes to balance the object. Then, as shown in Figure 6, a little multiplication and addition is necessary to obtain the final mass in grams. In the example above, the total mass is:

$$m_{total} = 3 \times 1 \text{ gm} + 1 \times 2 \text{ gm} + 2 \times 5 \text{ gm} + 2 \times 8 \text{ gm} = 31 \text{ gm}.$$

Finding masses in grams is a great way to practice multiplication, addition, and mental math.

A second way to get around using expensive standards is again to use washers but place them in packages of sets of 1, 5, 10, 20 grams, etc. The package can be composed of several washers wrapped in masking tape with enough tape or small washers to make an even 5 gm or 10 gm, etc. Either way, the cost of a washer is small enough that children can have a set of masses for a few dollars.

Mass vs. Weight

In everyday language, we talk about the weight of an object rather than its mass. Are these two words for the same thing? Technically, weight and mass are distinct concepts. In scientific terms, the **mass** of an object is the amount of matter in the object. Mass is measured in kilograms and grams in the metric system and in pounds and ounces in the English system. The **weight** of an object is the measure of the pull of gravity on that object. Sir Isaac Newton first explained the importance of gravity for the motions of the planets and for the fall of an object more than 300 years ago.

Because of the awareness of space travel, most children know that the pull of gravity is different on different planets and that there is essentially no gravity in outer space. Many museums and planetariums have exhibits that show your weight on the moon and various planets. For example, since the moon's gravity is weaker than the Earth's, the pull on an individual object would be less. Thus, a human being would weigh less on the moon than on the Earth.

How is the mass of an object affected by gravity? The mass of an object remains constant regardless of space travel since gravity does not influence mass. Since we use a two-pan balance to measure mass, both sides of the balance are equally affected by gravity. If an 11-gram pencil balances one 1-gram and two 5-gram standard masses on Earth, it will balance those same masses on the moon.

However, since most of us are likely to spend our lives on Earth, the distinction between mass and weight may be lost on many students.

We suggest two pedagogical alternatives with regard to the distinction between mass and weight:

1. Ignore it. This point is fairly subtle and eludes many adults.
2. Provide a simple explanation, but don't worry about it too much.

Manipulatives List

The Manipulatives List outlines all manufactured manipulatives and other materials needed to implement *Math Trailblazers* successfully.

Students explore shapes using geoboards.

Manipulatives List

Following are the manipulatives for first grade. There are several categories of manipulatives listed here:

Manufactured Manipulatives: a list of each of the manipulatives needed to implement fully the *Math Trailblazers* curriculum. Many of these manipulatives may be available already in your classroom or school.

Manipulatives which you need can be purchased:

- in kit form from Kendall/Hunt Publishing Company;
- in a kit configuration from Kendall/Hunt that allows sharing between classrooms;
- or as individual items from your manipulatives supplier.

Please contact Kendall/Hunt directly for additional information.

Other materials are needed for the successful implementation of the *Math Trailblazers* curriculum for the entire year. These materials are listed in three categories to aid in planning for the year:

- **Consumables** (edible or one-use items such as beans, paper cups, etc.)
- **Collectibles** (throwaway items such as magazines, egg cartons, jars, etc.)
- **School Supplies** (items usually available in classrooms such as tape, glue, markers, etc.)

Manipulatives for *Math Trailblazers* First Grade

Manufactured Manipulative, Classroom	Number per Group	TOTAL per Classroom of 30 Students
100 chart, large, poster-size	1 per classroom	1
*calculator	1 per student	30
connecting cubes	50 per student	1500
connecting links	50 per student	1500
cube, 1-inch	1 per student pair	15
easel paper, 1-inch square grid	1 per classroom	1
Mr. Origin	1 per student	30
pattern blocks, overhead		1 set
pattern blocks, plastic		1000
ramp	1	1
ruler, cm/inch, transparent	1 for classroom use at the overhead	1
spinners, clear plastic	1 per student pair	15
square-inch tiles, colored	25 per student	750
square-inch tiles, overhead	1 set per classroom	1 set
**wall chart, laminated: data tables & graph	1 set per classroom	1

*Students need a calculator with addition, subtraction, multiplication, and division with a constant operation function.

**The wall chart is available through Kendall/Hunt Publishing 1-800-228-0810.

Additional Materials or Equipment Needed for *Math Trailblazers* First Grade

Consumable Materials	Number Required
bags, paper	3 per student pair
bags, plastic	1 per student pair
beans	2-pound container per classroom
	100 baby limas per student pair
	40 large beans per student pair
	80 small beans per student pair
cereal, colored	1 box per classroom

Collectible Materials	Number Required
balls	1 per student pair
bowl, large, and 2 large containers	3 total "large containers or bowls" per classroom
boxes (tissue, cereal, etc.)	1 per student pair
cup and saucer	1 of each per classroom
cylindrical objects	10–20 per student pair
egg cartons	1 per student pair
jars	2 same-size jars per classroom
key	1 per classroom
magazines, newspapers, and food ads	
measuring cup, $\frac{1}{4}$	1 per classroom
paper cups, large	1 per student pair
pennies, nickels, dimes	40–50 pennies per student pair
	8 nickels per student pair
	5 dimes per student pair
scoop (a scoop that holds an appropriate number of baby lima beans—e.g., 40 to 70 beans for students to count)	1 per classroom
string	1 ball of white string or yarn and 1 ball of black or brown string or yarn
toilet paper core	1 per student pair
toothpicks	12 per student or 360 per class (1 box of 500)
toy cars	5 per classroom

School Supplies	Number Required
classroom calendar, large	1 per classroom
construction paper	1–2 pads (multicolored) per classroom
easel paper	1 pad per classroom
envelopes	5 per student
hole puncher, hand-held	1–2 per classroom
index cards, 3- by 5-inch	7 per student pair (100 or 150 per classroom)
paint and paintbrushes	1 of each per student
rulers, cm/in	1 per student
self-adhesive notes, 3-inch-square	3 per student (1 pad of 100)

The following supplies are used throughout the year:

colored pencils

crayons

glue or paste

markers

paper clips

scissors

stapler

tape

Literature List

The Literature List provides suggested titles and recommended reading of commercially available trade books, which are used in many *Math Trailblazers* lessons.

Students connect math and literature by reading a trade book.

Literature List

Math Trailblazers incorporates the use of commercially available trade books in many lessons. A listing of these trade books is provided here. There are two categories of books: essential titles and suggested titles.

- Essential titles are books whose context is used to develop and implement specific lessons. Instructions in the lesson guides incorporate the content of these books. Alternatives for teaching the lesson if the book is not available are also included in the lesson guides.
- Suggested titles are either possible alternatives to a preferred book or can be used to extend or enhance a particular lesson.

Unit 1—Welcome to First Grade: A Baseline Assessment Unit
Suggested Titles

- Adams, Pam. *There Were Ten in the Bed.* Child's Play International, Ltd., Sudbury, MA, 1998.
- Anno, Mitsumasa. *Anno's Counting Book.* HarperCollins Publishers, New York, 1992.
- Bang, Molly. *Ten, Nine, Eight.* Greenwillow Books, New York, 1998.
- Christelow, Eileen. *Five Little Monkeys Jumping on the Bed.* Houghton Mifflin Company, Boston, MA, 1998.
- Crews, Donald. *Bicycle Race.* Greenwillow Books, New York, 1985.
- Ehlert, Lois. *Fish Eyes: A Book You Can Count On.* Harcourt Brace, New York, 2001.
- Hoban, Tana. *Is It Larger? Is It Smaller?* Greenwillow Books, New York, 1997.
- Hutchins, Pat. *1 Hunter.* Greenwillow Books, New York, 1986.
- Morozumi, Atsuko. *One Gorilla: A Counting Book.* Farrar, Straus & Giroux, New York, 1993.
- Russo, Marisabina. *The Line Up Book.* Greenwillow Books, New York, 1986.

Unit 2—Exploring Shapes
Suggested Titles

- Ehlert, Lois. *Color Zoo.* The Trumpet Club, New York, 1997.
- Hoban, Tana. *Shapes, Shapes, Shapes.* Greenwillow, New York, 1996.

Unit 3—Pennies, Pockets, and Parts
Suggested Titles

- Aker, Suzanne. *What Comes in 2's, 3's, and 4's?* Simon and Schuster, New York, 1992.
- Carle, Eric. *The Very Hungry Caterpillar.* Publishers' Group West, Berkeley, CA, 1994.
- Caudill, Rebecca. *A Pocketful of Cricket.* Holt, Rinehart and Winston, New York, 1999.
- Freeman, Don. *A Pocket for Corduroy.* The Viking Press, New York, 1999.
- Langstaff, John. *Over in the Meadow.* Harcourt, Brace, Jovanovich, New York, 1992.
- Payne, Emmy. *Katy No-Pocket.* Houghton Mifflin Company, Boston, 1999.
- Walsh, Ellen S. *Mouse Count.* Harcourt, Brace, Jovanovich, New York, 1999.

Unit 4—Adding to Solve Problems
Suggested Titles

- Carle, Eric. *Rooster's Off to See the World.* Aladdin Paperbacks, New York, 1999.
- Merriam, Eve. *12 Ways to Get to 11.* Aladdin Paperbacks, New York, 1996.

Unit 5—Grouping and Counting
Essential Titles

- Dee, Ruby. *Two Ways to Count to Ten.* Econo-Clad Books, Topeka, KS, 1999.
- Hutchins, Pat. *The Doorbell Rang.* Mulberry Books, New York, 1994.

Unit 6—Measurement: Length
Essential Titles

- Hamm, Diane Johnston. *How Many Feet in the Bed?* Simon and Schuster Books for Young Readers, New York, 1994.
- Myller, Rolf. *How Big Is a Foot?* Dell Publishing, New York, 1999.

Suggested Titles

- Hightower, Susan M. *Twelve Snails to One Lizard.* Simon and Schuster, New York, 1997.
- Lionni, Leo. *Inch by Inch.* Mulberry Books, New York, 1995.

Unit 7—Patterns and Designs
Suggested Titles

- McGovern, Ann. *Too Much Noise.* Scholastic Inc., New York, 1967.
- Paul, Ann Whitford. *Eight Hands Round.* HarperCollins Publishers, New York, 1991.

Unit 8—Subtracting to Solve Problems
Suggested Titles

- Chwast, Seymour. *The Twelve Circus Rings.* Harcourt Brace Jovanovich, New York, 1996.
- Ehlert, Lois. *CIRCUS.* HarperCollins, New York, 1992.
- Johnson, Neil. *Big Top Circus.* Dial Books for Young Readers, New York, 1995.
- Spier, Peter. *Circus!* Delacorte Press, New York, 1995.

Unit 9—Grouping by Tens
None

Unit 10—Measurement: Area
None

Unit 11—Looking at 100
Suggested Titles

- Dee, Ruby. *Two Ways to Count to Ten.* Econo-Clad Books, Topeka, KS, 1999.
- Hoban, Tana. *26 Letters and 99 Cents.* Mulberry Books, New York, 1995.
- Gibbons, Gail. *Weather Forecasting.* Aladdin Books, New York, 1993.
- Medearis, Angela Shelf. *Picking Peas for a Penny.* Scholastic Inc., New York, 1993.

Unit 12—Cubes and Volume
None

Unit 13—Thinking About Addition and Subtraction
Suggested Title

- Hong, Lily Toy. *Two of Everything.* Albert Whitman Publishing, Morton Grove, IL, 1993.

Unit 14—Exploring Multiplication and Division
None

Unit 15—Exploring 3-D Shapes
Suggested Title

- Hoban, Tana. *Shapes, Shapes, Shapes.* Scott Foresman, Glenview, IL, 1996.

Unit 16—Collecting and Organizing Data
Suggested Title

- Ehlert, Lois. *Eating the Alphabet: Fruits and Vegetables from A to Z.* Econo-Clad Books, Topeka, KS, 1999.

Unit 17—Moving Beyond 100
None

Unit 18—Pieces, Parts, and Symmetry
Suggested Title

- McMillan, Bruce. *Eating Fractions.* Scholastic Big Books, New York, 1993.

Unit 19—Measurement and Mapping
None

Unit 20—Looking Back at First Grade
None

Games List

The Games List includes descriptions of games used in *Math Trailblazers*.

A student uses counting strategies while playing a math game.

Games List

Games are often used in *Math Trailblazers* to engage students in practicing basic arithmetic and other math concepts. A complete listing of the games for your grade and a description of the games are provided below.

Once introduced, these games can be used throughout the year for ongoing practice. We suggest that after the games have been introduced and played in class, they be added to a Games Menu, with necessary materials placed in a math center somewhere in the classroom so that students can replay the games during indoor recess, when they have completed other assignments, and at other times during the day. TIMS Tips in the lesson guides will remind you to add each game to the Games Menu.

Unit 1—Welcome to First Grade: A Baseline Assessment Unit
The Train Game in *Unit Resource Guide* Unit 1 Lesson 3 Pages 26–28
Students build a train of ten cubes by adding one, two, or three cubes. The player who places the tenth cube on the train wins.

Unit 2—Exploring Shapes
None

Unit 3—Pennies, Pockets, and Parts
Think and Spin in *Unit Resource Guide* Unit 3 Lesson 3 Pages 31–33 and *Student Guide* Pages 41–45
Students use a spinner and a ten frame to make and record sums less than ten. The first player to fill up all of his or her ten frames with sums of ten is the winner.

Unit 4—Adding to Solve Problems
None

Unit 5—Grouping and Counting
Care to Share? in *Unit Resource Guide* Unit 5 Letter Home, Page 1
Students share a pile of 12 to 20 objects among three, four, or five people. They write number sentences for the partitions and account for the leftovers.

Unit 6—Measurement: Length
None

Unit 7—Patterns and Designs
Balancing Act in *Unit Resource Guide* Unit 7 Lesson 5 Pages 34–36 and *Student Guide* Page 145
Students use pattern blocks to mirror symmetric designs on a game sheet.

Unit 8—Subtracting to Solve Problems
None

Unit 9—Grouping by Tens

Spin for Beans 50 in *Unit Resource Guide* Unit 9 Lesson 3 Pages 29–35 and *Student Guide* Pages 163–164
Students spin a spinner and take a specified number of beans from a pile. They keep track of their beans with ten frames, counting by tens and adding leftovers. The first player to accumulate 50 beans is the winner.

Guess My Number in *Unit Resource Guide* Unit 9 Lesson 6 Page 56 and *Student Guide* Page 171
A student selects a number and gives clues such as "higher" or "lower" to assist other players in naming that number.

Unit 10—Measurement: Area
None

Unit 11—Looking at 100

Arrow Dynamics in *Unit Resource Guide* Unit 11 Lesson 4 Pages 46–50 and *Student Guide* Pages 215–223
Students spin spinners and move accordingly on a 100 chart. They record number sentences for their moves. The player who gets closest to 100 wins.

Going to Extremes in *Unit Resource Guide* Unit 11 Lesson 4 Page 49
Students spin spinners and move accordingly on a 100 chart. They record number sentences for their moves. The player who gets closest to 0 or 100 wins.

Unit 12—Cubes and Volume
None

Unit 13—Thinking about Addition and Subtraction

Make Ten in *Unit Resource Guide* Unit 13 Lesson 1 Pages 16–23 and *Student Guide* Page 264
Students use a number deck to make sums of ten by pairing cards in their hand or asking other players for specific cards. Students determine the rule for the winner.

Make 100 in *Unit Resource Guide* Unit 13 Lesson 1 Page 19
Students use a number deck to make sums of 100 by pairing cards in their hand or asking other players for specific cards. Students determine the rule for the winner.

Doubles Railroad in *Unit Resource Guide* Unit 13 Lesson 3 Pages 34–35 and *Student Guide* Pages 269–275
Students spin a spinner and move double that number of spaces on a game board. The winner is the player who reaches the train yard first.

Unit 14—Exploring Multiplication and Division
None

Unit 15—Exploring 3-D Shapes
None

Unit 16—Collecting and Organizing Data
None

Unit 17—Moving Beyond 100
None

Unit 18—Pieces, Parts, and Symmetry
None

Unit 19—Measurement and Mapping
Mr. Origin Says in *Unit Resource Guide* Unit 19 Lesson 1 Page 19 and *Student Guide* Page 393
Students move their Mr. Origins according to directions specified by their teacher's Mr. Origin.

Unit 20—Looking Back at First Grade
None

Software List

The Software List outlines recommended computer software
used to enhance *Math Trailblazers* lessons.

Students use software to practice math facts and solve problems.

Software List

Software Titles by Topic

Patterns/Logical Thinking/Problem Solving
Math Concepts One . . . Two . . . Three!
Mighty Math Carnival Countdown
Mighty Math Zoo Zillions
Sunbuddy Math Playhouse
Thinkin' Things Collection 1
Thinkin' Things Fripple Town

Number Concepts and Counting
Combining and Breaking Apart Numbers
Grouping and Place Value
Math Concepts One . . . Two . . . Three!
Mighty Math Carnival Countdown
Mighty Math Zoo Zillions
Ready for Math with Pooh
Sunbuddy Math Playhouse

*Data Collection/Reading and Interpreting
Graphs/Probability*
Graphers
Math Concepts One . . . Two . . . Three!

Geometry
Math Concepts One . . . Two . . . Three!
Mighty Math Carnival Countdown
Mighty Math Zoo Zillions
Shape Up!

Measurement
Math Concepts One . . . Two . . . Three!
Mighty Math Carnival Countdown
Mighty Math Zoo Zillions
Shape Up!
Sunbuddy Math Playhouse
Trudy's Time & Place House

Understanding of Basic Operations
Combining and Breaking Apart Numbers
Grouping and Place Value
Math Concepts One . . . Two . . . Three!
Mighty Math Carnival Countdown
Mighty Math Zoo Zillions
Ready for Math with Pooh

Practice with Basic Operations
Combining and Breaking Apart Numbers
Math Concepts One . . . Two . . . Three!
Mighty Math Carnival Countdown
Mighty Math Zoo Zillions
Sunbuddy Math Playhouse

Programs for Illustrating
Kid Pix

Time and Money
Discover Time
Math Concepts One . . . Two . . . Three!
Mighty Math Zoo Zillions
Money Challenge
Sunbuddy Math Playhouse
Trudy's Time & Place House

Recommended Software for First-Grade Units

Unit 1—Welcome to First Grade: A Baseline Assessment Unit

Math Concepts One . . . Two . . . Three! provides practice with number sense. Students explore counting, estimating, comparing, and ordering numbers.

Mighty Math Carnival Countdown helps develop understanding of the basic operations and provides practice with counting and sorting sets by various attributes including numbers by size, more/less, and even/odd.

Ready for Math with Pooh develops early number concepts including number recognition, sequencing, patterning, addition, and subtraction.

Sunbuddy Math Playhouse is a memory game involving counting, tallies, and analog and digital clocks.

Unit 2—Exploring Shapes

Math Concepts One . . . Two . . . Three! provides practice with number sense, addition and subtraction with manipulatives and money, sorting objects and making simple bar graphs, and measuring and estimating time, money, length, temperature, and mass.

Mighty Math Carnival Countdown provides practice with counting, basic operations, and sorting sets on the basis of various attributes.

Mighty Math Zoo Zillions provides practice with basic operations, rounding, skip counting, and identifying even and odd numbers.

Ready for Math with Pooh develops early number concepts including number recognition, sequencing, patterning, and addition and subtraction.

Sunbuddy Math Playhouse is a memory game involving counting, tallies, and analog and digital clocks.

Trudy's Time & Place House explores time, the calendar, maps, directions, and geography.

Unit 3—Pennies, Pockets, and Parts

Math Concepts One . . . Two . . . Three! provides practice with number sense, addition and subtraction with manipulatives and money, sorting two- and three-dimensional objects to find the symmetrical half, and making simple bar graphs.

Mighty Math Carnival Countdown provides practice with identifying, counting, adding and subtracting money, and explores shapes, patterns, symmetry, area, perimeter, and fractions using pattern blocks.

Sunbuddy Math Playhouse is a memory game involving counting, tallies, and analog and digital clocks.

Trudy's Time & Place House explores time, the calendar, maps, directions, and geography.

Unit 4—Adding to Solve Problems

Combining and Breaking Apart Numbers provides practice with different number combinations that make up a target number.

Math Concepts One . . . Two . . . Three! provides practice with number sense, through counting, estimation, comparing and ordering numbers, as well as addition and subtraction with manipulatives and money.

Mighty Math Carnival Countdown provides practice with place value, counting, and basic operations, as well as sorting sets by various attributes, including numbers by size, more and less, and even and odd.

Mighty Math Zoo Zillions provides practice with basic operations while manipulating a fish in a tank, rounding, skip counting, and identifying even and odd numbers, as well as word problems.

Sunbuddy Math Playhouse provides practice with basic addition and subtraction facts.

Unit 5—Grouping and Counting

Grouping and Place Value practices grouping objects by twos, fives, and tens.

Kid Pix helps students draw, write, and illustrate math concepts.

Math Concepts One . . . Two . . . Three! provides practice with number sense, addition and subtraction with manipulatives and money, sorting objects, and making simple bar graphs.

Mighty Math Carnival Countdown provides practice with place value, counting, and basic operations.

Mighty Math Zoo Zillions provides practice with basic operations (adding and subtracting) with money, rounding, skip counting, and identifying even and odd numbers.

Money Challenge provides practice with money.

Unit 6—Measurement: Length

Kid Pix helps students draw, write, and illustrate math concepts.

Math Concepts One . . . Two . . . Three! provides practice with sorting objects, making simple bar graphs, and estimating and measuring time, money, length, temperature, and mass.

Mighty Math Carnival Countdown helps students explore shapes, patterns, symmetry, area, perimeter, and fractions using pattern blocks.

Unit 7—Patterns and Designs

Kid Pix helps students draw, write, and illustrate patterns.

Math Concepts One . . . Two . . . Three! provides practice with sorting two- and three-dimensional shapes, line symmetry, and identifying patterns.

Mighty Math Carnival Countdown helps students explore shapes, patterns, symmetry, area, perimeter, and fractions using pattern blocks.

Shape Up! provides practice with five geometric shapes.

Sunbuddy Math Playhouse provides practice with sorting musical instruments by an increasing number of attributes.

Thinkin' Things Collection 1 helps students explore various attributes of characters, a row of birds, and develop their spatial sense.

Thinkin' Things Fripple Town helps students explore patterns of various objects and make other patterns with the same attributes.

Unit 8—Subtracting to Solve Problems

Combining and Breaking Apart Numbers provides practice with different number combinations that make up a target number.

Math Concepts One . . . Two . . . Three! provides practice with basic operations (addition and subtraction) with manipulatives and money.

Mighty Math Carnival Countdown provides practice with counting and basic operations.

Mighty Math Zoo Zillions provides practice with basic operations while manipulating a fish in a tank, rounding, skip counting, and identifying even and odd numbers.

Sunbuddy Math Playhouse provides practice with basic addition and subtraction facts.

Unit 9—Grouping by Tens

Grouping and Place Value practices grouping objects by twos, fives, and tens.

Kid Pix helps students draw, write, and illustrate math concepts.

Math Concepts One . . . Two . . . Three! provides practice with counting, estimation, comparing and ordering numbers, as well as estimating and measuring time, money, length, temperature, and mass.

Mighty Math Carnival Countdown provides practice with place value concepts, basic operations (addition and subtraction), and developing the concept of equals and more and less with numbers up to 1000.

Mighty Math Zoo Zillions provides practice with basic operations (adding and subtracting), rounding, skip counting, and identifying even and odd numbers.

Unit 10—Measurement: Area

Math Concepts One . . . Two . . . Three! provides practice with estimating and measuring time, money, length, temperature, and mass.

Mighty Math Carnival Countdown helps students explore shapes, patterns, symmetry, area, perimeter, and fractions using pattern blocks.

Shape Up! provides practice with five geometric shapes.

Unit 11—Looking at 100

Combining and Breaking Apart Numbers provides practice with different number combinations that make up a target number.

Grouping and Place Value practices grouping objects by twos, fives, and tens.

Kid Pix helps students draw, write, and illustrate math concepts.

Math Concepts One . . . Two . . . Three! provides practice with counting, estimation, comparing, and ordering numbers, as well as basic operations (addition and subtraction) with manipulatives and money.

Mighty Math Carnival Countdown provides practice with place value concepts, basic operations (addition and subtraction), and developing the concept of equals and more and less with numbers up to 1000.

Mighty Math Zoo Zillions provides practice with basic operations (addition and subtraction) while manipulating a fish in a tank, rounding, skip counting, and identifying even and odd numbers, as well as word problems.

Unit 12—Cubes and Volume

Math Concepts One . . . Two . . . Three! provides practice with sorting two- and three-dimensional shapes, line symmetry, and finding the missing symmetrical half.

Mighty Math Carnival Countdown provides practice with identifying three-dimensional objects from various perspectives.

Unit 13—Thinking About Addition and Subtraction

Combining and Breaking Apart Numbers provides practice with different number combinations that make up a target number.

Math Concepts One . . . Two . . . Three! provides practice with addition and subtraction with manipulatives and money.

Mighty Math Zoo Zillions provides practice with basic operations (addition and subtraction), skip counting, identifying even and odd numbers, and solving word problems.

Sunbuddy Math Playhouse provides practice with basic addition and subtraction facts.

Unit 14—Exploring Multiplication and Division

Kid Pix helps students draw, write, and illustrate math concepts.

Math Concepts One . . . Two . . . Three! provides practice with counting, estimation, comparing and ordering numbers, as well as basic operations (addition and subtraction) with manipulatives and money.

Mighty Math Carnival Countdown provides practice with counting and develops understanding of basic operations.

Mighty Math Zoo Zillions provides practice with basic operations (addition and subtraction) and word problems.

Unit 15—Exploring 3-D Shapes

Math Concepts One . . . Two . . . Three! provides practice with sorting two- and three-dimensional shapes, line symmetry, and finding the missing symmetrical half, as well as estimating and measuring time, money, length, temperature and mass.

Mighty Math Carnival Countdown provides practice with identifying three-dimensional objects from various perspectives.

Unit 16—Collecting and Organizing Data

Kid Pix helps students draw, write, and illustrate math concepts.

Math Concepts One . . . Two . . . Three! provides practice with sorting objects and making simple bar graphs.

Mighty Math Carnival Countdown provides practice sorting sets by attributes including sorting numbers by size, more and less, and even or odd.

Sunbuddy Math Playhouse asks students to sort musical instruments by an increasing number of attributes.

Thinkin' Things Collection 1 asks students to identify various attributes of the characters and to observe a row of birds with various attributes and build the next bird in line.

Thinkin' Things Fripple Town asks children to copy a cookie pattern with correct orientations and to discover the similarities in several flags and make others with the same attributes.

Unit 17—Moving Beyond 100

Grouping and Place Value practices grouping objects by twos, fives, and tens.

Math Concepts One . . . Two . . . Three! provides practice with counting, estimating, and comparing and ordering numbers.

Mighty Math Carnival Countdown provides practice with place value and basic operations (addition and subtraction).

Mighty Math Zoo Zillions provides practice with basic operations (adding and subtracting) with money, rounding, skip counting, and identifying even and odd numbers.

Unit 18—Pieces, Parts, and Symmetry

Math Concepts One . . . Two . . . Three! provides practice with sorting and identifying two- and three-dimensional shapes, line symmetry, and finding the missing symmetrical half.

Mighty Math Carnival Countdown helps students explore shapes, patterns, symmetry, area, perimeter, and fractions using pattern blocks.

Shape Up! provides practice with manipulating and exploring five geometric shapes.

Unit 19—Measurement and Mapping

Math Concepts One . . . Two . . . Three! provides practice with estimating and measuring time, money, length, temperature, and mass.

Mighty Math Zoo Zillions provides practice with locating numbers and adding and subtracting on the number line.

Thinkin' Things Fripple Town provides practice with directions and coordinate maps.

Sunbuddy Math Playhouse provides practice with coordinate grids and compass directions.

Trudy's Time & Place House helps students explore time, the calendar, maps, directions, and geography.

Unit 20—Looking Back at First Grade

None

Recommended Software List–
Brief Descriptions of the Programs

Combining and Breaking Apart Numbers by Sunburst
This program allows students to explore the different number combinations that make up a target number. The teacher can change the size of the target number. In one activity, students transport vacationers to an island from the city using boats. Students choose the number of people to put on a boat and the number of boats that must be used corresponds to the number of terms in the final mathematical expression. The number of boats increases by level. In another activity students must pack sardines into several cans. Other activities illustrate how a number can be broken into parts as well. The program draws connections between student actions and numerical equations, helping students internalize the meaning of addition and subtraction. The program is recommended for grades 1–2.

Discover Time by Gamco
This program provides practice with identifying time in a game setting. Treasure is hidden in a cave. Students move pirates along a path trying to reach the treasure first. The pirates move when questions are answered correctly. Times are given on analog and digital clocks and written in clock symbols, e.g., 9:00 and as words, e.g., 9 o'clock. The preferences can be changed so that questions are about hour, half hour, quarter hour, and five minute intervals. The program allows the teacher to keep track of individual student progress on specific types of problems. For example the program shows the percent correct of all problems involving translating digital to analog clocks. Some reading is involved. The program is recommended for grades K–3.

Graphers by Sunburst
This program provides a data graphing tool for young students. The program allows even very young students to create pictographs, bar graphs, circle graphs, and data tables from data they have collected. It can also be used to provide practice in reading and interpreting different types of graphs. Students can write their interpretation of the graphs directly into an on-screen notebook to be printed out with the graph. The program is recommended for grades K–4.

Grouping and Place Value by Sunburst
This program develops the concept of groups by allowing students to use the computer mouse to move muffin pans and other containers and group objects on the screen into 2s, 5s and 10s easily. The program helps students count a large number of objects by skip counting. In one activity students find a target number by grouping, in another they package table tennis balls. In still another activity, students are given coins in denominations of 1s, 10s and 100s and they must buy items with exact change. Students exchange larger denominations for the next smaller by breaking up a 10. The program has many extension activities and is recommended for grades 1–3.

Kid Pix by Riverdeep—The Learning Company
This program allows students to create their own illustrations for many different applications throughout the curriculum. In mathematics, students can use this program to illustrate problems they have been given to solve or they can create and illustrate their own patterns or problems. The program is recommended for grades K–4.

Math Concepts One . . . Two . . . Three! by Gamco
This program is a collection of activities covering numeration, number sense, geometry, measurement, data management and probability, and patterning and algebra. Grade levels further divide each of the sections and there are numerous activities within each grade level. Many of the activities focus on developing conceptual understanding and connecting symbols with actions with the manipulatives. Teachers can keep track of student progress and choose grade levels for individual students. There are also supplemental non-computer activities available. The program is recommended for grades K–3.

Mighty Math Carnival Countdown by Riverdeep—The Learning Company
The program provides students with logic activities, basic operations, work with 2-dimensional objects, and place value. Each of the 5 activities is further divided into 13 to 26 different types of problems. Carnival Cars focuses on sets and sorting by attributes, using > and < symbols and distinguishing even and odd numbers. Snap Clowns practices the basic operations and helps students gain conceptual understanding of the operations that they are performing. Bubble Band focuses students' attention on place value. The beginning activities focus on the ones place but later students work in the hundreds and see how groups of 10 are traded. Giggle Factory focuses on number sense and the concept of equivalence. Students can work up to 1000 in these activities. Pattern Block Round Up uses the manipulative to pose questions about symmetry, area, perimeter and basic fraction ideas. The program is recommended for grades K–2.

Mighty Math Zoo Zillions by Riverdeep—The Learning Company
In this fun program based on a zoo theme, students visit five activities that promote problem solving and skill acquisition. Each of the activities has about 20 different types of problems. In Fish Stories, students connect word problems with mathematical symbols as they manipulate fish in and out of tanks. Stories range in what parts are missing, the size of the numbers and the basic operation that is practiced. In Gnu Ewe Boutique, students practice working with money. These activities range from identifying coins to adding and subtracting money and giving back change. In 3D Gallery students identify various 3-dimensional shapes. Annie's Jungle Trail provides practice in adding, subtracting, mental math, rounding, and identifying odd and even numbers. The last activity is Number Line Express. In this activity students locate numbers on the number line and then later move backwards and forwards and find missing addends. Students work on the number line to the 900s. This program is recommended for grades K–2.

Money Challenge by Gamco
Students practice working with money in a game-like setting. There are four activities to choose from. First, students can count money displayed on the screen. Another activity asks students to make a certain amount using the fewest coins. Third, students are asked if they can buy a certain item with the money they have been given. In the last activity, students are asked how much money they will have left after purchasing a given item. For each activity, the student can choose the set of money. The smallest set contains pennies, nickels and dimes while the full set contains all the coins and dollar bills. The program allows the teacher to keep track of individual student progress on specific types of problems. Some reading is involved. The program is recommended for grades K–2.

Ready for Math with Pooh by Disney Interactive
The activities in this program develop early number concepts. Students collect seeds for a garden by answering questions posed by Disney characters. The activities include number recognition, sequencing, and counting. The activity Wishing Well helps students develop counting as finding the cardinality of a set. Piglet's Cupcake Kitchen helps students develop the concepts of addition and subtraction as they decorate cupcakes. Other activities develop elementary patterning. The program is well suited and mathematically appropriate for the young learner. It is recommended for pre-K–1st grade.

Shape Up! by Sunburst
Shape Up! is a very versatile geometry program consisting of five sets of shapes. The user can choose to work with pattern blocks or tangrams designed to correspond to the manipulatives. Another set of shapes involves regular triangles, pentagons, hexagons, octagons, squares and circles. These shapes can be dissected and put back together in any desired fashion. The user can choose from two sets of three-dimensional shapes. One set is the platonic solids and the other a variety of shapes. Students can explore area, symmetry, tessellations, similarity and congruence. It allows users to view inside 3-dimensional shapes using the Transparent function. Any of the shapes can be moved and rotated. The teacher's guide includes an extensive implementation guide to use the program to its fullest capacity and an in-depth reference section. This program develops student van Hiele levels with opportunities to explore shapes more easily than working with concrete materials. The program is recommended for grades K–8.

Sunbuddy Math Playhouse by Sunburst
The program setting is a musical production. Backstage, the students can explore four mathematical activities. Test Your Memory with Tiny is a memory game with three levels. The first two levels involve counting while the third level involves matching digital and analog clock faces. Figure It Out with Hopkins practices addition and subtraction facts with increasing levels of difficulty. Sort It Out with Cassie is an excellent attribute game where students place musical instruments into boxes. At the third level there are several attributes and the boxes overlap. Go to Town with Shelby helps students understand how a coordinate grid system is labeled and also works on compass directions. The program is recommended for grades K–3.

Thinkin' Things Collection 1 by Riverdeep—The Learning Company
This program is not meant to develop numerical skills but rather general thinking skills. The program is divided into six activities. Three of these have very strong mathematical connections. In Fripple Shop, students must find the characters with specified attributes. At the more advanced levels, students must match up to four attributes using "and," "or," and "not." Similarly, in the activity Feathered Friends, students must build a bird with specified attributes that increase in difficulty and require pattern discrimination. Problems can be heard (by clicking the telephone), seen (by clicking the fax machine), or both by clicking on the door. The activity Blox-Flying Shapes develops spatial sense as students move shapes and change color, motion, and sound. The program is recommended for grades K–3.

Thinkin' Things Fripple Town by Riverdeep—The Learning Company
The four activities in this program focus on logical thinking, patterning, and directions. In Fripple Deliveries students learn relative directions as they maneuver a delivery van along city streets. Students learn about the four compass directions, left and right, and coordinate grids. Students copy a cookie pattern with various decorations and orientations in the activity Fripple Cookies. Spatial sense and symmetry are developed as well. Fripple Flags helps students distinguish attributes as they build flags to fit specific criteria. These activities have fourteen different types of questions each increasing in difficulty. In Fripple Skate Park students lead a skater along a path determined by signed numbers indicating forward and backward. Students observe the patterns formed. The program is recommended for grades K–3.

Trudy's Time & Place House by Riverdeep—The Learning Company
This program provides students the opportunity to explore clock and calendar time, map symbols, relative and compass directions, and geography. In the calendar activity students explore seasons and elapsed time as they develop an understanding of time units. In many of the activities the program uses a split screen. For example students manipulate a digital clock and the analog clock moves as well. In another activity students place map symbols on a map and a picture of the representation appears. In each activity students can choose from several difficulty levels and from explore or question and answer modes. The program provides a wealth of supplemental activities and is recommended for grades K–2.

Software Companies Addresses and Telephone Numbers

Disney Interactive
500 S. Buena Vista Street
Burbank, CA 91521-8139
1-800-228-0988
www.disneyinteractive.com

Gamco
The Siboney Learning Group
325 N. Kirkwood Road Suite 200
Saint Louis, MO 63122
1-800-351-1404
www.gamco.com
www.siboneylearninggroup.com

Riverdeep—The Learning Company
Attn: School Sales
P.O. Box 6121
Novato, CA 94948-9823
1-800-825-4420
schoolcustomerservice@riverdeep.net

Sunburst
101 Castleton Street
P.O. Box 100
Pleasantville, NY 10570
1-800-321-7511
www.sunburst.com

Parents and *Math Trailblazers*

The Parents and *Math Trailblazers* section provides suggestions and tips to help parents participate in their child's understanding of *Math Trailblazers* and to enhance its benefits for their children.

A teacher, student, and parent work together to solve a problem.

Working with Parents

As you begin to use the *Math Trailblazers* curriculum in your classroom, it is important that you give thought to how you will help parents understand the curriculum and how it works. Parents want assurances that the content and approaches of the school's mathematics program will not only educate and interest their children now, but also benefit them later in their educational careers when test scores and school admissions become serious realities. Parents' understanding and support of the curriculum can be a key factor in their children's success with mathematics. This understanding and support also play an important role in the successful implementation of this curriculum.

As a *Standards*-based curriculum, *Math Trailblazers* is very different from the mathematics parents learned in school. If parents are going to provide effective support for their children at home, they need to have a clear understanding of what *Math Trailblazers* includes and what your school hopes to achieve by using it. Most adults experienced a mathematics curriculum that focused on teaching facts and procedures for computing. In contrast, *Math Trailblazers* maintains a careful balance between developing skills, underlying mathematical concepts, and problem solving. Parents need to understand this balance. It has many implications for the work their children will do in class and bring home for homework.

Communicate to parents:

- how the varied contexts for solving problems in *Math Trailblazers* help children learn to use mathematics in meaningful ways;
- that current research supports the approaches used in *Math Trailblazers* for teaching math facts and procedures and that these approaches allow students to gain fluency with less drill and memorization than former methods and that retention will be enhanced;
- how practice with skills and procedures is distributed between homework, Daily Practice and Problems, and within most problem-solving activities in the program;
- how mathematical ideas are represented with manipulatives, pictures, tables, graphs, and numbers—and how these representations allow children to access the mathematics in varied ways;
- that *Math Trailblazers* encourages students to develop varied ways to solve problems—not just the solutions that adults might select; and
- that the activities in *Math Trailblazers* are designed precisely to provide their children with the varied skills that they will need in the workplace of the 21st century.

Most importantly, parents will also want to learn specific ways they can work with their children at home.

None of these things is likely to occur without a concerted effort on the part of teachers and the school to educate parents. Furthermore, getting parents on board early will save effort in the long term. We recommend that you anticipate potential parental concerns about a new math program and address them proactively through an ongoing parent education effort.

Built-in Tools for Communicating with Parents

Math Trailblazers provides several tools to help you communicate with parents about the curriculum.

Parent Brochure

A parent brochure in Spanish and English provides an introduction to the program for parents. The masters of these brochures are located at the end of this section. They have been designed for you to copy and fold, thus creating a two-sided brochure that can be sent home at the beginning of the year or used as a handout at a fall parent meeting.

Parent Letters

Parent letters are included at the beginning of each unit to give parents specific information about what their children will be studying. These letters describe the concepts presented in each unit and how parents or family members can provide follow-up and encouragement at home. A sample parent letter is shown in Figure 1.

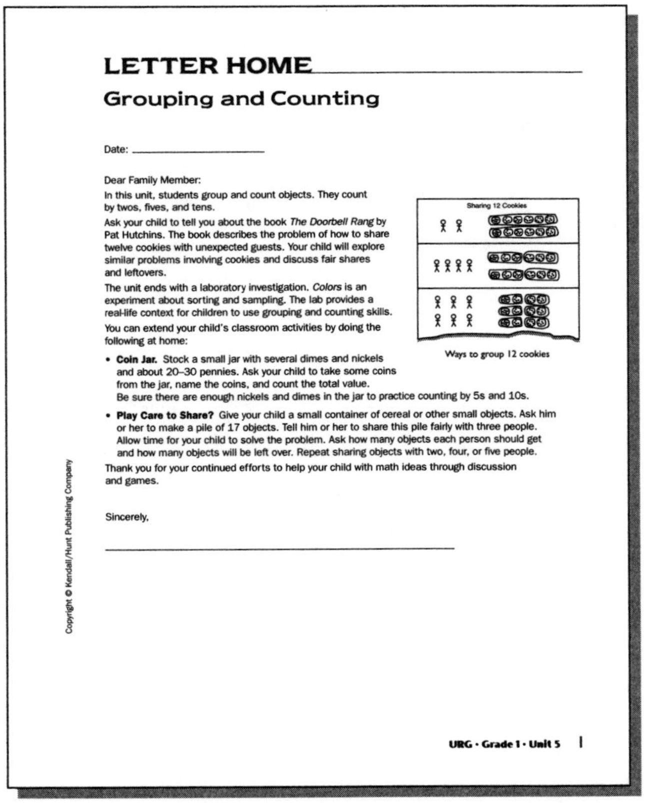
LETTER HOME

Grouping and Counting

Date: ____________

Dear Family Member:

In this unit, students group and count objects. They count by twos, fives, and tens.

Ask your child to tell you about the book *The Doorbell Rang* by Pat Hutchins. The book describes the problem of how to share twelve cookies with unexpected guests. Your child will explore similar problems involving cookies and discuss fair shares and leftovers.

The unit ends with a laboratory investigation. *Colors* is an experiment about sorting and sampling. The lab provides a real-life context for children to use grouping and counting skills.

You can extend your child's classroom activities by doing the following at home:

- **Coin Jar.** Stock a small jar with several dimes and nickels and about 20–30 pennies. Ask your child to take some coins from the jar, name the coins, and count the total value. Be sure there are enough nickels and dimes in the jar to practice counting by 5s and 10s.
- **Play Care to Share?** Give your child a small container of cereal or other small objects. Ask him or her to make a pile of 17 objects. Tell him or her to share this pile fairly with three people. Allow time for your child to solve the problem. Ask how many objects each person should get and how many objects will be left over. Repeat sharing objects with two, four, or five people.

Thank you for your continued efforts to help your child with math ideas through discussion and games.

Sincerely,

____

URG • Grade 1 • Unit 5 1

Figure 1: *Sample parent letter from Grade 1*

Information for Parents: Math Facts Philosophy

A letter for parents in English and Spanish that outlines the *Math Trailblazers* philosophy for teaching math facts is located at the end of this section. This letter is also located in the *Unit Resource Guide* for Unit 11 in first grade.

Homework Notes

Many homework assignments, especially in Grades 1–3, include a separate explanation for family members, outlining the purpose of the activity and providing hints for assisting the child. An example of such a note is shown in Figure 2. These explanations help parents feel comfortable with the content and goals of the curriculum. We encourage you to supplement the parent instructions with additional short notes of your own.

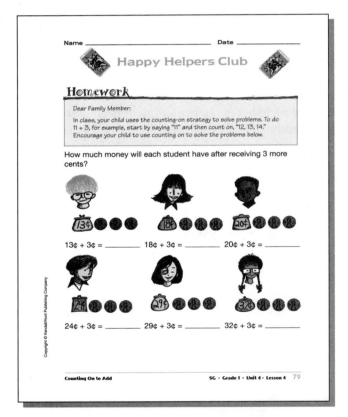

Figure 2: *Sample Grade 1 homework note for parents*

Special Programs for Parents

Math Nights

One way to help parents understand the goals and philosophy of *Math Trailblazers* is to organize special math-related events or presentations, such as a "Math Night," that focus on the topics and format from the *Math Trailblazers* curriculum. A Math Night program typically includes two or more problem-solving activities or math games for parents to try. These activities can be coupled with a short presentation by the teacher and other school personnel.

The following illustrate the types of activities in *Math Trailblazers* that have worked well in Math Night programs:

- sorting apples from *Data Collection* in the *Ongoing Content* in Kindergarten;
- parts of the *Pockets* activity in Unit 3 of Grade 1;
- a portion of *High, Wide, and Handsome* in Unit 4 of Grade 2;
- the *First Names* activity from Unit 1 of Grade 3;
- a portion of *Arm Span vs. Height* in Unit 1 of Grade 4; and
- the game *Three in a Row* from Unit 8 of Grade 5.

These activities can be adapted to involve parents in active problem solving. They also illustrate key ideas of the curriculum, such as the use of multiple representations of math concepts, the focus on problem solving, the broad range of mathematical content, and the strong connection with science. The use of one or more games as part of Math Night illustrates one way to engage students in practicing math facts. As part of their continued professional development and support for *Math Trailblazers* users, Kendall/Hunt Publishing Company offers assistance in planning Math Nights tailored specifically to the needs of your school. You may contact them at 1-800-542-6657.

It is usually helpful to complement the activities with a short presentation. This presentation might, for example, discuss the underlying philosophy of the *Math Trailblazers* program (see Section 1), discuss some of the key National Council of Teachers of Mathematics recommendations (see Section 5), discuss plans for future lessons, or provide practical suggestions for parents to work with their children, such as how to encourage children to explain their math thinking using manipulatives to model math concepts.

Another way to help parents understand a problem-solving mathematics classroom is to videotape a class session in which you can capture students engaged in some way: working collaboratively, collecting data, or explaining their thinking. This tape can be used in conjunction with Math Nights or borrowed for home viewing.

Family Math

Another good way to generate parent understanding of and support for a reform mathematics program is to organize a *Family Math* program at your school. *Family Math,* developed by Project Equals at the Lawrence Hall of Science, involves a series of classes in which parents and children come together to enjoy stimulating math games and activities. The program introduces families to key mathematical principles, involves parents as active partners in their children's education, develops students' critical and logical thinking skills, and connects mathematics to everyday life. These goals complement the goals of *Math Trailblazers*. As a result, parents who participate in a *Family Math* program are likely to have a good understanding of the approaches used in *Math Trailblazers* and will feel comfortable working with their children on mathematics. The *Family Math* book of activities can be ordered through various math publishers or supply houses, your local bookstore, or directly from the Lawrence Hall of Science. For more information about the program, including training for *Family Math* workshop leaders, contact:

Family Math
Lawrence Hall of Science
University of California at Berkeley
Berkeley, CA 94720-5200
(510) 643-6525 or (510) 643-6350
www.lhs.berkeley.edu/equals/

Roles for Parent Volunteers

Parent volunteers can be used in a variety of capacities to support the implementation of *Math Trailblazers*.

Hands-on programs, by their very nature, involve many manipulatives and other materials. *Math Trailblazers* is no exception. In addition to the commercially purchased manipulatives, many activities call for collectible materials, such as jars, container lids, paper towel cores, etc. The job of gathering and managing these materials can be eased with the assistance of a parent volunteer.

Many teachers use parent volunteers to assist with classroom activities. The parents can be assigned to work with particular groups of students or with individual students who need extra assistance. They can work on special projects or lesson extensions with small groups. Some teachers periodically invite several parents to assist with station activities, where student groups rotate from station to station. In many cases, it is simply just helpful to have an extra set of hands and eyes in the classrooms to assist as needed.

The roles parents play in providing support will obviously need to be tailored to your needs and the interests and capabilities of individual parents. There is little doubt, however, that cooperative parents are a valuable asset as you work with *Math Trailblazers*.

Math Trailblazers™

A Mathematical Journey Using Science and Language Arts

An Introduction for Families

A TIMS® Curriculum from the University of Illinois at Chicago

Published by Kendall/Hunt Publishing Company

How can parents talk with their children about math?

Your child will have a lot to share with you about mathematics. Here are some conversation starters to help your child communicate what he or she is doing in mathematics:

☞ What problems did you solve in math today? How did you solve the problems? Are there other ways to solve that same problem?

☞ Did you use any special materials in math today? What were they? How did you use them?

☞ Did you measure anything in school today? What did you measure?

☞ Did you collect data in math today? How did you record the data?

☞ Did you hear a math story today? Please tell me the story.

> "One of the things I've noticed … is that when he [my child] brings home an activity and he brings a measuring tape or something kind of special, he's excited about doing it. The fact that we're involved in the games—he loves that—and he's proud of what he's doing."
>
> **Parent**

You can contact the developers of *Math Trailblazers* at the following address:

 The University of Illinois at Chicago

TIMS Project
Institute for Mathematics and Science Education (M/C 250)
950 South Halsted Street, Room 2075 SEL
Chicago, IL 60607-7019
www.math.uic.edu/IMSE

KENDALL/HUNT PUBLISHING COMPANY
4050 Westmark Drive   Dubuque, Iowa 52002
www.mathtrailblazers.com

Development of *Math Trailblazers* was supported in part by the National Science Foundation.

What connections does *Math Trailblazers* make with other school subjects?

> "It seems a lot of this carries over to different subject areas. It's not just isolated to math."
>
> **Teacher**

In *Math Trailblazers*, children learn mathematics, in part, by applying it in many different contexts. This makes mathematics meaningful for students and models the way mathematics is used outside of school.

Science investigations are used often in *Math Trailblazers* to provide a context for learning and applying mathematics. Children design experiments; collect, organize, and graph data; and analyze experimental results in much the same way scientists do. Measurement of length, area, volume, mass, and time is done repeatedly within the context of scientific experiments. This strong connection with science engages students in rich problem-solving activities and introduces students to the tools and methods scientists use.

Math Trailblazers also has many connections with language arts—communication of math ideas in writing and orally is an integral part of every lesson. Children write journal entries, record data, and share ideas. They also read children's books and *Math Trailblazers* Adventure Books that connect with many class lessons. As children communicate their methods for solving problems and justify their answers, they better understand important math concepts. Their writing and other communication skills also improve.

Why is my child using calculators with *Math Trailblazers*?

The calculator is a tool used in appropriate situations to help your child explore number ideas and relationships, solve more complex problems, and explore mathematics on his or her own. The use of calculators is supported by the National Council of Teachers of Mathematics.

A curriculum for your children

The mathematics curriculum being taught in many schools today is very similar to the curriculum that was taught when the parents, grandparents, and even great-grandparents of today's school children attended school. Many of the math skills in that curriculum remain important today. But the world has changed considerably since the time of our grandparents. Advances in technology have created many other essential math skills that your children will need when they complete their formal schooling and enter tomorrow's work force. The National Council of Teachers of Mathematics recognized these needs when, in 1989 and 2000, it made a series of recommendations for updating math instruction in U.S. schools. *Math Trailblazers* was developed to reflect these national recommendations.

Math Trailblazers will prepare students to:

★ know and apply basic math skills;

★ solve problems using many different strategies;

★ be independent thinkers;

★ reason skillfully in diverse situations;

★ effectively communicate solutions to problems and methods for solving them;

★ work alone and in groups to solve problems.

Math Trailblazers was developed and tested over a seven-year period by a team from the Teaching Integrated Mathematics and Science (TIMS) Project at the University of Illinois at Chicago. Using the results of educational research and over 15 years of previous experience in curriculum development, the TIMS Project has written an innovative program that will prepare your children with math skills needed for the 21st century.

What is in the *Math Trailblazers* curriculum?

Math Trailblazers is a comprehensive curriculum that maintains a balance between the development of math concepts and basic skills. Students apply basic math skills while working on meaningful and challenging tasks. The math content of the traditional math curriculum is studied; but other topics—estimation, geometry, measurement, patterns and relationships, algebra concepts, and statistics and probability—are investigated at an appropriate level in each grade.

The curriculum includes different types of lessons:

Activities—explorations of math concepts and skills that use a variety of tools and methods.

Labs—extended investigations that use a simplified version of the method scientists use.

Daily Practice and Problems—items that provide practice in math skills and concepts.

Games—math games that build familiarity with math skills and concepts.

Adventure Books—illustrated stories that deal with math and science ideas.

Assessments—activities that allow the teacher and student to assess progress.

What is a *Math Trailblazers* classroom like?

When you walk into your child's *Math Trailblazers* class, you will probably notice that it does not look like the mathematics classroom you experienced when you were your child's age. Children might be working in groups, rolling cars down ramps, dropping water onto paper towels, or pulling jellybean samples from bags. As they work, children discuss different ways to solve problems. The room is filled with a feeling of excitement and discovery.

In a *Math Trailblazers* classroom, children are:

☆ learning mathematics by using it to solve many different kinds of problems;

☆ drawing on their own experiences and working with real-world problems;

☆ using concrete objects to understand abstract mathematical concepts;

☆ communicating mathematical ideas to their peers and teacher;

☆ gaining confidence in mathematics and developing an "I can do it" feeling.

Math TrailblazerS™*

Una Aventura en Matemáticas usando Ciencias y el Arte de Lenguaje

Una Introducción para Familias

Desarrollando por el Proyecto de TIMS—Teaching Integrated Mathematics and Science— (Integrando la Enseñanza de las Matemáticas y de las Ciencias) de la Universidad de Illinois en Chicago

Publicado por
Kendall/Hunt
Publishing Company

* Abriendo un camino de matemáticas

¿Qué conexiones hace Math Trailblazers con otras materias escolares?

En *Math Trailblazers*, los estudiantes aprenden matemáticas, en parte, aplicandolo a diversas situaciones. De esta manera las matemáticas se hacen interesantes y adquieren sentido.

Investigaciones científicas en *Math Trailblazers* proveen la oportunidad frecuente de la aplicación de las matemáticas. Los estudiantes diseñan experimentos; acumulan y organizan datos; hacen gráficas de datos; y analizan los resultados de los experimentos en una manera semejante a lo que hacen los científicos. Se hacen mediciónes de longitud, area, volumen, masa, y tiempo como parte de experimentos científicos. Esta fuerte conexión con la ciencia hace que los estudiantes resuelvan problemas como "científicos," usando métodos y herramientas de la ciencias.

Math Trailblazers también tiene muchas conexiones con el arte de lenguaje. La comunicación de ideas en matemáticas—a través de escribir, hablar, y dibujar—es una parte integral de cada lección. Los estudiantes escriben en sus diarios, registran datos, y comparten ideas. Ellos también leen libros infantiles y "libros de aventuras" que se conectan con muchas lecciónes. Los estudiantes mejoran en su entendimiento de conceptos matemáticos al comunicar sus métodos de resolver problemas y explicar sus respuestas. Sus habilidades en escribir y comunicar también mejoran.

¿Por qué mi hijo/a está usando calculadoras en Math Trailblazers?

Las calculadoras son instrumentos usados para ayudar a su hijo/a a investigar ideas con números y sus relaciones, resolver problemas complejos, y explorar la matemática. El uso de estas herramientas es recomendado por el Concejo Nacional de Maestros de Matemáticas.

¿Qué es lo que los padres de familia pueden hacer?

Su hijo/a tendrá mucho que compartir con usted acerca de matemáticas. Aquí hay algunos temas para iniciar conversaciones que ayudarán a su hijo/a a que él o ella comunique lo que usté esté haciendo en matemáticas.

☞ ¿Qué problema resolviste el día de hoy en tu clase de matemáticas? ¿Cómo lo resolviste? ¿Hay alguna otra forma de resolver ese mismo problema?

☞ ¿Utilizaste algúnos materiales especiales en tu clase de matemáticas? ¿Qué eran? ¿Cómo los usaste?

☞ ¿Mediste hoy algo en la escuela? ¿Qué fue lo que mediste?

☞ ¿Acumulaste algunos datos en matemáticas? ¿Cómo registraste esos datos?

☞ ¿Escuchaste alguna historia en matemáticas? Por favor cuéntame la historia.

> "Una de las cosas que he notado… es que cuando él [mi hijo] trae una actividad a la casa y trae una cinta métrica o algo especial, está emocionado para hacerlo. El hecho que nosotros estamos enredados en los juegos—le encanta—y está orgulloso de lo que está haciendo."
>
> **Un padre de familia**

Se puede comunicar con los diseñadores de *Math Trailblazers* a la siguiente dirección:

UIC The University of Illinois at Chicago

TIMS Project
Institute for Mathematics and Science Education (M/C 250)
950 South Halsted Street, Room 2075 SEL
Chicago, IL 60607-7019
www.math.uic.edu/IMSE

KENDALL/HUNT PUBLISHING COMPANY
4050 Westmark Drive   Dubuque, Iowa 52002
www.kendallhunt.com   www.mathtrailblazers.com

El desarrollo de *Math Trailblazers* fue ayudado en parte por la National Science Foundation.

Un programa para sus hijos

Los programas de matemáticas que se encuentran hoy día en muchas escuelas son muy semejantes a las clases que tenían los padres, abuelos, y aún bisabuelos de los estudiantes de hoy. Mucha del material de esos programas todavía se necesita hoy. Pero el mundo ha cambiado desde el tiempo de nuestros abuelos. Avances en tecnología han creado la necesidad de desarrollar otras técnicas especiales que sus hijos necesitarán en el mundo de trabajo del futuro. El Concejo Nacional de Maestros de Matemáticas reconoció estas necesidades cuando hizo una serie de recomendaciones para mejorar la enseñanza de matemáticas en las escuelas de los Estados Unidos. Hemos desarrollado el programa *Math Trailblazers* para incorporar esas recomendaciones nacionales.

Math Trailblazers preparará estudiantes para:

★ aprender y usar técnicas básicas en matemáticas;

★ resolver problemas usando varias estrategias diferentes;

★ pensar independientemente;

★ razonar con habilidad en diversas situaciones;

★ comunicar efectivamente tanto las soluciones como los métodos;

★ resolver problemas trabajando solos y en grupos.

El programa *Math Trailblazers* fue desarrollado y ensayado por un equipo del Proyecto de TIMS—Teaching Integrated Mathematics and Science—(Integrando la Enseñanza de las Matemáticas y de las Ciencias) de la Universidad de Illinois en Chicago. Han creado un programa innovativo que proveerá a sus hijos con los bases matemáticas necesarios para poder competir en el campo del trabajo en el Siglo XXI.

¿Qué hay en el programa *Math Trailblazers*?

El programa *Math Trailblazers* es un programa integral que mantiene un balance entre el desarrollo de los conceptos y las técnicas básicas de matemáticas. Los estudiantes usan las técnicas básicas mientras están trabajando con problemas interesantes y estimulantes. Se estudian los tópicos matemáticos de un programa tradicional; pero también se investigan otras materias—estimación, geometría, medición, patrones y relaciones, conceptos de álgebra, estadística y probabilidad—en un nivel apropiado para los niños.

El programa contiene varios tipos de lecciones:

Actividades—exploraciones de conceptos matemáticos y técnicas usando diferentes herramientas y métodos.

Laboratorios—investigaciones que usan una versión simplificada del método que los científicos usan.

Prácticas y Problemas Diarios—problemas breves que proveen práctica con técnicas y conceptos matemáticos.

Juegos—juegos matemáticos que estimulan familiaridad con técnicas y conceptos matemáticos.

Libros de Aventuras—historietas ilustradas que tratan con conceptos de las ciencias y matemáticas.

Evaluaciones—actividades que permiten al maestro y a los estudiantes evaluar el progreso.

¿Cómo es una clase de *Math Trailblazers*?

Si usted entra a un salón de clases *Math Trailblazers*, probablemente notará que no se parece al que usted asistía cuando tenía esa edad. En ese salón, los niños puedan estar trabajando en grupos, poniendo gotas de agua a toallas de papel, o analizando muestras de confites. Mientras los estudiantes trabajan, ellos discuten diferentes formas para resolver los problemas matemáticos. Se percieve en clases *Math Trailblazers* los sentimientos y la emoción de descubrimiento matemático.

En un salón de estas clases los alumnos están:

☆ aprendiendo matemáticas en la resolución de problemas;

☆ usando experiencias propias y trabajando con problemas verdaderas;

☆ usando objetos concretos para entender conceptos matemáticos abstractos;

☆ comunicando sus ideas de matemáticas a sus compañeros y maestros;

☆ adquiriendo confianza en las matemáticas y desarrollando un sentimiento de, "Yo sí lo puedo hacer."

INFORMATION FOR PARENTS

Grade 1 Math Facts Philosophy

The goal of the math facts strand in *Math Trailblazers* is for students to learn the basic facts efficiently, gain fluency with their use, and retain that fluency over time. In first grade, students focus on addition and subtraction facts strategies. By the end of second grade, students are expected to demonstrate fluency with the addition and subtraction facts.

A large body of research supports an approach in which students develop strategies for figuring out the facts rather than relying solely on rote memorization. This not only leads to more effective learning and better retention, but also to the development of mental math skills which will be useful throughout life. In fact, too much drill before conceptual understanding may actually interfere with a child's ability to understand concepts at a later date. Therefore, the teaching of the basic facts in *Math Trailblazers* is characterized by the following elements:

Use of Strategies. Students approach the basic facts as problems to be solved rather than as facts to be memorized. In all grades we encourage the use of strategies to find facts and de-emphasize rote memorization, so students become confident that they can find answers to fact problems that they do not immediately recall. In this way, students learn that math is more than memorizing facts and rules which "you either get or you don't."

Distributed Fact Practice. Students study small groups of facts that can be found using similar strategies. Practice of these organized groups of facts begins in the Daily Practice and Problems in Unit 11 and continues for the remainder of the year.

Practice in Context. Students continue to practice all of the facts as they use them to solve problems in the labs, activities, and games.

Appropriate Assessment. Units 11–20 include Daily Practice and Problems items that together provide assessment of all the addition facts. Students must solve addition fact problems and describe their strategies. Students' progress with the math facts can also be assessed as they complete activities, labs, and games.

Facts Will Not Act as Gatekeepers. Students are not prevented from learning more complex mathematics because they do not have quick recall of the facts. Use of strategies and calculators allows students to continue to work on interesting problems and experiments while they are learning the facts.

INFORMACIÓN PARA LOS PADRES
La filosofía de los conceptos matemáticos básicos en 1er grado

El objetivo de la enseñanza de los conceptos matemáticos en *Math Trailblazers* es que los estudiantes aprendan los conceptos básicos eficazmente, logren el dominio del uso de estos conceptos y mantengan ese dominio con el paso del tiempo. En primer grado, los estudiantes se concentran en las estrategias de sumar y restar. Para fines de segundo grado, se espera que los estudiantes demuestren tener dominio de los conceptos básicos de sumar y restar.

Las extensas investigaciones realizadas respaldan la aplicación de un enfoque en el que los estudiantes desarrollan estrategias para resolver los problemas de conceptos básicos en lugar de aprenderlas de memoria. Esto no sólo permite un aprendizaje más eficaz y una mejor retención, sino que también desarrolla habilidades matemáticas mentales que serán útiles durante toda la vida. Por lo tanto, la enseñanza y la evaluación de los conceptos básicos en *Math Trailblazers* se caracteriza por los siguientes elementos:

El uso de estrategias. Los estudiantes enfocan a los conceptos básicos como problemas para resolver en lugar de aprenderlas de memoria. En todos los grados, alentamos el uso de estrategias para hallar soluciones y ponemos menos énfasis en aprender de memoria, de modo que los estudiantes tengan la confianza de que pueden hallar soluciones a problemas de cuales no se acuerdan. De esta manera, los estudiantes aprenden que las matemáticas son más que tablas y reglas memorizadas que un estudiante "sabe o no sabe".

Repaso gradual de los conceptos básicos. Los estudiantes estudian pequeños grupos de conceptos básicos que pueden hallarse usando estrategias similares. La práctica de estos grupos organizados de conceptos comienza con la Práctica Diaria y los Problemas en la Unidad 11 y continúa el resto del año.

Práctica en contexto. Los estudiantes continúan practicando todos los conceptos básicos cuando los usan para resolver problemas en los experimentos, las actividades y los juegos.

Evaluación apropiada. Las unidades 11–20 incluyen una sección de Práctica Diaria y Problemas que en conjunto permiten evaluar el aprendizaje de todos los conceptos de suma. Los estudiantes deben resolver problemas de suma y describir sus estrategias. El progreso de los estudiantes con los conceptos básicos de suma también puede evaluarse a medida que completan actividades, experimentos y juegos.

El nivel de dominio de los conceptos básicos no impedirá el aprendizaje.
Los estudiantes seguirán aprendiendo conceptos matematicos más complejos ounque no se acuerden de los conceptos básicos con rápidez. El uso de estrategias y zcalculadoras permite a los estudiantes continuar trabajando con problemas y experimentos interesantes mientras aprenden los conceptos básicos.

Glossary

This glossary provides definitions of key vocabulary terms in the Grade 1 lessons. Locations of key vocabulary terms in the curriculum are included with each definition. Components Key: URG = *Unit Resource Guide,* SG = *Student Guide,* and TIG = *Teacher Implementation Guide.*

A

Approximate (URG Unit 12 p. 24)
1. (adjective) a number that is close to the desired number
2. (verb) to estimate

Area (URG Unit 10 pp. 4, 14; SG p. 246)
The amount of space that a shape covers. Area is measured in square units.

B

C

Capacity (URG Unit 9 p. 66)
1. The volume of the inside of a container.
2. The largest volume a container can hold.

Circle (URG Unit 2 p. 17)
A curve that is made up of all the points that are the same distance from one point, the center.

Circumference (URG Unit 15 pp. 22, 26)
The distance around a circle.

Coordinates (URG Unit 19 p. 4)
(In the plane) Two numbers that specify the location of a point on a flat surface relative to a reference point called the origin. The two numbers are the distances from the point to two perpendicular lines called axes.

Counting All (URG Unit 1 p. 5)
A strategy for adding in which students start at one and count until the total is reached.

Counting Back (URG Unit 8 p. 5)
A method of subtraction that involves counting from the larger number to the smaller one. For example, to find 8 − 5 the student counts 7, 6, 5 which is 3 less.

Counting On (URG Unit 1 p. 5 & Unit 4 p. 4)
A strategy for adding two numbers in which students start with one of the numbers and then count until the total is reached. For example, to count 6 + 3, begin with 6 and count three more, 7, 8, 9.

Counting Up (URG Unit 8 p. 5)
A method of subtraction that involves counting from the smaller number to the larger one. For example, to find 8 − 5 the student counts 6, 7, 8 which is 3 more.

Cube (URG Unit 12 p. 15 & Unit 15 p. 14)
A solid with six congruent square faces.

Cubic Units (URG Unit 12 p. 15)
A unit for measuring volume— a cube that measures one unit along each edge. For example, cubic centimeters and cubic inches.

cubic centimeter

Cylinder (URG Unit 15 p. 14)
A three-dimensional figure with two parallel congruent circles as bases (top and bottom) and a curved side that is the union of parallel lines connecting corresponding points on the circles.

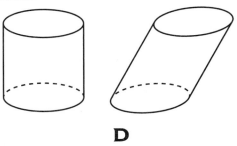

D

Data Table (URG Unit 3 p. 20)
A tool for recording and organizing data on paper or on a computer.

Name	Age

Division by Measuring Out (URG Unit 14 p. 4)
A type of division problem in which the number in each group is known and the unknown is the number of groups. For example, twenty students are divided into teams of four students each. How many teams are there? (20 students ÷ 4 students per team = 5 teams) This type of division is also known as measurement division.

Division by Sharing (URG Unit 14 p. 4)
A type of division problem in which the number of groups is known and the unknown is the number in each group. For example, twenty students are divided into five teams. How many students are on each team? (20 students ÷ 5 teams = 4 students per team) This type of division is also known as partitive division.

E

Edge (URG Unit 15 p. 35)
A line segment where two faces of a three-dimensional figure meet.

Equivalent Fractions (URG Unit 18 p. 36)
Two fractions are equivalent if they represent the same part of the whole. For example, if a class has 8 boys and 8 girls, we can say $\frac{8}{16}$ of the students are girls or $\frac{1}{2}$ of the students are girls.

Even Number (URG Unit 4 p. 16 & Unit 13 p. 41)
Numbers that are doubles. The numbers 0, 2, 4, 6, 8, 10, etc. are even. The number 28 is even because it is 14 + 14.

F

Face (URG Unit 12 p. 15 & Unit 15 pp. 26, 35)
A flat side of a three-dimensional figure.

Fixed Variables (URG Unit 2 p. 40, Unit 6 p. 4, & Unit 11 p. 58)
Variables in an experiment that are held constant or not changed. These variables are often called controlled variables.

G

H

Hexagon (URG Unit 2 p. 17)
A six-sided polygon.

I

J

K

L

Length (URG Unit 6 p. 17 & Unit 10 p. 21)
1. The distance along a line or curve from one point to another. Distance can be measured with a ruler or tape measure.
2. The distance from one "end" to another of a two- or three-dimensional figure. For example, the length of a rectangle usually refers to the length of the longer side.

Line
A set of points that form a straight path extending infinitely in two directions.

Line Symmetry (URG Unit 7 p. 31 & Unit 18 p. 16)
A figure has line symmetry if it can be folded along a line so that the two halves match exactly.

Line of Symmetry (URG Unit 7 p. 31 & Unit 18 p. 16)
A line such that if a figure is folded along the line, then one half of the figure matches the other.

M

Making a Ten (URG Unit 13 p. 4)
A strategy for adding and subtracting that takes advantage of students' knowledge of partitions of ten. For example, a student might find 8 + 4 by breaking the 4 into 2 + 2 and then using a knowledge of sums that add to ten.

$$8 + 4 =$$
$$8 + 2 + 2 =$$
$$10 + 2 = 12$$

Median (URG Unit 6 pp. 4, 23 & Unit 9 p. 67)
The number "in the middle" of a set of data. If there is an odd number of data, it is the number in the middle when the numbers are arranged in order. So the median of {1, 2, 14, 15, 28, 29, 30} is 15. If there is an even number of data, it is the number halfway between the two middle numbers. The median of {1, 2, 14, 15, 28, 29} is $14\frac{1}{2}$.

Mr. Origin (URG Unit 19 p. 4)
A plastic figure used to help childen learn about direction and distance.

N

Near Double (URG Unit 13 p. 4)
A derived addition or subtraction fact found by using doubles. For example, 3 + 4 = 7 follows from the fact that 3 + 3 = 6.

Number Sentence (URG Unit 3 p. 27 & Unit 4 p. 30)
A number sentence uses numbers and symbols instead of words to describe a problem. For example, a number sentence for the problem "5 birds landed on a branch. Two more birds also landed on the branch. How many birds are on the branch?" is 5 + 2 = 7.

O

Odd Number (URG Unit 4 p. 16)
A number that is not even. The odd numbers are 1, 3, 5, 7, 9, and so on.

Origin (URG Unit 19 pp. 4, 18)
A reference point for a coordinate system. If the coordinate system is a line, we can determine the location of an object on the line by the number of units it is to the right or the left of the origin.

P

Part (URG Unit 4 p. 23)
One of the addends in part-part-whole addition problems.

Pattern Unit (URG Unit 7 p. 21)
The portion of a pattern that is repeated. For example, AAB is the pattern unit in the pattern AABAABAAB.

Perimeter (URG Unit 6 p. 18; SG p. 100)
The distance around a two-dimensional shape.

Polygon
A closed, connected plane figure consisting of line segments, with exactly two segments meeting at each end point.

Polygons

Not Polygons

Prediction (URG Unit 5 p. 43)
Using a sample to predict what is likely to occur in the population.

Prism (URG Unit 15 p. 14)
A solid that has two congruent and parallel bases. The remaining faces (sides) are parallelograms. A rectangular prism has bases that are rectangles. A box is a common object that is shaped like a rectangular prism.

Q

Quadrilateral
A polygon with four sides.

R

Rectangle (URG Unit 2 p. 17)
A quadrilateral with four right angles.

Rhombus (URG Unit 2 p. 17)
A quadrilateral with four sides of equal length.

S

Rotational Symmetry (URG Unit 7 p. 31)
A figure has rotational (or turn) symmetry if there is a point on the figure and a rotation of less than 360° about that point so that it "fits" on itself. For example, a square has a turn symmetry of $\frac{1}{4}$ turn (or 90°) about its center.

Sample (URG Unit 5 p. 43)
Some of the items from a whole group.

Sphere (URG Unit 15 p. 14)
A three-dimensional figure that is made up of points that are the same distance from one point, the center. A basketball is a common object shaped like a sphere.

Square (URG Unit 2 p. 17)
A polygon with four equal sides and four right angles.

Symmetry (URG Unit 18 p. 16)
(See Line Symmetry, Line of Symmetry, and Rotational Symmetry.)

T

Three-dimensional Shapes (URG Unit 15 p. 14)
A figure in space that has length, width, and height.

TIMS Laboratory Method (URG Unit 5 p. 41)
A method that students use to organize experiments and investigations. It involves four components: draw, collect, graph, and explore. It is a way to help students learn about the scientific method. TIMS is an acronym for Teaching Integrated Mathematics and Science.

Trapezoid (URG Unit 2 p. 17)
A quadrilateral with exactly one pair of parallel sides.

Trial (URG Unit 6 pp. 4, 23)
One attempt in an experiment.

Triangle (URG Unit 2 p. 17)
A polygon with three sides.

Turn Symmetry
(See Rotational Symmetry.)

U

Using Doubles (URG Unit 13 p. 4)
A strategy for adding and subtracting which uses derived facts from known doubles. For example, students use 7 + 7 = 14 to find that 7 + 8 is one more or 15.

Using Ten (URG Unit 13 p. 4)
A strategy for adding which uses reasoning from known facts. For example, students use 3 + 7 = 10 to find that 4 + 7 is one more or 11.

V

Variable (URG Unit 2 p. 40 & Unit 11 p. 58)
A variable is something that varies or changes in an experiment.

Volume (URG Unit 9 p. 66 & Unit 12 p. 15; SG pp. 246, 247)
1. The amount of space an object takes up.
2. The amount of space inside a container.

W

Whole (URG Unit 4 p. 23)
The sum in part-part-whole addition problems.

X

Y

Z

Index

This index provides the unit number in parentheses followed by the page number for the multivolume URG (*Unit Resource Guide*). It provides page references for the SG (*Student Guide*), the AB (*Adventure Book*), and the TIG (*Teacher Implementation Guide*). Definitions or explanations of key terms can be found on the pages listed in bold type.

Assessment, SG 403–415, TIG 3, 12–13, 88–89, 149–188, URG (11) 8. *See also* Rubrics
  individual record sheets for, TIG 155, 182–187
  lessons designed for, TIG 157–158
  of Math Facts, TIG 159, 255–256
  observational. *See* Observational assessment
  overview of, TIG 176–182
  philosophy of, TIG 150–153
  portfolios and, TIG 159, 259, 263
  in scope and sequence, TIG 136–137
  units for, TIG 98–99, 159
  written, TIG 156–157
Assessment indicators, TIG 50, 154, 176. *See also* Observational Assessment Record, all URGs
Attitude, URG (1) 5
Attributes of shapes, URG (15) 16. *See also* Shapes
Average, URG (6) 4
  TIMS Tutor on, TIG 211–218. *See also* Central tendency, Mean, Median, Mode
Axes, TIG 86–87, URG (3) 35, URG (6) 25, URG (9) 67, URG (11) 60–62, URG (13) 49–50, URG (19) 4, 24–41. *See also* Horizontal axis, Vertical axis
  labeling, TIG 287–288, URG (5) 45
  scaled, URG (16) 4

B

Backwards, counting, URG (1) 10
Balance, URG (7) 31, URG (18) 16
Balance, equal arm, TIG 320–322
Balancing Act Game, SG 145, TIG 334, URG (7) 34–36
Balancing patterns, SG 139–140, 143–145
Balls (spheres), SG 313, **321**–325, TIG 78–79, URG (15) 4, **14**–19, 39
Bar graphs, SG 105–106, 109, 239, URG (2) 40– **41,** URG (11) 56, 60–62, URG (20) 26, 30.
  See also Labs
  grade levels and, TIG 288–289
  making, SG 28, 106, 177, 231
  reading, SG 179, 283–284, 297
  telling stories with, SG 341, 345
  weather, URG (12) 12
Base face of shapes, URG (15) 35
Base-ten place value system, TIG 194
Benchmarks, TIG 54–55, 229
Best-fit lines, TIG 228, 237–238, 290–291. *See also* Graphs
Betty Builds a Better Racer, AB 19–28, TIG 60–61, URG (6) 28–33
Big numbers. *See* Hundreds, Large numbers, 100
Borrowing, in subtraction, TIG 198
Boxes, URG (15) **14**–19, 28–35. *See also* Prisms (boxes), Rectangular prisms (boxes)
Buried Treasure, AB 93–108, TIG 86–87, URG (19) 43–51

C

Calculations, estimation of, TIG 221–227
Calculators, SG 72, URG (4) 4–5, 23–24, URG (11) 38, 40, 52, URG (20) 15
  "active" equals sign (=), URG (4) 24
  "hot" equals sign (=), URG (4) 24, URG (5) **18**
  Math Facts and, TIG 255
  mean and, TIG 218
  repeating equal key on, URG (12) 29
  scientific, TIG 194
  skip counting on, URG (9) 16
Calendars, SG 77, 408, TIG 52–53, 70–71, URG (2) 4–5, 10–11, URG (3) 12–14, URG (20) 12, 15
  counting on strategy and, SG 77, URG (4) 37
  problem solving with, SG 408
  weather and, SG 25–29, 227, URG (11) 56–66
Cameras, URG (2) 23
Canceling, TIG **225**
Canonical number sentences, TIG 267
Capacity, TIG 306, URG (9) 18, 67, URG (20) 15. *See also* Full of Beans Lab
Cards, counting on, URG (4) 36–37, 40
Care to Share? Game, URG (5) 1
Cartesian coordinates, URG (19) **4**
Cartesian products, TIG 273
Categorical variables, TIG **279,** 285. *See also* Variables
Centimeters, TIG 296
  square, TIG 300–303
Central tendency, measures of, TIG 215. *See also* Average, Mean, Median, Mode
Cents sign (¢), URG (3) 58. *See also* Money
Chicago, Illinois, AB 42, 49, 55, URG (11) 68, URG (11) 70
Circles, AB 104, 106, 107, SG 359, 362, 363, URG (2) 17, URG (15) 16, URG (18) 30–31, 36, URG (20) 25
  in fraction puzzles, SG 375–377
Circumference, SG **317–318,** URG (15) **22**–24, 26–27
Classroom, standards-based, TIG 93–94
Clocks, URG (2) 5, 39
Closeness, TIG 229–230
Cognitively Guided Instruction (CGI) problem types, URG (3) 5, 40, 57–60
Coins. *See* Dimes, Money, Nickels, Pennies, Quarters
Collaborative work, TIG 12–13
Colors, AB 9–18, SG 127–131, TIG 55, URG (3) 18–23, URG (5) 41–49
Colors Lab, SG 93–97, TIG 56–59
Combination foods, URG (16) 25
Communication, TIG 92, 99, 101, 103, 105, 107, 109, 111, 113, 115, 117, 119, 121, 123, 125, 127, 129, 131, 133, 135, 137, 259, URG (1) 5
Comparing, TIG 50, URG (3) 57–60
  area, SG 187–191, 201–202
  length, SG 7–9, 119–121, 317–318

more than/less than, SG 7, 9, 187–191, 247, 249, 255, 261

numbers, SG 7–9, 187–191, 247, 249, 255, 261

as problem type, TIG 271–272

shapes, SG 15–17, 313

subtraction as, URG (13) **5**

volumes, SG 247, 249, 255, 261

weather, SG 239–241

Computation, TIG 147, 200–203

Concrete approach to problem-solving, URG (14) 4–**5**

Connections

as process standard, TIG 92–93

in scope and sequence, TIG 99, 101, 103, 105, 107, 109, 111, 113, 115, 117, 119, 121, 123, 125, 127, 129, 131, 133, 135, 137

Constant ratios, TIG 237–238

Content standards. *See Principles and Standards for School Mathematics* (National Council of Teachers of Mathematics), Scope and sequence

Controlled variables, URG (6) **4,** 28–33, URG (11) 56, 58–59. *See also* Variables

Convenient numbers, TIG 223–224

Coordinates, URG (19) **4.** *See also* Cartesian coordinates, Graphing, Mapping

Corners of shapes, URG (2) 18, 22, URG (15) **16,** 31, 35

Could Be or Crazy? **measurement,** URG (6) 10, 54

Counters, TIG 248, URG (3) 24–29

Counting, AB 1–8, SG 3–5, 9, 37, TIG 50–51, URG (1) 15–19, 20–25, URG (5) 4, URG (14) 14–19

in arithmetic, TIG 192–193

assessment and, TIG 177–178

backwards, URG (1) 10

cubes, URG (1) 31–32

by five, SG 87, 353–354, URG (2) 40, URG (5) 22–28, URG (6) 4, 17–18, 25, URG (13) 12

grouping and, SG 83–97, 160–161

in home/store, SG 2–5, 32–33

by hundreds, SG 348–354

individual assessment record sheet for, TIG 183

money, SG 81, URG (7) 11, URG (11) 38, URG (14) 13

multiplication and, SG 295–299

numbers, URG (2) 10–11

by one, URG (1) 10, 13–14, 26–28

pennies, URG (11) 38

pockets, URG (3) 34–37

in problem solving, URG (3) 40

in scope and sequence, TIG 106–107

skip, SG 84–85, 87, 90–91, 167–169, 348–351, TIG 56–59, 60–61, 76–77, 250, URG (5) 8, 12, 15–20, URG (6) 8, URG (9) 16–17, 44–45, URG (10) 11, 38, URG (11) 12, 40, URG (12) 4, URG (19) 48, URG (20) 10, 22

software on, TIG 338

tallies and, SG 27, 32–33, 164

by ten, AB 77–93, SG 87, 167–169, 264, 279–281, 348–351, 353–354, TIG 82–83, URG (5) 22–28, URG (11) 20–25, URG (13) 12, URG (17) 12–22

by three, URG (13) 11

by two, SG 84–85, 351, URG (6) 10, URG (7) 10, URG (13) 10

volume measurement by, AB 57–68

Counting all strategy, SG 2–3, 5, TIG 247, URG (1) **5**

Counting back strategy, SG 157, TIG 64–65, 249, URG (8) 4–**5,** URG (11) **5,** 77

Counting book, URG (1) 23

Counting down strategy, TIG 250

Counting on strategy, SG 77–79, TIG 50, 56–57, 60–61, 248, URG (1) **5,** 11–12, 21–22, URG (4) **4,** 10, 34–40, URG (11) **5,** 77, URG (17) 29

Counting up strategy, SG 157, TIG 199, 249, 250, URG (8) 4–**5,** 31–32, 35–40

Cube models, SG **247,** 249, URG (12) 13–38

Cubes, SG 313, 319–324, 412, URG (15) **14**–19, 28–35

addition of, URG (5) 11

animals made of, AB 57–68, SG 259–261

assessment and, TIG 180

collecting, SG 319

counting, AB 82–84, URG (1) 10, 13–14, 26–28, 31–32

counting on with, URG (4) 36

identifying, SG **321**–323

individual assessment record sheet for, TIG 185

models of, SG 246–249

in scope and sequence, TIG 120–121

testing and, SG 313

towers of, SG 251–257

volume of, TIG 72–73, URG (12) 13–21, **15**

Cubic units, SG 246, 249, URG (12) **15,** 29, 33–38

Curriculum, standards-based, TIG 95

Curriculum and Evaluation Standards for School Mathematics **(National Council of Teachers of Mathematics),** TIG 15–16

Curved surface, URG (15) 26

Curves, TIG 290–291

Cylinders (tubes), SG 313, 315–319, **321,** 323–324, TIG 78–79, URG (15) 4, **14**–19

food shapes as, URG (15) 39

graduated, TIG 311–313

sizing, URG (15) 20–27

Daily Practice and Problems, TIG 48–49, 97, 145–148

Data, URG (2) 39–40, 40–42. *See also* Data analysis, Data tables, Graphs, Labs

aggregating, TIG 218

analyzing, TIG 291–292

assessment and, TIG 181

collecting and organizing, TIG 80–81, 283–284

in Daily Practice and Problems, TIG 147

graphing, TIG 284–291

individual assessment record sheet for, TIG 186

in scope and sequence, TIG 128–129. *See also* Data
analysis
software on, TIG 338
Data analysis, TIG 98, 100, 102, 104, 106, 108, 110, 112,
114, 116, 118, 120, 122, 124, 126, 128, 130, 132,
134, 136
Data tables, AB 9–18, 24, 27, SG 3, 5, 27, 32–33, 57,
59–63, 111, 117, 141, 161, 176–177, 189, 230,
233, 253, 316, 318, 326, 337, 400–401, TIG
54–55, URG (3) 17, 34–37, 41, URG (9) 21, URG
(16) 4, 22–30, URG (17) 10, URG (18) 11–12,
URG (19) 13, 24–41. *See also* Graphs, Labs
addition and subtraction using, SG 283–284
of colors, SG 94, URG (3) 18–23, URG (5) 37–40
of distance and direction, SG 111, 392, 395, 400, 401,
URG (6) 24–25
of doubles and halves, URG (13) 34
of foods, AB 74–76, SG 343
functions in, TIG 235–236
labeling, TIG 56–59
of length measurements, SG 104–106, URG (6) 15–19
of money values, SG 141
in Mr. Origin Says Game, URG (19) 18
for 100 seconds activity, URG (11) 52–53, 55
for partitioning ten, URG (3) 51–55
of rectangle area, SG 189, URG (10) 21
of survey data, URG (14) 20–26, URG (16) 12–16, **13**
variables in, TIG 284
of volume measurements, TIG 72–73, URG (12) 13,
18–19, 29–30, 38
of weather findings, SG 27, 230, 233–235, URG (2) 40
Decimals, TIG 17, 205–207. *See also* Fractions
significant digits in, TIG 232
Decimeters, TIG 296
Decomposing numbers, URG (11) 5
Dependent variables, TIG 280. *See also* Responding
variables, Variables
Derived number facts, URG (3) 40
Descartes, René, URG (19) **4**
Designing, TIG 62–63, 69, URG (2) 31, URG (10) 36–40
assessment and, TIG 178
individual assessment record sheet for, TIG 183
in scope and sequence, TIG 110–111
Dewey, John, TIG 16, 277
Diagonals, AB 36, URG (7) 35, URG (10) 33
Digit cards, SG 264
Digits, significant, TIG 222, 232
Dimes, SG 206–207, 209–210, 401, TIG 70–71, URG (6)
12, URG (11) 12, 15–18, 29–30, 34, 39, URG (12)
9, URG (14) 10, 13, URG (15) 10
Direction, URG (19) 48
distance and, SG 111, 392–401. *See also* Mapping
left and right, SG 392–401, TIG 86–87, URG (19) 4, 24–41
left, right, front, back, 393
from origin, URG (19) 14–22

Displacement, as volume measurement, TIG 311,
314–315
Distance, URG (11) 76, URG (19) 48. *See also* Measurement
of length
direction and, SG 111, 392–401
measurement of, AB 6, 19–28, 103–105, SG 103–111,
117, URG (1) 18, URG (6) 12, 14, 20–27.
See also Mapping
from origin, URG (19) 14–22
Distortion, TIG 214
Diversity
cultural, URG (16) 4, 27
in problem types, TIG 272
Division, SG 299, 301–302, 305, 407, 409, 412, 414,
TIG 56–59, 76–77, URG (5) 12–13, 29–35,
URG (11) 30, URG (14) 4–5, URG (20) 32
assessment and, TIG 180
estimation in, TIG 225–226
indicated, URG (18) 4
individual assessment record sheet for, TIG 186
Math Facts, TIG 143, 252
by measuring, SG 302
of money, SG 301
problem solving with, URG (14) 14–19, 28–32
problem types in, TIG 272–273
in scope and sequence, TIG 124–125
by sharing, SG 89–91, 301, 305, URG (6) 8, 11, 13,
URG (7) 9, URG (8) 11, URG (11) 17, URG (12)
9–10, URG (20) 27
stories with, SG 89, 299, 407, 412
of whole numbers, TIG 200–203
Doubles Railroad Game, SG **269**–275, TIG 335,
URG (13) 1, 34–35
Doubling, SG 265–277, 287, TIG 74–77, 78–79, 248–250,
URG (13) **4,** 13, 15, URG (14) 16, URG (15) 12,
URG (19) 13, URG (20) 11
card sets of, URG (13) 45–46
even and odd numbers and, URG (13) 39–46
halves and, URG (13) 31–37, **33**
identifying, URG (13) 24–30
Drawing pictures. *See* Labs

Edges of shapes, URG (15) **16,** 35. *See also* Cubes,
Rectangular prisms (boxes), Shapes
Eighths, SG **387,** 389
Empty *versus* **filled ten frames,** URG (3) 27–28
Energy from foods, AB 73–76
Equal arm balance, TIG 320–322. *See also* Balance
Equal fractions, URG (18) 22–27. *See also* Fractions
Equal parts, TIG 84–85
Equals sign (=), URG (4) 24, **30.** *See also* "Active" equals
sign (=), Calculators

Mental math, TIG 82–83, 222–223, URG (13) 16–23
Metric system, TIG 295–298
Midnight Visit, The, AB 29–40, TIG 68–69, URG (10) 30–35
Millimeters, TIG 296
Missing parts problems, URG (3) 5, 42–43, URG (13) 5
Mississippi River, AB 48
Missouri, AB 48, URG (11) 72
Mistakes, errors *versus,* TIG 227
Mode, TIG **211, 215.** *See also* Average, Central tendency, Mean, Median
Modeling, TIG 56–57, 72–73, 265–266
Models, cube, SG **247,** 249, URG (12) 22, 24–25
Money, SG 79–81, 141, 205–213, 401, TIG 55, 69–71, 70–71, URG (6) 12, URG (7) 11–12, URG (11) 5, 12, 15–18, URG (12) 9, URG (14) 10, 13, URG (15) 10, URG (17) 11. *See also* Dimes, Nickels, Pennies, Quarters
    addition and, SG 81
    assessment and, TIG 177
    in Daily Practice and Problems, TIG 147
    division of, SG 301
    grouping, URG (11) 36–44
    individual assessment record sheet for, TIG 182
    mental math and, TIG 222–223
    partitioning, URG (11) 26–34
    problem solving with, SG 65, 141, 205–211
    in scope and sequence, TIG 102–103
    software on, TIG 338
More than **relationship,** TIG 50–51, URG (1) 18, 29–34, URG (2) 12, 14, URG (3) 10–11, 28, URG (4) 12, URG (9) 24–28, 45–46, 46, URG (12) 24
Motion, TIG 319–324
Mr. Origin, SG 392–401, TIG 86–87, URG (19) 1, 4. *See also* Mapping
    number line and, URG (19) 24–41
Mr. Origin Left/Right Lab, SG 395–401, URG (19) 24–41
Mr. Origin Says Game, SG 393, TIG 336, URG (19) 14–22
Multidigit numbers, URG (4) 24, 34
Multiplication, TIG 56–59, 76–77, URG (13) 27, URG (14) 4–5, 10, URG (17) 9, 11, URG (18) 9, URG (20) 25
    counting and, SG 293–299
    estimation in, TIG 222–223
    individual assessment record sheet for, TIG 186
    Math Facts, TIG 143, 250–252
    problem solving with, SG 293–294, 299–305, 303–305, 406, 409, 412, 414, URG (14) 14–19, 28–32
    problem types in, TIG 272–273
    volume calculation by, TIG 309–311
    of whole numbers, TIG 200–203
Multi-step logic, TIG 11

Name grid pattern, SG 133–137
National Bureau of Standards, TIG 323
National Council of Teachers of Mathematics (NCTM), TIG 2–3, 8–10, 15–16, 90–95, 150–151, 191–192, 246
National Research Council (NRC), TIG 278
National Science Education Standards **(National Research Council),** TIG 278
National Science Foundation (NSF), TIG 15
Native Americans, AB 54–55, 95
Nature, shapes in, URG (2) 21
Navajo Indians, AB 95
Near double, URG (13) **4,** 13. *See also* Doubles Railroad Game
New Mexico, AB 53, URG (11) 74
Newspaper headlines, SG 173–174
Nickels, SG 211, 213, 401, TIG 71, URG (5) 24–25, URG (6) 12, URG (11) 17–18, 38–39, 42, URG (14) 13, URG (15) 10
Nonstandard units, AB 29–40, SG 7–9, 100–109, 111–121, 182–185, 392–401, TIG 60–61, 68–69, 295, URG (6) 14, 34–43, URG (10) 12–17, URG (20) 15
Notation, fraction, URG (18) 4
Number cards, URG (13) 21
Number facts, URG (3) 40
Number line, SG 395–401, TIG 86–87, 204, URG (9) 66–67, URG (18) 4, URG (19) 14–22, 24–41
Number operations software, TIG 338
Number patterns, TIG 66–67, URG (7) 25–28, URG (9) 39, URG (18) 10, URG (20) 29
Numbers, URG (1) 11, 13, URG (3) 10, 14–15, URG (4) 11. *See also* Counting, Hundreds, 100, Partitioning
    basic concepts, URG (3) 5
    comparisons of, SG 7–9, 187–191, 247, 249, 255, 261
    convenient, TIG 223–224
    counting, AB 1–8
    doubling, SG 265, 267–277, 287, URG (13) 26–27. *See also* Doubles Railroad Game
    even and odd, SG 68–69, 279–281, TIG 56–57, 74–75, URG (4) 11–12, 14–19, **16,** URG (5) 10–11, 13, 18, URG (6) 9, URG (9) 44, URG (12) 8, URG (13) 14, 39–46, URG (20) 9
    facts about, TIG 195–196
    halving. *See* Halves
    large, TIG 82–83, 179, 185, URG (8) 4, 32, URG (9) 68, URG (17) 4, 23–26
    leftover. *See* Leftover numbers
    multidigit, URG (4) 24
    naming, URG (8) 12, URG (9) 15–17, URG (11) 19, URG (15) 12, URG (20) 26
    in the news, SG 173–174, URG (9) 58–63
    ordering, TIG 50, URG (1) 31–33, URG (20) 31

ordinal *versus* counting, URG (2) 10–11
partitioning, SG 204–213, TIG 54–55, 56–59, 64–67,
   193, URG (3) 49–56, URG (4) 30, URG (5)
   29–35, URG (8) 20, 29–34, URG (17) 18
part-whole relationships of, URG (3) 38–47
software on, TIG 338
two-digit, TIG 64–65, URG (4) 34, URG (9) 38, 53–57
whole, TIG 3, 17, 140–143, 196–203
Number sense, TIG 17, 70–71, 147, URG (11) 5, 51–55
Number sentences, SG 38–39, 242–243, TIG 54–57,
   64–65, 267, URG (2) 12–13, URG (3) 27–28,
   41, URG (4) 13, URG (5) 8–12, URG (7) 9,
   URG (8) 13, 20–21, 23–28, URG (9) 26–27,
   URG (11) 13–14, 23, 26–34, 47–48, 79–81,
   URG (13) 10, 18
   addition, SG 49–51, 205–210, 212–213, URG (4) 4,
      28–32, **30,** URG (14) 11, URG (15) 11, URG (16) 9
   from data, SG 237
   for doubles, SG 267–268, TIG 74–75, URG (13) 28
   multiplication, URG (14) 4
   for partitioning ten, URG (3) 49–56
   of penny arrangements, SG 57, 59, 61, 63
   pocket counts and, SG 47–53
   for purchases, SG 65
   solving, SG 408, 410, 413, 415
   subtraction, SG 149–158, 205–206, 209–210, URG (8)
      4, URG (9) 11
   for ten frames, SG 38–39
   for tens, SG 205–206
   writing, SG 38–39, 47–65, 75, 77, 173, 205–215,
      219–220, 243
Numeration, TIG 192–194
Numerical variables, TIG **279,** 285. *See also* Variables

Observational assessment, TIG 29, 153–155, 160–161,
   169, 176. *See also* Assessment indicators, all URGs
Odd numbers, SG 68–69, 279–281, TIG 56–57, 74–75,
   URG (4) 11, 14–19, **16,** URG (5) 10–11, 13, 18,
   URG (9) 44, URG (12) 8, URG (13) 14, 39–46,
   URG (20) 9
Oklahoma City, Oklahoma, AB 49, URG (11) 72–73
One-dimensional patterns, URG (7) 4
One-fourth, URG (18) 18, 42, URG (20) 31.
   See also Fourths
One-half, URG (18) 16–17, 39–43. *See also* Halves
100, TIG 70–71, URG (9) 24–28, URG (11) 5, URG (18) 8,
   11, URG (19) 10–11
   adding, URG (17) 27–32
   Arrow Dynamics Game and, SG 215–223
   assessment and, TIG 179
   counting to, URG (10) 11
   Make 100 Game, TIG 335, URG (13) 19

number sense for, URG (11) 51–55
numbers larger than, TIG 82–83, 130–131, 179, 185,
   URG (17) 4, 23–26. *See also* Hundreds
partitioning, SG 204–212, URG (11) 20–25
100 Chart, SG 167, 217, TIG 66–67, 70–71, URG (5)
   17–18, 20, URG (9) 15, 42–51, URG (11) 5, 22,
   40, 46–50, URG (14) 17, URG (20) 15, 22
Ordering numbers, TIG 50, URG (1) 31–33, URG (20) 31
Ordinal numbers, URG (2) 10–11
Origin, AB 95, 99, 102. *See also* Mapping, Mr. Origin
   coordinates and, URG (19) **4**
   Mr. Origin Says Game and, URG (19) 14–22, **18**
Outer space, TIG 324
Ovals, SG 375–377, URG (18) 30–31

Paint-blob pictures, URG (7) 35
Pairs, SG 265, URG (13) 24, 28. *See also* Doubles
Parallels in shapes, URG (2) 18
Parents, working with, TIG 4, 349–362
   brochure for, TIG 355–358
   communication tools for, TIG 351–352
   Math Facts information for, TIG 359, 361
   programs for, TIG 353–354
   Spanish language materials for, TIG 357–358, 361,
      URG (Spanish letters)
Partitioning
   fifty, SG 213
   money examples of, URG (11) 26–34
   numbers, SG 47–63, 75, 148, 404, TIG 54–55, 56–59,
      64–67, 193, URG (3) 49–56, URG (4) 30,
      URG (5) 29–35, URG (8) 20, 29–34, URG (9) 60,
      URG (11) 5, URG (17) 18
   one hundred, SG 204–212, URG (11) 20–25
   sets, URG (18) 34–43
   shapes, URG (2) 34–36, URG (18) 28–33
   ten, URG (13) 16–23
Part-part-whole **model of subtraction,** TIG 64–65
Part-part-whole **relationships,** SG 49–63, 75, 148–153,
   404, URG (13) 10–11
Parts, TIG 84–85, URG (18) 4. *See also* Fractions
   assessment and, TIG 177, 181
   individual assessment record sheet for, TIG 182, 187
   missing, URG (13) 5
   problems solving in, URG (3) 5
   in scope and sequence, TIG 102–103, 132–133
Part-unknown **subtraction,** URG (13) **5**
Part-whole **fractions,** TIG 204
Part-whole **relationships,** SG 51, 75, 148, 404, TIG 57,
   84–85, 271, URG (3) 38–47, URG (4) 4, 13,
   21–26, **23,** 28–32, URG (5) 9–10, URG (11) 5,
   URG (13) **5,** URG (18) 4, 17, 34–38. *See also*
   Fractions

Math Facts, TIG 143, 248–249, URG (9) 10, 12, 14, URG (11) 5, 8, URG (18) 7, 10, URG (19) 11
    number sentences for, SG 52–53, 149–158, 205–206, 209–210, URG (3) 28, URG (11) 26–34
    partitioning numbers and, TIG 193
    problem solving with, SG 151–153, 279–281, 285, 289, 308–311, 328–330, 405, 410, 413, URG (8) 4–5, 12–13, 35–40
    problem types in, TIG 270–272
    in scope and sequence, TIG 112–113, 122–123
    separate—result unknown, URG (3) 5, 57–60
    take-away, URG (8) 14–17, 29–34, URG (9) 45–46, URG (17) 8
    from ten, URG (14) 11
    of ten, TIG 70–71, URG (11) 77, 80–81
    of whole numbers, TIG 196–203
    whole-part-part model of, URG (8) 18–28
Sum, URG (13) 16, 23
Surface, curved, URG (15) 26
Surface area, TIG 303. *See also* Measurement of area
Surveys, SG 331, 337, TIG 80–81, URG (14) 20–26, URG (16) 4, 12–16, 22–30
Symbols, TIG 204–205, 266–267, URG (9) 4, URG (10) 28, URG (11) 56, URG (19) 45
    fraction, URG (18) 4
    for patterns, URG (7) 22
    in problem solving, URG (14) 4–**5**
Symmetry, SG 139–140, 143, TIG 62–63, 84–85, URG (7) 29–33, **31,** 35, URG (10) 38, URG (18) 4, 14–20, **16,** 24, 27, URG (20) 30. *See also* Line of symmetry, Line symmetry, Shapes
    assessment and, TIG 181
    individual assessment record sheet for, TIG 187
    in scope and sequence, TIG 132–133

Tables. *See* Data tables
Take-away subtraction, URG (8) 24–25, 29–34, URG (13) **5,** URG (17) 8
Tallies, SG 27, 32–33, 164, 242–243, 337, 343, TIG 52–55, URG (2) 40, URG (3) 16, 21, URG (11) 56, 58, URG (14) 23, URG (16) 25
Target numbers, URG (9) 18, 45–46, 49–50
Teacher Implementation Guide (TIG), TIG 24, 39
Teacher Resource CD, TIG 24, 40
***Teaching Integrated Mathematics and Science Project* (TIMS),** TIG 15
***Telling* rubric.** *See* Rubrics
Ten, SG **294,** URG (17) 8–9, URG (18) 8, 11, URG (19) 10–11
    addition and subtraction of, TIG 70–71, URG (11) 77–83

    as benchmark, TIG 54–55
    counting by, AB 77–93, SG 87, 90–91, 167–169, 264, 279–281, 348–351, TIG 56–59, 70–71, 82–83, URG (5) 4, 22–23, 25–28, URG (7) 11, URG (9) 45–51, URG (10) 38, URG (11) 20–25, 40, URG (13) 12, URG (20) 10
    in estimation, TIG 223–224
    greater than, URG (3) 28
    grouping by, SG 160, 163–165, 348–351, TIG 66–67, 114–115, 179, 184, URG (9) 5, 11, 36–41, URG (17) 4, 12–22, URG (20) 29
    Make Ten Game, SG 264, TIG 335
    making, TIG 50, 74–75, URG (8) 4, URG (13) **4,** 12, URG (16) 9
    multiples of, TIG 64–65
    partitioning, URG (3) 49–56, URG (8) 31
    powers of, TIG 205
    subtraction from, URG (14) 11
    using, SG 279–281, TIG 248–249, URG (13) **4,** URG (16) 9
Ten Frame Flash Game, URG (3) 27–28
Ten frames, SG 35–43, 87, TIG 54–55, 64–67, 193, URG (3) 5, 24–29, 58, URG (5) 25, URG (8) 31, URG (10) 8–9, URG (11) 28–30, URG (13) 49
Ten percent benchmark, TIG 229. *See also* Accuracy, Approximation, Estimation
Tensland, AB 77–92, TIG 82–83, URG (17) 12–15
Testing, AB 20, TIG 88–89, 158, 255–256, URG (20) 3, 21–32
Texas, AB 50–52, URG (11) 73
Think and Spin Game, SG 41, TIG 55, URG (3) 31–33
Three, counting by, URG (13) 11, URG (14) 14–19
Three-digit numbers, URG (17) 18
Three-dimensional shapes, TIG 180, 186, 303. *See also* Balls (spheres), Cubes, Cylinders (tubes), Prisms (boxes), Rectangular prisms (boxes)
Tilting, URG (2) 22
Time, SG 225, TIG 70–71, 100, 102, 104, 106, 110, 112, 114, 118, 132, 136, URG (2) 4–5, URG (8) 10–11, URG (9) 10, URG (11) 51–55, URG (20) 15
    calendars and, URG (2) 4, 39
    in Daily Practice and Problems, TIG 147
    for math study, TIG 13–14
    software, TIG 338
TIMS Laboratory Method, TIG 11, 48, 52–53, 60–61, 66–67, 76–77, 80–81, 86–87, URG (5) 4, URG (14) 20–26, URG (16) 4. *See also* Labs
    analyzing data (phase 4) in, TIG 291–292
    beginning investigation (phase 1) in, TIG 281–282
    collecting data (phase 2) in, TIG 283–284
    graphing data (phase 3) in, TIG 284–291
    in process standards, TIG 92–93
    science view of, TIG 277–278
    TIMS Tutor on, TIG 277–294
    variables and values in, TIG 279–281

TIMS multidimensional rubric. *See* Rubrics
TIMS Tutors, TIG 3, 189–210
   Area, TIG 299–304
   Arithmetic, TIG 191–210
   Averages, TIG 211–218
   Estimation, Accuracy, and Error, TIG 219–234
   Functions, TIG 235–240
   Journals, TIG 241–244
   Length, TIG 295–298
   Mass, TIG 319–324
   Math Facts, TIG 245–258
   Portfolios, TIG 259–264, URG (3) 6
   TIMS Laboratory Method, TIG 277–294
   Volume, TIG 305–318
   Word Problems, TIG 265–276, URG (3) 5–6,
      URG (3) 40
Topography, URG (19) 4
Train Game, The, TIG 51, URG (1) 26–28
Translating patterns, SG 126, URG (7) 16–17
Translations, TIG 267–268
Trapezoids, SG 20–23, URG (2) 4, 17, 21, 28, URG (3)
   11, 13, URG (7) 29–33
Trends, TIG 237
Trials, URG (6) **4,** 13, 22–23, URG (7) 9, URG (11) 52–53
Triangles, AB 99, SG 13, 17, 19–23, 359, 362, 371, 392,
   395–397, URG (2) 4, 17, 21, 28, URG (3) 12–13,
   URG (15) 17, URG (19) 28, URG (20) 28
Tubes, URG (15) **14**–19. *See also* Cylinders (tubes)
Tucson, Arizona, AB 56, URG (11) 68, 75
Turn-around facts, URG (12) 30
Turning, URG (2) 28
Twelve, URG (11) 13
Two, counting by, SG 84–85, **294,** TIG 56–59, URG (5) 4,
   17, URG (6) 10, URG (7) 10–11, URG (9) 44–45,
   URG (13) 10, URG (14) 14–19, URG (19) 28, 48
Two-digit numbers, TIG 64–65, URG (4) 34, URG (9) 38,
   53–57
Two-pan balance. *See also* Equal arm balance
Two times (multiplication), URG (13) 27. *See also*
   Doubling

Unequal fractions, URG (18) 22–27
Unequal parts, TIG 84–85
United States Department of Agriculture (U.S.D.A.),
   SG 338, URG (16) 1, 15, 17, 26, 30
Unit Resource Guides (URG), TIG 24–38
   Adventure Book lesson guide, TIG 36
   answer keys, TIG 38
   background, lesson, TIG 28
   daily practice and problems, TIG 30–31
   lesson guides, TIG 32–35
   Letter Home, TIG 25

   observational assessment record, TIG 29
   student pages, TIG 37
   unit outlines, TIG 26–27
Units. *See also* Measurement of area, Measurement of
   length, Measurement of volume
   of area measurement, TIG 68–69, URG (10) 4
   cubic, SG 246, 249, URG (12) **15,** 29, 33–38
   fractions and, TIG 206
   of length measurement, SG 113–115, 117, TIG 60–61,
      TIG 295–298
   of measurement, URG (10) 34, URG (19) 45
   of money, URG (11) **29**
   nonstandard, AB 29–40, SG 7–9, 100–109, 111–121,
      182–185, 392–401, TIG 60–61, 68–69, 295,
      URG (6) 14, 34–43, URG (10) 12–17, URG (20) 15
   size of, URG (9) 64–69
   square, TIG 300–303, URG (12) 17. *See also* Square
      inches
   standard, URG (6) 17, 51–56, URG (10) 4
   of time, SG 225, URG (2) 4–5, URG (11) 51–55
   of volume measurement, TIG 72–73, 306
University of Illinois at Chicago (UIC), TIG 15
USA map, SG 241
Using doubles, SG 265–268, 277, 287. *See also* Doubles
   Railroad Game, Doubling
Using ten, SG 279–281, TIG 248–249, URG (13) **4,**
   URG (16) 9

Values, TIG **279.** *See also* Money, Place value, Variables
Variables, AB 22, TIG 80–81, URG (6) **4,** 24–25,
   URG (16) 4, 14. *See also* Arrow Dynamics Game
   categorical, TIG **279,** 285
   changing, URG (6) 28–33
   controlled, URG (6) **4,** 28–33, URG (11) 56, 58–59
   in data tables, TIG 284–285. *See also* Data, Data tables
   dependent, TIG 280
   fixed, AB 22, TIG **280**–281, URG (2) **40,** URG (6) **4,**
      28–33
   functions and, TIG 235–240
   heights as, URG (12) 17
   independent, TIG 280
   labeling axes and, TIG 287. *See also* Graphs, Horizontal
      axis, Vertical axis
   locations as, URG (11) 68–76
   manipulated, TIG 239, **279**–280, 284, 287
   mass as, TIG 319
   numerical, TIG **279,** 285
   responding, TIG 239, **279**–280, 287
   in TIMS Laboratory Method, TIG **278**–283
   volume as, TIG 307
   weather, URG (2) 39–**40**
Velocity, TIG 319

Vertical axis, TIG 287, URG (3) 35, URG (6) 25, URG (9) 67, URG (13) 49–50, URG (19) 4
Visual approach to problem solving, URG (14) 4–**5**
Visual imagery, URG (3) 26
Volume. *See* Measurement of volume

Wagreich, Philip, TIG 15
Weather, SG 227–241, URG (11) 18, URG (12) 12
    in autumn, SG 25–29, TIG 52–53, URG (2) 37–45
    calendar of, SG 25–29, 227
    comparing, SG 239–241
    data table of, SG 230, 233–235
    graph of, SG 231
    location and, AB 41–56, TIG 70–71, URG (11) 68–76
    problem solving using, SG 237–238
    recording, URG (2) 5
    weekend chart of, URG (2) 44, URG (11) 66
    in winter, SG 229–239, TIG 70–71, URG (11) 56–66
Weather 1: Eye on the Sky Lab, SG 25–29, TIG 52–53, URG (2) 37–45
Weather 2: Winter Skies Lab, SG 229–239, TIG 70–71, URG (11) 56–66
Weekend weather chart, URG (2) 44, URG (11) 66
Weight, TIG **324**
What's in That Pocket? Lab, SG 55–63
Whole numbers, TIG 3, 17
    computation with, TIG 200–203
    operations of, TIG 140–143
    subtraction and, TIG 196–199
Whole-part-part mat, SG 148
Whole-part-part model of subtraction, URG (8) 4, 16, 18–22, 18–28, 35–40
Wholes. *See* Fractions, Part-whole relationships, Whole-part-part model of subtraction
Width, URG (9) 17, URG (10) 4
Word problems, SG 279–281, 285, 289, 293–294, 299–305, 328–329, 405–406, 409, 412–414.
    See also Labs, Problem solving
    TIMS Tutor on, TIG 265–276, URG (3) 5–6, 40
World of Cubic Animals, A, AB 57–68, TIG 72–73, URG (12) 33–38
Writing. *See* Math journals
Written assessment, TIG 153, 156–157

X-axis. *See* Horizontal axis

Y-axis. *See* Vertical axis

Zero, AB 105, URG (3) 35, 52, URG (9) 17, URG (12) 9